THOMAS CRANE LIBRARY
QUINCY MA

CITY APPROPRIATION

THE CALL OF

SOLITUDE

Alonetime in a World

of Attachment

Ester Schaler Buchholz, PH.D.

SIMON & SCHUSTER

SIMON & SCHUSTER
Rockefeller Center
1230 Avenue of the Americas
New York, NY 10020

Copyright © 1997 by Ester Schaler Buchholz
All rights reserved, including the right of reproduction
in whole or in part in any form.

SIMON & SCHUSTER and colophon are registered trademarks
of Simon & Schuster Inc.

Designed by Leslie Phillips
Manufactured in the United States of America

1   3   5   7   9   10   8   6   4   2

LIBRARY OF CONGRESS CATALOGING-IN-PUBLICATION DATA
Buchholz, Ester Schaler.
The call of solitude : alonetime in a world of attachment /
Ester Schaler Buchholz.
p. cm.
Includes bibliographical references and index.
1. Solitude. I. Title.
BF637.S64B83   1997
155.9'2—dc21   97-20698
CIP
ISBN 0-684-81874-4

The author gratefully acknowledges permission to reprint the following:

Excerpt from *Tao Te Ching* by Stephen Mitchell, translation copyright 1988
by Stephen Mitchell. Reprinted by permission of HarperCollins Publishers,
Inc. New York.

Excerpt from "I'll Walk Alone," by Sammy Cahn and by Jule Styne, © 1944
Morley Music Co. Copyright renewed, assigned to Morley Music Co. and
Cahn Music Company. All rights on behalf of Cahn Music Company. Ad-
ministered by WB Music Corp. All rights reserved. Used by permission.

Excerpt from "Inner Peace," by Rosalie Cutting, reprinted from *Parabola,
The Magazine of Myth and Tradition,* Vol. 17, No. 1 (Spring 1992).

"Solitude," from *Now We Are Six* by A. A. Milne. Illustrations by E. H.
Shepherd. Copyright 1927 by E. P. Dutton, renewed © 1955 by A. A. Milne.
Used by permission of Dutton Children's Books, a division of Penguin
Books USA Inc.

155.92
BuCH

ACKNOWLEDGMENTS

Thanks. I begin with that word because a fear of mine in having an open forum to express gratitude is that I shall forget someone whom I should remember. My first thank-you is to those who have helped me to author this book but who go unmentioned. They will remember.

My debt is large. It is to family, friends, patients, students, assistants, colleagues, mentors, and strangers. It is to my agent, Susan Golomb, who had trust in my ideas at the beginning and who always has excellent and penetrating advice. Thanks also go to my editors three, headed by Mary Ann Naples. I do not know if I'm in an enclave of the publishing world of Simon & Schuster that is everywhere else obsolete, or if we are witnessing a renaissance where once again writer and editor are a closely knit unit. Mary Ann leads a dream team—Laurie Chittenden and Carlene Bauer. What writer wouldn't love and appreciate his or her words read seriously and diligently, or to be offered a thought, phrase, or word that inspires new thinking? I received all that, as well as directions to cut-cut-cut, with tact and concern. Mary Ann and Carlene worked day and night on these tasks, although Carlene was kind enough to say that reading the book gave her plenty of alonetime.

My family—father, Harry Schaler; mother, Rose; and sister, Vida—was intense. But from early on everyone had the intuitive sense and obvious need at times to leave one another alone, even in our small apartment. Nothing much may have come of this had I not met and married Leonard Wolf. He, an only child, through his absorption in music, his end-of-day wish to unwind, concentrating on the newspaper, and his interest in and love of people led me to a room of *his* own and to a new look at my own work. Day-to-day life with Leonard, coupled with theoretical, clinical, and field observations, had me exclaim, "Eureka!"

Of course, I had home tutorials for many years. When Gary, my eldest son, went to camp, it was as if I had lost a limb. But he was quite enthralled with this leave-taking, and traveling far and wide continued to be his wont. At eight months, David was arguing with me about doing things himself, and if I wanted him to eat and go places, I had to listen. Phillip made some peace with his differences—being learning disabled

—by the time he was nine years old, when he told me that he did not mind being lonely.

In the throes of writing the earliest version of this book, I could not have done without the quick and most critical first readings of chapters by Gary and his wife, Linda, and David and his spouse, Jeanne. Leonard caught mistakes in chapter after chapter, and then on the rewrites. Without mercy, I taxed family, colleagues, and friends—to name some, Mort Gladstone, Elizabeth Krimendahl, Gary Rosenthal, Dorienne Sorter, Jill Stein, and Athena Foley—to read parts of the book. But Barbara Gol, friend and colleague, faithfully read every chapter, challenging ideas while always encouraging the process. Caroline Chinlund and I together published the first article on alonetime. Indeed, when I conceived the idea for this book, we were going to do it together. I enjoyed our work together, but I am also gratcful that she knew before I did that this was my project and I had to pursue it myself.

Nevertheless, I never could have ventured forth as thoroughly as I tried to if not for my fellow researchers and students, including, foremost, Heidi Maben and Edith Tyson, as well as Rochelle Catton, Josh Friedman, Elizabeth Helbraun, Stephen Hoff, Maya Memling, Cathleen Patterson-Dehn, Jim Racine, Karen Roser, Susan Schwartz, and Susan Tomasi. This list is partial and leaves out many coconspirators from my classes, not to mention Lisa Jones, my videographer of parents and babies. All the parents and babies I've viewed and interviewed over the years are fresh in my mind and deserve gratitude. New York University, and especially Deans Daniel Griffiths and Ann Marcus of the School of Education, who sponsored my research through developmental grants, provided the space to compose with intellectual freedom. I am grateful.

I do not mention the actual names of patients, and none of them are recognizable in the disguised and composite descriptions that I use as case examples. But I am beholden to them, going back to my internship days. I am indebted to the many whose struggles with and pleasures in alonetime gave me more positive reinforcement than any analyst deserves.

In my schooling and analytic training, I have had dozens of mentors. To all of them I am thankful, but two stand out in the context of this book. Frank Lachmann in 1988 told me about Anthony Storr's writings on solitude and whetted my appetite for the topic. Anthony Storr's eloquence on the subject reached further psychologically than that of any before him. I hope I add to his barrier-breaking thoughts. I also credit Esther Menaker as a role model for holding truth above politeness, for loving to question the obscure and the obvious, and for encouraging my own rebellious nature.

Starting with Lisa Lau, who helped me to prepare the proposal and some very early drafts of chapters, I was inordinately lucky to find assistants of the highest caliber. Charlotte Butzin and David Serlin are master decipherers of language, lines, and arrows, given my preference for composing in longhand. I am obliged to Charlotte for her grasp of film lore and unremitting loyalty, and to David for his knowledge of history and literature. Both were ever ready to question and correct gaps in my experience. Adding to my knowledge about the !Kung society from the Kalahari Desert was University of Wisconsin professor Herbert Lewis, and I recognize his help as well.

In the end, of course, I take full responsibility for what is placed in print and what is left out. As the careful reader will notice, I add my own land mines to explode any remaining anbivalences surrounding aloneness. These loaded points leave no doubt as to my position on alonetime: sensations and memory traces of this peaceful state evolve in the womb; the need is both developmental and biological, both unequivocal and ubiquitous. My psychoanalytic colleagues may be the first to holler because I use broad strokes and may not afford proper due to psychology or psychoanalysis. Because this is a biography of a need, I felt I could leap over time and place to chart alonetime's comings and goings. I have to admit that this presumptuous expedition was always great fun, particularly in discussing the topic with strangers, when our eyes connected and I heard in their sigh of relief that we both had caught on to a longing for good and all in life.

E. S. B.
New York City

For those whose lives
I know in love and
in silence and slow times—
Leonard, Gary, David,
Phillip, Benjamin, Jacob

and
to Vida

CONTENTS

There is another Loneliness
That many die without—
Not want of friend occasions it
Or circumstance of Lot

But nature, sometimes, sometimes thought
And whoso it befall
Is richer than could be revealed
By mortal numeral—

EMILY DICKINSON

INTRODUCTION

Achieving inner calm while feeling centered is a human goal that is never easy to master. But why of late do serenity and peace of mind seem further from reach than ever before? The world appears very busy, and finding moments to catch up with ourselves looks to be almost impossible. Something has occurred to change life's circumstances, to make peaceful, restorative time terribly elusive.

As a child, I loved books containing visual games of discovery, in which a boldly designed field, forest, or farm held purposely obscured fauna of all sorts. The observer tried to identify creatures that were hidden in trees or integrated into the texture of flowers and barn doors. Once sighted, the images became immediately obvious. Much later, while teaching a graduate psychology class, I became focused in a similar way on the story of child development. As I was describing bonds of attachment, a given in child psychology, I paused and thought: Something else is in this picture. Why is attachment continually linked with situations of stress? Why do babies, so dependent when awake, require so many alone hours in sleep? If relationships are supposed to provide us with penultimate satisfaction and are considered *the* significant factor in establishing emotional well-being, then why are there so many problems surrounding them? And how, then, are people able to endure and succeed—even reasonably well—with minimal ongoing relationships?

There seems to be no intelligible, unifying message in answering all of these questions. Right now we live in a society that touts independence yet fears alienation. We focus on infants' and toddlers' attachment needs, while more and more, children are rejected and neglected. Despite our constant emphasis on love, relationships, and family values, those who marry face a 50 percent chance of divorcing or separating. But to begin to clear up these ambiguities, we need to understand the intricacies of our fears when alone.

Interestingly, in contrast to attachment, people view time alone and solitude with greater trepidation. The reasons for the fear of being alone are many. Some fears self-generate; most are taught. In setting out to dispel the latter, I call to mind philosophers, theologians, psychologists,

[15]

poets, and writers who have already explored this territory. I also turn to the new biological findings that shed light on how infants are inherently able to adapt and even to regulate some of their needs and emotions themselves, in addition to having them regulated by others. I shall show throughout the book that we are born ready to do things on our own as well as to connect to others. Both needs—to be alone and to engage—are essential to human happiness and survival, with equally provocative claims. Without solitude existing as a safe place, a place for long sojourns and self-discovery, we lose the important sense of being self-regulating individuals.

Gratifying aspects of time alone and self-regulation are precisely illustrated in Lynn Hall's novel *The Solitary*, in which seventeen-year-old Jane Cahill goes to live by herself. Hall writes of Jane's decision:

> For the first time in her memory she was independent of time. Seven o'clock, get up. Eight-thirty, be in her seat in her first class . . . Saturday, up early to get her part of the house-cleaning done so she could go to her Saturday job. Sunday, go to Sunday school and church to placate Uncle Doyle . . . The bits of time that weren't demanded of her by others, Jane used to pull herself in herself in whatever solitude she could find . . .
>
> The joy of her aloneness was growing daily more evident to Jane. The tiny luxuries of waking in the mornings, lying in bed until she'd had time to plan her day, eating what she wanted for every meal, . . . eating when she was hungry, not when someone else decreed that it was mealtime, being in control of her day. That, she thought, was the key.[1]

As Hall suggests, being alone gives us the power to self-regulate and adjust our lives. When Jane questions the value of solitary life she turns to a friend, Iva, who from her own lone life concludes: "If I was God and running the world, I'd try to make it so everybody, men and women, had to live alone for awhile, take care of themselves, support themselves, learn their own strengths, if you know what I mean."[2]

I am not the first to pay attention to alone experiences. Philosophers of old charted aspects of this terrain. Emily Dickinson called it "another loneliness."[3] Each generation seems to create individuals, and sometimes groups, who speak out in favor of solitude. To name a few: Buddha, Euripides, Marcus Aurelius, Saint Jerome, Saint Augustine, Wordsworth, de Tocqueville, Thoreau, Virginia Woolf, Thomas Merton, Giacometti,

Doris Lessing, and most recently Philip Koch. Certain psychiatrists, psychoanalysts, and psychologists also have written on the experience of solitude. Among those whose work I explore—from Frieda Fromm-Reichmann and Donald Woods Winnicott to Clark Moustakas and Anthony Storr—I find both rapport and room for differences.

Finding truth and God, as well as creativity and a return to the self, has been suggested as the reward of time spent alone, but mostly for select groups of people, like artists and the spiritual. In this book, I suggest more. From clinical evidence and from what I have read and researched, it seems that all those who are unable to be alone or make little room for being alone hamper their ability to find a sense of inner ease, at best, or, at worst, end up dependent on others or drugs in unhealthy ways. My psychological position is closest to the philosophical one of Philip Koch, who defends solitude and encounter as coexisting needs in adulthood. The problem, however, affects children as well. Ask the youngster behind the bedroom door slammed shut, or the adolescent glued to earphones, or those hiding out in bathrooms. When I was young, I could go out alone with ease. Play areas were safer, video games were nonexistent, and television was not so ubiquitous and was more or less restricted to set times. Tranquillity in nature was more accessible, and every free minute was not supposed to be programmed.

The psychological and physical consequences that result from shrinking times alone range from self-centeredness and lack of resourcefulness to disorders concerning eating and sleeping, and mood swings that relate to over- and undercontrol of our selves. There is no denying that many of our social and psychological "diseases" are primarily disturbances in self-regulation. As with hysteria in Freud's time, the most prevalent mental health problems today—such as depression and hyperactivity—reflect our times and cultural stresses. When we feel overcrowded by others' wishes and feel overly busy, we may relinquish the time to regulate our needs. We skip meals and sleep, or constantly eat and frequently doze. Bemused college professors report that students, claiming inadequate time to prepare themselves at home, brush and comb their hair in class. Not all problems that I discuss—including poor attachments, type A personality, sleep deprivation, and depression—stem entirely from the conflict of having to satisfy two seemingly disparate needs. However, all the conditions that I name are complicated and exacerbated by inadequate time alone.

Prior to the eighteenth century, before the advent of crowded cities, television, and faxes, people had time to wander, in the Wordsworthian sense, "as a cloud."[4] And even not so long ago, one didn't have to carefully consider where to find privacy. Learning was often a solitary pursuit with time for reflection, a far cry from the overcrowded classrooms, *Sesame Street* episodes, and computer exchanges of today. I am *not* suggesting going backward in time. I am proposing a careful examination of the things we lose as we sacrifice time alone to technology and increasingly complex lives.

In a *U.S. News and World Report* issue, Neil Postman cautions that by the year 2053, people will have lost their social skills.[5] He sees the home computer as the future center for all activities, from early childhood education to a range of interpersonal connections, including making friends. Peter Cochrane believes that computers of the future will talk and listen to their owners with apparent feeling.[6] Indeed, the *New York Times* reports that scientists have already built machines capable of reading human emotions.[7] Historians tell us that alienation in the workplace started over two hundred years ago with the introduction of industrial machinery into workers' lives. So, to what do we owe the accelerating departure from close human contact that we see today? Although we know that part of the reason lies in the technology explosion, the motivation and willingness to give up direct socialization is less visible. Looking at aspects of Euro-American social history from the post-Freudian era to postmodern times, we shall see that the escape from direct, face-to-face contact (*f2f* in computer language) is largely a reaction to social change and an escape from psychological messages that ignore, underacknowledge, or neglect our basic need for aloneness.

When the prevailing culture dictates how to use all free time, the sense of the aloneness need gets lost, even repressed, and is acted out in ways that range from inconvenient to bizarre and even destructive. The *New York Times* predicts that in our current sped-up, information-oriented climate, we are heading toward an era "when portable phones, pagers and data transmission devices of every sort will keep us terminally in touch" and there will be much that we will forfeit.[8] Hilariously oversized communication planners, in which one notes *all* daily activities, are carried by those who resist pocket computers. In bizarre fashion, climbers questing solitude on the top of Mt. McKinley whip out handheld radios to call home.[9] Even more in the extreme, patients' experiences have shown to me deep and disturbing disruptions in people's lives when aloneness needs are continuously frustrated. For instance, little children stop speaking to maintain control, and adults leave their families and disappear for a time. As a clinical psychologist and psychoanalyst, I have witnessed the enormous psychological benefits of time alone and how such time strengthens attachments.

Some still insist that love is salvation and aloneness condemnation. I recognize now how difficult it is for people to acknowledge aloneness as having a value equivalent to attachment. The other day, a colleague sent me an article that corroborated my ideas about the value of being alone. At the same time, she scolded me on my views: "I shall never agree with you about children needing time alone. It is only through *constant* closeness to their *mothers* that children learn to feel secure." One reviewer of my work raised a question about an adolescent's need for time alone: "Is it not a fact that it is *not* 'downtime' in the abstract that counts, but what transpires in that solitude that matters? An adolescent could well be contemplating suicide rather than developing resilient strategies. How are we to assure that reflective time will be employed for positive reflection?" My response is straightforward: we cannot guarantee that solitude will be used for "positive reflection" any more than we can guarantee relationships will exist without abuse or sadism. Yet we do not ever seem to question the value of relating in a similar way. The reviewer's query reflects this enduring prejudice against aloneness.

How can relationships, for example, which are such a large part of life, be punishing? Or does this explain the saying "To live is to suffer"? Then again, is it aloneness that causes suffering? It is clear to everyone, even without scholarly support, that the wrath of person upon person is more devastating than the wrath of nature or God. Though aloneness has been considered in texts before, most writing about it is philosophical, and so it remains a relatively open area to ponder. Certainly, psychology is only beginning to distinguish aloneness from loneliness and to recognize the importance to infants of emotional states besides attachment.

Not all children denied early bonding are failures in life or relationships. For example, I recall an experience that I had early in my psychoanalytic practice. During the treatment of Evelyn, a successful schoolteacher who had survived the Holocaust, I discovered that she was born prematurely and that she had lived in an incubator in pre-Nazi Germany for her first six months of life. Hospitals and pediatric wards in Germany in the late 1920s were not as they are today. A child in an incubator experienced little human contact beyond being fed and kept clean. Granted, this person sought help because she had difficulty expressing her emotions. Nevertheless, how had she, without primary affectionate connections, managed to proceed in a difficult life with the fortitude, moral integrity, and ability she displayed? These and other questions about aloneness began to formulate in my mind and caused me to investigate the phenomenon much further.

My own discomfort with popular notions on aloneness suggested to me that I take the journey of discovery by following a typical paradigm: find my own solitude by seeking a leave of absence from teaching and a sabbatical from patients for six months in order to contemplate and compose. Then my thought changed direction. I had read books combining an author's reclusive pilgrimage with a discussion of solitude. Given that most perspectives were different from mine—that time alone is a lifetime developmental need—writerly seclusion did not seem the way to go. I was already convinced of the personal value of aloneness. But what happens to this need when one feels flooded by work and outside demands? I knew of unusual people, like Ludwig Wittgenstein, who managed in even the most imperfect solitude to think their own thoughts.[10] During the course of war, he wrote his greatest book. Thus, I determined, better I should risk the dangers of lack of time alone to figure out the risks of overconnectedness.

Somewhat afraid of the absolute pressure of my busy life, I gave myself a jump start by beginning writing during a vacation period. But soon after, I began the hectic life of school, home, children, grandchildren, stepchildren, husband, and friends. At certain times, writing was part of a frantic schedule (when the book was edited on my stationary bike, for example). The car became an office, half hours were used to compose paragraphs, and research and reading were squeezed in between patients. At other times, the writing itself became perfect solitude. Going off to write on a Saturday, skimming through books leisurely, or watching a relevant film turned into a soul-soothing sojourn, like spending time in a monastery or a temple. A patient of mine mentioned something writer Grace Paley said about composition: "We write to know about that which we know."

By being conscious of a need for time alone, my mind stepped in to fill the void. From the start, I knew this time was essential, but I did not realize to what degree. I found that sex, hunger, and thirst were subordinate to my quest for solitude. Beloved engagements, like "playing hooky" with friends or going to the theater, became second best to a night at home. Nor did I think that the need would appear in me so strong and outspoken, or that there would be some who absolutely denied anything other than attachment as significant in life. At the same time, when I discussed the topic with others, I was surprised by the numbers of people who were intrigued and in agreement with me. Their everyday stories helped to fuel me during moments of depletion. I also learned that I slowed myself down automatically when I felt about to burst with things to do. After I responded to my need, panic dispersed and I found that work moved at a restful pace and almost everything was completed anyway. This may be basic knowledge, but it was news to me, since I was used to seeing people who plowed over inner signals to slow down. On the other hand, my irritability and selfishness index rose whenever I was pressured by demands, as did my ability to say no to requests for my time. After a good weekend of sleep and relaxation coupled with work, the irritability and selfishness diminished, but not my need to say no or my need for solitude. Throughout the writing of the book, I was reconfirming in my heart and soul the basic necessity of time alone.

But we require other forms of information, also, in order to demonstrate *external* proof of a fundamental human need. First, we must find facts that support the need over time and in the culture, to understand how and why a basic need would defy discovery and not appear rudimentary. We have to establish that the need is bred in the bones, and animal studies are helpful in this approach. We need strong and corroborating research and clinical data, too. Evidence from aberrational behaviors can tell us much. For example, zoologists inform us that what we see in extremes of behavior are exaggerations of normal animal (and human) nature. Certainly, there are examples, such as autism, of excessive alone states. To sketch the aloneness landscape, I have chosen to use historical, sociological, ethological, biological, and psychological sources as well as my own personal experiences. There are pitfalls to you, the reader, in my taking a heterogeneous approach. My aim, though, is to show how these diverse areas contribute to one core theme that is inextricably woven into human nature but that has been obscured by decades of focusing elsewhere.

I have set out to demonstrate in Part One of the book why being alone is necessary in human development, from childhood to adulthood and beyond. Specifically, I discuss various reasons how and why society steadily devalues solo time, and then demonstrate that our view of aloneness should not be that of a place fraught with peril but of one that offers peace. *Aloneness should be distinguished from loneliness.* That—and because society's emphasis on attachment has undermined solitude—is why I have coined my term "alonetime." "Alonetime" is a new word for a vital need and state of being. In this way, I affirm in language that aloneness is a biological and psychological essential and just as important as the heavily documented need for attachment. By my definition it includes *the need to retreat psychologically (and at times, physically) in order to modify stimulation and to constitute or reconstitute how one functions — by oneself.* I go on to show that the appeal of the wild in sanctuaries and lone pursuits continue in modern times, even though by now attachment needs have overshadowed and displaced the concurrent need for alonetime. I recognize the strong dual messages common to all religions and philosophies: one must be connected to the world and people but should also reach a spiritual peak through solitude and meditation. Sometimes these paradoxes add to people's perplexity, yet people who acknowledge their different needs, for alonetime and togetherness, are better able to negotiate the confusion these teachings may create.

During the past century, so much has changed in terms of the way aloneness has been handled by society and the individual. From the early 1900s, psychoanalysis gave additional life to bonding theories. During World War II, reactions against the separation of parents and children, and the rising numbers of orphans, added to fiercely held attachment messages. As a countermeasure to the mistreatment of children, psychoanalysts and developmental psychologists emphasized the need for attachment as the major force in life. But to the old question "Is the bond with mother the one significant factor that shapes the child, the adult, the parent in his or her relationship?" my answer is an emphatic *no.*

In Part Two of the book, I build my argument for aloneness as an equal and urgent developmental need. I review the most recent psychological and psychoanalytic discourse, dipping into the exciting new research in neonatology and infancy, which shows that fetuses and infants actively initiate periods of isolation, and I find confirmation for the parallel needs for attachment and aloneness. After infancy, it becomes apparent that the school-age child, teenager, and adult also need alonetime for physiological and psychological growth.

In the last section of the book, Part Three, I reconstruct alonetime in diverse cultures and modern society, as well as examine relationships within and without the analyst's office. We learn how love has been distorted by unreasonable expectations for attachment. For example, how can couples at moments of intense closeness suddenly find themselves disenchanted? In the experiences of my patients, we find some solutions that resolve painful dilemmas between partners. Differences between the sexes may, in part, account for the relational needs that emerged with increased magnitude after the feminist movement took hold. Whether men and women think in opposites about aloneness in couplehood is debatable, but I believe alonetime is an equivalent need for men and women and often enhances both love and responsibility. While couples have trouble earning solitude, acceptable alone space has always been reserved for those engaged in creative endeavors. Beyond school years, only dedicated artists and performers can inhabit this space, but alonetime is necessary for *all* human development. In discussing extreme alone states, I use studies of autism, pseudoindependence, and isolation in an attempt to probe every corner of the alone experience.

Above all, this has been a personal odyssey, and I have encountered many psychically dangerous obstacles. The cases of loneliness, abandonment, disillusionment, and fragmentation among people completely alone were intimidating enough and became my Scylla, but in 1996, facing my sister's death and my social dependency on other humans became my Charybdis. How could I surmount these significant barriers, which pitted the consistent need for human contact against the need for peaceful aloneness and companionship? To overcome all the harsh and highly visible messages that the fear of aloneness delivered, I found that I needed to resist the siren call of attachment. In babyhood we require close, constant, and caring encounters. I was not saying that babies need less. Therefore, I had to become intimate with the attachment literature before I could add my perspective. My log entries reassured me that others traveled some of the same waters, and those statements served as the buoys. Although I knew that I could bolster my clinical experience and research with that of others, no one sails the exact seas of another. I had to find my own Ithaca.

Saying that, I would like to revive a time-honored custom. While rereading Bertrand Russell's *History of Western Philosophy*, I noted that this brilliant scholar begins his book by apologizing to the reader for not being a specialist on such an enormous topic. Without any claim to brilliance, I, too, need to beg the reader's indulgence. In my proof of alonetime as a basic need, I cover vast canyons of knowledge, extrapolating from them what I see as major themes in order to support my thesis. Unavoidably, I give short shrift to many subjects. But while I may have given limited attention to the fullness of the material and treated history less adequately than I might, I hope that I have also conveyed the steady significance of the need to be alone as shown throughout culture, time, and human development.

Perhaps the videotaped words of a former child prodigy, Glenn Gould, who abruptly stopped performing piano concerts, best sums up the interplay of achieving harmony between the two needs: "I don't know what the effect in ratio would be but I've always had a sort of intuition that for every hour you spend with other human beings, you need x number of hours alone. Now what that x represents, I don't really know, whether it be 2 and $7/8$ hours or 7 and $2/8$ hours, but it's a substantial ratio."[11]

Within this framework, ours is not an either/or world, where growing up always means losing attachments and separation always means bearing loneliness. This book begins to lay the foundation for both through a new view of alonetime, which claims that each and every one of us needs time alone. Some people may crave many hours by themselves; others may find sufficient solace in small doses of separate time. Regardless of the dosage, solitude is a deep, soothing, and persistent call in life.

PART ONE

Preconceived Notions

and New Thoughts

About Aloneness

CHAPTER 1

Fear, Helplessness,

and Loneliness

The word loneliness prevents us from entering into a complete understanding of that state. The word associated with past experience, evokes the feeling of danger and creates fear; therefore, we try to run away . . . you will see that the word has extraordinary significance for most of us. Words like . . . loneliness—what an astonishing influence they have on us. We are slaves to such words, and the mind that is a slave to words is never free of fear.

J. KRISHNAMURTI, *On Fear*[1]

THE QUIET CONTAINMENT in the stretch of time before birth hardly prepares us for the dependent helplessness immediately after. Seeds may be planted within that state of helplessness—the seeds of fear—and if they are allowed to blossom and spread, they could well interfere with a wonderful inner garden of alone life experiences. Those fears, together with social preconceptions and today's myopic focus on bonding needs, keep hidden a vital awareness of the need for alonetime.

Nevertheless, the need for alonetime remains and influences our lives. Some of the ways it expresses itself can be quite surprising, and illustrate the "return of the repressed." Desires that are repressed unconsciously by fear, anxiety, and social taboos can reappear in other guises, such as psychosomatic illnesses. This is a long-accepted concept in psychoanalytic thinking, and today scientific evidence shows that traumas (for example) that are totally denied can disrupt functioning and cause stress reactions that consequently affect physical well-being. A disguised enactment of the aloneness need may be seen in the behavior of computer buffs who spend countless hours transmitting messages and receiving information over the Internet while all by themselves—*alone*. Lured by pressures to interact, yet starved for private time, are people perhaps responding to the computer as a modern-day holy grail that will fulfill both needs? While personal computers are, by definition, single-user tools, many of the high-tech computer phrases—communication highway, World Wide Web, Internet, and the like—suggest connectedness to others. Conversations that can be interrupted by a one-way click of the switch are hardly equal to spoken dialogue, nor is meeting in cyberspace the virtual equivalent of holding hands. If alonetime is a vital need, shouldn't its claim nevertheless be highly visible, for how can something essential to life not always be palpable?

The fact that a basic requirement for life is not consistently recognizable is not unusual. Take thirst. Most often we get enough to drink through normal ingestion. Therefore, we are not automatically attuned to a deprivation. But even people in the state of dehydration do not necessarily feel thirsty. So it is with the need for alonetime. In the past, the need for alonetime had been more or less satisfied in the natural course of things. Few today recognize this profound loss. The majority of people are not fully aware of the present decline in alonetime, due in part to objective realities. World population has doubled since the 1950s. In cities across the world, including those in the United States, great urban crowding and globalized economies have revolutionized social relationships. World-renowned historian Eric Hobsbawm thinks the social and economic upheavals just in the third quarter of this century brought about the most profound revolution in society since the Stone Age.[2] Complex technological inventions have invaded all parts of private and public life. Every economic market is now interconnected. No longer can individuals depend on themselves for subsistence through agriculture, hunting, or herding. Even our basic way of refreshing ourselves in alonetime—sleep —has become constantly threatened by stress and noise.

Mother nature gives aloneness a high priority, viewing it differently than does American culture. For instance, nature built in a system that monitors sleep-wake cycles, called "circadian rhythms"—those internal clocks that help to regulate our day and evening cycles, affecting many behaviors including sleeplessness and wakefulness. Sleep is nature's way of ensuring alonetime. But given the rise in the number of sleep-disorder clinics and the sale of soporific drugs, even this one fundamental outlet for alonetime is in trouble. Sleep is invaluable. When, however, days are overcrowded with obligations, normal sleep hours are used to fulfill responsibilities. Sleep and alonetime's greatest disturber is fear. It blinds us to a need for time alone and forces the need to struggle for recognition.

Of course, people may request solitude, but wanting it and receiving it are two different matters, especially if one is not an ascetic or an artist. Invariably, alonetime meets with social questioning, if not censure. Even worse, people associate going it alone with unnecessary risk taking and antisocial pursuits. Whether listening to patients talk about their partners, or students about their lovers, family, or friends, I am struck by their expressions of gratitude if they receive "time off" to engage in their own pursuits—be it exercising or studying for an exam. Like prisoners who are granted parole before they deserve it, they feel their freedom is a gracious gift. Therefore, they have a hard time ever suggesting the possibility of spending a relaxing day alone.

When I was in kindergarten, my first report card read *S* (satisfactory) for how well I played with other children and *I* (needs improvement) for how I played alone. I didn't know it then, but that *I* was my first step toward discovering the complex nature of alonetime. I didn't understand what was wrong with my school behavior, especially since I always loved playing alone with dolls or just sitting imagining things and doing nothing. Wasn't I correct to assume that in school the name of the game was socializing? Furthermore, the unfamiliar made me scared to be alone, and I felt lonely. What seems strange in looking back is that I felt lonely among my classmates, but not in the true alonetime when home playing by myself. So alonetime is *not* the same thing as loneliness.

Loneliness is the most obvious risk of aloneness, and deep childhood fears of abandonment and neglect may be evoked by the idea of being alone. Terrors of night and darkness remain coupled with solitary sleeping. And sleep itself is interrupted by nightmares filled with embedded guilt and worries, which at times seem insurmountable. Discontent, ennui, and a deep sense of alienation can cause some people to rush into connectedness. For others, death anxiety may be avoided only by keeping oneself preoccupied or immersed in activity. If we can count alonetime as a pressing need, then despite countless obstacles, it will emerge and reemerge. When we confront the unconscious and conscious fears that I believe have derailed and obscured a need to be alone, will the general public provide confirmation—as my patients do in safe surroundings—of their persistent pursuit of alonetime? Given our present vocabulary, the battle will be uphill.

The Language of Alonetime

Language we use to describe being alone has changed. "Alone" did not always mean an absence of others. Originally, "alone" signified a completeness in one's singular being, as the word was coined in medieval times.[3] "Alone, by oneself," in modern dictionaries, goes with "retirement" and "seclusion"—being apart from others. "Solitude," the favored synonym of "aloneness," seems the politically correct term for the alone state; nevertheless in dictionary definitions it connotes "isolation" and "loneliness," as if they were potentially barren states.[4] All current meanings of "alone" imply a lack of something and conjure up pangs of loneliness. "Solitude," moreover, is an adult term. Philosopher Philip Koch and I seem closest in our positions of all the authors I've encountered.[5] He opposes solitude to loneliness; he sees the possibility of relating and aloneness as coexisting, and added difficulties to women in securing solitude. He reviews the arguments for and against solitude. But since his definition of solitude intimates knowledge of a populated world from which one turns away in order to reflect, he still is presenting it as primarily an adult harbor.[6] His understanding implies that someone else is available and suggests the presence of a self-organization sufficiently advanced either to have taken in or to have retreated from another. In contrast, I state that, especially for the young child or the infant, quiet soothing is sought not just as a disengagement from society, but for aloneness itself. Children do not *always* have to actively seek a solitude: when they are very young, alonetimes appear naturally. As they grow and find themselves intruded upon when alone, privacy and aloneness will take on more elusive tones.

"Solitude" also resonates resolution, and in that sense a conquering of fear. In religious terminology, "solitude" typically means the experience of oneness with God. Such esoteric heights require a knowledge of freedom, nature as repose, and creative urges. So it may be. But filled with such mixed messages, the word "solitude" cannot express the full dimensions of the need. "Alonetime" expands this conception, for it begins as a natural rhythm, a cycle in the connectedness and disconnectedness of life, a way of achieving homeostasis (stable inner equilibrium), a continuity with the earliest states of existence. "Alonetime" recognizes levels and degrees of disengaged consciousness, as will be shown, for example, in trance states. This places autism, alonetime's most extreme representative, on a continuum. Thus, my word "alonetime" includes the baby's faraway stare as well as the contemplative's embrace of religious unity. "Alonetime" captures the full and pleasurable essence of the experience because it not only incorporates all aspects of the need from infancy through old age but also, as a new word, is spared years of negative connections and ambivalences.

The psychological importance of changing the language of aloneness needs to be emphasized. In everyday parlance, "aloneness" and "attach-ment" are paired as antonyms. "Aloneness" represents the negative op-posite of "attached," that is, "alone" equals "not attached." With attachment being a desired state, not being attached immediately as-sumes a contrary, which in linguistic circles is called a "marked" state.[7] If we put "alone" in its own dimension as a positive term, then we can separate it from its negative opposites, "isolated" and "lonely." "Alone" and "attached" are then viewed as separate states of being, not marked as opposites. Similarly, "attached," "related," and "intimate" are desirable terms, and the marked antonyms, or undesirable opposites, are "merged," "smothered," and "symbiotic." The goal is to free, or unmark, "alone" as a contrary to "attached," and to make it more dynamic on its own descriptive plane. As "hot" is opposite to "cold," neither being inherently positive or negative, "attached" and "alone" portray two equal states, each valuable and pertinent. This psycholinguistic shift would help us in accepting alonetime as a positive need, distinguishing it from loneliness, which is a consequence of ruptures in relationships or too much immersion in aloneness, just as "merged" or "smothered" depict an overemphasis on an attachment need. The remarkable fact is that, despite bias in language, admonishments about evils of the solitaire, and the long-taught and sometimes unshakable fears associated with alonetime, a desire to be alone remains.

Society's Negative Thrust

Along with language barriers, societal demands instill fear of going it alone. Why does society ardently decry alonetime? Could it be that the lure to be alone is so great that strong countermeasures are always em-ployed?[8] Although adults differentiate between being alone and being lonely, the way we speak indicates that this knowledge is lost to the cultural pull for social attachment. Statements such as "Be good or I'll leave you alone" or "Stay alone in your room until you know how to behave" serve as threats because early on we are taught to believe that aloneness is not desirable. Indeed, it is made frightening. As my youngest son, Phillip, was told by a camp counselor, "Behave or I'll put you into the woods and Freddie Krueger will get you!" Even friends and relatives imply to adults as well as the young that "if you dress, talk, eat, or smell like that you'll have no friends—you'll be lonely." These messages are geared to "civilize" us. They work because they resound with our social longings for companionship and fears of being without it. Obviously, it is in society's interest to foster connections as, by definition, societies depend upon *co*habitation for perpetuation.

It is also in our interest as individuals to be connected. Being single sets off fear of matelessness or childlessness. One need not be a scientist to know—as do sociologists, anthropologists, and evolutionary biologists—that the continuation of the species is a primary goal of all animals. Without relationships, society as we know it would cease to exist, and no generations would follow—both in humans and in the animal kingdom. Biologically, parents and children must foster connections or else children may die. Therefore, fear of being alone is a biological imperative.

I teach a psychology of parenthood course that explores reasons for becoming a parent across the animal kingdom and cultures. The basic reason to procreate, from an evolutionary point of view, is to ensure survival of the species. The psychological reasons gleaned from interviews and broad-based surveys vary from "wanting to share our love with another" to "providing grandchildren" to "ensuring a lack of loneliness" to "having someone to play with" to "saving the marriage" to "It's what I'm supposed to do." Society's relentless directive to mate and produce offspring—pronatalism—is evident everywhere, reverberating, for example, in advertisements and television.

It's the most natural thing in the world for a woman to want to be a mother—isn't it? Not necessarily, according to research done by Judith Teicholz, clinical instructor in psychology and psychiatry at the Harvard Medical School in 1980.[9] The topic first gained her attention when she noticed in the *New York Times* that Hugh Downs had received an award for being Non-Father of the Year from a group named the National Alliance for Optional Parenthood.[10] She realized that people need to have options about such an important decision as parenthood. "I decided to design a study that would really evaluate what seems to be a negative stereotype of a woman who didn't want to have children," she said.[11] Many would have us believe that a woman who chooses not to have children has made a poor feminine identification and adjustment, and has not internalized the basic values and mores of society as a whole, because she has rejected the value of motherhood.[12] The results of Teicholz's study show that these are not givens.

To sociobiologists, sexual attraction leading to copulation is the evolutionary adaptation that ensures continuation of the species. For mammals, more than sexual fervor is required for couples to stay together long enough to raise a child.[13] Society, according to genetic and anthropological thought, has what might be called a nomadic instinct to explore and live on one's own. Alternately, social scientists describe a herding instinct that may trigger fear of being ostracized when going it alone and impede people's desires to explore solo or assume an independent stance. Instinct has been linked to tribal groupings. At least since we stood up-right, humankind has banded together. However, are herding or tribal formations any more instinctive than wanting to "do our own thing"? The behaviors of newborns tell us no. Disturbing an infant's routine can make parents' lives miserable. Among the first words of toddlers are "my turn," "I do it," "mine." These words are heard in most families with one child or more whether parents do or do not stress competition. Children instinctively define their singular as well as group selves.

Crucial evidence exists to support the notion that being alone itself is an imperative. Ages ago, our species learned that lone survival required very special skills. Hunting in a group, settling in communes, trekking together, and herding with others increased opportunity to survive. Conditions equally required people to learn how to forage and live on their own resources. In parts of the Amazon or Central Africa today, alone survival skills are handed down from one generation to the next. Our own soldiers are taught survival skills for use when in hostile territory and separated from their command. These lessons in self-preservation are not part of typical childhood education in Euro-American societies. Yet the desire to learn in this regard has to be implanted in us, as is demonstrated by the number of young people and even adults who seek the lone challenges presented by organizations such as Outward Bound. By not treating the teaching of these skills as everyday imperatives, society keeps alonetime secondary to attachment. We need to teach these skills, both for personal survival and for daily pleasure and health.

In the lives of risk takers, the lure of alonetime never stops. In 1993, Borge Ousland, a thirty-one-year-old Norwegian explorer and professional deep-sea diver, made one of the most difficult treks in polar history. Pulling a three-hundred-pound sled, he skied alone to the North Pole, over more than six hundred miles of drifting ice. His only companion, his sled, held his food, stove, tent, sleeping bag, spare clothing, and navigation and maintenance gear. It also carried equipment to scare off polar bears. Once or twice a week he communicated with his base camp by radio. His goal in conquering the North Pole was to see if it could be done alone, without outside help. After his extraordinary solo trek of fifty-two days and eleven hours, he said: "I had feared I would be lonely; I had never spent so much as a single night alone in a tent before, much less been on a lone expedition. But being alone proved to be one of the greatest experiences of the entire trek."[14]

If alonetime is challenging and gratifying, and necessary to self-reliant existence, what makes many of us vulnerable to the fears that dissuade us from this important path? The human baby, though not as dependent and helpless as many parents believe, is still very much under the control of adults. Parents have enormous power. One psychoanalyst[15] declares that the basis of adult fears is the childhood terror of parental power over life and death. Fairy tales like Hansel and Gretel depict the horror of premature abandonment by parents.

Bonding may seem more attractive than time alone, yet I claim that these conditions are equally important. To account for this disparity, I believe we have to understand both a baby's initial alone capacities and helplessness, and the degree to which the latter may shape the psyche, not only in babyhood but throughout life. Parents, we know, cannot always or instantly meet the needs of a baby. Times occur when babies are too cold, too hungry, too hot, too wet, too stimulated, too unengaged, too sleepy, too alert. Great relief comes when that powerful other reads the baby's signals and changes its environment. As someone grows up, he or she may associate being left alone with an inability to fulfill his or her own needs. It is no wonder, then, that the need to connect soon takes precedence over desires for aloneness. But make no mistake: people are *taught* to want to relate, just as alone needs require positive reinforcement. And sometimes people overlearn the relating lesson.

Erich Fromm tells us of "incestuous symbiosis,"[16] whereby we inextricably merge with a parental figure. An all-powerful mother figure may become worshiped in a group, culture, or cult, as in the case of Argentina's Eva Perón. Or a father figure can lead a nation, as Fromm described the Germans' blind obedience to Hitler, or as we have seen more recently, messianic leaders can inspire mass suicides. People in general may, out of fear of assuming responsibility for their own life, shy away from empowering themselves and remain slaves to their mythical pasts.

How are our alone needs overshadowed by fears of helplessness and separation? Other situations can also feed feelings of helplessness. For example, humans are not innately equipped as some species are to function at night. Naturalists see fear of the dark as basic to our species' development.[17] Helplessness and darkness go together. Though humans have somewhat conquered darkness with fire and electricity, they have not completely conquered fears of the dark, as fans of the vampire stories of Anne Rice will attest. Fearing being alone in the dark sometimes leads to fear of sleep, and therefore affects alonetime. According to one author, the average number of hours spent in sleep by age seventy is two hundred thousand.[18] But this is not true for those with troubled thoughts.

Sleep and Fear

Guilt about "being bad" may augment fears about sleeping alone. When children have misbehaved they often feel ashamed and may wish to be unseen and think they deserve to be isolated. Parents sometimes reinforce this association with long, alone time-outs as punishment. Eugene Field's poem about a little boy who sees things at night illustrates the scared and agonizing sleep time fears that guilt breeds:

> Mother tells me Happy Dreams! and takes away the light,
> An' leaves me lyin' all alone an' seein' things at night! . . .
> It almost alluz when I'm bad I see things at night! [19]

In the past, sleep traumas were thought to occur when a person was overpowered by a demonic mare or evil incubus or succubus. Nightmares today may relate to psychological conflicts, but they are simply scary dreams that wake someone from sleep. Believe it or not, there was a time during the Romantic period of the late nineteenth century when bad dreams were in vogue. Percy Bysshe Shelley and his followers gave great score to the private self, and nightmares were a means to explore the dark side of that self. In order to follow the lead of nineteen-year-old Mary Shelley's fearless writing, and her groundbreaking novel about Dr. Frankenstein's monster, frightening dreams were not to be shunned. Some went so far as to defy the vegetarian regime touted by Shelley and ate large quantities of raw meat to induce dreadful and bizarre dreams. But most of these seekers of night terror experienced little more than indigestion from the rich food, unlike another Romantic poet, Samuel Taylor Coleridge, who had suffered since childhood from daytime trauma and shocking dreams and could soothe himself only by overdosing with laudanum.

Modern dream researchers see nightmares as connected to childhood themes, particularly feelings of helplessness. A recent study shows that individuals with repeated nightmares (more than one per month) are prone to high levels of annihilation anxiety—fear of being overwhelmed or engulfed in a basically dangerous situation.[20] Sleep, our guardian of alonetime, may be interrupted when the needs for attachment and being alone reach an unresolvable impasse. When we innocently steal into the alone caverns of sleep, we open ourselves to inner or outer destruction, and *this* is why many people distrust sleep.

The psychological avoidance of dreams and sleep might be considered an extreme form of fear of being alone. In babies and toddlers, this fear is often reinforced. For some babies, sleep can be more frightening than it is for others, and the ensuing need for comfort may easily become habitual. Sleep problems in babies are sometimes constitutionally based, as with sensory-processing difficulties and digestive problems, or they may develop as the result of illness.[21] With innate problems, sleep troubles may erupt. But even without inborn disturbances, natural sleep may be disrupted. Caretakers can all too easily fail to recognize the infant's ability to disengage from others. Take a friend baby-sitting for my grandson. New to the situation, he determined that because Benjamin was happy playing, he didn't need any nap, and continued engaging him for eight hours straight. The toddler was so exhausted that the second his parents came home and his mother lifted him, he was asleep. Knowing the right time to give comfort, or how to allow babies and toddlers to find their own biological rhythm, is not easy. If they resist being put down to sleep, most often after a few minutes of fussing they settle down. In my work as parent consultant—and even when I briefly hosted a parent-information radio show—the most popular question asked by parents was how to get their children to sleep.

Sleep

Sleep is the great protector of alonetime. In the anatomy of sleep, the quiet efficiency of this state of alonetime stands out. After loss of sleep, our brain waves change to a slower wave activity, and REM sleep (those rapid eye movements that connote dreaming) takes over. That REM is the making up of the lost motor and visual brain activity in sleep, an attempt to organize and catalogue the information of the day. When sleep becomes a battleground, it loses its gentle quality and its potential healing benefits. Research on the psychological and physiological aspects of sleep is still in the preliminary stage, but we do know that sleep offers stress reduction and physiological regulation, and appears to be crucial to maintaining normal body temperature and conserving energy.[22] In any case, debate is ongoing about the amount of sleep people need. When we make fun of friends who sleep nine or ten hours, remember that before artificial light was used to extend work and play hours, people went to sleep when darkness fell and arose with the rising sun (in many climates easily nine to twelve hours).

Both sleep and rest deprivation elicit compensatory responses.[23] But so does work overload. From what my friends and colleagues tell me, I'm not the only one who in the wee hours bolts upright with the knowledge of an incomplete task. The information highway may already be causing a traffic jam in our brains. Several high-powered people tell me they have stopped entering their E-mail and the Internet, for a while at least. They plan a moratorium in order to finish work that has a higher priority. Although both working in the dark of night and sleeping would qualify as alonetime, they offer different degrees of gratification. A peck on the cheek is far less satisfying than a soul kiss if the need is for intimacy.

Sleep is not necessarily passive alonetime. Currently, neurologists hypothesize that this activity is a way for the brain to organize itself. We learn as we dream![24] As sleep expert J. Allan Hobson points out, learning is probably part of active sleep. The idea that by osmosis we absorb knowledge from books placed under our pillow before an exam may be far-fetched, but an analogy exists in real life. When people say they will "sleep on it," they awake sure of their decision in the morning. During sleep, the person is off the receiving line, dealing with little or no information from the environment.[25] Sleep visualizations may serve a process similar to the imagery that performers use to prepare for competition. Though many a joke or song composed in dreams turns out to be sheer nonsense, people are also inspired by their dreams.

Not many besides Freud himself have felt comfortable interpreting their own dreams. Most ignore dreams or look for interpretations and guidance in dreams and life from powerful others—analysts or mystics. Yet, is not the acceptance and understanding of an individual's unconscious, although in part a process helped along by others, in the last analysis a solo task? Dreams can be private riches, the source of poetry and insights. Heraclitus of the ancient city of Ephesus wrote to his students: "We must not act and speak like sleepers . . . The waking have one world in common, but the sleeping turn aside each into a world of his own."[26] Thus even the earliest scientists understood this alone world of the dream, and the hopes, fears, and memories it houses. We can attempt to share our dreams, but in truth we have only ourselves to confirm these inner flights.

Existential Meanings of Loneliness

Existentialists grant it as fact that humans are ultimately alone. No one else can experience another individual's feelings and thoughts or face another's death. From the existential viewpoint, people must deal with this loneliness, and often do so with escapism. According to existentialists, individuals employ elaborate defensive systems in order to avoid the pangs of being alone.[27] Despite attempts to distract themselves from dealing with life questions, people sometimes experience a loneliness anxiety (fear of being alone) that pushes them into seeking activity with others. Loneliness anxiety, according to this theory, should be distinguished from true loneliness, which stems from acknowledging and facing the reality of being alone. True loneliness, as opposed to loneliness anxiety, can be a creative force.[28] The distinction between loneliness anxiety and true loneliness in existential thinking is akin to my differentiation between loneliness and aloneness.

According to existentialists, true loneliness, while seen as healthy and productive, is still something we need to grit our teeth to bear. It is at first unwelcomed and later tolerated. I see aloneness, on the contrary, as healthy, necessary, and initially not painful. It is one of our first sensory experiences with antecedents in a cozy, comfortable womb state. We *learn* to fear this state when confronted by helplessness at birth. If early experiences of aloneness are unduly threatening and reinforce helplessness, sometimes even turning out to be dangerous, attachment needs become overwhelming. Fear will henceforth be associated with alonetime. Saint-Exupéry's Little Prince knows this fear well, and he charmingly tries to dispel anxiety about making solo journeys through life. In his travels to this planet, he learns not to be afraid to make friends, take responsibility, "waste" time, or to be sad, and finally to go his own way.

Boredom: Me and My Shadow

The Little Prince was committed to establishing the importance of doing nothing or of simply watching a sunset. Clearly, society has been afraid of endorsing such solitude, or "idleness." The Puritans believed that an idle mind is the devil's workshop. The last words of a seventeenth-century treatise on behavior are "Be not solitary, be not idle."[29] And Johnson tells Boswell similarly: "If you are idle be not solitary, if you are solitary be not idle."

The state of mind Johnson fears, implying a moral sin, is boredom. According to literary critic Patricia Meyer Spacks, "acedia"—the medieval term for the sin of sloth and idleness—was proclaimed by theologians of those times as the root of many evils. Boredom brings on the "danger of insufficient engagement with life's obligations and possibilities."[30] Later on, boredom reflected a sociological rather than a moralistic problem. With more leisure time, those among the landed gentry sought ways to pass away the hours agreeably. In Spacks's view, our growing emphasis on the inner experience is one cause of boredom's rise. For if we fear an inner inadequacy, a meager interior life, then we struggle to avert boredom at all costs.

Despite these efforts, boredom seems to be a widespread phenomenon of our time. How to explain this? People have more leisure time—but are also busier. Most have access to washing machines, convenience foods, and other ways to reduce actual work hours. On the other hand, women saved from some carrying and cleaning chores work longer hours at jobs and may be also the major caretakers of children. Rest time is typically TV time. We fill up to avoid boredom, but this alienates us further from ourselves. Inner boredom is bred from being out of touch with emotions. Boredom is a common experience, a signal to reach deeper into our feelings or to challenge ourselves to do more than we have been. One can happily do nothing, or be engrossed in a project, but anxious escapes from doing nothing are frequently boring! Being afraid to be bored can also keep us from being alone. This state of affairs suggests that we are losing access to the richness of inner life. Perhaps we forget being bored silly as a child. While the imaginations of children are sparked by doing nothing, they also intuitively know the dangers in feeling bored too much of the time. Boredom is a form of alienation that stems, in part, from the individual running from self-knowledge. Eagerness to act can be a knee-jerk reaction to sidestep perpetually being "bored to death."[31] In 1988, Anthony Storr, a psychoanalyst and fellow of the Royal College of Psychiatrists, wrote an important book that recognized both the creative aspects of and the treacherous route in finding oneself through aloneness. In *Solitude*, Storr stated: "Human beings search for meaning through the use of imagination and solitude, through separation [and] isolation and finally come to a sense of coherence by the end of their lifetime, narrowly escaping the label of mad."[32]

The running from self-knowledge—being alone with oneself—is not truly safe. According to some physicians, the nervous activity associated with type A behavior can actually cause death.[33] "Hurry sickness" is the name for the frenzied, nonstop, hasty behavior that takes pleasure out of life and can lead to headaches, high blood pressure, and heart attacks. Young children who are described as type A are less likely to recognize the signs of fatigue than those who are easygoing. Could it be that the determination to be occupied constantly is a misdirected attempt to stave off death? Alonetime for some has the connotation of the long sleep of death, as seen in the origin of the word "cemetery." The word derives from the Greek *koimētērion*, meaning a sleeping place or dormitory; later, Christian writers would use it to describe the Roman catacombs and then churchyards for burials.

Death: The Dreamless Sleep

Even if one hired the most eloquent spin doctors, it would be difficult for aloneness to escape a bad press completely. Yet, as we explore fears of death, it is important to keep in mind that being alone is a very different state from that of death (moreover, the peace of death is not always viewed as loathsome). But I think that the fear of nothingness, of our breath being snuffed out, of being without others to confirm us and validate our reality and save us from the madness of being solely in our own head, stems not only from terror of helpless abandonment but also from a realization that we may learn to want the peacefulness of our own company to the exclusion of others.

When the need to disengage and be on our own is misinterpreted, we experience a split between two essential aspects of ourselves. An anxiety-ridden conflict ensues between the pull to relate to that which is outside of us and the pull to know and be one with ourselves. Dread of being alone, as Coleridge's Ancient Mariner chants,[34] is not exactly on the same scale as a general distaste for dreaming, lone pursuits, being bored stiff, or having time to kill. Rather, this dread is a soul-searing association with death. The ultimate fears of alienation and death make us disavow the aloneness need. Existential philosophy tackles both fear of alienation and death anxiety. Alienation in existentialist theory is difficult to describe, partly because the idea has been misapplied. Contrary to popular belief, alienation is not separateness from others or from God, but a fundamental loss of connection with oneself that leads to a sense of not being in the world. Renowned philosopher David Potter has said: "The alienated person . . . feels that objects dominate him, and that he is a 'victim' of his sensual 'animal' desires."[35] Alienation, then, is self-estrangement. Existential philosophy, which is rooted in Socratic dialogue, seeks to transform an individual's sense of alienation first to a relationship with oneself and then to what religious philosopher and existentialist Martin Buber describes lyrically as connectedness and commitment—an I-thou relationship to the world. Modern life encourages fears of aloneness by neither honoring the inborn desire to be alone nor providing skills that will aid us in lone pursuits for their own sake. Thus we are encouraged to turn away from the essential core of our being. This premature deadening makes us all the more fearful of actual death.

How we handle death as a people reveals much about who we are as a whole.[36] Cultural attitudes toward death from medieval times to now have been endlessly reviewed.[37] Death in earlier times was part of everyday experience, for death was like a voyage to another place. Nor was death unfamiliar. Graveyards were near dwelling places and people intrepidly walked or sat among the dead. The familiar death people sometimes witnessed in the Middle Ages came from frequent exposure to people dying. In familiar death, corpses are not automatically feared, contagious, or dangerous. During the Renaissance, as sinfulness became more and more incorporated into the gospel, several authors[38] recorded a sharp rise in fear of death. Our modern approach to death is significantly altered, and we like to encounter death indirectly, in sterile isolation. Longer life spans have kept many people (until the AIDS epidemic, perhaps) from ever experiencing the death of a relative or friend except when all were well along in years. Despite some healers' and authors' courageous work,[39] in the abstract, the idea of death is frightening. A picture of a rather tame Death is portrayed in a seductive manner by Fredric March in the film *Death Takes a Holiday*. No grim reaper he, but a rather likable fellow. In our times, people outside of war zones are sheltered from the absolute finality of death, and death is presented as sufficiently ludicrous so as to become alien. Current films often make a mockery of it. Rather than protecting us, this glib treatment may be scaring us and giving us increased reason to exile the thought of death from our active lives.[40]

In *The Denial of Death*, renowned scholar Ernest Becker states: "The final terror of self-consciousness is the knowledge of one's own death."[41] People cannot live heedless of their fate because self-consciousness is part of the human condition. Children are not unaware of death. At age four or so, they begin to realize that life isn't forever. However, most children —unless confronted head-on, as in war-torn countries, through early personal loss, unbearable pain, or unusual anger—are able to suspend and deny the reality of death. Those who feel safe feign becoming mortally sick, shot, or vanquished and then resurrect themselves and reenter their unself-conscious play space and daydreams fearlessly. In contrast, adults fantasize freedom from the tomb yet inevitably stumble upon the angst of mortality. Adults do have greater realization of life's ending than children, but the young are fearful of abandonment and separation and in far greater need for others to offer perspective on what the real dangers are. Little wonder that aloneness, tied to punishment and desertion, is greeted with ambivalence.

The Two Sides of Aloneness

Associative fears color our view of being alone and inhibit us from consciously valuing its pleasures. We already know that desires are not halted by external pressures and fears. AIDS, for example, like sexually transmitted diseases in ages past, only partially curbs or distorts an appetite for sex. If alonetime is a basic need, social messages and fear won't keep one from fulfilling it. My clinical work teaches me this every day. I see patients drawn to trying out being alone who are inwardly cowed, having been taught that it is something to fear. Excerpts from my patients' experiences show varied moments of alone states:

- Elaine is home by herself. Suddenly she feels scared and panicky; she rushes to the telephone to call a friend.
- George is driving along the highway; he begins to feel isolated, uneasy, and unsettled. He pulls into a motel, goes to a bar, and orders a stiff drink.
- Laura is driving alone on the same highway as George; she is filled with a sense of well-being, a rush of completion. She holds these good sensations deeply and fully within herself.
- Jim is at home alone. The familiar room, the quiet surroundings, begin to touch him and he is aware of a feeling of ease, an inner well of acceptance.

Elaine and George are *lonely*. They are in need of solace and companionship. Laura and Jim are *alone*. They chose a time for reflection and solitary thought. While superficially these experiences appear similarly isolating, they actually represent completely different states. Laura and Jim value alonetime; Elaine's and George's learning was derailed.

When Elaine began treatment, she felt being on her own at night meant that she was completely unlovable. If the phone didn't ring, it confirmed her belief about being a nuisance and hard to stomach. Calling someone dispelled the fears of loneliness for the moment. However, having several friends who were always glad to hear from her did not allay her fears for longer than the evening. Interestingly enough, she craved alonetime. She was like other members of her family, who sought free time and kept people at bay.

George's story is more complex. This ambitious young man learned to be afraid when he was very young. His mother had terminal cancer and died when he was ten, but he frequently went to bed worried even before that loss. His older sister had juvenile diabetes before treatment for the disease had been refined. More than once he witnessed her in a coma. Worse still, many days he returned home from school to find the house empty and a note saying his sister and mother were in the hospital. George was an excellent and imaginative student and, later, businessman, but he associated his strengths and lone accomplishments with others' sickness, suffering, and death.

◆   ◆   ◆

According to George, his sister had difficulty separating and striking out on her own. What people associate with sickness and loneliness often explains why they think of themselves as fragile and weak and why they have fostered excessively attached behaviors. Loneliness is described as the "inner worm that gnaws at the heart,"[42] a state that paralyzes our spirit and compromises our soul. While being lonesome is usually normal and transient, something often related to missing a specific someone, loneliness can be overwhelming and feel everlasting.

Psychologists and psychiatrists have seen loneliness as a precursor to psychosis, an anxiety so terrible that it has no redeeming features. I challenge this assumption. Although psychosis may at times be a resolution for an unhappy life, the disturbed thinking of the psychotic lies on a separate plane than even the most excruciating loneliness. When loneliness turns to mental illness, it is accompanied by either deep depression or a hostile withdrawal into one's own isolated thoughts. There are situations, too, when people become disoriented in strange surroundings or find themselves confined alone for unusual periods of time through choice or circumstance. Obsessive ideas can then take hold of the mind and lead to psychotic thinking.

Withdrawal from life is beyond loneliness, as is documented in Michel Negroponte's film *Jupiter's Wife*. Maggie, the heroine of the film, lives among the "gods" (thus her nickname) and the homeless of Central Park. She and her dogs survive through her wit and wiles and the help of interested New Yorkers living on the Upper East Side of Manhattan. The primary relationship, however, for this solitary person is with Jupiter, to whom she listens through earphones. Yet loneliness by itself is not what causes Maggie's disregard of reality. Her disillusionment began with re-

jection from her perfectionist mother and was reinforced after abandonment by her intimate friend John, the father of the two children whom
she ultimately left. Maggie illustrates the devastating compromise of a
reality that attempts to balance the extreme separateness in both unending solitude and dismal relationships.

Unlike the angst of alienation or the restlessness of boredom, loneliness, in its pining for others, carries with it a distinct brand of unhappiness. Feeling lost, unloved, bereft, and doomed weaves its own circle of
hell. At its worst, it is the terrifying separateness of an individual lost
from community and equally alienated from the inner core of self. One is
not as helpless as in depression, but often equally hopeless. Having been
there and treated many patients in that place, I have my own understanding of the condition. Loneliness is a complex combination of moods.
There is extreme *withdrawal* that portends severe pathology. No one is as
lonely as Hannibal the cannibal in *The Silence of the Lambs* or the title
character in Camus's *The Stranger*. Different degrees of loneliness are felt,
as are varying states of aloneness. Given that, should we consider all
loneliness as negative? For loneliness sometimes has its place.

Controversy surrounds the question of what causes intense, relentless
loneliness. Some think that negative states of mind, like boredom, are at
the root. Many insist that social support and relationships are crucial as
buffers against these feelings. However, clinical work has shown that
relationships are not the perfect cure for loneliness, since negative experiences with others can initiate lonely feelings. One look at the artist Edvard
Munch's portrayal of a couple in several versions of his work *The
Lonely Pair* clearly demonstrates this. The couple touches side by side
while each of the pair looks off to a separate distant horizon. Munch
himself bore severe loneliness, caused in part by a panicking fear of being
suffocated by closeness. To avoid intimacy, he preferred aloofness, even
living without connections. Munch was not alone in his apprehension.
There is a different school of thought that sees overengagement, rather
than insufficient relationships, as the cause of loneliness. Early overindulgence in infancy and childhood, where the caretaker fills every spare
moment in the child's life, could breed loneliness in adulthood. Described
as "egotistic desolation,"[43] this situation keeps one from developing the
self-sustaining alone side of life.

As we have seen, lonely people fall into different clusters. There are
those who feel and think differently than the majority, and they may find
ways to band together. Gays and lesbians, for example, have overcome
societal estrangement by forming their own impressive networks. Their

status in society today, though less than perfect, is a far cry from the one depicted in the 1928 book *The Well of Loneliness* by Radclyffe Hall. Banned at the time of publication, it is about a woman's courage and despair in attempting to overcome the imposed stigma of homosexuality. She recounts the longing for her mother's love in an episode of missed closeness between them: "They had gazed at each other as though asking for something, as though seeking something, the one from the other; then the moment had passed—they had walked on in silence, no nearer in spirit than before."[44]

Cultural determinants of loneliness, such as homosexuality, have been politicized and nationalized. In certain instances, such determinants have been used to describe Americans as a whole. A group of sociologists in the 1960s, headed by David Riesman, characterized Americans as "other-directed" and overly concerned with popularity and how others evaluate them.[45] Paradoxically, the other-directed person, like the alienated, remains a lonely spectator looking outwardly for approval but "never com[es] close to others or to himself." In contrast, powerful writer Phillip Slater asserts that Americans put too much emphasis on individualism.[46] In his view, the pressing desires for engagement and dependence become thwarted because of American society's ever-present commitment to individualism. Thus, pursuing one's bliss can lead to disconnection, boredom, and loneliness. Could both Riesman's and Slater's theories be true? Certainly, both are in tune with the popular concept of inordinate narcissism leading to ostracism. I see, however, a central flaw in these theories. They begin with the premise that aloneness and attachment are either/or conditions. The needs for social acceptance and to be one's true self are at odds only when they are pitted against each other and interpreted as opposites. People thrive best when they achieve an equilibrium between both states of mind. Faced with so many theories about the dangers and benefits of the individual self alone, many people paradoxically do not have sufficient alonetime to allow these ideas to simmer. Thinking, however, may be becoming a lost art. But what about adolescence, a time when young people have scads of time for rumination?

Adolescence may not be the first time one discovers aloneness, but I don't remember feeling a complete and utter loneliness before then. Bouts of loneliness were a painful part of my teenage years, and I knew others felt similarly. Sometimes I didn't understand how anyone survived without a constant companion. Yet even the friends with whom I spent most of the day did not always share my thoughts and feelings—even with them, I could feel estranged. As Octavio Paz suggests:

It is true that we sense our aloneness almost as soon as we are born, but children and adults can transcend their solitude and forget themselves in games or work. The adolescent, however, vacillates between infancy and youth . . . He is astonished at the fact of his being, and this astonishment leads to reflection . . . The singularity of his being, which is pure sensation in children, becomes a problem and a question.[47]

This adolescent problem may be deeply troubling, but not until one faces separation from parents and changing intimacies with friends can there emerge the particular desolation of loneliness. Some adolescents retaliate against new circumstances in their relationships and assume an angry and rejecting stance when caught between a parent's desire to push them away and then to hold them back. Feeling utterly abandoned is a different story. What ultimately altered my Technicolor world to a dull gray was the death of my father. At age fourteen, I didn't stop to realize the extent of the void.

Healthy although painful loneliness is a reaction to a sad occurrence, linked to mourning and recovering from trauma. This transient state of withdrawal is to me a natural protective hibernation that many people employ on the way back to engagement with others. Stepping back from the world and slowing down the metabolism of stimuli acts like sleep to regird emotional energies. Still, some people choose loneliness over closeness, unwilling to risk intimacy. But what happens to those born less socially adept, or shy? My son Phillip, for example, who seeks companionship as well as time alone, falls in the continuum of a shy child, which could have augmented his aloneness need.[48] Research demonstrating the genetic and neurological bases of intelligence and social behavior suggests that to a degree the individual's need for aloneness may be "hardwired" (that is, in our brain cells) before nurturing takes over.

Shyness, by itself, while signaling greater sensitivity to stimulation, does not prevent the urge or capacity to relate or preclude a social network; it just makes it harder to create one, as Monroe's and Patrick's stories show.

Monroe, born with neurological problems, was always shy around strangers. As he grew older, he witnessed others able to play ball, follow directions, and understand conversation. He felt like a third wheel and had a lot of catching up to do. He didn't want to go to nursery school, and his mother let him stay home. He played by himself in the playground, and his parents ended up making sand castles with him. When company came, he went to his room; no one objected. Later his teachers suggested to the family that Monroe needed to be taught how to play with others, but the family said, "He gets too upset; let's wait." Monroe began to tell stories about how everyone picked on him. He exaggerated how nasty and rude the other children were to the adults. He thought that he was better than the others, and his parents concurred. Consequently, Monroe grew up with almost no friends except the adults in the family. No one minded, least of all Monroe, who complained about being lonely but kept himself occupied on his own. His shyness was fostered as a way to avoid contact with anyone other than the immediate family.

Another child, Patrick, also had learning disabilities. He was so shy[49] that at three months, when someone addressed him in an elevator, he blushed. When he saw other children in day care doing things he couldn't, he held back. But in the play yard, he laughed when children splashed him with water or raced after him, and they started to like his sense of humor. His parents didn't think he should be allowed to run away when he couldn't do something, and always included him in their social functions. He decided himself to go to a camp, even though he knew the kids would tease him because, at age ten, he could not read. He said that he could handle being left out sometimes. In high school, however, Patrick began to want to join groups and made a few friends. When he began to live on his own, he expanded the number of friends in his circle.

◆   ◆   ◆

Monroe's shyness was too avidly supported and thus undermined any courage to go it alone, but Patrick persevered. This simple determination—the undaunted spirit of resolution possessed by characters in Shakespeare's historical plays—is a self-will and fortitude that gives one the spunk to brave life.

Ernest Becker speaks of this heroism as a fading but necessary virtue in all of our lives. Rejection, annihilation, separation, loneliness—whatever fears we may have, there is an accessible cosmic heroism that enables us to face them head-on. What the poets and skeptics bring to our awareness is how the cyclical nature of creation—emptiness-life-death-life—

makes living a double-edged sword. We face death in life and life in death. Cosmic heroism, for Becker, is a "scientific-mythical (religious) construction of victory over human limitations." [50] It is us joining into the creative life force despite its mysterious and unpredictable nature.

In *Women Who Run with the Wolves*, Clarissa Pinkola Estes identifies and runs with the wild man and woman in us. She, too, discusses the inevitable cycles of life:

> Among wolves, the Life/Death/Life cycles in nature and fate are met with grace and wit and the endurance to stay tight with one's mate and to live lone and as well as can be. But in order for humans to live and give loyalty in this most fit manner . . . one has to go up against the very thing one fears most. There is no way around it, as we shall see. One must sleep with Lady Death. [51]

Becker and Estes seem poles apart in their approach to life and death. Becker is by admission "morbidly minded." Estes is vitally ensconced in the joy of nature. Yet many meeting places are found in their work. Both writers embolden the reader by reminding them that the helplessness of childhood doesn't have to shape his or her later choices. Facing our worst fears, and gaining a reconciliation with our natural fate, is lightened by an appreciation of alonetime. Once we've stood our ground with death, this appreciation becomes easier and motivates us to seek actively and indirectly whatever else we fear, be it solo adventures, creative pursuits, peaceful sleep, or meditation.

Nature, culture, and social training have taught us to be afraid or feel helpless when we are alone. As powerful as these lessons have been, desires for alonetime persist, and often we fear what we wish for the most. Loneliness has varied meanings, and is not necessarily the result of immersion in alonetime. It can be an angry turning away from others, coupled with devastating feelings of isolation, or merely a transitory condition. As a child I feared being lonely while craving alonetime as well. This tension between these two apparently disparate feelings poses a mystery that I will continue to explore throughout the book.

CHAPTER 2

Wilderness, Wanderlust,

and "Wild" Animals

Old Mr. Hacker lived alone in the city. He used to like it, but not anymore. The people upstairs were always making a racket. Somebody played a loud radio next door. The elevator was often broken, and the stairs were hard to climb. The streets were full of garbage . . . "I wonder what it would be like to live in the country?" he said to himself. At night he began to dream of villages and fields, and of wind moving through the branches of big trees.
JAMES STEVENSON, *Mr. Hacker*[1]

How silent, how spacious, what room for all, yet without place to insert an atom; in graceful succession, in equal fullness in balanced beauty, the dance of the hours goes forward still. Like an odor of incense, like a strain of music, like a sleep, it is inexact and boundless. It will not be dissected nor unraveled, nor shown. Away, profane philosopher! Seekest thou in nature the cause?
RALPH WALDO EMERSON, "The Method of Nature"[2]

W E ARE BORN WANTING and needing time and space alone to process the stimulation around us, as we also learn quickly to revel in and long for attached and related times. From the proximal and the distant we learn different lessons. Rhythms of animal and human life, escapades across land and sea, retreats into the wilderness, and quiet times spent with nature reinforce what we already know from deep inside: alonetime is vital to our peace and existence, a route open to us for survival.

When Schopenhauer wrote *Studies in Pessimism* in the early 1800s, he, like Mr. Hacker, complained about city noise: "The most inexcusable and disgraceful of all noises is the cracking of whips—a truly infernal thing when it is done in the narrow resounding streets of a town. I denounce it as making a peaceful life impossible; it puts an end to all quiet thought."[3] What was a personal peeve to Schopenhauer has become a world problem in the 1990s: "Noise is becoming a threat to human health, and as such, ranks among the foremost environmental problems in the industrially developed countries."[4] Some say that "people consider noise to be the main local environmental problem";[5] certainly city noises like police sirens, alarms, delivery trucks, construction sounds, and (at worst) gunshots incessantly invade most quiet moments.

Ultimately, our storybook friend Mr. Hacker finds the best of possible worlds. Experiencing the jarring intrusion of excessive stimulation, he discovers the peace he longed for in the country—but *too much* of it. This dilemma is resolved after he becomes closer to nature, finding the quiet of the country and companionship through hosting several animals. All ends well. Other fictional examples in this chapter will illustrate how wilderness, wanderlust, and animal behavior confirm the aloneness need and demonstrate ways to find connection as well.

The love affair with nature of which Ralph Waldo Emerson speaks implies a far greater involvement in alonetime. For him and other Transcendentalists of the 1820s and 1830s, communing with nature was essential to gain "inward illumination and spiritual insight."[6] Tidal pools, empty fields, winding streams, rocks, mountains, trees, and oceans evoke endurance, peace, and contentment that circulate, cool, and calm the system. Something sacred fills these wide open spaces, and human hearts have been privy to this for eternities.

What could Mr. Hacker have in common with the fertile minds of the nineteenth century, such as Emerson, Henry David Thoreau, and Herman Melville? Actually, quite a lot, beginning with a common solution to feelings of being overcrowded and needing peaceful time. People with access, from every walk of life, choose nature in order to clear their heads and create a private wilderness.

Throughout history, we see individuals who have tired of the confines of civilization and voiced a longing for free, unpolluted space. These desires—as William Cronon, author and University of Wisconsin professor, tells us—are aspects of the "problems" with wildernesses, our trying to create wildernesses only after we have destroyed them.[7] His portrayal of wilderness in American society is as a makeshift invention—a cough drop remedy for culture's common cold. His concerns suggest a population of Dorothys running and chasing after wizardry instead of searching for solutions within home and community.[8] While acknowledging the experience of wilderness as something outside ourselves and as a symbol of shedding the confines of civilization, Cronon asks, why not keep considerations of nature a must at all times—even as we mechanize the world? Is it that aspect of wilderness—a place for redemption and renewal—that, unbeknownst to most, temporarily gratifies the ongoing need for alonetime? Could it be that which wilderness represents? Our unsocialized feelings, wanderlust, our roots in nomadic existence, and our resistance to social mores seem part and parcel of a suppressed wish for alonetime. Perhaps, as well, the attraction to and sometimes fear of wild beasts is actually the desire to be free and unfettered, a feeling bred in our bones.

Alonetime, I will show, fuels and is fueled by feelings and experiences that put us in contact with nature and the wild. First hear the story of a neighbor of mine in the country that awakened me to the fact that it isn't only city dwellers who are short of private time.

Mark, age thirty-two, known as a family man, did not play ball, gamble, or drink. He kept two jobs to support his wife, mother, and several children. His comings and goings were as reliable as the tide. A modern-day Jimmy Stewart (in *It's a Wonderful Life*), he found nothing too much for him—helping a neighbor paint his house or getting up in the middle of the night to feed and change the baby. When he didn't arrive home one night, everyone presumed he had a terrible accident. After checking with the hospital and police, the family feared that he had run off with someone. Not the case, as one month later he returned with a beard, suntan, and more-than-sheepish grin. Although he had never known the inside of a tent or hiked in the woods, he went camping on his own for those four weeks and returned with the muscles to show for it. Relatives and friends found his explanation limp, but he was sincere in the telling: "I didn't know how to say, 'I've had enough!' I just needed a vacation from work, friends, and children. It was the wrong way to do it, but the only way I knew how. And I hate to admit it because it won't make you happy: being alone there in the backwoods was the best thing that happened to me for years." Mark, once pulled out of despair, actually was glad to be home. The experience managed to change the family's lifestyle from hectic to downscaled.

◆ ◆ ◆

Clearly, more reasons than sexual passion, midlife crises, or drug addiction cause adults to run away from home. Mark is not alone in his wish. Across the country people are looking to simplify life, in and out of the city, by reducing the accumulation of *things* and reestablishing priorities.

Wilderness and Solitude — Confusion and Clarity

Though they did not experience the same kind of crisis that Mark did, the Transcendentalists were in a rebellion of sorts against current social and church practices, and believed that the combination of an inner journey and contact with nature would be reenergizing. Transcendentalism —the religiophilosophical teachings of a New England school of thought best represented by Emerson in the mid–nineteenth century—had no unified voice, but certain themes stand out in Transcendentalist writings. One is freedom. Another is the belief that divine truth can be obtained through examination of the inner mind. The "tonic of wilderness," as Thoreau called it, is not just a creation of the Transcendentalists but a repetitive theme throughout history. It is alive in the wisdom of philosophers and poets of ancient Greece, the preachings of the Middle Ages, the writings of Jefferson, Shelley's poetry, the exuberance of Willa Cather, and the concerns of people of our not-so-distant past. But changes in geography make finding a link with nature a particular concern today, as Archibald MacLeish tells us: "Wilderness and silence disappeared from the countryside, sweetness fell from the air, not because anyone wished them to vanish or fall but because throughways had to floor the meadows with cement to carry the automobiles which advancing technology produced."[9]

How do wilderness, wanderlust, and animal life—human and nonhuman—inform our understanding of alonetime? Freud saw individuals at war with civilization, resigning themselves to the sacrifices demanded by society because they could not exist in isolation. I see the wild and the tamed, the social and the asocial, residing side by side.

Unfortunately, confusion between isolation, loneliness, alonetime, and seclusion has penetrated our understanding about wilderness. In the fast track at the end of this century, trailblazing has become like summer camp, no longer offering the same opportunities for an interchange between challenge and solitude. Some critics of the wilderness theme, such as Hansford C. Vest, go to great lengths to distinguish between types of solitude—one artificial and the other actual wilderness solitude. Vest writes pejoratively on the former—alone qua alone. He sees feeling all alone as an untrue encounter with wilderness, stating that it portends withdrawal from society. Yet he recognizes the *world* of nature as worth preserving and sees a desire for wilderness solitude as a positive and ingrained human need.[10] Ambivalence about wilderness echoes a failure to properly value alonetime. If alonetime is seen to be as fundamental as any other need, why should it not be subject to overindulgence? I would not, however, call being isolated in the woods necessarily gluttonous.

Sometimes this search takes wilderness too far and ends in tragedy, as in Christopher Johnson McCandless's trek to Alaska. A likable young man and honor student, McCandless plunges into the wilderness to escape the bonds of civilization and, perhaps, his seemingly overbearing parental ties. McCandless apparently explored wildernesses unfrequented by others and was overcome by the elements. In the language of a true mountaineer, Jon Krakauer, a journalist and mountain climber who wrote about McCandless's youthful derring-do, describes the intoxication of his own alone challenge: "A trancelike state settles over your efforts; the climb becomes a clear-eyed dream . . . The accumulated clutter of day-to-day existence—the lapses of conscience, the unpaid bills, the bungled opportunities, the dust under the couch, the inescapable prison of your genes—all of it is temporarily forgotten."[11] Just before the tragic end of his life, McCandless *did* want to return to the world, but in his initial disconnection with people who care we see the unempathic pursuit of single-minded goals, and perhaps the selfishness of youth. What this account primarily reinforces is that the desire to explore the wild, take risks, and go it alone is encoded in our genes—as Krakauer states, a "convergence of chromosomal matter, parent-child dynamics, and alignment of the cosmos."[12]

Strangely, Krakauer, who in his book questions himself putting his personal life and limb in jeopardy, again risks everything to scale Mt. Everest. This failed attempt at great adventure cost the lives of climbers even as experienced as he. Peter Hillary states that many mountain climbers are "more motivated than experienced," suggesting that the call touches a primordial spirit, some remnant of the untamable part of our aloneness wishes.[13] Such feats would never be tackled without that brave side of us. Would daring and death-defying acts be diminished in reconstructing alonetime if one knew that such states were reachable by other means?

In maintaining wilderness as an illusion of some lost perfection— William Cronon suggests—we are alienating ourselves from the urban or suburban real world; for the sake of necessity and convenience, we must learn to locate alone contentment in our *everyday* lives and avoid the literal escape to wilderness proper as the only solution. The wild inside and outside of oneself can be integrated. Home then includes the everyday place we live in *and* nature. Cronon's lessons demand an awareness and acceptance of our immediate environment, ourselves, and the wilderness—in other words, engagement with others and alonetime. Betsy Berne, writing in *The New Yorker,* laments the loss of such refuge.[14] All her friends are exhausted, everyone is too busy, no one has sufficient sleep. These upper-middle-class thirty-to-forty-year-old people may be single, married, working in offices or at home. Along with lack of sleep there seems to be an overdose of the "amount of human interaction." Her brother is in the worst of positions as he plays gigs on the road. When he's not traveling in a group or playing, he just "hangs," which means drinking all night with fans. How did the expression "hanging out," which suggests relaxation, come to mean nonstop interaction? A lot has changed.

City parks are not providing the wild space of ancient rock-ribbed hills. The free and easy lives of the wandering minstrels of yesteryear have become jam-packed with activity. So I, like many of the fortunate, have found other spots in which to hang out, read, and relax. In a country retreat, I listen to the rain and watch it pour down on the skylight as I reflect on wilderness and its connection to being alone. Nearby, my husband is reading *Moby-Dick.* Yet, of course, we are both experiencing a form of alonetime. Reinforcing this idea that one can be alone *with* people, my husband says, "Let me show you this passage from Melville's novel":

> I had noticed that Queequeg [Ishmael's "savage" companion] never consorted at all, or but very little, with the other seamen in the inn. He made no advances whatever; appeared to have no desire to enlarge the circle of his acquaintances . . . Here was a man some twenty thousand miles from home, by the way of Cape Horn, that is—which was the only way he could get there—thrown among people as strange to him as though he were in the planet Jupiter; and yet he seemed entirely at his ease; preserving the utmost serenity; content with his own companionship; always equal to himself.[15]

Out of the blue, my husband chose to read *Moby-Dick,* reminding me of a solitude I envisioned in adventures at sea at age fifteen. Melville taught me then that I could be enthralled with an adventure novel (without boy-girl romance) in which the main character was contemplating life and isolation. Without having read *Moby-Dick*, I would have lost important knowledge of the world of men, wild adventures at sea, and managing alone.

Wilderness solitude is not what my weekends in the country are about, although I feel at rest with myself and my surroundings. It is not sufficiently remote. But the other day, I walked alone in Bartholomew's Cobble, a historical nature preserve in Massachusetts, several miles from the house. Small caves in the Cobble may have been used from time to time as temporary shelters by nomadic Indians. I found a rock in one of the caves to sit on, from which to watch a stream, and later lay down on a flatland that was equally quiet. There I mused about those here before me, enjoying the empty moments and feelings of awe.

Alonetime brings forth our wishes to explore, our curiosity about the unknown, our desires to escape from another's control, our will to be an individual, our hopes for freedom. Alonetime is fuel for life. Both nature and civilization have been viewed as enemies of the people—one needing to be tamed, the other too taming. While living near hospitals, remote from predators, with ease of communications, it becomes easy to hail the benefits of civilization. Sustained by gratifications of alonetime, explorers of nature's wild side feel equally enriched.

Wanderlust from Childhood

Touching nature while musing at the Cobble had a familiar ring, and triggered very early memories of imagining myself as an animal freely roaming everywhere. My wanderings, fed by fairy tales and picture books, seem to confirm what other children say about themselves and their need for wild places. Could there be an actual ache in a child's heart for "places with no roads . . . but plenty of space, animals, and rocks?"[16] My grandson Benjamin, riding on the Metro in Washington, D.C., when he was less than two years old, opened his hands as if reading a book. "I'm reading a book," he said. "What's it about?" asked his father, David. "I'm in the ocean," replied Benjamin; "I'm swimming with the dolphins. They're throwing their food all around." Charles Darwin wrote about the indelible stamp of early origins embedded in the human mind and body. Maybe well before adulthood, children sense that, in nature, exploration and freethinking interlock close to animal origins, removed from people's demands. We have to pretend and go into the woods to follow this thread of the alonetime need.

Besides the political message in Washington Irving's story "Rip Van

Winkle," there was also the man who slept in the woods for twenty years, escaping the nagging of his wife. In her secret garden, Mary Lennox[17] explores from different angles the lone place Maurice Sendak[18] paints in *Where the Wild Things Are*. When Sendak's hero, Max, dons his wolf suit, his room becomes a jungle and he visits the wildest places and creatures. Frances Burnett's Mary searches calmly for herself. I have seen overprotective parents interfere at the slightest sign of anxiety in a wish to spare their children. In that scenario the anxiety accelerates. Coming to terms with our own demons is like marching bravely into the unknown, like knights of yore. Indians likened this bravery to that of the eagle, bear, or wolf. If animal spirit is akin to being alone, we need it in order to develop moral courage!

Picture books, like *Mr. Hacker,* or, better yet, fairy tales and full-length children's books, are far less subtle than adult books in recognizing the individual's need for alonetime. No one compares to Huckleberry Finn, the archetypal loner romanticized in American fiction. Twain writes:

> He slept on door-steps in fine weather and in empty hogsheads in wet; he did not have to go to school or to church, or call any being master, or obey anybody; he could go fishing or swimming when and where he chose, and stay as long as it suited him; nobody forbade him to fight . . . In a word every-thing that goes to make life precious, that boy had.[19]

Naturally, I emphasize aloneness found in children's fiction and being alone's interaction with exploratory interests, survival skills, and personal courage. Although in most examples, the literature illustrates that the need for aloneness exists alongside that for bonding, children's books demonstrate the alone need with a resounding clarity that is sometimes forgotten in everyday life. There is another theme—going it alone—in myth and imaginary writing that speaks of survival and courage and reverberates the trials of religious seekers, shamans, and Native Americans on vision quests. Only alone will one make the self-discovery that leads to personhood.

Did you ever try or pretend to be lost? As I was growing up, I played that game, admittedly mostly without risk. When I wandered aimlessly, I wasn't far from home and I knew what the majority of the signposts were. As an adult, I play the game differently. I like to think that I shall find my way in any strange place with my own internal homing pigeon device. But except for walks or cross-country skiing in the woods, I have not entered the wilderness of the dark unknown alone and far from help. *New York Times* editorial writer John Markoff, however, suggests that, even for adventurers, getting lost is a lost art:

> Wilderness is supposed to be a place where, compasses notwithstanding, there is always the possibility of getting lost, where one must pit one's wits against the elements to survive. Now the elements barely have a chance. A dazzling array of new technologies, including hand-held global positioning satellite receivers and computerized altimeters, make it possible to know where you are within 300 feet.[20]

True adventurers, unlike me, do not just rove the untamed caverns of the mind; they wander intrepidly into deep wilderness. In fiction, from the epic of *Gilgamesh* to *Gulliver's Travels,* the risks of solo explorations reach dramatic proportions, exemplifying the high stakes involved in achieving personal freedom. In real life, however, some people make lives of exploring, such as nomads, who never stand still for long. These groups have enhanced alone skills.

Alonetime, Bred in the Bones

The trekking of any current nomadic group cannot match the hardships of ancient hominids, who wandered the continents over a million years ago. Historically, according to mathematician, teacher, poet, and historian Jacob Bronowski, we were all nomads until the time he calls the most powerful of social transformations. Life changed after the Ice Ages of over twelve thousand years ago, when suddenly there was fertile ground all over Europe and Asia. Along with the realization that the environment could be controlled in terms of planting and hunting came the dawning of settled civilizations: "And you have actually to travel with [those nomadic survivors] to understand that civilization can never grow up on the move."[21]

I do not question Bronowski when he states that the "largest single step in the ascent of man is the change from nomad to village agriculture."[22] It is much easier to build, invent, engineer, and create when settled in one place. Even when humankind discovered the benefits of nonmigratory social groupings, however, this did not alter people's needs and wishes to be alone. Other means to satisfy these desires—such as religious practices—were incorporated over time. Moreover, everybody did not renounce the alone urge or give up their desire to explore or their love of wilderness.

Itinerants, tinkers, and mountain people have for years wandered nomadically over sand, hills, and valleys; they are bound to realize alonetime in foraging, sleeping without electric light, and walking between villages. The alone experience reaches new limits when the traveler is going solo. The desert wanderer is a special breed, contending with heat, wild winds, and absence of water. "He . . . never felt alone in the miles of longitude between desert storms. A man in a desert can hold absence in his cupped hands knowing it is something that feeds him more than water."[23] Expansive and explorable space, whether of sea, land, or air, is what beckons to humankind and emboldens us with the spirit of adventure. Democratic vice president Hubert Humphrey noted these needs over thirty years ago: "There is in every American, I think, something of the old Daniel Boone—who, when he could see the smoke from another chimney, felt himself too crowded and moved further out into the wilderness."[24]

Is it only the pioneer spirit that gives us itchy feet? The desire to keep on the move seems more primeval than that. Even so, if evolutionary psychologists are correct in assuming that living in groups helped to shape the human brain, then shouldn't one equally suppose that the million years of wandering may be also programmed in our genes, adding impetus to an alonetime need as expressed in wandering adventurously? As aloneness has an adaptive value in people, so it does in many other species. There is some truth to the notion that lions travel in packs, but in actuality "pride members are usually scattered singly and in small groups that change from day to day as individuals come and go on their own initiative."[25]

Animals and the Call of the Wild

Little, however, puts one as in touch with the animal alonetime need as Jack London's Buck. Buck went from his great "demesne" (estate), where the "whole realm was his to roam as he wished," to being a caged animal with a rope around his neck. It was through his misadventures that he came into his own again and learned recovery in alonetime, love, and the "call of the wild": "He was sounding the depths of his nature, and of the parts of his nature that were deeper than he, going back into the womb of Time. He was mastered by the sheer surging of life, the tidal wave of being, the perfect joy of each separate muscle, joint, and sinew in that it was everything."[26] It is in this wilderness that Buck finds his true self among the wild wolves who cross "alone from the smiling timberland."[27]

This story of Buck's affinity to the lone wolf and the wolf pack is fiction. There are other stories from animal observation and ethological studies that relate a similar picture of a basic need for alonetime across species. Elizabeth Marshall Thomas,[28] an anthropological writer, translated her thirty-year love affair with dogs into an unusual solo adventure with canines. This is not Charley traveling with John Steinbeck,[29] the dog following man's whims. Rather, it is a woman traveling in the dogs' shadow. Thomas follows dogs on foot and bicycle, night and day, trying to capture a dog's inner spirit. One revealing episode occurred when she camped in a shallow cave by herself to observe wolves. Wolves are both lone and family creatures who carefully raise their young. Nevertheless, in order to survive (find food for themselves and kin), parents leave the pups alone in a safe den. Usually, one adult would be left to guard the den. Pups seeking a playmate might try to engage the baby-sitter. This proved impossible, for the wolf caretaker typically spent the entire time on a ledge by itself asleep or in a resting state.

Thomas's descriptions verify that there is no exaggeration in the stereotype of the lone wolf. She feels closest to dogs' innermost secrets, however, in another episode, when she and one of her dogs silently and separately stare into space:

> To sit idly, not doing, merely experiencing, comes hard to a primate (at least one raised in the latter half of the 20th century), yet for once I wasn't among primates. At last, as dogs learn to live among our kind, it came to me to live among theirs. In the late afternoon sun we sat in the dust, or lay on our chests resting on our elbows, evenly spaced on the hill top, all looking calmly down among the trees . . . No birds sang, just insects. Off in the silent, drying woods a tree would now and then drop something . . . While the shadows grew long we lay calmly, feeling the moment, the calmness, the warm light of the red sun.[30]

Despite the obvious enjoyment conveyed by Thomas during her vigils, she still insists that primates feel "pure, flat immobility as boredom, but dogs feel it as peace." Yet, as a child I recall content, absent gazing at dust motes floating in air. And growing up, I remember seeing many human primates who enjoyed lying on beaches, coasting on rafts, or just resting on the front stoop. Perhaps Thomas wasn't considering the days before the invention of the cellular phone.

In observations of primates, aloneness needs get lost. Primates, our closest relatives, are known to form loyal groups, rear their young with affection, and mourn loss, but I propose another look at laboratory studies of monkeys. In the early days of primate studies, Henry Harlow[31] studied mothering needs in rhesus monkeys—though his original intentions are reported as attempts to find a way to isolate baby monkeys from mothers to prevent the spread of a virus.[32] He invented surrogate feeders made out of cloth, as well as some from an uncovered wire hanger. The wire hanger held a bottle of milk and the baby monkeys fairly consistently seemed to choose the cloth over the wire. The monkeys in most studies were separated from mothers and peers. The aftereffects on the animals were such that those who were just fed—with no contact either by cloth or "cousin"—adjusted, if at all, with hardship and lasting social deficits back to the fold of mother, sister, or brother.

These scientific paradigms were interpreted as proof of the all-powerful need of attachment to future survival. Naturally, by taking all companionship away, Harlow was asking for trouble. An interesting aside to this is that monkeys who were nurtured by the cloth surrogate mother did not have such a hard time readjusting to social life. Certain readers of Harlow interpreted this symbolically, as if the monkey somehow made the connection to the cloth as an object representing mother. But how can we say these cloths were transitional objects—things that reminded them of mother? This interpretation seems an exaggeration of attachment motivation. Without a doubt, the clinging and grasping reflexes that monkeys display significantly help in the formation of bonds and attachment. Remember as well that monkeys ultimately need to know how to cling to and grasp on to tree branches and vines on their own as well as on to parents. Thus, in the instance of the surrogate, cloth mother, these same reflexes—which were probably contributing to monkeys' alone survival and satisfying alone needs—were interpreted as safely transferable to forming relationships. I maintain that the innate relating and aloneness skills of these monkey babies parallel those of human babies. Either for social gain and survival or to foster freedom and survival, these early grasping behaviors remain reciprocal and central to all primate development and serve the law of self-preservation.

Even taking into consideration the fact that wide differences in behaviors of alonetime and relational needs in primates have been recorded, the resistance to accepting such a range of behaviors as normal is formidable. Orangutans are believed to be the most solitary members of the ape family, capable of perching high up in trees for long times alone. One ethologist[33] does not see this as speaking for primates in general or for our species at all; furthermore, he writes: "The human race as a whole . . . is *social to the core*" (emphasis mine). What transpires at the zoo may prove otherwise. When I stroll through some of the large "natural" zoos, I watch the primates grooming, mating, playing, and teasing one another or visitors—*and* just as readily hiding, turning their backs on playmates and pedestrians, and hitting the glass of the cage when a camera flash disrupts their solitude. Paleontologist Stephen Jay Gould acknowledges our link to other animals best, but perhaps his most significant lesson simply affirms Darwin's aphorism that we should "never say higher or lower" when describing different species: "And if we abandon the venerable chain of being, we lose the most promising frame for viewing human culture in biological terms as an extension, almost a necessary one, of longstanding evolutionary trends."[34] This broader view embraces a wide range of behaviors that connects us to the whole of the living world. Instincts to be social and be alone are so fundamental that they bind us to all within the kingdom of animals.

Wilderness, wanderlust, *and* alonetime interact. Our desire to explore, to wander and discover the unknown and the wild, are corollaries to alonetime. Alonetime and together time require a harmony that is frequently found in wilderness experiences. When we solve the equation between our outer surroundings and innermost wishes, equanimity resides within oneself. The adventure continues and leads next to a way of life that seems inclined toward the direction of aloneness and asceticism.

CHAPTER 3

Hermits, Monks, and

Philosophers:

Self-Regulating Solitaires

My soul at times,
in this silent cell,
continues to furnish
me with beauty.
ROSALIE CUTTING, "Inner Peace"[1]

O N AN EXCURSION TO THE Monasterio de Santa María de Pedralbes in Spain, I entered the large and mostly undecorated main sanctuary and was stunned by the quiet. There I began to formulate the questions for this chapter. How does the search for God overlap with the search for solitude? Does fear of alonetime diminish after learning it is possible to take charge of emotions and bodily needs? Does this coordinate need for regulating oneself occur both in religious and in philosophical solitude? When we pursue the teachings of those who have secluded themselves as an escape, a retreat toward God or a pursuit of knowledge, is there a common thread to follow? The most difficult question is perhaps unanswerable: why are suffering and denial often integral to the spiritual and philosophical journey? Philosophy has changed. Was it that, within this metamorphosis, the importance of alonetime diminished, or was it the solitary life that caused disillusionment in and of itself?

The Rise and Fall of the Solitary Life

The exact origins of monastic life are lost in antiquity. Some believe the source to be India—from which evidence in the sacred writings of Hindus dates as far back as 2400 B.C.—later spreading to China, Japan, and

Tibet by way of Buddhist monks who renounced the world yet traveled far and wide. Schemes of self-torture and other practices devised by these ancients were mirrored by the Christian ascetics of the desert. Another influence on Christian monks was the Essenes (the ascetic John the Baptist was probably one),[2] a Jewish sect that established a celibate, monastic-style community near the Dead Sea as early as the second century B.C. and practiced character building through self-mastery. Saint Anthony's own austerity in the desert has earned him the title "Father of Monasticism." But in order to understand the demise of solitude's fervent call, we must briefly explore monastic life and follow in the philosopher's footsteps.

The intense period of the monastic movement in Europe began with Saint Benedict, who actually never founded a monastery, as the story goes. In about 530 A.D., he lay down his *Rule*—a set of dicta concerning monastic practice—atop Monte Cassino, between Rome and Naples. Presumably his organizational skills and his *Rule* gave shape to the beliefs of disparate introspectives, recluses, and hermits, bringing new life to the monasteries. They changed from being only places of retreat to centers of learning and models for personal life that balanced prayer and work, social engagement and solitude. Rules of the order enjoined silence and useful employment when the monks were not in divine service. Benedict's *Rule* is still observed today around the world.

Let us reflect on the devotional practices and sleep patterns of monks, for in fact the monks, among the most solitary of creatures, disciplined themselves about sleep. A simple question and important aside: if people are frequently alone in their meditation, as would be expected, then will their need for sleep decrease? The Benedictine monks slept no more than from 8 P.M. to 2 A.M., and in other orders only four hours of sleep were allowed, the rest of the time spent for the good of community or in meditative prayer. It makes sense that long periods of meditation (with or without dozing, we do not know) would lessen the time needed for sleep. People who meditate in modern times also claim fewer hours in sleep than ordinary folk and speak of the many gains from alert consciousness these states provide. The life of the ancient solitary monk has much to convey to us about needs for alonetime and social engagement.

Monk and theologian Thomas Merton's insight as to how monasteries functioned overall further illuminates the ways these medieval orders balanced needs to bond and to be alone:

> Within the impenetrable walls, the monasteries were filled
> with life. Despite the vows of silence, there was time allowed

for chanting or reading aloud. The noises of everyday chores
—beating carpets, washing clothes, repairing shoes—were evident at times. The peacefulness and lack of direct communication did not dispel the inhabitants from feeling a sense of
family.[3]

Culture has historically eased natural tensions by establishing institutions and social codes such as religious practices, siestas, and ritualized
meditation to ensure alonetime without ignoring a need for others. The
relationship of the individual to God is one solution to what some call
the paradox of aloneness and relatedness. But that solution was most
apparent within a less self-conscious era that accepted paradox as part of
the natural rhythms in life, and one without the lures of the megatropolis.

Both "monastery" and "monk" stem from the same Greek word,
meaning "alone" or "single." When local people told me about a "monastery" in Barcelona, I was surprised to discover a convent. Prior to this, I
was aware only of the common usage of the word "monastery," as applied to a house used exclusively by monks. Later I found out that the
term came to include the abbey, the priory, the nunnery, and the friary,
and in this broad sense is synonymous with "convent." The source of
"convent," however, is from the Latin convenire, which means to meet
together.[4] When I found out that these two words used as names for
similar places combine in their origins the two basic human needs to be
alone and to be together, it was a poetic revelation. Here was further
recognition that society was looking for a place of reconciliation for these
two paradoxically different, but equally valid, simultaneous desires.

The history of convents is similar to that of monasteries. For most
male orders there was a comparable sisterhood. The life of a nun held
attraction. But consider this call to the convent:

> Do you think there is no difference between one who spends
> her time in prayer and fasting, and one who must, at her hus-
> band's approach, make up her countenance, walk with a minc-
> ing gait, and feign a show of endearment? The married woman
> has the paint laid on before her mirror, and, to the insult of
> her Maker, strives to acquire something more than her natural
> beauty. Then come the prattling of infants, the noisy house-
> hold, children watching for her word and waiting for her kiss,
> the reckoning up of expenses, the preparation to meet the out-
> lay, a message is delivered that her husband and his friends
> have arrived. The wife, like a swallow, flies all over the house.

She has to see to everything. Is the sofa smooth? Is the pavement swept? Are the flowers in the cup? Is dinner ready? Tell
me, pray amid all this, is there room for the thought of God?[5]

Ironically, this feminist, equal-opportunity doctrine came from Saint Jerome, writing in A.D. 400. He wanted to lure the women of Rome to the
convent, and it is said that he succeeded in convincing thousands.
Thoughts of forgoing a busy life may have been as much the attraction
as was salvation. Later Jerome himself gave up all his secular goods to
live in the vast solitude of the desert. "Others may think what they like
and follow each his own bent. But to me a town is a prison and solitude
paradise."[6]

I, too, was tempted at age ten to seriously consider entering a nunnery.
But the perplexing and perennial problems of humankind—the problem
of the relationship of people to nature and morality, the problem of fate,
and the problem of death—were not my foremost concerns. Nor were
those my thoughts at age nineteen, when I dreamt that nuns actually
captured and cloistered me despite my fighting against them. Instead, I
was thinking of the escape from a world where others' demands seemed
overwhelming and yet the need and desire to remain with people was
equally profound. Moreover, I was tremulous and wary about the idea of
such an absolute withdrawal from the world.

Notwithstanding an undying urge to reach the peace of aloneness, we
sense the danger in an unmitigated pursuit of solitude. Certain dangers
may be far more injurious than imagined or innate fears. Alone, we can
become as entranced with our own reflection as Narcissus. A minister
interviewed on the *MacNeil-Lehrer Report* stated that inward contemplation is selfish and that the good Christian is *always* community centered!

In answer to the central paradox of an active, outer versus a quiet,
inner life, Trappist monk Thomas Merton[7] chose a solitary one, believing
that was the only way once a person became aware that alonetime is
undeniable. Yet Merton found his vocation and his identity when he
discovered, in recuperation from an illness, the benefits of extended rest.
He believed that the religious hermit or just simply anyone who is determined to find solitude will find an identity beyond belief in the search
and a way out of loneliness. At the same time, Merton saw his solitude
as "a gift of himself to God." This twentieth-century monk experienced
all that comes with such a decision—fear and angst, the vision of truth
and God in solitude, the specter of self-centeredness, and the difficulty of
balancing contemplation with society.

Merton suffered early loss. His mother died when he was six, his father when he was sixteen. Beginning years were sprinkled with travel and separation, including frequent stretches of time away from his younger brother. A life that started with considerable disadvantage changed into one with an enormous longing for alonetime as well as commitment to important causes. Why is this so? Is it settling for second best, as some might claim? Not at all. Merton may have followed a pathway opened to him due to loss of family connections, but to do so comfortably there must be basic motivation to explore that direction. In solitude, uninterrupted by others' demands, one can experience the self-care and self-regulation that perhaps were missing from childhood and gain as well an inner peace and direction.

Of course, religious orders fundamentally rely on the attachment and dependency needs of their followers for cohesion. But for religion to have its greatest appeal it must also provide time for prayer, meditation, and self-empowerment. A cursory glance may suggest that Judaism is unlike other great religions that offer long stretches of private time, when one is cocooned from outside stimuli and external demands. True, modern Judaism does not provide a formal system for individual reclusiveness. Yet even beyond the enduring prayer of Orthodox males, and despite Judaism being a family- and society-oriented religion, significant time is set aside for solitude. The book of Genesis lays this foundation. Within the creation story, God established Saturday, the Shabbat, as a day of rest, a day to be set aside from all other days.[8] A day set aside and apart may not be actual alonetime as interpreted by current society. But if we check back at the original rabbinical sanctions against work, lighting lights, ordinary play, or even cooking on that day, this was the obvious intention. Traditionally, the Shabbat was the time to contemplate one's life and the scriptures.

Contemplation is often described as the preferred mode to achieving spiritual peace and closeness to God. Found originally in the scholarly writings of rabbi, philosopher, and physician Maimonides (Rabbi Moses ben Maimon, 1125–1204), the *vita contemplativa* of communion with God gained momentum in the mystical and meditative Hasidic treatises of the sixteenth century and perhaps primarily from a charismatic figure of that time, Isaac Luria, who established the Lurianic Kabbalah. (Kabbalah is considered by some an esoteric and mystical discipline within the Jewish religion that speculates on the inner life of God and human consciousness.) Although Luria's spiritual point of view is much debated among Jewish leaders, similar practices are part of the meditative Eastern religions, as they were in the philosophies of ancient Greece.

When five years old, I was taken to an Orthodox synagogue. I couldn't understand how people sat in one spot talking to themselves for so long. In Orthodox Jewish tradition, men and women are separated in the synagogue, in part so that concentration is not interrupted by sensual distraction. However, as a very little girl I was permitted on some occasions of celebration to accompany my father into the sanctuary, forbidden to women. A constant hum and buzz of monologue rose from the mouths of those with heads bent in prayer. Were they, as they seemed, oblivious to all else surrounding them? One memory of the synagogue remained with me because in it there was something puzzling. Why did those engrossed in prayer so often have fear and strain in their eyes? "Are all these people sad?" I asked my father. "No, they just want rest and the strength to do good deeds," he replied—what I later learned Herman Melville called "a Tahiti of the Soul."[9]

In the heydays of the monks, as in Melville's time and even in my childhood, these escapes were easily accessible not only in a place of worship but outside as well. Now, we are at far greater risk of giving up the important growth that occurs in alonetime for amusing technological stimulation. In a time when worldly goods are instantly replaceable, people lose touch with the ephemeral nature of life. Eventually, even the monks of old gave up self-reflection for the tangible. Monks once sought solitude for a simpler life and a way to combat Rome's self-indulgence. But they only fell prey to the same sin. Monastic life met its downfall from engaging in greedy, bigoted exploitation of others, which was fostered by wealth and internal corruption.[10] No one better or more humorously described this than Geoffrey Chaucer, who quotes a monk no longer enamored with meditation, dressed in frills with a love knot on his wrist, en route to Canterbury:

> And his opinion here was good, I say,
> For why go mad with studying all day,
> Poring over a book in some dark hall,
> And with one's hands go laboring as well.[11]

Asceticism and Self-Regulation: The Quest for Inner Power

Chaucer's monk adopted some of the fancy dress of society, but in order to feel in charge of bodily and emotional needs, one must be able to renounce quick fixes or unearned comforts. This is the province of the ascetic. Ancient Greeks used "ascetic" to describe athletes who practiced self-denial to gain control over their bodies and in their sport. Later the word was associated ecclesiastically with someone who seeks holiness through self-modification and with people who put wisdom above secular pleasures.

The ascetic and the solitary seem to go hand in hand. Marx,[12] for example, believed that wars are caused by excessive wants, particularly of money. The only reason people pursue money is to satisfy undisciplined bodily needs. Plato held this opinion as well. In his thinking, contemplation is raised to the highest plane with the belief that "man could live on very little money if his wants were reduced to a minimum."[13] We all know that religious philosophers of India and Tibet have mastered the control of bodily needs in their solitude, indulging in little beyond rice and meager offerings, as their purpose is to dispense the gift of wisdom. Equally famous for their cult of abstinence were the Stoic philosophers, who gained their label from the Greek name for the porch upon which disciples and their founder, Zeno, debated. The controlled, calm Stoic is the self-regulator par excellence. Not surprisingly, one of the greatest practitioners of this movement was also a seeker of alonetime.

Marcus Aurelius (born A.D. 121), the last distinguished philosopher of Stoicism, wrote about achieving inner power and controlling and improving moral character. He thought obtaining outward pleasures, even from vacation retreats, was unnecessary and a mark of excess: "For it is in thy power whenever thou shalt choose to retire into thyself. For nowhere either with more quiet or more freedom from trouble, does a man retire than into his own soul."[14] This absolute renouncement of earthly pleasures and desire for total management of regulatory functions may seem out of touch with the imposition of today's culture. But within the Stoic culture resides a message for modern society and our great problems with self-regulation.

Maureen, a patient of mine, thought she was obtaining inner power through alcohol but she was running from loneliness, intimacy, solitude, and her religious background. When she courageously joined Alcoholics Anonymous (A.A.), she was able to use the group connection, being alone, and quiet time as an arena for self-rescue. Remembering her early connections to religious thought and prayer, Maureen found a way to reverse her sense of powerlessness and loss of inner regulation and realized that her dual needs for affection and alonetime were not automatically clashing.

◆　◆　◆

In June 1995, Alcoholics Anonymous had its sixtieth birthday. A.A. was founded in 1935 by Dr. Bob (Smith) and Bill W. (Wilson) on the first day of Dr. Bob's sobriety, in a time period when even public confessions retained a sense of anonymity. As in most institutions that embrace religious themes, in A.A. there is a place for both the individual's private and connected self. In fact, one worry among A.A. veterans is that today A.A.'s effectiveness is being challenged, with members expecting unconditional love instead of taking responsibility for themselves.[15] A recent *New York Times* article shows how one man handles his need for group support and inner mastery. This recovering thirty-two-year-old alcoholic goes to A.A. meetings, but prefers chatting on-line with fellow alcoholics: "On the Net, feelings are true," he states. "It's more about self-help."[16] In a session with me, Maureen confirms the dual needs for alonetime and attachment:

> "At first, the idea of A.A. meetings was sissyish. This may sound awful—I'll say it anyway—not even God could make me give away my life. All the time I secretly thought my drinking was one thing that was solely mine, and I was sticking my tongue out at all the Goody Two-Shoes. I'm not sure how, but I finally felt things differently. Yes, the group in a way was holding my hand, but I had to do this myself."

◆　　◆　　◆

Despite alcohol fortifying the dual illusion of social ease and being on one's own, addictions inevitably weaken one's self-reliance and group skills and leave one feeling impotent and still questing for inner power. Maureen's struggle to find individual space while remaining part of a whole reappears eloquently as a perplexing dialectic in the philosophical and religious writings of Ernst Cassirer, Ernest Becker, and Karen Armstrong.[17] However, the basic dualistic need in human nature has come under harsh attack in different guises by those who strongly lobby for one side or the other: "The asserted absolute independence of man, which in the Stoic theory was regarded as man's fundamental virtue, is turned in the Christian theory [which supports community] into his fundamental vice and error."[18]

The need for alonetime offers no answers as to how or whether we should believe in ourselves, a single divinity, the stars, or nature—or live a contemplative or active life. But within people's philosophical and religious struggles and quests for power is a desire for inner control granted through alonetime and maintaining connectedness. Yet even today sometimes, despite all that scientific evidence tells us, people still feel as powerless as in days of old and consult visionaries, philosophers, and mystics for direction in life. Those pursuits of power are important in a book on alonetime because the very quests themselves provide the self-regulation gained in doing things on one's own. As is clearly demonstrated in myths and fairy tales—when Sir Lancelot finds Excalibur, Aladdin his magic lamp, or Cinderella her fairy godmother—the magic releases the individual's solo power. Without the glass slippers, Cinderella would not have had the confidence to attend the ball; until then, her mental self-image was of a scullery maid. Frank Baum's *The Wonderful Wizard of Oz* is perceptive: we know what to do and how to do it when we feel in touch with our own personal magic.

The attraction of the mystical and supernatural lies in its promise of extra power. But we are vulnerable on such pathways. Cultists such as the Mansons and Koreshes of the world will always have their followers. If the end result of pursuing mysticism reveals that we have followed a deceptive trail, then we had better know why we set forth in the first place. Cults that offer protection and individual growth attract audiences because they seem to embrace both needs; half the hangers-on seek dependent attachment, the others wish to adopt and incorporate the power of the leader. One might think that the introduction to the world of rational idealism would have diminished the following of false idols, but it hasn't. Rational thought through philosophizing grew in importance in the sixth century B.C. as a means toward power through self-knowledge.[19] Yet the interplay of magic with science, while seemingly disharmonious to the contemporary mind, continues to live. For as long as people feel unable to regulate their environment (internal or external) they will look to cults, the occult, and spirits.

Philosophy has changed, and it is no longer simply a meditative science. The downfall of the great monastic movement and the death of the self-reflective philosopher provide further insight into why solitude no longer abides comfortably in people's minds. In both instances we see excesses enacted in the seeking of solitude that were predicted by those who warned against such endeavors. What philosophy of old tried to do was restore reason and control to human existence. These quests for a solution to the problems of humankind brought excessive solitude in two great thinkers' lives. German philosopher Friedrich Wilhelm Nietzsche took a dramatic and revolutionary stand in his attempt to decipher what was behind all motivations and human values. He determined that behind all behavior is one reducible source—"the will to power." In conflict with Charles Darwin, Nietzsche maintained that enhancement of power is more important than preservation of life. And to obtain this power, he agreed with the Greek philosophers that one must endure pain, discomfort, and give up pleasures in favor of self-discipline. Only this puts man above the beasts and leads him to the joyous confirmation of a creative existence.

Friedrich Nietzsche led a revolution in philosophy by submerging himself in philosophical arguments. The individual's personal experience —subjectivity—became the object of thought, and philosophizing— thinking inwardly and alone—exemplified philosophy. Power comes from within, and the inner power sustains us against our insignificance in the world.

The influence on existentialism of Protestant and Danish religious philosopher Søren Aabye Kierkegaard was as profound as Nietzsche's was on philosophy in general. Rather than power being the major thrust in life, it was the freedom and value of the individual. Søren Kierkegaard's Christianity and abjuration of all but the religious life came from what Hannah Arendt called a "cruel psychological addiction to reflection."[20] Rejecting even his fiancée, he searched in solitude for connection to God. This religious "poet" lived and preached a neomonastic creed. He believed that everyone had to make an *either/or* choice in life between the aesthetic (devoted to art, music, and the like) and the ethical (seeking happiness in marriage or a profession). However, Kierkegaard, favoring a love of music and art, also believed in a union with God, and it is for the sake of that choice that he secluded himself.

Both men died very much alone. Kierkegaard was trying to undo a sin committed by his father—the cursing of God. Nietzsche was escaping the hypocrisy of his time. In religion and philosophy their influence has been inspirational to many and misleading to others. Nietzsche's political message has been read as a harsh call to embrace a world of (Nazi) supermen, while others see that he was grappling with the problems of modern-day life before they became evident to most. The fact that he saw the will to power as a chief motivating force of both the individual and society was prophetic, considering that this century has heralded two world wars and the long-lasting Cold War.

Against friends' advice, Kierkegaard and Nietzsche entombed themselves in solitude. Their brilliance led them to realize there were remarkable discoveries awaiting them in that private space. Their personal stories reveal the pitfalls in the fine and intricately detailed route necessary to follow when we are seeking a *balanced* picture of aloneness and attachment in life. One can become addicted to solitude and introspection as easily as overly dependent on relationships.

Learning from the Ancients

As we have seen, we in the West must struggle for solitude. But no teachings have recognized a place for alonetime in everyday life as completely as have the Eastern philosophies. Combining action, interaction, and solitude seems to be their way. Through meditation one seeks answers, through meditation one reaches nirvana. Yet it is not the individual who reaches the supernirvana *(parinirvana)* state of perpetual peace and total serenity who is most admired. It is the "bad" one, called *nisattva,* who refrains from the final step and goes back to the world. This seems to suggest the importance of community and the need to give special notice to those who relinquish total tranquillity. Buddhism, the ancient doctrine of India, is still alive after twenty-five centuries, and its doctrines or methods (dharma) were formulated around 600 B.C.,[21] originally by the son of an Indian raja, Gautama Siddhartha. Siddhartha, like many of the philosophical and spiritual leaders, was a great traveler. Journeys on the way to truth or salvation are undertaken alone, guided by God or wise men, frequented along the way by friends as well as hardships.

Pilgrimages in the old sense still occur today, but they are more brief. We see in people's walks and runs attempts to escape the hectic pace of life and rid the mind of excess. The sojourns do not equal the many-month hikes of ancient times for sustained thought.[22] Buddhists, however, continue to live in a state of pilgrimage because life is a search. For example, Zen Buddhism teaches the dangers both of attachment (even to one's teachings) and of withdrawal from ordinary life. The whole system of Zen "is nothing but a series of attempts to set us free from all types of bondage."[23] All the same, in meditation one must take care to not become overly caught up in self. In a *zendo*—the place where, for several hours a day, the recluse sits in the lotus posture meditating—one monk, who is usually on guard with a stick, does not hesitate to strike the shoulders of anyone who is not manifestly awake. This flagellation is not considered a punishment, but rather a prod to bring individuals into the place where they move past illusions and experience humility and detachment. A patient of mine who was inclined to seek self-punishment as a way to justify his alone needs first cultivated the stick and then found curative ways to satisfy this need and others.

Lance, a Caucasian African artist, suffered from frightful and haunting obsessions spurred on by his intense religious upbringing. His images rivaled those of a Stephen King novel: being dissected in a bathtub, eyes floating from heads, and heads turning into skeletons. His imagery was not primed by movies or TV, as he led an ascetic life without either, both for idealistic and financial reasons. Instead, he was plagued by guilt, occult stories, and the harsh circumstances of his childhood. From boyhood he felt that the oppression of black people in his country was wrong. Farmers and school chums filled his mind with tales of black men chopping up little boys after stealing them off into the woods. There were kindly black workmen on his father's farm whom he learned to love, yet he feared their revenge. His father, in contrast, was a frugal and brutal man whose temper had often caused Lance injuries. Lance's mother loved him and clung to him throughout his childhood. It was breaking away from her that caused him the greatest pain and guilt as he didn't know how to disengage himself and also maintain closeness. This drama was reenacted in his interactions, and proved central to his life. Lance's wife, Lizabeth, an artist in her own right, had a different sense of family life. Lance's resolution was to make family a convenience that shouldn't interfere with one's own social activities or separate time. Together you did very little—no need for two people to care for a child simultaneously. One is enough, so the other can do his thing. His wife disagreed. Family life was sharing. They had enormous fights over these issues, with Lance walking out. As Lance in therapy began to consider another picture of his wife and child, one that contained a three-way dialogue, and as he became better able to negotiate for time alone to pursue his art, he discovered that he had to find some way to channel his abundant sense of guilt.

Guilt is never totally abated, but his was destructively debilitating. Two resolutions occurred. One was that Lance decided to teach art without pay in a local public school. Many of the children were black or Hispanic. He also began to meditate. Lance's meditation practices at first became excessive. He found himself courting the stick and chastising himself as well. When finally he encountered someone he thought was an unjust master, he was able to reconsider his time meditating. He found another group—and this one offered family retreats.

The enormously violent feelings Lance was carrying since childhood were stilled when he felt justified in following some of his own preferences. Meditation was an apt way, because he felt so bound by others' wishes that, before, only anger allowed him to walk away and be alone. He went too far with meditation at first, and even that became enslaving. When he recognized this, the whole pattern of his life changed.

◆   ◆   ◆

How strange that self-inflicted pain so frequently accompanies a search for selfhood. Is there another accompanying inner need represented by the theme of suffering often present in solitary, religious, and philosophical devotions?

Guilt, Suffering, and the Will to Be Alone

One psychologist's opinion is that "all the animals in the world are psychologically less distinct from one another than one man is from other men."[24] So it is with individual requirements for peace and interaction. These differences, by the very nature of our upbringing and our ultimate destiny, may turn into guilt-ridden, agonizing internal dilemmas, and no one has treated them as poignantly as cultural anthropologist Ernest Becker. Becker calls it the "nexus of unfreedom" and correctly places part of the origins of this problem within the intensity of early relationships. This is similar to what early psychoanalysts claimed: people are mesmerized by their initial caretakers to feel magically protected. For Freud, those childhood feelings were at the bottom of the appeal of God and religion. Otto Rank, once a member of Freud's inner circle, who broke from traditional psychoanalytic thought, presents an alternative and more rounded picture. Rank, as much philosopher as psychoanalyst, grasped the ontological sense of individual helplessness and the subsequent desire to be part of something bigger: "a feeling of kinship with the all."[25]

Rank also understood the will to become oneself. At least as many children don't follow in the footsteps of caretakers as those who happily take that course. Within our makeup resides an evolutionary pressure to achieve self-definition and interrelatedness.[26] The need to stand alone can come under attack in our own mind, first out of guilt toward those from whom we are individuating, then out of fear of being alone and the consequences from both. Either may cause suffering.

Whether suffering is as necessary as alonetime in order to achieve one's creativity, find a true self, or obtain redemption through salvation is a question as old as the story of Job. Why does there seem some natural affiliation between pain, solitude, and contemplation? Perhaps it is an ill lesson learned from childhood, when the soothing rhythms of inner life are interrupted by needs impossible to fulfill ourselves and our cries go unanswered. There are those who have suggested that suffering is the beginning of metaphysics.[27] In pain people have greater awareness of separateness, and from that alone place may question life and seek greater control over other adverse conditions. Medical anthropologist Arthur Kleinman connects the limits of control over one's life with pain. Although he realizes that no explanation for human suffering is ever adequate to account for all moral and spiritual questions, he explains that recognizing suffering and pain as resistance to having one's autonomy overrun may add to general understanding of this complex experience. He informs us as well that "the development of chronic pain . . . sanctions a transformation in . . . experience. The pain becomes a means of resisting . . . [A] sense that . . . [the] world is not . . . [one's] own . . . is replaced by illness behavior."[28] Novelist Milan Kundera identifies suffering as akin to a person's self. "I feel suffering, therefore I am" is his stated philosophy, since pain is never transmittable to another person and is uniquely one's own.[29]

The ascetic discipline can intervene to the struggling solitary's benefit. If guilt breeds suffering and fear of punishment, the vows of discipline and self-mortification beat the "jailer" to the punch. Self-denial and flagellation bring back humility and say to the defied "father," "I am not much," and, "Don't think I'm trying to defeat or excel you." The idea of inflicting one's punishment before it's meted out may be what is behind the well-known social notion of initiation by suffering; whether in mythology or fraternities, personhood is achieved after hardship. Many of the notable monks and philosophical ascetics who followed this path— Saint Jerome, Saint Francis of Assisi, Marcus Aurelius, and Siddhartha— came from homes of wealth and comfort. The casting aside of earthly goods resonates in the thinking of these great independent men, who perhaps wanted to liberate themselves from dependency and inhibiting relationships.

Remember this as well: the initial womb sensations that link us to alonetime are ascetic by nature since few possibly perceived outer trappings, or stimuli, are connected to this steadily contained minimal environment. Buddhism recognizes this and suggests its pupils study infancy.

Whatever pleasure comes with this homeostasis may become one standard for later harmonious moments sought in solitude, ascetically. Whether in a remote, faraway stillness or in the very center of a community, the hermit or itinerant monk resides in us all.

Little in modern society provides the stillness necessary to recover from the inevitable insults and assaults of daily life. Cultures, as do individuals, have the potential to draw strength from past lessons as they move forward. Something terribly important is at stake if society ignores ancient wisdom and common sense and continues to lose sight of the meaning and value of alonetime. Let us trek onward and see how society embraced psychological messages that by neither design nor intent nevertheless veiled the need for time alone.

CHAPTER 4

Abandonment,

Attachment, and Theory:

A Half-Told Tale

There was a certain power in her [mother's] healing that I, as a child, felt was beyond my capacity to comprehend, the way I, as an adult, cannot comprehend the largeness of the universe, the number of its stars, parlance—Fathers and sons, brothers and sisters, family circles go off together to bond . . . I could not fathom how such a terribly sick woman could get well . . . I could not understand how pills and a changed environment were helping when her family's love had been of no use . . .

Because of her . . . [depression] it was impossible for her to be with us all the time. I always maintained the notion that I deserved a mother and could someday have mine . . . I never abandoned the ideal of a mother. She gave me ample opportunity to ostracize her completely. Why did I "turn out"? Why did my brother "turn out"?

KAYE GIBBONS, *Sights Unseen* [1]

STANDING IN FRONT of graduate students as a teacher of psychology and supervising advanced psychoanalytic work year after year, I wondered: how do children emotionally survive when raised in homes where parent-child attachment is not reliable? Gradually, I became aware of my own uneasiness in presenting the theories of relationships and maternal attachment that increasingly dominated clinical work. What was missing in the picture? Clearly not all children denied early bonding wind up as failures in life or in their ability to form relationships. And since some bonding is far from optimum, those who bond in the early part of their lives may court disastrous attachments later. I needed light shed on this puzzlement. But to achieve illumination, I knew I had to question time-honored foundations and a mainstay in child psychology: bonds of attachment. It took me many years to understand that another central need ran parallel to the necessity to bond and attach. This need, though operative even in children's lives, is obscured by the social-political message to bond.[2] These discoveries, in fact, have a psychological story.

The Prelude

Once upon a time, no psychoanalytic or psychological theories existed. No one even had particular concerns about attachment or child development. Boys and girls grew up experiencing minimal attention, whether or not they were happy, well adjusted, or loved. Physical survival was worry enough. But by the last part of the nineteenth century, everything began to change. Freud started to formulate a theory of psychosexual development and wrote that children's development coincided with different stages of sexual motivation from birth to puberty. In the year 1878, G. Stanley Hall became the first American to receive a Ph.D. in psychology (from Harvard University). His thoughts concentrated on adolescence, a time of life that was barely acknowledged until then. Little did anyone realize that these sciences of the mind and behavior were going to proliferate and influence future decades in countless ways, including the care of our children.

The Story

Before the curtain rises on *Perestroika*, the second part of Tony Kushner's Pulitzer Prize–winning play sequence *Angels in America*, an old Russian revolutionary walks onstage proclaiming, "For life we need a theory." "Any theory," no particular theory, he makes clear. As the play unfolds, other characters discover that theory doesn't always fit day-to-day life. People never fully understand their impact on the world, or the world's impact on them. Nevertheless, as Kushner's play states, we don't have the choice of standing still. We spin on, and theory changes as we move and redirect our thinking.

So it is with psychoanalytic theory, one of the most encompassing theories influencing our understanding of the human condition. Although a strong countermovement prevails to deemphasize Freud's impact, it is no longer possible to deny his influence on all of us in our day-to-day pursuits.

To illustrate the power of psychoanalytic theory, try imagining that Oedipus is just another Greek king from mythology, or a world without pediatrician and author Benjamin Spock, whose psychoanalytic slant to his pediatric advice sent the powerful message that young children, even infants, deserve credit for having sexual feelings and curiosity about sexual matters. Since then, we readily see the humor in an oft-told joke about the four-year-old child who asks his mother where he came from. Being an enlightened parent versed in Freud and Spock, the mother proceeds to tell him the facts of life, to which he replies, "Yeah, but where do I *really* come from, Buffalo or Chicago?"

New parents seeking modern methods of child rearing readily turn to authorities. Because of this propensity, a prolific popular literature on what is best for children at particular ages prevails. Today's parenting literature is fed by infant research, child development theory and research, and, most significantly, formulations on bonding and attachment derived from psychological and psychoanalytic theory.

But in days gone by, parents were not paying attention to theories of child development that catered to the special needs of children. Children went from being seen and not heard to being looked at and listened to with intensity, and this change can be explained in part by evolution. Selection theory, for instance, predicts that when families are abundant with children, parents devote less time and energy to them. The desire to parent, even in humans, is thought to be bound to survival of the species, and this behavior at times seems to outweigh individual survival tactics. Human parents experience less urgency in their duties as caretakers when they realize that continuation of the species is ensured by the sum total of offspring. But when family size began to decrease in the early 1900s, parents had more time to coddle their offspring. Eventually, an individual child was considered precious, increasing the odds for continuing a family line as sheer numbers of children per family decreased. This paralleled a new emphasis in child development theories.

Consciously or subconsciously, the theories of our generation shape our behaviors. In fact, the less we question cultural messages—the zeitgeist of our times—the greater their influence. When a theory takes hold, often something else gets lost. We automatically incorporate powerful theory because it is based on attempts at truth and thus suggests answers to fundamental questions. However, because knowledge is never complete, theories are just what they purport to be: plausible assumptions. And thus it is with attachment theory—the theory that stresses connection above everything else in life. The notion of attachment as the dominating need distorts expectations of relationships, as it did for one of my patients.

Jane, in the middle of a heartbreaking divorce, consulted me after five years of five-days-a-week psychoanalysis. She was a top-notch lawyer who seemed to have her act together until an event disturbed her equilibrium. She and her analyst seemed at odds as to how she should respond to her physician husband's having had an affair with a nurse. Jane, understandably devastated, sorrowfully recalled other humiliating experiences, in which her father or brother belittled her publicly or took advantage of her generous nature. Her analyst added fuel to the fire by reinterpreting her past experiences with her husband on vacations, during decision making, or even during lovemaking as proof of what Jane had called her pusillanimous nature and self-punitive, masochistic character.

Jane's husband, apologizing for the affair, explained it as a last-ditch effort to avoid a commitment to Jane and raising a family. Jane, in a two-times-a-week termination phase of therapy, was now advised that she needed continued intense psychoanalytic years to work out the destructive masochism and the insecure attachment to her father that dominated her life, causing her to make poor interpersonal choices.

A bit of background might help to explain why initially Jane was angry enough to seek an immediate divorce. Her husband's nurse lover blurted out the news of the affair to Jane at a Christmas party. Though the affair was already over, the shock sent Jane into a tailspin and she immediately filed for separation. Her husband's apology and attempts at reconciliation finally persuaded Jane to the point that she decided to go away to the seashore to think. She thought the separation from her husband important, and he, after protests, concurred that maybe it was a good test of their love for each other. Jane's therapist, however, said that Jane was running away! Why couldn't she work her problems out in treatment? What was she concealing? Jane felt she needed to gain her mind back. There was too much outer noise confusing her own thoughts. She returned after three weeks of time alone, love for her husband restored. He, too, while alone, had searched his soul and rediscovered his devotion.

Jane consulted me not knowing whom to believe: her prior analyst or herself. Her own instincts were to trust her husband again, and I sided with them. Now, over ten years later, I received the latest Christmas card from the couple, telling me that one of their two children is having a dance recital.

◆   ◆   ◆

In the beginning days of psychoanalysis, poor nurturing practices were finally coming under public scrutiny. Developmental theorists joined the effort to broadcast the damage from untimely separations and insecure attachments. Later, theorists reacted to changing lifestyles and greater numbers of abandoned children. Specifically, some psychoanalysts welcomed premises that equated faulty attachment with psychological problems because they were seeking a theoretical model to fit the picture of emotional abandonment that their patients were depicting to them. In other words, it seemed quite plausible that to have solid relationships—a prevailing benchmark of emotional maturity—individuals required stable ones in childhood.

For Freud, the patriarch of psychoanalysis, these early attachments were essential, but even more essential was an individual's ability to break away and achieve from emotional independence an ability to form mature attachments and self-sufficiency. Despite Freud's recognition of the importance of the bonds of love, his concentration on an individual's intrapsychic (inner-mind) processes led latter-day psychoanalysts to criticize his psychological theories for ignoring the interpersonal realm.

Interestingly, Freud did not facilitate this independence for his special and youngest daughter, Anna. He made the decision to be her analyst, and her tie to her father convinced her of the wisdom of this.[3] It is compelling to ponder Freud's ambivalence about independence and attachment when one realizes that he broke his own rules to make his daughter a companion for life. Freud's behavior implies that he was reluctant to allow his daughter her separate space for fear of losing continued immortality through a brilliant disciple. Freud spoke of autonomy and practiced it in his self-analysis. But his most important contribution to the recovery of mental health was the establishment of a treatment that required another person—a therapist—for progress.

Attachment Under Stress

Responding to the intricacies of attachment is never simple. Our current understanding of attachment became convoluted by the negative effects of extreme separation.[4] In England during World War II, Anna Freud and her friend and patron Dorothy Burlingham participated in a therapeutic nursery established to care for children who were separated for various lengths of time from their parents due to the war. The astute observations of these two women led to the important discovery that seemingly unaffected children actually have very profound reactions to separation from parents, ranging from mild responses to extreme devastation. The reactions of the child, of course, depended upon many factors, including the age and stability of the child, the nature of the parent-child relationship prior to separation, and the length of time of separation. Anna Freud and Burlingham also discovered that reunions with parents were not necessarily happy. More often than not a child reacted with anger or aloofness, making it difficult for the attachment to be reestablished.[5]

Similar sagas of enforced separation were germane to attachment and maternal-deprivation theories. In the 1940s, observations of children confined to institutions fueled activist and psychologist Margaret Ribble's thinking. In her book, she gives an account of institutionalized children who showed stunted physiological and psychological growth.[6] This marasmus—the failure to thrive—prevented infants from functioning in age-appropriate ways. Need for the sole and constant attention of one caretaker is the foundation of her theory of maternal deprivation.[7] New perspectives on attachment theory like Ribble's did not initially capture consumers' imaginations. To appreciate the forcefulness of the arguments in its favor, we must contemplate the struggle.

At the turn of the last century, the main authority on child care was physician Luther Emmett Holt.[8] His methods echoed the philosophy of the day, before attachment was in vogue. According to Holt, children did not require stimulation, and rocking was only a pernicious habit; he discouraged soothing since he believed that infants needed to cry in order to exercise their lungs. Spanking children to achieve this benefit was acceptable. Later in his career, after observing poor hospital conditions, he was sufficiently brave and ethical to revise his thinking. He noticed that certain infants lying quietly in cribs manifested a steady loss of strength and weight. Eventually, the children starved to death. Autopsies performed on large numbers of such children found no obvious physical cause of death. Dr. Holt discovered that when these children were not left dormant, and instead were stimulated by gentle touch (friction, not spanking), they regained their will to live. Then he began to recommend that nurses hold children and walk the corridors with them. It was he who actually discovered and named the illness marasmus and who saw that touch prevented it. Twenty-five years later, a prominent clinician from France made similar observations at a time when many of his colleagues were prepared to listen.

A contemporary of American researcher Ribble was psychiatrist René Spitz, who, with research associate Catherine Wolf, directly observed and compared infants raised in foundling homes to infants reared at home or in nursery settings, cared for by their mothers. He used the term "hospitalism"[9] to describe his findings on children hospitalized for long periods of time, deprived of "stimulation by any person who could signify a mother representative."[10] Hospitalism is characterized by lessened physical health, heightened reactions to infection, and lowered intellectual progress. Equally disturbing to Spitz was another syndrome he observed in infants six to eleven months old after separation from their mothers. He labeled these phenomena "anaclytic depression," a depression based on thwarted dependency needs.

Margaret Mead, reacting to the implication that all degrees of maternal separation in early childhood were potentially damaging, commented in her typically frank fashion: "The campaign against maternal deprivation has become a subtle form of anti-feminism in which men, under the guise of exalting the importance of maternity, are tying women more tightly to their children."[11] As is pointed out by those who have traced women's rights in the context of the politics of psychology, a dilemma resides in feminists who debunk psychological theory. Yes, many of these traditional theories are echoes of eras in which women were denied full recognition, but some of these same theories recognize the importance of women and their touted forte—relating.

Psychology at its best, and psychoanalysis as conceptualized, offer liberty to both men and women—upon reflection and introspection—to choose, change, and actualize. Ironically, attachment theory was originally meant to stand as an alternative to theories that rely on love as the key to relating. Attachment theory, based on observations of animals and humans, was purported to be an evolutionary theory that does not claim to be analogous to a romantic relationship, as it is founded on the need for security, not sexual intimacy.

John Bowlby, a psychoanalyst whose name is synonymous with theories of attachment, makes a distinction between attachment *theory* and attachment *behavior*. Attachment theory defines "the propensity of human beings to make strong affectionate bonds to particular others" and explains how unwilling separations and loss give rise to anxiety, anger, depression, and emotional detachment.[12] Attachment behavior, most apparent when a person is frightened, fatigued, or sick, is defined as "any form of behavior that results in a person attaining or maintaining proximity to some other clearly identified individual who is conceived of as [comforting and] better able to cope with the world."[13] In Bowlby's view, attachment was not meant to be a synonym for the term "social bond" or to apply to all aspects of the parent-child relationship,[14] yet the general public, and even a few practitioners, have absorbed a different message. Now the terms "attachment" and "bonding" are interwoven into the framework of relationships.[15]

It may seem strange that Bowlby—a stubborn, self-motivated, and determined man whose very headstone on the Scottish isle of Skye reads "To be a Pilgrim"—is the father of a theory that pays secondary attention to self-reliance. Some believe his thinking was shaped by his own distancing parents: a physician father absorbed in work and a free-spirited mother who left his care to nursemaids and nannies.[16] But he was anguished by the unmistakable effects of extreme and careless separations that he observed in various species of animals as well as people. Bowlby's break from the psychoanalytic rank and file was in part forced upon him as his ecological theories were seen as heresy by a field struggling for recognition of the power of inner dynamics.

Fortuitously, Bowlby joined with the developmental psychologist Mary Ainsworth, who, like him, also experimented with attachment patterns, carefully watching and conducting psychological research on children's behaviors with strangers.[17] Ainsworth, childless herself, traveled the globe early in her career to observe mothers and children. A marriage between psychoanalytic theory and developmental attachment theory offered great possibilities to Bowlby and Ainsworth. Although ultimately they concluded that multiple ties could work for children, the emphasis in their findings on attachment needs occluded other important discoveries. According to Ainsworth, all that seemed important was

> the sensitivity of the mother in responding to the baby's signals of need and distress and to his social signals, and the promptness and appropriateness of her response; the amount of interaction she has with him and the amount of pleasure both derive from it; the extent to which her interventions and responses follow the baby's timing rather than her own; the extent to which she is free from preoccupation with other activities, thoughts, anxieties, and griefs so that she can attend to the baby and respond fully to him; and finally and obviously, the extent to which she can satisfy his needs, including his nutritional needs.[18]

Ainsworth was asking a lot from a mother. In her studies, she labeled some maternal care insecure and anxious and correlated this to the inability of children to handle time away from their mothers. Children who were rated as more avoidant of their mothers' attention, according to her research, seemed to have been raised in insecure environments.

However, avoidance behavior can be appropriate to a situation, conducive to growth, and certainly adaptive to circumstances. One behavior in response to a mother's leave-taking may not in and of itself be more positive than another. Take Cynthia, forty-five, who lost her mother at age two. She describes never having played with dolls and not having a child because she feels she never learned parenting skills. This explanation, however, does not account for the full truth: others in Cynthia's situation are able to form close attachments, bear children, and aptly care for them. Cynthia herself raises birds and is very nurturing to them. She is also celebrating her twenty-fifth wedding anniversary. While growing up, Cynthia's hard-earned self-reliance and self-sufficiency became motivating and rewarding. Thus, her lack of interest in raising another person stemmed not only from attenuated attachment feelings, but also from the gratification she derived from aloneness and personal pursuits. The choices Cynthia made are examples of an adaptive lifestyle.

It may seem an almost heartless thought that, outside of sleeping hours, a baby needs unengaged time. In very early years, the helplessness and dependency of children are so profound that children require inordinate amounts of hands-on attention. Nevertheless, through the ages, astute mothers have said things like, "Just leave her alone for a few minutes; she needs to settle herself." Moreover, parents would be better prepared to provide care themselves, or through substitute caretakers, if society recognized parents' need for time off from child rearing. If society accepted the naturalness of such yearnings, then realistic expectations and sufficient caretaking facilities might be demanded and created to protect our children truly.

In fact, absolute attention to attachment misses the critical fact that individuals, even infants, are resourceful in their abilities to find solo comfort. Take a screaming newborn boy observed in the nursery as he is being weighed. The observer, unseen by the infant, puts a finger in the baby's hand. The baby grips the finger—a reflexive response. The crying infant then moves the finger to his cheek. He then turns his face so he is fully resting against a warm hand. Ardent attachment theorists might say, "Aha, the baby is being soothed by the contact." Surely, the connection is important, but the baby is not attaching to a person. As a survivor in a shipwreck might attach himself to a floating wooden plank, the baby comforts himself by grabbing something in his environment that is readily available. This "independent" act of hand and face movement precedes behaviors learned from a two-person relationship.

Potent damage occurs when parents take the attachment message too literally, perhaps to satisfy their own yearnings for closeness. Many people say that they wish to have children just in order to have a caretaker down the road. This may be a part of the life cycle, but not the best reason to procreate. These parents may fail to recognize a child's equal need for distance, and place inordinate need on their children. In the early 1940s, sensing the growing importance of parental attachment, Philip Wylie captured in unusually scathing, volatile language the paralyzing effects of overintrusive mothering. Could the case now be made for fathering? He said, "Our society is too much an institution built to appease the rapacity of loving mothers. If that condition is an ineluctable experiment of nature, then we are victims of a failure."[19] Mothers are society's, psychology's, and individuals' scapegoats when all emotional problems are interpreted as stemming from under- or overprotected childhoods.

Strikingly, the message conveyed by many psychoanalysts and psychologists to a receptive general public was, "Bond, attach, connect, or else!" I, too, even as a clinician, at one time fell for the siren call of attachment theory. Who doesn't have complaints about their childhood? It seemed quite rational to a budding psychoanalyst that if we concentrated on the attachment message, we could ensure a society of emotionally healthy children and adults. But I kept seeing patients whose treatments didn't quite coincide with the expected secure attachment leading to lack of avoidance behaviors.

Edna chose psychoanalysis in order to find a way back to her family and simultaneously her own life. Her several years spent to gain relief from severe symptoms of anxiety, depression, and sexual inhibitions follow more than the one track in this vignette.

Edna, the longed-for girl in a family with three sons, was loved by both her parents. In the beginning of treatment, every time Edna spoke of her parents' love or hers for them, she would weep. A concert singer who married and moved miles away from them, Edna contributed money from time to time to subsidize the family. Nevertheless, she was plagued by feelings of deep betrayal of her siblings, mother, and father. It was especially her mother whom she felt she deserted. She told stories from early childhood of her and her mother's hopes clashing. Her mother thought she should study teaching, but she liked music. Her mother wanted her to play outside, but she preferred to read. None of these differences made for huge or unusual battles. Basically, she felt their love and support, but she knew she needed to follow a dream that was unlike any within her family. Originally, there wasn't room for her own wishes to exist side by side with her family's, but when the family heard how well she sang, they demonstrated pride in her accomplishments. Despite their growing appreciation of her, she still felt a need for maintaining great distance.

◆   ◆   ◆

I found it interesting that Edna became a soloist. I also learned through her analysis that absolute rules about attachment can be challenged. She had faith in the security of her family's love for her, but she knew that their desires for closeness far outweighed hers. This made her sad, worried, and enormously guilt ridden—as she still clung to old expectations for perfect family harmony. While decision making frightened her, she wanted to be her own person, and she eventually realized that she needed to give her parents the same freedom. Another patient of mine said it best: "I no longer expect my father to jump in response to me, since I recognize that he, too, has his own world."

In our own age of throwaway children, to disagree at all with attachment theorists and to suggest that parents and children may need further recognition of their alone needs may be met with skepticism. However, I am *not* advocating that parents shed their responsibilities and allow children to fend for themselves. I am proposing that by not recognizing the pressing need for time apart, we set ourselves up for parental failure and guilt and we limit development of our children's capacities to brave it alone. Attachment theory was born from watching the anguish of children's unhappy separations.[20] It was a theory of *attachment under stress*. Because the time was ripe for society to take a new look at child care, some scientists and clinicians may have initially overprescribed instant bonding, ignoring those lengthy periods of time when very young children flourish in peaceful aloneness.

The Plot Thickens

So far, I have emphasized how unidimensional statements about attachment made by psychoanalysts and developmental psychologists have impacted culture. Yet culture has also influenced psychoanalysis. As our divorce rates grow, so does the amount of slogans for keeping people related, ranging from "The family that prays together stays together" to "Reach out and touch someone." Families change, and with women in the workplace a need for alternative child care increases. Simultaneously, cognitive psychologists and sociologists keep convincing parents that stimulation through heightened play experiences and peer interactions is important. But within these arguments lies the need to constantly occupy children. Slowly but surely, children lose time to muse rather than to be amused. Parents program not only activities but also "quality" parent-child interactions. The lovely, unhurried pace of childhood is being suffocated as children glue themselves to television shows they "need" to watch. Perhaps TV protects against fear of loneliness and fearful fantasies, and provides company. But the great luxury of childhood—free, safe, and unprogrammed alonetime—is being eroded. In thinking about this invasion into childhood, I have wondered about the decided shift of focus in society. For example, how responsible is my field and the media's great interest in psychology for the changes in the way people think about relationships and the development of the self?

Emphasis in psychoanalysis on the importance of relational love and interconnectedness augmented the negative focus on loneliness, which now stood in opposition to people needing people. When women began to make their imprint on psychoanalysis, one of the first criticisms of Freud was that he understood neither women nor the importance of the emotional mother-infant connection to all other relationships. With the door now wide open to psychoanalytic critique, other challengers marched in, seriously questioning Freud's fundamental conceptions of sex and aggression. One strong and lasting group affirmed that forming a cohesive self superseded sexual and aggressive motivation—the self psychologists. Reformed psychologies began to influence film, theater, magazine articles, and soap operas to suggest closer ways of mothering, greater intimacy between men and women, altered perspectives on the role of a "manly" man, and the development of self. I thus interweave these new threads into the story about the impact of psychoanalytic thinking.

Melanie Klein, a theorist from Europe and Anna Freud's chief rival, climbed the ranks of the male psychoanalytic network. As someone who stated that relationships with others begin at birth, arising from the initial feeding experience, Klein can be considered the mother of a most important theory of relationships, called "object relations."[21] Even now, Klein remains one of the most controversial analysts of her time. She was a woman who hated her mother, analyzed her children, and used them to provide clinical examples of her theories. These theories are filled with ideas of early fantasy life and nasty internalized feelings of envy, guilt, and aggression toward others (the objects). Nevertheless, her ideas are stimulating and creative. Whereas Freud's concentration on unconscious processes sometimes left analysts forgetting that there was more to individuals than their intrapsychic life, his daughter Anna's focus was on conscious processes and normal development. Thus it was Klein who remained closer to Freud, her father in theory, by plunging into the depths of aggressive feelings of sadism and hatred. On the other hand, Klein's sense of the infant as capable of experiencing life was perspicacious and very modern in describing babies, from birth, as interacting with their surroundings by both perceiving and often incorporating how others feel. This goes beyond the state of attachment, which is connection for safety's sake. In the psychoanalytic office of Melanie Klein nothing interrupted the work of patient and analyst. They were in a world unto themselves. Through Klein, her contemporaries, and her disciples, psychoanalysis entered a two-person field. The connection between patient and therapist came out of the closet. No longer would established techniques of Freudians—symbolized by the analyst in a chair thinking his thoughts and the patient on the couch in a separate fantasy world—predominate.

Writing in the United States from the late 1920s through 1949, Harry Stack Sullivan gained prominence with his own interpersonal school of psychoanalytic thought.[22] Sullivan's beliefs were distinct from and sometimes even contrary to Freud's. In this country, in particular, he is credited with bringing both relationships and a self-system—as an organization of experience—under the scrutiny of psychoanalysis.[23] Yet, due to the highly specific nature of his use of the term "self," he is largely neglected by self psychologists. While Sullivan's focus was primarily on the pros and cons of mother-and-child connections, he included the influence of peer relationships on self-development. The latter is just now having its deepest impact on relational theories and society. Among the new experiences that continue to emerge and shape personality, none seemed as important to Sullivan as intimate relationships to a peer. Loneliness, which Sullivan believed the most painful of human experiences, results when interpersonal needs are unmet.[24]

Once again, in contemplating a theorist's basic premises, background plays a part. For Sullivan's theories may have been fueled by his own lonely childhood. Growing up in farm country without sufficient friendships, he complained about this loss to those who knew him well. Moreover, his frequent contact with schizophrenic patients and his own bout with schizophrenic symptomatology taught him about radical and painful withdrawal. Repeatedly, from a place of extreme stress—in this case, loneliness and the anxious isolation of the psychotic mind—came information on how people need relationships.

Erich Fromm, a psychoanalyst with a strong social consciousness, also concerned himself with loneliness. His thoughts[25] lent understanding to how people could follow the murderous and racist ideas of a Hitler. According to Fromm, people craving security are afraid to be on their own. It is dependency on others' approval that makes people willing to be led by an authoritarian dictator. Then they can leave the control of powerful (especially aggressive) feelings to group decisions. Adolescents who follow cult leaders are described as having similar motivations. In coming to this conclusion, Fromm described individuals as trying to re-create their womb existence. He saw this as the one time in life that people felt truly secure and safe. For Fromm, only before birth is the human organism one with nature and in paradisiacal harmony. The central feature of the human condition is that each individual after birth is fundamentally and abjectly alone; the womb is a state of *connectedness* bliss. Connection may be the fact of womb life, but it cannot be the subjective experience in utero, as will be discussed in Chapter 6.

Within Fromm's relational model, the inner life of the individual is dominated by powerful passions and pretenses that serve to overcome loneliness. Unlike Sullivan, who considered this emotion the unhappy curse of mankind, Fromm believed people needed to accept it in order to have a true productive flowering of their potential. He accepted living comfortably with aloneness—but as an achievement possible particularly in later life.

The place of aloneness in the accomplishment of strong and satisfying selfhood was derailed by the ardent relational, two-person psychoanalytic therapists rebelling against the one-person psychology of Freud and perhaps, inadvertently, by some of the contributions of self psychologists to psychoanalytic thinking. Heinz Kohut, a Chicagoan by way of Vienna, provided leadership for the self psychology movement. Nevertheless, he gave impetus to a theory in which human relatedness remains so primary to the survival of the self that self psychologists speak about the external influences that remain with us by becoming internal as "selfobjects." Kohut's assertion that the *other* is the *oxygen* for the self demonstrates the strength of the attachment message in self psychology. Esther Menaker, one of the few remaining psychoanalysts to have been analyzed by Anna

Freud, clarifies Kohut's contribution to psychotherapy; she makes proper note of how Kohut emphasizes the self growing developmentally within the family matrix. While his theory brings to light a healthy side to narcissism and self-focus it also portrays an ongoing sense of the infant self as lacking resilience and constancy. Thus, the self of Kohut's baby does not seem capable of being alone, separate or differentiated from others.[26]

Jean Piaget, the noted Swiss psychologist, would disagree. Picture, in contrast, the nutrients that toddlers receive on their own in a classroom. Observing high-spirited children in a different setting, we see in action other *necessary* sources of substance for a developing self besides a specific other. A nursery-school teacher, for example, knows the pleasure young children derive from belonging to a small community apart from primary caregivers. Although children need time to separate from home and family, in this new world almost everything is child sized and adjusted to children's needs and interests. Within the inviting space of an effective preschool class, children can explore socially, physically, imaginatively, and intellectually—frequently in solo endeavors. Juxtaposed in the classroom are spaces to be together and alone. Some professionals might link this social and cognitive development to securely attached behaviors and say that all learning in the classroom is an extension of the mother-child interaction. Nevertheless, Piaget might be the first theorist the teacher would cite in supporting the classroom space as a metaphor for young children's developmental needs.[27]

Piaget emphasized the need children have for interaction with the world of *things* in order to develop the capacity to reason. In the earliest period of newborn life, the sensorimotor period, the child's own body is an object of exploration. It begins to connect through smell, taste, and touch with things in the world around it. If we focus for a moment on the image of a baby with a rattle—curious, delighted, repeating over and over the act of waving its hand, hearing sounds, looking at the object—we can see a child at work on learning in aloneness, with a very keen attention.

Margaret Mahler, a pediatrician-turned-psychoanalyst, had an all-embracing interest in together and separate times. The early part of her career was spent trying to unravel the mysteries of childhood schizophrenia and autism. Through her involvement she saw extremes of relatedness and unrelatedness, from clinging symbiotic ties in the child with schizophrenia to ceaseless withdrawal in a child with autism. From her observations of nondisturbed youngsters in a Greenwich Village nursery school, she organized her ideas on separation-individuation. This foundation of early relational concepts described stages in the development of emotional "object constancy," or how children go from needing absolute closeness with a primary caretaker to being able to function on their own when the beloved other (object) feels positioned in one's mind and heart and is thus forever constant.

Mahler was always searching for integration between normal and pathological behaviors. In her last systematic formulations,[28] she describes phases and subphases in the child's march away from mother (separation) and toward independence (individuation). She defines continuous stages in which babies go from a more merged to a more separated state.[29] Within this separation-individuation process, she emphasized periods of time when children experience their greatest separation fears. Even in the popular scene this was referred to as separation anxiety and became the cornerstone to understanding people's hesitancy in forming *and* leaving close relationships. Comparatively, I maintain that close ties and separateness are not mutually exclusive and that a sense of separateness is within us from the start.

Conclusions and New Horizons

As early as the 1950s, Lois Barclay Murphy, who did her work at the famous Menninger Foundation in Topeka, Kansas, studied coping and resiliency in children longitudinally.[30] Murphy's work, largely neglected by others until the 1970s, tells us that there are many variables that help children overcome bad experiences, other than just secure and stable relationships: for instance, a child's ability to communicate, capacity for play and fun, resources for discharging tension, and facility in satisfying his or her own needs. These endowments are part and parcel of the ability to be alone. Adding to this viewpoint, contemporary studies of infants debate Mahler's early merged stage, suggesting that from birth babies are their own persons. Self psychology, although interested in the self in the context of relationships, still promised to be the missing link between identity formation and attachment to parents. Therefore, without systematic intention, both theories—Mahler's and Kohut's—provided an entranceway for analysts to peer into and see a need for close time *and* alonetime.

Viewing aloneness as a developmental need parallel to attachment offers a way to resolve paradox and reduce pathologizing. Then we are able to regard achieving a balance between experiencing closeness and experiencing aloneness as elementary, essential, and natural. In the ever-growing hectic pace of today's world, attachment and aloneness needs, just like those deprivation stories of children under stress, loom larger than life. People openly complain about unsatisfactory time to relate. Though hidden from view, our aloneness needs also yearn for attention. If these needs are silenced, there is inner rebellion.

Attachment theory and psychoanalytic self and relational theories began to solve the puzzle of how we grow and develop into warm and loving adults. Aloneness theory, which broadens our understanding of patterns in relating and the development of the self and self-reliance, is the missing part of the jigsaw puzzle. In Part Two of this book, we seek the references for this revisionary story from psychological development, psychoanalytic theory, research, and professional experience.

PART TWO

The Need for

Aloneness

CHAPTER 5

Silence, Sharing Secrets,

and Change: The Other Half

of the Psychology Story

There were some kinds of silence which implied very sharp hostility and others which meant deep friendship, emotional admiration, even love . . . I think silence is one of these things that has unfortunately been dropped from our culture. We don't have a culture of silence . . . Young Romans or young Greeks were taught to keep silent in very different ways according to the people with whom they were interacting. Silence was then a specific form of experiencing a relationship with others. This is something that I believe is really worth cultivating. I'm in favor of developing silence as a cultural ethos.

MICHEL FOUCAULT, *Politics, Philosophy, and Culture* [1]

IF ONE WISHED FOR additional proof of how ingrained psychology is in our culture, one would not have to look further than *Consumer Reports*. [2] In the midst of rating coffeemakers and cars, they collected data from four thousand outpatient clients who sought psychotherapy. This in-depth survey revealed, among other things, that the longer people stayed in therapy, the more they felt improved. (Tell that to the insurance companies!) Thus, as psychology and psychotherapy are part and parcel of many people's lives, how their messages have changed tells us a lot about what is expected of human nature. In this chapter, I am interested in how old ways—and often the newer ways—discriminate against alonetime. I also visit alonetime's partner, self-regulation, in the realm of psychology, psychoanalysis, and everyday life, all the while searching for a balance between attachment and alonetime. Along the way, I keep in mind a strong response, even rebellion, to twentieth-century scientific and social conditions.

Typically, we give pause when we see—besides the usual wish for better relationships—conspicuous statements of withdrawal and silence in film, theater, sculpture, or painting.[3] But the antipathy of the artistic elite to popular culture's embrace of stimulation has not caused any tremors in my field. Silence, I had almost forgotten until recently, is not incorporated into psychoanalytic training as it once was.[4] The patient's and analyst's silences were once important aspects of the psychoanalytic hour and worthy of symposia and innumerable articles. This has changed; interaction between patient and analyst is now in the forefront. This time, I take you behind the curtain of psychoanalysis and psychology. As we now realize, my world has influenced yours, infiltrating just about every cultural corner.

Change and the Culture of Psychology in America

Psychologist Robert Fancher claims that every healing profession—even every school of healing—produces its own culture.[5] Each culture extends beyond the therapeutic milieu. For example, ideas infuse the mind and practices of all those trained in psychoanalysis, and, "repeating [them], the student becomes a mythmaker too."[6] A case in point is a budding male analyst, in the process of choosing a new therapist, who came to me for a consultation.

> Dalton, a middle-aged male and a psychiatrist in psychoanalytic training, knew he needed to return to psychoanalysis. His relationship of ten years was turning sour. His mate, Jim, was jealous of the creative turn Dalton's life was taking since Jim was no longer participating in every inch of Dalton's productivity. The two had stopped writing poetry and having sex together. Yet neither went anywhere socially without the other. Although they didn't share a bed, they did spend long hours talking, eating meals, and taking vacations together. Dalton felt Jim's admission that he no longer loved or even liked his partner indicated his own—not his mate's —bad nature. In fact, Jim had accused Dalton early in the relationship of not caring sufficiently, and now the proof was apparent.
>
> Dalton came to me to improve and maintain his relationship and to keep this partner, who he hoped would once again help him to be in touch with his vigorous self. In his words, Dalton

wanted almost a selfobject, or someone he could count on even when he was away.[7] In training as a self psychologist, he was learning a lot about a "never-ending need for psychological dependency." Dalton related that he wanted a treatment that would reestablish that kind of partnership. I admitted a problem in rote following of a set formula.[8] I confessed to being integrative in my approach (exploring and rethinking theory in the context of clinical data rather than adhering to one dogma). At the same time, I was open to confrontation or questioning when and if he felt that I had been unresponsive or had misunderstood him. At first, Dalton appreciated this openness, but upon reflection he said that psychotherapy with me conflicted with his training. When I supported his desire for uninterrupted time, he responded that his friend was probably correct in insisting that Dalton's wish for a half hour or so of silence—no talk and no TV—was evasive. I wondered with him what he might be evading. He didn't know. Discussing the feelings that were occurring in the therapy between us was not fruitful for him. Later, I asked whether Dalton thought silence brought a calming element to his life. This angered him. Of course, nothing in self psychology militates against silence—alonetime or silence can serve selfobject functions as can a book, exercise, and so forth.

I didn't think Dalton's version of immersion in another was an accurate picture of self psychology either, but it seemed best for Dalton (and me) that we part company. Though he said his relationship helped him to maintain a "consolidated sense of himself," he described himself as feeling a lack of vigor and spontaneity. Inwardly, I knew I was not the right one to mold him into a relationship. I was viewing his actions as a narrow defense of his beliefs; he saw his actions as an allegiance to a central school of psychoanalytic thought that, he stated, conformed to "respected social values of loyalty in relationships." Dalton was correct to seek help elsewhere and probably saw me as too rigidly following my path. Times have changed. Analysts of old were never wrong and might have tried harder to convince Dalton to change his "faulty" perspective.

◆   ◆   ◆

Dalton represents strict adherence to a doctrine—mythmaker extraordinaire, an exponent of the trickle-down process of theory, in which what is learned well is perpetuated in word and deed. Once psychology in the United States claimed its stake in the early to mid-1900s as the scientific discipline with proof that childhood experience has a profound and lasting effect on development, many of its myths colored the messages delivered to parents and teachers. Psychological insight, says historian Ellen Herman, is the "creed of our own time,"[9] as we have seen. To illustrate how the public succumbs to word of scientific change, let us take one last look at an exceptionally strong message that underplayed attachment in the American tabloids and periodicals before today's attachment teachings.

John B. Watson—1915 president of the American Psychological Association, professor at Johns Hopkins University, and parent trainer—had far-reaching ideas on children's behavior and needs. Some of his thoughts seem prescient—he believed, for example, from observing newborns that conditioning began early in life, probably in the womb. Detached behavior, he theorized, could allow an infant to discover the world independently. In his earliest writings, his theories reflected Freud's concept of an inherent sexual drive. But his later theories did not subscribe to innate responses and placed all learning at the foot of a mechanistic stimulus-response theory—behaviorism. Since all was learned equally and inadvertently by repeated actions, parents should be wary of what they do with their children. Watson's antiseptic approach ruled out hugging, fondling, or kissing infants. In keeping with his approach and that of L. Emmett Holt, Mrs. Max West, through the auspices of the United States Department of Labor Children's Bureau, wrote advice and guidelines to parents under the heading of *Infant Care*. The publication's philosophy demanded almost superhuman infants: "A baby should be taught to blow its nose, to submit the tongue and throat to inspection, [and] to gargle."[10] Mrs. West asserts:

> An older child should be taught to sit on the floor or in his pen or crib during part of his waking hours, or he will be very likely to make too great demands upon the mother's strength. No one who has not tried it realizes how much nervous energy can be consumed in "minding" a baby who can creep or walk about . . . the mother . . . will need to conserve all her strength, and not waste it in useless forms of activity.[11]

Against this backdrop, parents toilet trained children by age one in the 1930s. It is astounding that people in their seventies and eighties who were raised according to Watson's rigid guidelines have nevertheless become wonderful people. I doubt that all of them needed to resuscitate on the analyst's couch.

The families of the Depression era and World War II, however, did face confused grounding in parenting. And depending on whether they were avant-garde, like the title character in *Auntie Mame,* or self-absorbed, like the parents in one of Eugene O'Neill's or Tennessee Williams's plays, their practices as mothers and fathers ranged from the permissive to the harsh and the neglectful. Grown-up children of those generations of parents eventually made themselves heard. I was one of them. When I was in graduate school in the mid-1960s, a cultural revolution unfolded in the United States, especially in the university environment. Sit-ins, strikes, and marches against the A-bomb were all part of my education. But within the psychoanalytic kingdom, at least from the sheltered eyes of a potential disciple, all seemed fairly copacetic.

The Sounds of Silence

Until the 1970s, dissidents who had potential to shatter the inner sanctum, like "fallen" analysts or feminists like Karen Horney, stepped aside to form their own groups of theorists and practitioners. Many of the challenges from within were incorporated into the ongoing system. But ultimately the rumbles and roars from the inside and outside—feminist and civil rights protests—made their way into the caverns of psychoanalysis and affected theory to such a degree that certain basic tenets turned 180 degrees.[12] In asking the famous question "What do women want?" Freud left the task of responding to others. When women finally had sufficient voice to answer, they shouted from various directions. Along with medicine and advertising, the feminine position on relationships in its apt socialization of psychoanalytic theory masked the equally essential alone nature of individuals. Silences, privacy, and secrets—especially the analyst's—were obliterated. Before, therapists were trained to follow the abstinence rule. Just as patients were expected to abstain from many pleasures and changes during the course of treatment, so, too, therapists were expected to keep their personal needs, thoughts, and life stories private. This silence was not always meant to rehabilitate alonetime; rather, the main aim was to inspire regression. For quite a while, these silences provided comedians with wonderful images of analysts asleep behind the couch or preparing their income tax returns. Among the wittiest portrayals were the celebrated dialogues between Elaine May and Mike Nichols. In one, patient Nichols complains of seeing the analyst as his mother. His despair is hardly lifted when analyst May admonishes him when he leaves about keeping warm and not forgetting to eat chicken soup.

In time, as psychoanalysis wove in the relational thread, analysts became less self-conscious about telling personal stories and began to view them as conducive to cure. Some interpret this new openness as chumminess or the feminization of therapy, but in learning more about most old-school therapists (Freud included), we see how they broke their own rules while professing the absolute necessity for rigid boundaries and impersonal therapy sessions. In Victorian society, mandates from therapists were embarrassingly difficult for the patient to challenge. Without formal pronouncement, the 1960s feminist theories and the self psychology of Kohut brought a change in the authority of analysts that paralleled changes in the way the world viewed authority and the supremacy of rational thinking. Who, in fact, is the truly dependent one: the patient seeking aid or the therapist receiving a fee? Who is in charge: the analyst interpreting material or the patient supplying the material?[13] Freud's wish to make his science of the mind equivalent to the rational, "hard" sciences of chemistry and biology was acknowledged as impossible.[14] The objectivity of the analytic laboratory gave way to the subjectivity and relativism of a mostly democratic working alliance.[15] Analyst and patient, now trying to interact on more equal footing, could form a bond to solve the mysteries of the mind. Subsequently, the attachment theme all but drowned out the important other chord of alonetime.

Let me reveal another backstage secret about the world of psychoanalysis and its welcoming of rational and attachment theories. My informant is Merton Gill, recently deceased psychoanalytic pioneer, who felt that the psychoanalysis of the 1960s was ripe for a transfusion and that new blood had to be interpersonal. Gill believed, as I do, that as teachers we should halt further "vampire" tendencies that seek total domination of one theory over another and move toward reconciliation and harmony between the one-person and two-person psychologies. Gill's training, however, represented a different philosophy. One prominent female psychoanalyst in the 1950s lectured to him, describing the pristine ways that analysts should treat patients:

> The analyst's office should be spare and bare. She [the prominent analyst] also believed that an analyst should not participate in any public activity, such as taking a position on an issue ... In [Gill's] first course in analytic technique, the instructor

. . . said that in the ideal analytic situation the analyst would be behind a screen and his or her voice would be disguised so that the patient would not know the sex of the analyst. Furthermore, as it soon became clear, the disguise would hardly be necessary for the first several hundred hours because the analyst should preferably say nothing during that time anyhow.[16]

This is strangely predictive of the computer-programmed therapy that I've seen. Talk about silence and alonetime! Indeed, the first analysis that I underwent followed the idea that "uh-huh" was a major verbal concession on the part of the analyst. I spent far too many years in that deprived atmosphere and remember the most helpful day in my analysis as the occasion when my analyst broke parameters and suggested that I call immediately to get an application to college because I'd been hemming and hawing for too long about it. Despite that exception, the code of abstinence was still primary throughout my early years of graduate training. Strangely, or perhaps not, these anxiety-laden treatments in which many patients regressed to a state of helplessness produced analysands more loyal to their analysts than many sons to fathers or daughters to mothers—once again attachment under stress.[17]

Nevertheless, in the abstinence rule and the silences, opportunities existed for lone adventures into the unconscious. A nineties book,[18] *We've Had a Hundred Years of Psychotherapy and the World's Getting Worse*, written by well-known Jungian psychoanalyst James Hillman and journalist and screenwriter Michael Ventura, points a finger at psychotherapy for making the world a worse place in which to live: "The vogue today, in psychotherapy, is the 'inner child.' The child archetype [in Jungian jargon] is by nature . . . disempowered . . . The thing that therapy pushes is relationships . . . You just can't make up for the loss of passion and purpose in your daily work by intensifying your personal relationships."[19]

I also know what they mean when they describe the passivity of a "therapized" middle class. While welcoming greater interaction in therapy, I, too, ponder the loss of the alone spirit once provided by a healing climate that fostered solo inner voyages. Hillman notes classical psychoanalysis as an exception to current trends away from quiet introspection. The silence of the therapist was an appropriate party line; the silence of the patient was a different matter indeed. With few exceptions, the patient's silence was *resistance* in the days before the changes of the 1970s. After all, a talking cure relied on speech, and since the analyst's lips were partially sealed, the process depended on the patient to provide all of the juicy material by free association. A close-lipped patient was nearly always negative, and conferences and papers[20] debated the intricacies of this resistance. Were patients aggressive, obstinate, anxiety ridden, seductive, sexually inhibited, anal-erotic, or all of the above and more? In earlier times, therapists always blamed the patients; quiet was rarely seen as provoked by the silence of the analyst, and certainly not as a positive expression[21] of the patient's inner world.

In the patient's use of silence, however, there resides a continuity with culture and religion.[22] For example, in the Grimms' fairy tale "The Twelve Brothers," a sister stops speaking in order to protect her brothers and show love. Cordelia, King Lear's faithful daughter, says, "What shall Cordelia do? Love and be silent . . . my love's more richer than my tongue."[23] Regulated silence is also an important part of most religious ceremonies. The Quakers come together in silence as they await the inner light. Similarly, in religious meditation, all speech stops. Therapists of the 1960s and 1970s began to accept that silence provides a rich vein. Eventually, they became intrigued within this silence, designating it as "preverbal expressions." The silence, however, remained something to analyze and convert into language. For me and others, many silences in therapy, as in life, are also a turning away to take stock, to appropriately express a depth of feeling beyond speech, or register a discovery in a way stronger than spoken language, through true "in-sight."[24]

Silences today are as rare inside the analyst's office as they are outside. Adults from all social strata would have trouble entering a psychoanalyst's parlor without the intention to talk. Time is money and for some the meter starts the first second of the forty-five-to-fifty-minute hour. Demystified analysts might also have some difficulty simply sitting back and waiting. Although self-reflections are still foremost in the process, analysts, too, may feel the idea of being seen but rarely heard somewhat outmoded. Patients, analysts might reason, would want more substantive interventions for their time and money. Clearly, time—not silence—is golden. Indeed, object relations theory, female psychology, and self psychology still feel like taking in a breath of fresh air, as all bring a different approach to treatment that promises more authority to patients. But another lifeline to theorists, patients, and, I think, the population in general appeared in the late 1950s and 1960s, yet few at the time appreciated its vitality.

The Skill to Separate

In mid–twentieth century England, pediatrician-turned-psychoanalyst Donald Woods Winnicott spoke with a new voice about alone experiences: "In almost all our psycho-analytic treatments, there come times when the ability to be alone is important to the patient. Clinically this may be represented by a silent phase or a silent session, and this silence, far from being evidence of resistance, turns out to be an achievement on the part of the patient."[25] Fearlessly for his time, psychoanalyst Winnicott saw silence and alonetime in a positive light, but few carried forth his ideas. However, I question how he places aloneness within a relationship: "Perhaps it is [with the analyst] that the patient is able to be alone for the *first* time" (emphasis mine).[26] Maybe in the analytic session patients will dare to express the alone need and re-create this experience from the earliest of their silent hours. But to me, such alone experiences are part of the course of life and more rudimentary than Winnicott's learned "capacity to be alone" or Freud's "infantile narcissism" or Mahler's concepts of a baby's "normal" autism. Winnicott, though, is rightly credited as the first person to name the capacity to be alone as a significant psychological variable. Instead of following the growing fashion of togetherness and attachment, which characterized the 1950s, he considered the ability to be alone as a vital sign of maturity in emotional development. He felt that it was imperative for the child to discover a private and personal life.

Winnicott's deep familiarity with healthy babies and mothers enabled him to see the creativity that stems from a child's state that he called "going-on-being," a demand-free experience during the early months of infancy. I interpret going-on-being as among the first meditative, free-floating states—not necessarily from an environment created by the mother, but certainly secure and safe. It is a calm condition basic to human nature that later supports the formation of a recognizable self.

A modern-day psychoanalyst and psychiatrist, Thomas Ogden,[27] who has studied autism extensively, reworks early theories while making room for his own contributions. Ogden believes, as I do, that a baby creates a self-generated, sensation-dominated consciousness throughout early development. To Ogden, that environment is personal isolation, separate from the mother's province as supplier of everything. However, in his description the role of personal isolation is mainly a buffer against the "strain of . . . [being] alive in the . . . [world] of human beings."[28] His theory seems to evolve from the context of pathology, since the failure of the mother to "compete" with this personal isolation might very well lead to autism. Parents naturally add essentially to a child's interest in living and knowledge of how to function in relationships or alone. But simultaneously, babies are equipped to provide a self-comforting sensory environment, the start of the mind-body connections necessary for learning, creativity, and survival from within.

How does one, for instance, survive the Holocaust, a time that, according to Elie Wiesel, "has to do with silence, even with silence in the words we say, a silence beyond the words, the deepest silence in us"?[29] Surprisingly few survivors of the Holocaust seek psychotherapy.[30] Nevertheless, this is not to say they are without posttraumatic symptoms, and scores of former hidden children in groups all over the world share tales of anguish and strength. From a sociological perspective, besides lasting memories of loved ones are traits of tenacity[31] and enduring silence that helped survivors toward success after and even before the Holocaust. We already know that denial of one's emotional truth may lead to dire consequences. Yet adjustment in life, for some, does not always come from reviewing and rewitnessing over and over again scenes of the past, because, in forever tearing open scars, people run the risks of rewounding and possibly even renumbing themselves.[32] Many survivors of all types of trauma, instead of classifying their symptoms as pathological, accept them as normal, given their life circumstances.

Within these thoughts resides a general message. In creating norms for behaviors, we need to take into account context, or how people are able to overcome, adjust, and lift themselves from trauma, and to respect self-righting abilities.[33] As an example, within the normative standards of mental health, alonetime and solitary solutions are not sufficiently valued, despite the self persisting in the foreground. Health professionals are actually not that different from the average person. Like a relative or companion, they may see the self-possessed introspective person as less malleable, less normal. Thus, equally in the context of parental expectations and demands of compliance, how can one avert donning what Winnicott called a false self and allow a true self to emerge? Children who are allowed to express negative feelings and are given time to think about consequences, private play time with freedom of imagination, and the right to question authority even in the midst of obedience have the opportunities to develop a true and personal self. However, if insecurity is fostered as the basis for attachment, healthy development will not take place.

Training for Dependency

Psychotherapists, too, can be like the parents who enjoy and miss their children, and rather than use empathy as a way to understand, may overly sympathize and take away self-reliance. Analysts can become intrusive by not recognizing a patient's boundaries and self-sufficiency, and parents can do the same. Let's take a backward step and, in doing so, intertwine the clinician with the parent because both—in understanding children and adults—incorporated the fruits of Mahler's theories. One of Mahler's vivid observations was of a "normal autistic" and "normal symbiotic" state in babies.[34] Here is the question in this finding: how could a healthy baby be autistic? Actually, Mahler was remarking on an ongoing normal condition of life: the baby's contented moments of alonetime as recorded in the faraway gaze. But if we replace the word "autistic" with "alone,"[35] then we see that Mahler recognized periods of a baby's normal alone contentment from the time of birth. Unluckily, "autistic" is the label that stuck and one that continued to be associated with severe pathology. On the other hand, although "symbiosis" is also a term used to describe disturbed states, clinicians were willing to view infancy as an appropriate time for enmeshed attachment, and thus "symbiotic" proved acceptable. In very early babyhood, intimate contact with the parent does prevail, although "in unison" or simply "connected" would be more descriptively apt.[36]

Babies may emotionally and physically experience their strongest sense of power—in regulating parental behavior—as well as helplessness in the early months, even though attachment to others develops over time, and protection and safety are lifelong concerns. In Mahler's view, individuation and attachment depend upon the mother's response and are always seen in dynamic tension with each other. Individuation in this formulation can derive only from a secure attachment: mother where you expect and want her to be. But I believe that one overenlarged concern in psychological and lay circles is separation anxiety. While many consider unresolved separation fears from inadequate attachments as a major deterrent to achieving stability in childhood and adult life, other psychologists, including me, believe the picture is off balance and that secure attachment is not only the outcome of engagement—for example, feeling a sense of self-mastery helps a lot.

Parents themselves may reinforce separation fears by inadvertently socializing their children to have intense responses to leave-taking.[37] Current literature suggests that the cries and protests during separation times result from lack of "attachment security," or separation anxiety. Rather, many such protest behaviors are often unintentionally encouraged by parents who anxiously hesitate when saying good-bye. Different ways exist for parents to reduce infant and toddler separation protests, such as sticking to a bedtime ritual and not over and again returning to kiss a child good night. But, if handled with trepidation, bedtime and leave-taking rituals become negatively conditioned behavioral responses. While parents need to be sensitive to children's insecurities and fears, a debilitating factor ensues when parents' own worries translate into a back-and-forth departure dance.[38]

Adults may try to heal old wounds by overidentifying with a sad child, or unwittingly begin to enjoy the sense of importance conveyed upon them by children who protest about being without them or alone. Children's fears escalate when they feel reason to be afraid through their parents' own deliberations and doubts about leaving them alone, and the result is a decrease in a child's capacity to be alone. According to Jerome Kagan, an influential developmental psychologist from Harvard University, "A century ago, the protesting cry of the one-year-old following maternal departure was classified as similar to the willful disobedience of the adult. Today the same act is linked with the anxiety and sadness that follow loss of sweetheart, spouse, or parent."[39] We have as a society added a poignancy to simple farewells that rivals the histrionics in old-time films.

Kagan believes that a mother's empathy can also be invasive and is not the end-all and be-all for a child's future mental health. He would like to see less attention paid to early experience.[40] Reading one of his books in the 1980s, I was jolted into recognition of something residing deep within my mind: some of us are overtrained for dependency. All infants develop according to the mores of their culture with more or less sufficient survival skills. Thought of that way, our culture's version of good attachment is not any more perfect or privileged than its way of making music, art, or literature.

A direct link between an incident in a child's past and adult behavior is neither to be ignored nor a given. Development obviously is not totally without structures that are preserved from earlier phases. Looming within the conscientious parent is fear of a misstep. Yet as Kagan suggests, "It is unlikely that every actor in the first scene of the play has a role in the second act."[41]

Personality Traits and Alonetime

Love is not all that is integral to psychic well-being. Work and creativity equally sustain healthy existence. Anthony Storr, in his departure from the relational nature of the analytic experience as the one means of correcting self-esteem from unempathic mothering, is not claiming that solitude or aloneness, like attachment, is a rock-bottom need. However, Storr does confirm how much *certain* individuals need alonetime—those individuals who are shaped by alonetimes in the parent-child relationship and perhaps genetically endowed in temperament to prefer solitude.[42] For Storr, alonetime may resonate with avoidance behavior in the baby, but he does not see it as basic throughout life or with origins in the womb.

Without discussing an ongoing alonetime motivation, Storr singles out two of Jung's basic personality types—extroverts and introverts—as needing alonetime, calling attention to the way in which society makes extroverts of us all. Nowadays this process begins at a young age as children increasingly become video performers in front of amateur photographers, and the men and women on the streets gain instant exposure for life events ranging from the ordinary to the prurient. Not too long ago, I heard about a three-year-old who said to his father as he put the video camera away: "Daddy, look at that tree. It's good sometimes not to see things through the camcorder." Out of the mouths of babes!

The experimental work of a maverick and critic of aspects of psychoanalytic theory strengthens the case for an inner-directed need for alonetime. Credit Hans Eysenck, no more a conformist than Jung, as the person who brought introversion and extroversion to the limelight. Eysenck, a German-born psychologist, studied in England and remained there after being exiled at the start of the Second World War. His biographer, H. B. Gibson, portrays him as a child with enormous self-confidence who defied a lashing by his music teacher by biting into the maestro's thumb and refusing to let go.[43] Eysenck himself tells of when he was nine years old and visualized people in authority in various sexual positions, which enabled him to debunk adults in his mind.

Eysenck's personality model, which differentiates adults into introverts and extroverts, rests on his belief that such characteristics are innate.[44] He is the sole psychologist to have written volumes about the adult propensity to seek out and disengage from others. Sensitivity to stimulation forms in his eyes the foundation of whether people become introverts or extroverts.[45]

From personality tests of seven hundred soldiers in the hospital, he extrapolated characteristics of introversion and extroversion through factor analysis. He noted immediately that these traits had already been described by both Freud and Jung. Freud had written, "An introvert is not yet a neurotic, but he finds himself in a labile condition; he must develop symptoms at the next relocation of forces, if he does not find other outlets for his pent-up libido."[46] Jung stated, "It is a mistake to believe that introversion is more or less the same as neurosis. As concepts the two have not the slightest connection with each other."[47] Jung's ideas were borne out by Eysenck's study. The introverted soldiers were no more seriously disturbed than the extroverted. What is most interesting is that Eysenck's four categories of personality—neurotic introvert, neurotic extrovert, stable introvert, and stable extrovert—are all used to describe a continuum of normal personality and temperament, including even neuroticism. Therefore, Eysenck and Jung established introversion—inner-directedness, that which I call a character trait related to the need to be alone—as a progression in human nature.[48]

Secrets

Sometimes the desire for aloneness is not obviously part of a person's life and even enters the picture while a patient demonstrates strong needs for attachment. My oversight of these needs further clouded one situation.

Julie was a thirty-five-year-old retailer who had been in several long-term relationships. She reported that her prior analytic experience resolved a painful relationship to her mother. But after four years, she was in analysis three to four times a week with someone who never took a vacation day or a holiday. Therefore, as the new analyst who took a vacation, I initially represented the bad, unempathic mother. Needless to say, anger, fear of separation, and resentment of authority figures peppered the early months of the new treatment. A consistent fear of aloneness was radically emphasized when she refused to attend a concert by herself. However, her protests seemed too much. Only in later phases of treatment was I able to juxtapose the protests to other actions of Julie. Once, without much ado, she journeyed off solo in her car to various showrooms nationwide.

As I now look back, even in the first weeks of treatment Julie had inadvertently made known her satisfaction in being by herself as a child and an adult. In recounting a series of very early losses —a move to a new neighborhood at age two, the death of a family friend who was like a beloved uncle, and her mother's subsequent depression—she mentioned that, on many other occasions, just by chance, contented alone experiences were interrupted by crisis. Thus, alone experiences were negatively reinforced and became confused with anxious times. In fact, when alonetime as a topic was finally broached head-on, it turned out that Julie was keeping secret and private most of her pleasant alone experiences, fearing they would be contaminated by unhappy events or she would be chastised for failure to express sufficient feelings of caring.

◆ ◆ ◆

Alone needs cover the complete life cycle and live in everyone. This is suggested in the clinical observation of a self psychologist, Russell Meares, a professor of psychiatry at Sydney University in Australia. "Privacy" and "secrecy" are key words for Meares. Borrowing from Winnicott, he calls the play space an essential private area for exploration, where individuals learn to be "distinct and separate from others."[49] He sees secrecy and the ability to lie as necessary characteristics in the achievement of individuality. These endowments, which Meares sees beginning at age three and a half, are the elements that supply us with a conscious understanding of privacy. For him, secrets are pearls to give others on the way to obtaining intimacy.[50]

When we realize that a secret is something we can keep from others, we recognize something elementary, silent, and powerful. From time to time, we control these processes within our own mind. An example of an infant's behavior might clarify this point. Little Benjamin, nine months old, has learned that some "toys" are off-limits. He knows also that when he chews on certain objects they will be taken from him. However, he likes to chew on keys. One small key, his favorite, is securely fastened in the lock, but one day he manages to undo it and grab the key. When he suspects that his mother is watching nearby, he hides the key in his hand and crawls as fast as possible away from her to rest in a new spot and explore the key. Suddenly he sees Mom again and takes off; surely he knows it is necessary to keep his actions secret if he is to enjoy his loot.

Frederick Buechner, a pastor and novelist, writes in his memoir, "I have not only had my secrets. I am my secrets. And you are your secrets."[51] When people choose to put their lives into words varies. Some do this quite publicly, while others speak to analysts or only themselves about who they truly are. Comfort is derived through validation from others, especially after revealing painful thoughts. The confessional works.

Talk shows that group people together who share the same dark "sin" may in a similar way reassure a large audience. Yet the invasion of privacy is becoming so ordinary that it is beginning to shock even the publicity-hungry public and is calling people to action in attempts to protect a private self. *High Tech Snoops* was an NBC News[52] report that documented workers at all levels of employment—from police officers to executives at a hotel gymnasium—who were spied on by hidden cameras. Employers even photographed employees in the nude. The rationalization is that companies have the right to screen for activities such as drug exchanges, and the truth is that possible legal means to prevent surveillance have been defeated. It is estimated that at least 20 million people are viewed from concealed cameras that are impossible to detect, whether the surveillance equipment is on helicopters in the air or attached to bosses' tie clips in the office. If Big Brother watches and collects data, secrets may be few and far between.[53]

Our Body, Our Secrets

One exception may be the intimate goings-on inside our bodies, which are completely hidden from others unless we choose to share inner sensations. The body is the bridge between oneself and the outer world; according to Freudian theory, our body ego is the first image and experience of ourselves.[54] Others note that our first bodily sensations are both from the outside and inside.[55] Therefore, we are from early on privileged with information about ourselves. This could be the foundation for feelings about the self, its regulation, and alonetime as the body is seen as giving us form more than other objects.[56]

A book on the importance of alonetime needs to consider the bodily habit kept most secret—masturbation. Although Freud's discovery of infant sexuality went a long way to change pediatricians' thinking about the normality of masturbation, self-stimulation was and remains a taboo to many, especially those who are raised in strict fundamentalist religions. Even within psychoanalytic ranks there are mixed responses, particularly given the legacy of earlier theory, which regarded patients' masturbatory practices as abnormal.

The great authority on adolescence G. Stanley Hall joined the numbers of those who condemned the secret practice of masturbation, seeing it as an evil acting "on human nature like a worm upon fruit in producing premature ripeness."[57] Yet he not only saw swimming as most whole-some and beneficial for heart and lung, but advocated nude bathing for youths, dispensing with even the scantiest of suits.[58] Before the great Erik Erikson, Hall pleaded for a transition period in which adolescents could mature in peace and concentration. But he could not break with the Victorian belief that the dreadful vice of masturbation must be curbed. On the one hand, he viewed the cautionary tales of masturbation leading to insanity as horror stories. On the other hand, Hall, who had his own adolescent trauma, feared anything that might signal a precocious imagi-nation—and intense sexuality might be just such a signal. He came down on the side of those who saw masturbation as sad, weak, sinful, and self-abusive. Nevertheless, few besides him wanted to discuss masturba-tion with candor and plainness, or believed that ignoring or denying its existence was pure hypocrisy. In the end, however, he joined forces with others who thought this solitary pleasure led to extreme isolation and, eventually, moral and physical stunting. I was lucky: my mother told me only that it made you bowlegged!

Societal censure, of course, was prevalent historically (since biblical times—the sin of Onan), but masturbation was not actively discouraged until the late sixteenth century, by Catholic and Protestant pedagogues. These teachings were followed by a period in the nineteenth century in which children were viewed as pure and asexual. The constant cultural seesaw makes sexual rights and wrongs change. Sentiment today is mixed, but still rather grim, except in the situation of an elderly woman overheard in a supermarket by one of my students. As I was lecturing about the pros and cons of masturbation in connection to self-regulatory behaviors, Rachel, a student, described this encounter:

> Two elderly women were standing in the checkout line. One said to the other: "Mildred, you look absolutely marvelous! I have never seen your skin so bright. What have you been doing?" Mil-dred replies softly: "I've been masturbating one hour a day." "What?" asks her friend in a louder voice—obviously a bit hard of hearing—"I didn't understand, but whatever it is I must come over so that you can teach me how to do it."

◆ ◆ ◆

Masturbation is more often still linked to guilt and shame. Let's con-sider that former surgeon general Joycelyn Elders may have lost her appointment in 1994 because she broke a silence about masturbation in the context of psychological and social considerations. I see alonetimes of fantasy and bodily satisfaction as occurrences that maintain health and reduce tension. Currently, many psychologists and psychoanalysts would support Dr. Elders's view that masturbation is normal and a reasonable alternative for anyone, especially one not ready or able to commit to a sexual relationship.

Please do not hear me incorrectly: because I am a romantic as well as a realist, I know little compares to the pleasures derived from sex that feels like it's the right fit, especially when accompanied by love. I also know that masturbation is not just a substitute and can even be a part of a sexual relationship in the service of intimacy. I have heard it said that masturbation is like going back to a childhood game; other people, after the demise or desertion of a lover, insist that it's too far removed from what they truly want. They prefer nothing to take the place of conjugal lovemaking. Masturbation is not everyone's cup of tea. But the better we know ourselves,[59] the more we realize that no one is exactly like us, or able to satisfy all that we need. Self-soothing is just one form of self-regulation.

Self-Regulation — A Mainstay of Life and Alonetime

Self-regulation is now a buzzword in psychoanalytic circles. This is interesting because for a long time in psychoanalysis, the idea of control (and, essentially, regulation is synonymous with control), even as in the word "will,"[60] was not taken to kindly. After all, wanting one's own control—not necessarily the control of others—was associated with compulsivity. Being a control freak connoted an anal character. And I agree with *The Language of Letting Go*,[61] which tells us we can't manipulate events, relationships, or life. Nevertheless, a place exists for self-control.

Freud, in his writings on the origins of psychological structures, implied control outside the realm of obsessive-compulsive behaviors. The infant requires a stimulus barrier "to control" excessive stimulation disruptive to equilibrium. Equilibrium, or homeostasis, itself suggests that organisms attempt to control their inner balance. This decrease of stimulation unmistakably reinforces self-control. Early Freudian theories on the reduction of sexual and aggressive tension were really self-regulation theories. Frederick Perls, originally trained as a Freudian, created a whole approach to life via Gestalt therapy[62] based on principles that aimed to restore self-regulatory skills to individuals. A firm believer in individuals both doing for themselves and listening to what others want, he tried to find a balance in such choices in people's lives. Self-regulation themes lost popularity in traditional psychoanalysis for a time, until Kohut refocused the field on self-soothing techniques and self-regulation acquired in a situation of caretaker-child regulation.

The behavioral psychologists, however, never stopped elevating control.[63] For example, renowned behaviorist B. F. Skinner summarized his thinking by saying, "The evolution of culture is a gigantic exercise in self-control."[64] Watching pigeons feed, he demonstrated how varied schedules of rewarding behavior produce corresponding patterns of response, and thus developed his famous theories on "operant conditioning." In other words, the more often someone says thank you to a child after the child hands the adult something, the more likely the child will give thanks when receiving something. Does this sound more like brainwashing than self-control? But think of it another way. All through life we take in and make use of bits and pieces of information that feed ourselves, and in the deciding of what we take in and expand on exists a personal freedom.

People who feel they have some control over who they are and what they do claim greater happiness.[65] The best and most self-fulfilling experiences in life are rarely passive or receptive, and they will often occur when we are alone and self-disciplined.[66] And it is in our very earliest environment—alone in the womb—where we first begin this learning and choice making. Changing our understanding of psychological origins —the goings-on in the womb—will confirm the idea that our love of silences and solitude is an inborn capacity reinforced in fetal life. Since we are about to learn of this initial environment, why not suspend thought and imagine yourself free-floating in soothing harmony, evoking a state that conscious memory has long neglected?

CHAPTER 6

Rhythms, Sensations,

and Womb Life

For a fetus is a benign tumor, a vampire who steals in order
to live.

CAMILLE PAGLIA, *Sexual Personae*[1]

Birth was the death of him.

SAMUEL BECKETT, *Three Occasional Pieces*[2]

For no king had any other first beginning; but all [human beings]
have one entrance into life.

THE WISDOM OF SOLOMON[3]

THROUGHOUT THE BOOK so far, I challenge the widely held myth that
the intricate fetal experience only establishes attachment of baby to
parent. While evidence abounds of expectant mothers who form an emotional link to the life within, the animation of the single fetus actually
begins in a psychological environment of aloneness. This is not to say
that the womb is a void without any input from outside, that signals to
the fetus's senses are entirely absent, or that my viewpoint is "matrapho-
bic"—trying to exclude the significance of the maternal connection from
the event.[4] Sensations are experienced by a prenatal being who is virtually
alone, and these womb sensations appear to the fetus as neither initiated
nor barred by others. Besides, other initiated womb happenings are as
arbitrarily dealt as cards in the unseen hand of the computer version of
solitaire. Relationships with inanimate objects such as placenta, cord,
fluid, and the uterine wall are experienced as rhythms, shapes, and
sounds that later may attach to specific people or form the repertoire of
dreams and imagination. This protected peaceful state, which is also
characteristic of aquatic mammals, marks our beginnings. Conditions of

disconnection, separateness, and independence are experientially primary at this stage, but the tables turn after the fetus is born. It takes years of development outside the womb for that whole to be restored. No matter how unlike the awaiting world, these many months of conditioning have left their imprint. Therefore, in describing the nature of this conditioning, I will discuss fetal capacity to feel and be aware in order for early imprints to register and have some impact on later development.[5]

The self-feeding embryo rapidly, intricately, and dynamically evolves in the early weeks of pregnancy into a fetus. Once the implantation takes place and a placenta is formed, fetal circulation begins, the heartbeat pulses, and only somewhat later exchanges of gas between maternal and fetal circulations occur. Yet, with few exceptions, embryologists, developmental psychologists, and psychoanalysts neglect the meaning of this time during which the human psyche lives in alonetime. Generally, psychologists focus their attention on the newborn, seven months after the occurrence of self-generated movement. What part of this seven months of neural and motoric development is visible in future behavior? When we examine fetal life will there be suggestions of alone, or self-regulating, behavior?

Over one hundred years ago one physician laid claim to the rarely explored life of the fetus.[6] Wilhelm Preyer was an enthusiastic investigator whose curiosity about embryonic exploits began with the pregnancy of his wife. Only part of his work is translated into English, so its influence was felt more in his native Germany than in the United States. Much of his work was on animal embryos. His conclusions were extrapolations from findings arising from laying his hands on and listening through a stethoscope to a woman's abdomen. He postulated from these relatively crude methods that the human embryo moved its limbs by seven weeks.

He divided fetal movements into two main groups: involuntary and voluntary. The explicitness of his distinctions is still in dispute, but Preyer's descriptions appear comparable to current observations. Involuntary movements he labeled passive, irritative, or reflexive. Voluntary movements were named expressive, instinctive, and ideational; the latter he thought came only after birth. However, he saw self-regulatory actions in fetuses' instinctive movements—for example, getting into the most comfortable position in the smallest possible space. Voluntary movements all have a purpose and they do not always immediately follow a stimulus. Innovative and prescient, he saw early movements giving rise to sensations that leave memory traces in the cerebrum. It is not until the last half of this century that scientists were able to document some of his exceptional insights. These lay the groundwork for my discovery and understanding of alonetime satisfaction (along with security through connection) as learned responses in the fetal period.

We need to accept a semblance of consciousness and memory in the fetus and infant in order to understand an active need for alonetime. Moreover, according to Stanley Coren, "For the infant in the womb . . . the dream state [REM sleep] provides a form of theater, a relatively continuous flow of sensory stimulation."[7] With this priming newborns are ready for action and able to stare straight into the eyes of the person holding them. And I have seen this happen, with minute-old babies maintaining the gaze for as much as sixty seconds. Why then wouldn't the fetus, only hours earlier, be as cognizant of its surroundings? Therefore, I continue to explore the notion of consciousness at birth and intention and memory in infants.

Historically, the facts are few on fetal experience, and the reality of fetal consciousness has always at best been considered an old wives' tale. Midcentury, a French gynecologist spoke openly of his memory of birth, including the painful feeling of forceps gripping his head. In Europe and the United States, Frederick Leboyer, who claimed knowledge of his unpleasant birth experience, preached a method of delivery that would guarantee, he thought, birth without trauma.[8] He held little doubt of the baby's consciousness:

> The newborn baby is not at all the unconscious little thing we have assumed it to be for such a long time. We assumed that a newborn baby doesn't feel, doesn't see, doesn't hear, has no emotions. It is just the opposite . . . A baby still has a consciousness which is wide open, not conditioned . . . This consciousness is unprotected and fully open.[9]

Speaking passionately about the rough entry of neonates, he proposed a delivery procedure that included soft lights, music, placing the baby in water, and in some instances an underwater birthing. This immersion method did have the appearance of a soothing process. Unfortunately, mishaps were reported. Physical risks, as far as hospital administrators were concerned, ultimately outweighed the psychological gains, and few gynecologists, pediatricians, or midwives adhere to these techniques today. In the latter years of the 1990s we have the greatest evidence of fetal and infant awareness—but not, correspondingly, more attention paid to the consequences of this alertness as such.

I ponder what in womb life marks our nature and the need for alonetime. Cutting the cord may signal separation to the mother, but to the baby it may be a different type of loss. The newborn leaves the unusual calm of a world devoid of wants, to enter one of aching needs. The womb, as a metaphor, may best stand for constant, basic satisfaction and a sense of empowerment. It is also seen by some as a simile for autistic withdrawal. When I tell a close colleague and friend that I'm writing about the fetus and contemplating womb experience, he says, "Ester, don't go psychotic on me." Troubled, especially schizophrenic, individuals do scrunch their bodies into a fetal position with and without thoughts of returning to the womb. But many of us as well go off to gentle sleep at night in fetal curls. To some, the womb represents a wish for total care. But Samuel Beckett, as evident in the epigraph at the beginning of this chapter, saw another meaning. His womb metaphor holds the memory of an alone freedom, safety, and truth that is compelling.

A Universal Metaphor for Death, Separateness, and Life

The womb, pregnancy, and childbirth are universal metaphors. Unlike the cross, the flag, or the shield, they cut across religion, culture, and time. The womb, described as cave, tunnel, and the deep, is at once Mother Earth and the underworld. Hellenist scholar Ruth Padel, who writes about the vivid divinities of ancient Greece who found a place inside and outside the mind, strikes an important chord that existed for Athenians between the mind, the womb, and the nether world. Like the womb, the mind is penetrable. But so is Hades:

> In Greek culture, as others, women are identified with the interior. The culture generally confined and guarded its women. The house was a woman's place. Middle-class women spent most of their time indoors . . . "House" is also, from early times, an apt word for Hades . . . Hades which is a *muchos* [women's quarters] . . . suggests not only parts of the house that hold women, but also recesses contained within them.[10]

Other scholars[11] liken the womb to hell's gate and monstrous births, as part of or in opposition to images of restoration and growth of an idea. Hence, the word "brainchild." Womb life and birth are transformations. Change is so intense that old labels ("embryo" to "fetus," "fetus" to "infant") actually die. Freethinking scientist Carl Sagan called attention to near-death experiences that occur cross-culturally as possibly being explained with reference to birth experience. He believed that the tunnel light so frequently referenced both in myths and people's accounts relates to the glowing light fetuses see as they propel into the world. Oscar, Gunter Grass's tin-drumming protagonist, believed he was a fully conscious fetus and described his entry into the world as first seeing the light.[12] Beckett says birth is death. Others say dying recapitulates being born. Sagan's idea of similarity between birth memories and near-death experiences draws on the work of a physician, Stanislav Grof, who regressed patients back to their births with LSD.[13] Grof thought pregnancy had four perinatal stages: experience in the womb, the onset of labor, entering the birth canal, and entry into the world. It is stage three, when the infant comes through the birth canal, that he believes is simulated by near-death experiences.

Age-old wisdom and poets thus remind us that even in the most powerful of life symbols—the womb and birth—we cannot exclude connections to death. Certainly, the blissfulness of the womb experience may be sufficient reason to find a death wish in human nature. Psychology, too, picked up on this theme—somewhat unidimensionally—and, I think, cast a pall on alonetime. Freud's consuming despair and anxiety during the years ending World War I led him to rewrite his theories on the pleasure principle (love and sex) as the prime human motivator.[14] Rethinking his grandson Ernst's preoccupation with a sophisticated peekaboo game,[15] Freud interpreted the "gone" aspects of the play as representations of Ernst's anger and revenge at his mother's leaving him. In actuality, the *fort-da* game was quite ingenious. Ernst took a toy on a string and repeatedly made it disappear, shouting, "Oooo" (interpreted by the child's mother and Freud as *fort*, meaning "gone"). And when it reappeared, he squealed at its reappearance with the word *da*, meaning "there." Freud saw more than a will to mastery in his grandson's active handling of the disappearance act. Indeed, he believed the game represented repressed hostility over a mother's separating, and used that as a beginning simile for life-and-death struggles in human existence. He called this destructive side of the human condition Thanatos, as opposed to the life force, Eros. Thanatos's aim is to "unbind and break down living matter, eventually reverting all living organisms back to their simplest forms," that is, death, and thus Freud saw in human nature the death wish.[16]

Although Freud saw this as the beginning of people's ability to delude themselves, this is also the continuation of an internal human dialogue that, once undertaken, goes on forever. We incorporate aspects of the world and others whether they are in our midst or lost from us. This ability to imagine those out of sight, those far away, and even those dead adds another source of courage on a spiritual or philosophical journey into alonetime.

Putting aside Darwinian perpetuation of the species, the death instinct is on a day-to-day level best understood as the need to balance the stress of perpetual connectedness to outside stimuli with a restorative aloneness. Freud's observations on the death wish have been interpreted as an organism's desire for peace—the Nirvana Principle—sleep, and altered consciousness, and as a relief of stress.[17] In my theory the fear of death—even the existential fear—gains momentum because it buries a wish for utter calm and fulfillment. Similarly, the bliss of merger, where two blend indivisibly into one, sublimates the other to the point of vaporization. Humans want to recapture the inner solitude, as well as the connectedness, of womb life. Terrors, unsuccessful attachments, vulnerabilities, and false teachings distort this initial alone experience. Similarly, destructiveness and a desire to remove oneself from social interaction are recurrently linked. Serial killers may be loners, but battery and deaths result equally, if not more, from within the family milieu. Let us contemplate this: could it be that because humans, like our animal counterparts, are aware of the possibility of alone survival, evil acts are performed with impunity? Combine that knowledge with an overinflated or undervalued sense of self and one could engage in self-destructive actions. But heroism also depends upon the knowledge of alone capacities, omnipotence, and the willingness to self-sacrifice for the sake of others. The destructiveness in reckless deeds has most to do with uncultivated morality and with empathy unlearned in the course of life.

Since alone travel is depicted most frequently as treacherous or malevolent, with fearful associations to loneliness, whence arises the courage, determination, and overpowering need to be on one's own? Preparedness to be alone begins within the lone womb experience and our initial positive feelings connected to early inner sensations. As we grow older and learn about the attachment of fetus to womb and mother we formulate the metaphor: womb equals attachment to mother. But before this, in our subjective preverbal memories rests the grounding for the need and ability to be alone. I see initial womb learning as a time of establishing self-righting capabilities—like the ability to soothe ourselves. Freud was surprised that within the early months a baby learns to be satisfied even before obtaining a wanted object. He proposed the infant capable of imagining what was not there. The baby appeared temporarily soothed just by noticing his mother on the way to supplying food. Maybe our imaginative ability gets a jump start in the solitude of the womb.

Life in the Womb

I have had patients and friends who claim to remember their womb life. When I first heard such a story, I was disinclined to believe it, though the woman who told it spun an intriguing tale. Sarah was a mother whom I met in the park while we "aired" our sons. We became good friends and one day, talking about newborns, she asked if I remembered before I was born. I didn't, but she proceeded to tell me about her early memories. I listened, wondering if she were inventing her dramatic saga of fighting her way down the birth canal to be born. She included moments when she felt her heart stop, saw a cord float around, and pushed herself headfirst into the hands of a midwife. It was as if she had done all the work. I never forgot her compelling story—nor did I completely accept it until much later, when a patient described a less vivid but nonetheless equally thought-provoking account of prenatal life.

> Alfred, middle-aged and immaculately groomed, hardly seemed the type to remember positive and poetic remnants of beginning life. A lawyer caught up in the absolute facts of life, he sought treatment to resolve a work crisis that placed him in a moral and psychological dilemma. One day, however, he described moments of repose that he typically used to resolve problems. Trying to understand why they weren't working in the present situation, he outlined how naturally he stepped into a state of reverie, and in fact demonstrated this. I commented on his ease in meditating and that it seemed a special gift. Pooh-poohing this, he stated matter-of-factly that he "envisioned how to do it from the time [he was] in the womb."
>
> "Could you repeat that, please?" I said, nonplussed.
>
> Alfred described many shades of light and dark. He recounted his early pictures of a serene environment as true memories, and believed that the shadows and patterns he conjured up when relaxing reflected different parts of the womb. Most potent was the inner sense of calm that he reproduced by shutting his eyes and focusing on patterns of light. I had noticed that his breathing was most gentle, and asked about that. He did not concentrate on

breathing at all. Rather, he focused on following the light and regaining a sense of floating in space. He said this was his first memory and that he used it from babyhood to put himself to sleep.

◆   ◆   ◆

For a time, I put aside my thoughts about this atypical session with a patient. Nevertheless, in one way or another I would time and again find occasion to think about the fetal environment. The work of another psychoanalyst gave rise to my formulating definitive ideas about womb life. For about one year before beginning her actual ethological research on the fetus, Milan physician, child psychotherapist, and psychoanalyst Alessandra Piontelli studied ultrasound scans and learned how to interpret them.[18] (Ultrasound is a nonradiological and noninvasive technique.) Just recently, I had occasion to view some of her images.[19] Intrauterine life was Piontelli's Galápagos, and her unusual and fascinating observations confirmed several previously unclarified beliefs of mine:

1. The fetus experiences a sense of pleasure as it floats freely within the amniotic fluid.
2. The sense of impotence and helplessness at birth appears in striking contrast to intrauterine freedom.
3. Soothing rhythms and activities are primary in the womb environment, and many of these are self-initiated.
4. Except in twins, initial attachments are to things, not people.
5. Priming for an alone need occurs in the womb.
6. Alone space is evident.
7. Attachments to others may also be given impetus by the sounds of parents' voices and the felt rhythms of the mother's movements and breathing.
8. Most important, the fetus seems to be exercising choice.

So, it is important to recognize that the fetus is neither separated nor autonomous. It is the illusion of free movement and self-initiated gratifications that stick with us as the first memory of contented alonetime. Fetuses touch other objects in the womb, besides their own bodies. These bodily sensations become original input and later prototypes for behaviors. Swallowing, sucking, moving, touching, grasping, and hiding are all actions performed in the womb by the fetus. These actions are both purely pleasurable and protective measures. We now know that the first experiences of sensations are in utero, and some sensory functions seem in place as early as twelve to sixteen weeks. Among his amazing pictures of life before birth, photographic explorer Lennart Nilsson captured a fourteen-week-old fetus putting his hands together and sucking his thumb. Intrauterine experiences like that provide the critical mechanisms for distinguishing between self and other bodily boundaries[20] and establish sensory pathways in the brain. With this learning our brain changes; thus neuronal structures that are the key to later mental processing appear in the fetal stage.[21] Early alone sensations are likely to be registered in the nervous system as well. What are precursors for attachment behaviors, since the psychological atmosphere favors aloneness? Think back to Harlow's monkeys in Chapter 2 and the necessary grasping reflexes that favor attachment, and recall what was stated about the nature of early attachment. We are ready at birth to respond to things and to people, and both aid adaptation.

Considering how many centuries it took for children's rights to be acknowledged, it is not surprising that the idea of a fetus having even a rudimentary personality is met with incredulity. One debate in the psychoanalytic community and elsewhere concerns the question of when the infant reaches psychological awareness. Some practitioners believe that this awakening occurs only after five to six months of life or accompanies birth itself, but most consider only contact with other people as tantamount to thinking, feeling, imagining, or being self-aware. Awareness of a "not me" in the womb may seem out of the question. Yet actually it was Freud who wrote, "There is much more continuity between intrauterine life and earliest infancy than the impressive caesura of the act of birth would have us believe."[22]

This idea, quoted in Piontelli's book *From Fetus to Child*, is potent in her description of eighteen-month-old Jacob, who was brought by his parents to her therapy office. He never seemed to stay still and explored her small office nonstop. The parents reported that night and day he also searched, with little time for sleep. Piontelli suggested to Jacob that he was looking for something lost, and with this Jacob came to a halt. Later in the session she said that he was afraid not moving meant death. The last two weeks prior to his birth were spent with a dead co-twin, who had died in utero. Piontelli assumed Jacob experienced a terrible loss. This was one of several pivotal occurrences that led her to intrauterine studies of twins as well as singletons.

The nature of the twin connection had already whetted my interest in fetal experiences years ago, during the analysis of a forty-eight-year-old woman.

For several years I worked with Ethel, an extremely depressed patient who had lived on and off in orphanages. The frequent tragic stories of her background seemed sufficient narrative to account for her depressed visage, so only well into treatment did she reveal that she, during her first pregnancy, had carried twins, but one was stillborn. After she herself experienced an intense period of mourning facilitated by her sharing of the loss, she confessed that the living co-twin's behavior often seemed resigned and despairing. Yet it was her daughter's treatment of potential friends that most concerned Ethel. Her daughter initially responded to children's advances toward friendship and then after a brief acquaintance turned away from them to further withdraw into books. I asked if her daughter was aware that she had been a twin. My actual thinking was that her daughter might have been suffering a conscious burden that formed a stumbling block to success in friendships. Instead, her mother told me she had never informed her daughter for fear of upsetting her. Then, I wondered out loud if her daughter didn't indeed still have unconscious memories of her twinship. After contemplating this idea, Ethel sent her daughter to therapy. Later, Ethel reported to me that she told her daughter about the pregnancy and loss. This bright and sensitive child quickly pieced together why she was always trying to match potential friends to some vague, indefinable standard and was thus always disappointed. Even though becoming quite sad, the daughter experienced relief from this knowledge.

◆ ◆ ◆

Ethel's daughter's fetal experience was one of attachment and loss—but it speaks to some form of conscious self prior to birth. Science is only now uncovering nature's secret that individual characteristics make themselves known in utero and continue in life. The womb view begins to reveal what is required for adaptation to the light, actions, and sounds of day. Piontelli's in-depth studies further point to where a personal, individual self and alonetime begin.

Watching twins in utero points out the diversity among fetuses. Even in the enclosed boundaries of the womb, twins do separate things, except in one example of monozygotic (MZ), or uniovular, twins, who in this case share, besides the same ovum, the same placenta, chorion, and amniotic sac. These extremely rare uniovular twins are not even a membrane apart, and the only thing closer, rarer, and with greater fetal risk is Siamese twins.[23] One MZ set from Piontelli's description were born to rather neglectful parents and followed a strange course of development. In the womb, as was to be expected, they practically fused together—this is the closest that two distinct humans come to symbiosis. Outside the womb, they also "stuck" together and found little to interest them beyond the confines of their rooms, but this pattern was as much a product of being unattended to as of their twinship.

Those twins whose genetics are different would not be expected to share similar traits, but as Piontelli illustrates paradoxically in later studies, identical twins may be less alike at birth than later on in their development. The descriptions highlight the fact that even twins are unique individuals and that each takes to the womb environment and shares it quite singularly. For some twin pairs the close womb quarters evoke rivalry that can escalate to violence—not too long ago a columnist writing about twins reported evidence of one punching another while in the uterus.[24]

No trace of sibling rivalry is observable in the activity of Alice and Luca, another twin pair studied in utero. They are often head-to-head, stroking each other and even appearing to kiss. But little Luca, the male, is active, alert, and independent in his motions and first to leave the crowded womb quarters, while Alice, the larger of the two, is slow to move and sleepy. In the womb Luca always takes the initiative; first he strokes Alice, then she responds. At four, Luca is still a most advanced child who likes doing things alone but in crowded spaces with others feels claustrophobic.

The following extracts of ultrasonic observations of a singleton fetus named Giulia are from the thirteenth and thirty-fifth weeks of pregnancy and again will demonstrate the continuity between pre- and postnatal life. Obstetricians are the commentators.

> She is moving her tongue all the time . . . here is her mouth again . . . she has opened it again . . . opening it and closing it . . . and sucking her tongue . . . now she has brought her hand in front of her mouth again . . . she is sucking her palm . . . now she is sucking her thumb! . . . Let's look at what she's doing with her other hand . . . it is still there right in between her legs . . . she is still opening and closing her mouth . . . swallowing . . . she must be hungry . . . she is swallowing the amniotic fluid non-stop . . . again . . . again . . . gulping enormous quantities of it . . .[25]

Giulia, at three years old, seen in treatment with Piontelli, continued showing her insatiable appetite. After one session, for example, she gulped down a tin of Coke in one breath. Less than twenty years ago it was believed that more by accident than design the fetus imbibed amniotic fluid.[26] Now we know fetuses self-feed to varying degrees. How seemingly self-sufficient this system appears, and how self-motivated is Giulia: "Look what she is doing now . . . licking the placenta again . . . my God . . . she is really wild this time . . . look . . . it just goes on and on."[27] As a seven-year-old, according to a verbal communication of Piontelli, Giulia displays the same sensuous traits that she exhibited in the womb, choosing pleasures and food before all else.

Not all babies are as at ease in their intrauterine world as Giulia, who floated peacefully in the amniotic fluid, rocked herself to sleep at times, and kept her hands between her legs. Among the three singleton fetuses and eight twins Piontelli reports on in her book, one experienced a risky change in the uterine environment that altered active behavior to docile. Another, it was speculated, may have been influenced by his mother's fluctuating adrenal hormonal levels due to the enormous anxiety she was experiencing. As if he, too, felt her angst, he clung, huddling against the uterine walls or to the cord for dear life. Each fetus has its own way of movement and activity, each responds to stimuli differently, and each is obviously formulating its own rhythms in order to handle the environment.

The uterus is definitely a place for learning about life and one's capacities, and these behaviors that are carried into postnatal existence fall under the principle of continuity in behavior and temperament from inside to outside the womb.[28] One summary of an intrauterine study states, "The final general observation is one of continuity between fetal and infant behavior."[29] The researcher goes on to claim that "this is so elementary and not requiring of emphasis except that some still see the fetus as a passive intrauterine passenger."[30] Fifteen years ago, when on occasion I made mention of personality variables—including fear or confidence—beginning in the womb, some of my audience would look at me as if I were preaching witchcraft or astrology. But now many think about the last two-thirds of pregnancy as learning experiences for prenates.

The continuity we have discussed between prebirth and after is not evident in one emotional area, or so it seems. It is said that in the first few weeks of life, an infant cries anywhere from 50 to 150 minutes a day. Yet through ultrasound it is rare to see anywhere near that level of discomfort or need to signal a want in the expressive facial movements of a fetus. In *Behavior of the Fetus,* Jason C. Birnholz notes:

> Given the consistency of the intrauterine environment, including continuous nutritional and respiratory support via the placenta [and self-feeding], one may conclude the fetus can cry, but rarely does so unless provoked by some abrupt noxious stimulus, such as sharp needle contact [by error only in these days of ultrasonic guidance] during amniocentesis.[31]

What exactly is the womb environment like? While it is still in part mysterious, evidence is accumulating on its nature. Terra incognita[32] it may be, but the mammalian prenatal environment is probably more climate controlled, predictable, and accommodating than most places on land or sea or in air. Never again in life—not even for astronauts—is one's physiology so regulated. Despite the incredible hookup to the mother, in which vital blood, gases, nutrients and vitamins, steroid hormones, and antibodies pass from one system to the other, this is the first opportunity for solo adaptation to life. If one interprets the setup concretely, yes, the fetus is not truly alone and is, in fact, highly protected in this adventure. Nevertheless, as fetuses adapt—and adapt they must —they are making their own first movements to self-regulate and they are, in their eyes and mind, not doing it in the context of a personal relationship. They adapt due to internal rhythms and environmental demands.[33] Let me explain this further.

When little fetus Giulia was initially observed ultrasonically, at thirteen weeks, her tiny movements seemed coordinated to her mother's. At thirty-five weeks her "pacemaker"—internal circadian rhythms—was different. Her active times (which in fetus Giulia's case were few) were not in correspondence to her mother's, nor was the rate of her "breathing" motions. The respiratory movements of Giulia's chest followed their own pace. "Why can't it sleep when I do?" mothers often complain in the later months of pregnancy. But this complaint may not be telling us of a baby's individuality, for the baby could easily be lulled to rest with the mother's movements and awake when she's still. Fundamentally, however, womb observers of twin pregnancies confirm—as, typically, no two fetuses are alike—that mother is *not* the pacesetter. If she were, there would not be differences between twins or siblings in activity levels. My mother made this clear when she would joke about how my tempo was quicker than hers. "They must have switched you in the hospital," she would say any time I was too frisky.

Some parents hope to set a very fast pace for their children by stimulating them in the womb. One institute offers, as part of parent education, a course of instruction that includes ways to talk and sing as two examples to the babe in the womb.[34] Supposedly, this leads to a better-oriented child, a more connected mother, and possibly a more intelligent baby. Madeleine, one of Pascal Bruckner's fictional characters in the absurdly hilarious and sardonic book *The Divine Child*, certainly had this in mind:

> Having read somewhere that the mothers of Einstein and Oppenheimer had sung three hours a day during their pregnancies, she made a habit of crooning traditional ballads and old French folk ditties . . . She avoided cripples, hunchbacks, and tramps, abstained from watching violent movies on TV and thought only positive thoughts. Every day, she would pick up grade school primers and force herself to read them in a loud, clear voice . . . Finally, by tapping the tip of a pencil on her teeth, she sent him encouraging morse code messages that said "Whatever you may be, boy or girl, I love you, you are already the best."[35]

The results of such experimentation are not yet apparent. My scientific judgment tells me that the cushioning and barriers to stimulation of the uterus serve the important purpose of preparation for alonetime. The way in which Madeleine stimulated her baby in utero sounds more like science fiction than science. But in my opinion instructions to parents on how to engage through ongoing stimulation to the fetus may be precipitous interventions without sufficient knowledge of potential aftermaths. While preparing for attachment, we could also be robbing people of the primary opportunity to prepare for alonetime and alone resiliency. Babies will soon enough have to adapt to a wide range of stimuli. In studies of premature infants, it is apparent that fetuses lack the readiness to face strong stimulation. By watching premature infants, we are provided with further clues about what is and what isn't learned in utero.

Fetal Infancy

Even in casual observations of children considered by their obstetricians to be premature, it is obvious that the early arrivals not only are smaller in size and weight but seem miles apart from full-term cohorts in level of alertness. Many barely open their eyes during the first two weeks of life, and they typically have little interest in gazing at others. This alerts us to the importance of continued alone experiences. Preterm babies (thirty weeks) are thought to spend and require far greater time in REM sleep than full-term (forty weeks). Four states of sleep and wakefulness have been recorded through ultrasound in the infant: quiet sleep, active sleep, quiet awake, and active awake. One child in my study of three infants over a two-month period was only a couple of weeks early. Though not premature, medically speaking, she nevertheless showed differences in alertness and sleepiness, being not as tuned in or awake as the other newborns. But by the end of the two months of observation, she had caught up to the others: "She knows who we are now," her mother reported. "If she's crying a little bit and I start to talk to her, like right before I pick her up, she stops."

Among those to profoundly study "fetal infancy" was the renowned Connecticut physician and psychologist Arnold Gesell. He was instrumental in setting the "norms" for child development that, though now modified, are still referred to today. Gesell believed that "the growth career of a pre-term fetal-infant is demonstrated to adhere closely to the developmental time schedule of the full-term infant."[36] He illustrated this development pictorially, giving a reader the opportunity to see the change from repose to activity as the fetal infant reaches full term. At twenty-eight weeks, an infant placed on a smooth, moderately soft surface seemed weak and somewhat relaxed. Gesell notes the infant's relaxed nature, the drowse that is neither awake nor asleep, and the "fetal huddle," or staying in a ball-like repose. At thirty-four weeks he describes this shift in responsiveness in brief flickering eye movements—which he called "after pursuits" because they followed a presentation of a dangling ring. Even at thirty-seven weeks he observes the composed face as less alert and more tranquil than that of the full-term infant.

Although birth, even preterm, changes the equilibrium of as well as the stimuli to a fetus, Gesell was primarily studying the development of motoric competence as it related to his belief in the importance of neuromotor equipment. Gesell believed that our tool-making capacities distinguished us as humans. Inadvertently, while taking a careful look, he noticed the varied sleep-wake cycles, signals of pleasure and discomfort and composure that he felt "undoubtedly occur in utero."[37] These intuitions came before the advent of technology, but we now have confirming evidence in the form of filmed expressions of preterm neonates. Innovative researcher, infant expert, and author Tiffany Field's work shows that in fetal infancy, facial expressions were markedly similar to those of full-term infants, displaying interest, disgust, sadness, and crying.[38] Remarking on these similarities and generalities, I must also emphasize the specific individual differences between infants.[39]

For the second time, I am privileged to be nearby at the birth of a grandchild. My first grandchild, Benjamin, was amazingly alert, self-regulating, and attentive to his environment from the start, while his younger brother, Jacob, still seemed to rest in the lacuna of the fetal state a few hours postbirth. When I bent down to kiss him gently, he started. When I picked him up, his face showed discomfort. His lips parted—would he cry? Not if I allowed him to settle into a comfortable sleep again. In that stage of deep sleep, he could be gently passed around to eagerly awaiting arms. His expression changed when he was in utter repose in his cradle or cradled. Then a smile lit up his face. His contentment and quietude were apparent.

At this stage, Jacob shut out stimuli and gently signaled alone needs more than Benjamin had. Perhaps, too, the ability of fetus and infant to retreat into a protective state of alonetime provides what I referred to in Chapter 5 as a stimulus barrier—the psychic ability to ward off noxious stimuli.[40] People defend themselves against trauma by erecting this biologically based barrier. Think of how totally bombarded a baby would be without a threshold for stimuli, as described above (reactivity and alertness), and the ability to retreat to an alone state and form a protective shield. An infant can either passively or actively avert stimuli, as is seen in fetal studies of infants covering ears and eyes, even in utero. Hourlong visits with newborns reveal them responding to the everyday (like being undressed) or being faced with stressful events (like a too-bright light or a sibling's jealous slap) with changes in blood pressure and heartbeat as well as in posture. At first, many may try interactive skills (emotional signals to caretakers) to restore equilibrium, but they readily fall back on other behavioral strategies. Infants are able to withdraw from stress by turning or arching away or even losing control over posture (slumping down). No adult has the knack as fine-tuned as a baby's for glazing over an unwanted stimulus. Thus, not only will neonates move their bodies to adjust, but it was found that "stimuli affected the neonates' level of consciousness."[41] They return to sleep or engage in an activity directed toward a decreased level of arousal. Infants enter life with the ability to dispel stimuli through their alonetime skills such as staring vacantly or dozing. Life, however, provides challenges that require caretakers to assume the role of a protective shield and add support to these rudimentary capacities.

The stimulus barrier, or *Reizschutz,* as Freud conceived it, was a series of cells or a membrane that shields us and then sheds itself.[42] He at one time thought of it as literally something neurological. This special "envelope" that saved deeper membranes from dying related to an ability to alter consciousness and concentration. In prior writings, he saw it as a primitive defense, a psychological structure that everyone employs until individuals develop more complex coping and defense systems.[43] Often, while I write this book, I am oblivious to sounds and smells, and I have even forgotten my internal needs.

Level of Awareness: The Mind-Baby Connections

Freudian theory suggests the existence of infant consciousness. But is there scientific evidence to back this up in fetal life? The quick and successful adaptation of the neonate to life demonstrates a repertoire of complex perceptions and self-regulatory skills that are observable and recordable and must also be apparent before birth. I will show how specific input appears from several corners:

1. perceptual skills of the fetus
2. proprioceptive reactions and body awareness
3. hypnotic studies—perhaps the most controversial reporting to some

Some unusual experiments on fetuses inform us that their perceptual skills are sufficiently developed to enable them to learn prior to birth. A typical learning paradigm is "infant habituation"—an infant responds to stimuli and then shows bored disinterest and no response. But what about the fetus? One group of researchers ingeniously applied the base of an electric toothbrush to a mother's abdomen and induced fetal movement. Within fifty applications of the vibrations the movement of the fetus stopped.[44] The fetus had tired of the interesting sound, and indeed, by thirty-two weeks was no longer even surprised by this particular external noise. Eavesdropping by ultrasound observations, we learn that the fetus does hear and recognize voices and sounds from the outside, and responds in movement. Voice recognition is confirmed by what happens after birth. A book read aloud continuously to a fetus is remembered, as measured by interest on the part of the newborn to concentrate on that story rather than others. The mother's voice as well as the father's voice is preferred by newborns. A videotape taken just after baby and parents leave the labor room portrays this by now well-accepted phenomenon of a baby's having taken in specific sounds. The baby readily turns its head in the direction of Dad's voice as opposed to any other. The presumable explanation is that the newborn recognizes the voice from before, the one it heard from inside the womb. Sociologist Beth Rushing, who feels a newcomer to solitude, describes her experience as similar to the womb experience: "You're floating on your back in water, and you hear what's going on around you, but in those muffled voices like adults have in Charlie Brown specials on television, and you're glad because you're closing your eyes, weightless, about to fall asleep or into a trance because it feels so good to be alone with your thoughts."[45]

Proprioceptive Reactions and Body Awareness

However, all is not la-di-da in the womb. Some of the happenings are rigorous training for the outside world—tuning up our proprioceptors. The prefix "proprio" means "one's own," and according to *Taber's Cyclopedic Medical Dictionary*, a proprioceptor is a receptor that responds to stimuli originating within the body itself, especially to pressure or stretch movement.[46] Proprioceptive sensations keep us aware of the activities of muscles, tendons, and joints, and of balance, or equilibrium. These sensations enable us to recognize the location and rate of movement of a body part in relation to others. They also let us judge the position and movements of limbs, without using our eyes. Although fetal movement is different from what occurs postnatally, impulses for conscious proprioception[47] are present during womb life. How else would a newborn so quickly be able to turn away from overstimulation, or toward a fascinating event? An infant's movements are in readiness at birth to react to environmental changes—for example, knowing to respond when the body is too hot, too cold, or hungry.

Besides the fact that these movements appear to be instrumental in the subsequent organization of upright locomotion, muscle firings are part of spontaneous movements that register their impact on the brain, which will several months later transform these proprioceptions into a more articulated task. By twelve weeks in utero, rotation of the head and trunk and hand-to-face movements occur. Shortly thereafter, the mouth opens and eyelids open and close. At eighteen weeks the baby can be seen exploring various parts of its body with its hands, including primitive thumb sucking. Observers of the fetal state witness mobility that is goal oriented, smooth, and coordinated. Moreover, spontaneous movements are visible as well, and other rhythmical and cyclical motions in the fetus that later are apparent in the newborn.[48]

Why is proprioception, or awareness of our bodies, so essential to consciousness? According to Antonio R. Damasio, professor of neurology and head of the Department of Neurology at the University of Iowa College of Medicine, our bodies are our minds:

> For the biological state of self to occur, numerous brain systems must be in full swing, as must numerous body-proper systems. If you were to cut *all* the nerves that bring brain signals to the body proper, your body state would change radically, and so consequently would your mind. Were you to cut only the signals from the body proper to the brain, your mind would change too. Even partial blocking of brain-body traffic causes changes in mind state.[49]

Earlier, Ida P. Rolf, founder of the Rolfing technique, in which physical pressure is used to realign the body, stated, "Physical personality is not something separate, strange, or different from psychological personality, but part of a . . . psychophysical entity."[50] For some, the whole mind begins with the body—which is one of our best informants on the state of emotions. The baby in utero moves far more—two to three times more often—than the mother is aware.[51] Substance abuse, including alcohol and smoking, reduces fetal movement—and, we can thus say, self-regulation and even perhaps consciousness. What type of consciousness has its antecedent in fetal life? To answer this question, we can take a glimpse at dream and hypnotic studies performed on term and preterm babies.

Hypnotic Studies

Babies, preterm and term, spend more time in the active, REM state than in the deeper, quiet sleep. This may be because the long alonetimes of sleep in a baby's life seek balance and because these active phases of REM sleep are thought to be when the baby's brain develops and consolidates the enormous learning that takes place. As psychologist David Chamberlain insists, "Infants appear to be in business for themselves, dealing with compelling phenomena originating and being perceived from within."[52]

Hypnotic studies, though slim in number and to be treated with some doubt, are based on the belief that a fetus uses an active mind and thus pose interesting questions and deserve further follow-up. Some of these studies combine the idea of birth trauma with attempts to retrieve patients' conscious experiences at birth. In Grof's LSD experiments he regressed patients, thinking that they would uncover traumatic births. On these occasions, private and secret events, hitherto unremembered by the regressed person, were validated against external memories of other people involved in the actual births.[53] By contrast, Chamberlain is among a group of therapists, midwives, and parents who have witnessed individuals regress through hypnosis or drugs back to birth experiences that were not traumatic events for an infant. His study looked in depth at ten mother-child pairs and included questions about their birth memories. The group of children had never heard any stories of their birth. He found substantial matching between the extended narratives of both mothers and children under hypnosis. More startling is that in his thirteen-year study, both mothers and children indicate that it is the baby who is in charge of birth. Louis, our antihero from *The Divine Child*, certainly controlled his destiny and was determined not to leave his comfortable quarters: "Imagine the fate lurking . . . on earth . . . birth is the first victory of death—Fontaine [the gynecologist] who had blanched, now bleated: 'Louis, come on out, we have no time to waste.' The same atrociously shrill voice [of Louis] repeated, 'Go fuck yourself. I'M NOT COMING OUT.' "[54]

As incredible as Louis's story sounds, it is noteworthy that Chamberlain reports small children saying that they tried everything they could to "get out" and even had a sense of a crying person (mother) whom they were helping: "Tests of memory indicate the ability of newborns to remember color patterns . . . A further sign of memory at birth is seen in the ability of adults to remember the head and shoulder sequences of their own deliveries."[55] Who yet knows for sure whether babies are mostly inclined to resist or go with the hormonal tide and venture through the birth canal? Certainly the imperative of uterine contractions and mother's pushing leaves them, unlike Louis, little choice. Chamberlain advocates increasing the sensitivity to babies' awareness at birth. I have witnessed my own children's and other children's birth, and crying or discomfort was not evident except in response to a handler's stimulation for a reaction.

Intrauterine experiences provide the initial mechanisms for preserving boundaries between oneself (one's mental images) and what is outside the body. Translated into words: "Where I begin and where I stop. I am who I am, alone and connected, in touch with things and floating free." In the womb, the fetus has neither an awareness of harmony with others nor an aloneness that states, "I am all by myself," per se. But fetuses can sense an equilibrium, which is recorded in their smiles of satisfaction, quite apparent pre- and postbirth. The inability of people to recognize the pleasure in a newborn baby's smile as inwardly motivated —"Merely a gas bubble"—suggests a narrow, egocentric vision of grown-ups, in which the infant's gratification can revolve only around the care-taker.

Womb observations and fetal development offer a major insight into our need for alonetime as maturing adults. This viewpoint values aloneness as a given physiological and psychological dimension emanat-ing from the intrauterine period. Both childhood and wombhood speak about our style of reacting and acting. They provide some input that *may* characterize later feelings and behavior. Most of all, in wombhood rests the foundation for alonetime needs. Next we trace those and patterns for attachment from infancy.

CHAPTER 7

The Baby, the Child,

the Adolescent . . . Then Us

These are the hills, these are the woods,
These are my starry solitudes;
And there the river by whose brink
The roaring lions come to drink.
ROBERT LOUIS STEVENSON, "The Land of Story Books"[1]

When at home alone I sit
And am very tired of it,
I have just to shut my eyes
To go sailing through the skies
To go sailing far away
To the pleasant Land of Play.
ROBERT LOUIS STEVENSON, "The Littlehand"[2]

BILL GATES AND STEVEN SPIELBERG, please answer: What would you be today if your childhood had been filled with all the wonderful creations you are providing for the young of the world? Would your imaginations have taken off the way they now do if twenty-four-hour programming were available? If knowledge were as accessible as an apple from a tree, would you have pondered and sought after new learning? If virtual reality could fulfill every dream, would you have spent time daydreaming? If you had been able to play high-tech games of cops and robbers, cowboys and rustlers, space adventures, and make-believe, would you have bothered creating your films and software? Will the fin de siècle 1990s produce its own version of a Woody Allen, George Lucas, or Gene Roddenberry?

Are we downloading our inventive, originative minds into the maze of an irretrievable cyberspace and permanently changing the parameters of friendships? I am asking, I know, questions with answers that only time will reveal. Yet, for people growing up with fairly constant TV, being without it feels like losing a friend. Computer children find company in the chat rooms; while they may be alone pursuing mechanized friends, they often don't experience this as alonetime. Perhaps to reflect on private thoughts seems old-fashioned. Some think we have already put children's minds in danger, and maybe the mature mind as well.[3] Adults not only sleep with earplugs and eye masks but take walks with plugs in their ears. Touch-Tone phone responses lead us to home delivery of newspapers or disclosures of bank balances and are a Kafkaesque threat if we need to truly make contact with someone. If we lose sight of ourselves, we can become as panicked as some patients do when they realize that they have lost the ability to know how they feel or what they want.

> Frieda, a talented actress and writer, finds her career blossoming and her friendships rich and consuming. However, she spends her limited free time and almost all social time drinking. She doesn't become drunk, but she is inebriated enough to forget things. Her best friend, a noted stage lighter, takes cocaine. Neither of them knows what they want life to bring them. Frieda cannot look inward enough to answer the question "What am I feeling now?" She knows that, growing up, she courted being alone—all her dreams of acting and writing were born in those moments. Yet today she runs from such time as if it were the plague.

◆   ◆   ◆

Being on the fast track has removed Frieda from her sensory knowledge. But why do we run from ourselves? The phrase "Stop and smell the flowers" was incorporated into the culture because many people have forgotten how to reach their senses. And since our senses teach us who we are and what we feel, the restoration of alonetime has much to offer. This book, however, is not so much a cautionary tale as a tug on the sleeve to pause and think about the value of time alone. In this instance, it is alonetime's place in our lives as we grow up that requires reassessment. To do this, I shift the prism through which we view motherhood and parenthood, and offer research that captures the baby's contributions to its own welfare and children's intuitive knowledge of themselves. I also show, in different forums, alonetime as basic to the ways we survive our childhood.

From Devotion to Desertion? — Childhood Then and Now

Child watchers focus mainly on the importance of the close relationship of mother to child. But when their gaze is unremitting, it makes me reflect on the infant, the older child, the adolescent, and even us as adults retreating when the presence of others begins to feel overbearing. And they themselves bring to light the self-determination of the developing infant, child, and ultimately adult person. Stories of children with handicaps sometimes best emphasize the power that self-determination wields. These are the against-all-odds youngsters whose wills, despite disabilities that limit and confine contact (blindness, deafness, and so forth), prevail beyond expectations. From another perspective, observations reveal that mothering is not always gentle and caring.

Parallel insights from animal research, which show periods of time when monkeys deliberately leave their offspring alone, make the human need for aloneness seem ever more real. Mothers do not always display the same behaviors. In the animal kingdom, offspring born at off moments—too soon after another litter or during hard times—create variations in protective and nurturing habits. Although most mammals feed and groom their own, in monkey societies members share child care as well as abandon the job. According to an article by Sarah B. Hrdy in *Natural History,* the observable variations in child care range from devotion to desertion: "Infanticide, abortion, cannibalism, these are altogether natural lapses from imagined natural laws. Why is it only in the last two decades that researchers have begun to view such behaviors as other than aberrations?"[4]

Pat Barker's *Regeneration* suggests that we should distrust "the [convention] that nurturing, even when done by a man, remains female, as if the ability were in some way borrowed, or even stolen, from women."[5] Nowadays, reports in the daily news of the numbers of children of small age left alone living in squalor, or of a Susan Smith, who like Medea sacrifices her children to gain revenge over her betraying husband, tell us that we should know better than to assume that all mothers are instinctively nurturing.

We are not ready-made social animals, although we are born fitted in ways that encourage socializing. Caretakers—through loving exchanges, feeding, playing, and discipline—work hard to "civilize" children. Newborns are more inner directed than outer, but it doesn't take long for them to increase their responsiveness to attentive outsiders. And for most, once they get the hang of relating, it is fun and rewarding. But if people were truly social animals, I believe social conditions would be far better than they are, and concern for others' welfare would not have to be something preached from pulpits, monitored by courts and police, or promoted by charities. Human nature seems weighted as much in the direction of isolation as companionship. This is not only true today, but also part of our history. In his psychohistorical studies, Lloyd de Mause[6] characterizes various modes of parenthood from the earliest times to today. Ancient civilizations are painted as primarily infanticidal. He cites authorities who describe how, in ancient Greece and Rome, children could be seen left out to die in clay pots placed in front of houses. When Abraham (through the angel of God) spared Isaac, parenthood was freed, at least symbolically, from the then all too natural condition of child sacrifice. If parental love and attachment were natural to humankind, why would it be necessary to have such a strong reminder as the fifth of the Ten Commandments, "Honor thy father and thy mother, that thy days may be long upon the land which the Lord thy God giveth thee"?

I do not completely share de Mause's pessimistic view of the history of parenthood. Successive generations contain a wide array of parental practices, for sure—from pampered Little Lord Fauntleroys to orphaned Oliver Twists. In each era, overprotection, abuse, and neglect—as well as love—are observable among parents. What is remarkable to me is the fact that scores of great and able people of earlier centuries were raised through the help of strangers (such as wet nurses) and siblings whose other priorities allowed relatively little attention or time for sentimental attachments. Here again it may be the significance of the need for contact —touch—that comes into play. Touch is helped by attachment, and vice versa, but as I have already stated, they are not the same. And again, at certain points in history, wrapping infants in swaddling clothes instead of hands-on touching may have offered comfort, contact, and protection over and above direct family fondling.[7]

Moreover, even in today's so-called enlightened age of parental practices, with a plethora of child-development books and parenthood gurus reaching out to parents, treatment of children varies from empathic to insensitive. It is far harder to be empathic to another's needs if a major need of your own goes unnoticed. Parents are given small indication that they have separate needs—a paragraph or two in parenthood books may discuss the topic of parents needing time to themselves. This hardly measures up to the warnings about the consequences of inadequate bonding.

We might also need to think about how avoidance behaviors on the part of children may be consistent not only with a culture's child-rearing patterns, but also with the demands placed on the grown person. Unchallenged attachments are not the answer for everyone. Robert Hinde, an ethologist whose work was the foundation for some of Bowlby's formulations, takes another look at fear of strangers and separation anxiety. He argues for allowing children (and, implicitly, adults) who favor avoidance and ambivalent attachments their singular developmental patterns, explaining how in certain instances it may be the most adaptive mode. What about the person who works night shifts? The world traveler? The foreign correspondent? How will he or she balance the needs for rest and needs for family? There has to be more than one way.

Childhood is where this book began. It is where we continue the exploration. In my childhood, I had the dilemma I see facing patients and friends today. If I relish alonetime, will I be thought antisocial? Will the gods notice and curse me with a friendless life? When I feel that I am happier alone than socializing with others, will I be left mateless? Who would take care of me when necessary? Maybe I did not articulate my fears and thoughts as such, but I knew full well that sometimes I preferred to be alone rather than in play groups, and sensed that this was not a feeling you could admit to just anyone. Alone desires are taboo. Reflect upon libraries blacklisting *Huckleberry Finn*. Ostensibly this is a reaction to the book's racism, but it could well be that "[Huck] is too independent, too rebellious and self-willed for adults who wish to see children as helpless, innocent creatures, blank slates on which to scrawl whatever obscenities they like."[8]

I also fought against alonetime in childhood. Sometimes when I nagged my sister to play with me, I was protesting too much and was relieved when she said no. You see, I was ambivalent. While I took to heart my father's insistent desire for sisters to be close, I also felt like doing my own thing. Reading Robert Louis Stevenson's poems brought me to his "Land of Counterpane." His China Seas, deserts, and the like were lone, imaginary pursuits. Notwithstanding whines for companionship, attention, and help, I loved my solitary time. Looking back, I remember that every day held many such hours. When I was very young, I played with a one-inch Kewpie doll that I put in a box with cotton protection surrounding it. It was my "incubator baby," and no one else could play with it. Climbing and walking across dangerous precipices, staring blankly out the window, and silently composing stories about the unknown neighbors were taken for granted. Though I dreaded my sister's starting kindergarten, thinking that I wouldn't survive without her, when she left I did not always miss her. Instead, I reveled in more space and time to spend as I pleased.

To make alonetime scary, I had to conjure up a negative association that had less to do with aloneness and was more connected to help-lessness. For me, this fear was actually born of claustrophobia, symbol-ized by a time when polio was endemic and the vaccine against it was still unproven. Pictures of children with polio unable to move from their metal tunnel—an iron lung—had me, even at six years old, testing myself for pains in my legs. Images of remaining isolated, left alone, caged up in a smaller compartment than any zoo animal, became my aloneness metaphor and what spurred me on to dress quickly and not dawdle when threatened to be left alone. Recently, I interviewed a woman who as a teenager experienced being in an iron lung due to polio. Besides knowl-edge that relatives had died from this disease, her worst times resulted from being absolutely dependent on others and always having people —doctors, nurses, family, friends—around her. She described teaching herself a tuning-out technique that served her well, as it allowed her to feel self-sufficient and unbombarded.

When young, I worried about not always being part of the "in" group, but not enough to cause me to work at it. I always had best friends. Yet I knew that I was consoled not only by sharing or learning the latest gossip. I loved early mornings by myself, make-believe games, fantasizing to radio programs. No one, however, until I was an adolescent, spoke openly of what they did alone or of liking to be by themselves; they just enacted it fearlessly, recklessly, and secretly. Solitary games—such as writing a letter to a celebrity or imagining oneself as heroic and saving the country from an atomic bomb explosion—were invented to explore daring and nerve. But even so, when I shared secrets in my teen years, I learned about how much alonetime occupied people's lives. My ongoing observations of children and adolescents tell me that desires are not that different now, although certainly against the current grain.

Baby watching[9] outside of experimental conditions is a child psychol-ogist's spellbinding busman's holiday. The mutual engagement, locking of eyes, sharing of expressions and sounds, suggest the intensity of this first human exchange. Emphatically, it is a mutual exchange, although infant researchers until the late 1960s primarily registered parental (mother) input. In my professional baby watching, I see a less-told se-quence in this story of consuming infatuation. Even in the beginning moments of discovery and bonding there are separate times. The baby coos, the mother coos back. The mother smiles, the baby grins in response. Then the baby slowly turns away and gazes and coos at another object. The mother tries to reconnect, but the baby is content to be distracted. Sometimes it is the mother who loses concentration and the baby who attempts to reengage. Some master baby watchers, although principally concentrated on attachment, describe an attachment pattern that includes periods of disengagement.[10] Those who look closely see great variety in a newborn's levels of activity and alertness.

Professionals seem to agree about six different levels of consciousness:[11]

1. *Deep sleep*, with regular breathing and little movement, thought to have a restorative function that rests and arranges an immature nervous system and offers respite from most stimulation.
2. *Light-active sleep*, with REM (rapid eye movements) and less regular breathing. This state is associated with dreaming, more evident in neonates than older infants, and is a time for brain differentiation and growth.
3. *Drowsy wakefulness*, with its shallower regular breathing and some movement. Babies usually can be easily aroused to an alert state from here, or drift back into sleep if given alonetime.
4. *Alert awake*, when babies are calm yet bright eyed, and while not excited, attentive and responsive to stimuli. This quiet alert time is initially short lived.
5. *Alert active or fussing*. Babies can be distressed, but also self-soothed or soothed by others back into an alert quiet state. Stimulation may work negatively in that it provides too much and may cause crying.
6. *Crying*. Researchers have identified at least four types, including pain, hunger, boredom, and discomfort.

Both researchers and child caretakers—who recognize the differences between states and signals, including crying—are able to gear their social exchanges according to the infant's receptivity. Parents have needs to hold and make contact with their babies. But, of all the above important states of consciousness and vital social and nonsocial behaviors, the alone periods of time are given least attention.

Research

When psychologists play detective, as I am in uncovering alonetime, we need the facts—the research to back us up. In the 1950s, a clinical psychologist in Michigan, Clark Moustakas, decided to study loneliness.

He did not know what to expect, but he presumed that he would be looking at gloom.[12] Instead, children taught him that even in the setting of a hospital room, being lonely at times had many positive moments. By an examination of phenomena that made clear that loneliness is more than just a state of despair, his rich study actually described what I name alonetime.[13] Against the current dictum, he divided aloneness into positive and negative feeling states. Without accepting alonetime as a vital and ongoing basic need, however, he began to create a database for accumulating and studying good alone experiences.

Silence and uninterrupted time provide possibilities for children, an open time to be prince or pauper, adventurer or faithful friend. In a rural Midwestern community, a graduate student in nursing, Marita B. Hoffert, decided to inquire into the nature of children's solitude.[14] She spoke in depth to fifteen nine- and ten-year-old boys and girls and their families. Children were asked about the meaning of spending time by themselves: When do they choose this? What do they know about spending time alone? Reflecting the negative connotation of current vocabulary, Hoffert's children responded positively to "by yourself" more than to "alone" and had longer stories to tell about such experiences. To elicit dialogues on aloneness, she used drawings they had made of the times they chose to be by themselves. All children had a special place to be alone: hiding in a tree, playing in an alley or backyard, going to bed or a bedroom. One entry into alonetime for school-age children is boredom. One of Hoffert's interviewees, Bryan, prefers staying home alone rather than going to a boring hardware store with his parents: "Being bored [without having anything] to do moved Bryan into and out of solitary time."[15] Children were prompted by having nothing to do or courted doing nothing if they could get away with that. Like being alone, being bored is deemed bad. You can hear it in the language: "bored to death" or "to tears" or "to distraction" and "bored silly" or "stiff" or "sick" are the negatives. But an English psychoanalyst, Adam Phillips,[16] reminds us that the capacity to be bored is an achievement. Being bored, he says, is being underwhelmed and understimulated, and allows one necessary escape and replenishment. Proving this, another participant in Hoffert's study, John, found that being bored led to drawing or painting at his desk, to finding space to practice his art, to inner solitude.[17] A young girl, Linnae,[18] when bored by "stuff" or people, secluded herself to listen to music, read, draw, or play basketball by herself.

In Hoffert's conversations, she discovered that a difference exists between people discussing being "alone" and those who speak of being "by oneself." I find that as well. For some, being "alone" feels like a forced separation. "I stayed home alone. It was okay, but I wished I had been asked to the party," a wistful patient tells me. "When I learned that going to the gallery opening was just another excuse to start a night of bar hopping, I chose to stay home by myself," said one analysand, who found it far easier to differentiate her wants from those of others these days. Since taking up the study of alonetime, I routinely survey all ages and nationalities of children and students, and sometimes ask strangers about their recollections of being alone. Initial answers are often negative, but when they are prodded to write descriptions of early experiences of alonetime, the tone of the remembrances changes:

> "I really don't remember being alone as a young child. (I shared a room with my annoying younger sister!) The first time I remember being alone is as a thirteen-year-old, when I finally got my own room. I would sit on my bed, read a favorite book, and often drift peacefully in and out of sleep—often dropping the book on the floor and not realizing it till hours later!"

> "My first alonetime was probably at about four years old. I just remember playing with my toys in my room by myself. Mom was in the living room with my sisters. I was glad to be by myself— but I wasn't sure I should be so happy."

> "At three years old, I looked out a window, waiting for my mother to come back. Ironically, I wasn't scared. I just stared outside."

> "I can remember being in my crib with a bottle of milk and having the sensation of not liking the taste of milk. I don't know if this counts as an alone experience, but it's an early memory and I think I was alone. Throughout my childhood (I'm not sure when this started, but definitely by four) I would sit on the inside ledge of the windowsill in the living room and stare out the window and daydream. I could do this for fairly long periods of time."

◆   ◆   ◆

Some of the children I know are like a friend of mine from childhood, who escaped family society by going into the bathroom for long stretches, reading or reflecting. Funnily enough, many adults confess that this retreat is still a favorite hideout.

How many of us (other than in the therapist's office) easily admit to being bored by people? And whereas children, when bored by siblings, can shut down or shut out others, what can a father do who admits to his therapist his grown daughter bores him? One friend I have makes no bones about having had enough of people—but to mask his genuine requirement for reduced stimulation and alonetime, he always announces his retreat belligerently. In a climate that accepts little in human relationships beyond attachments, we need to continue to look to children to inform us when the emperor is without clothes.

Feeding the Capacity to Be Alone

Children have always operated with an intuitive sense. However, only in the past thirty years have scientists credited infants with five senses: smell, vision, hearing, taste, and touch. All these senses contribute to infants' and children's growing awareness of their inner and outer worlds. But what some have called a sixth sense [19] continues to be overlooked. Proprioceptors, as I previously discussed, signal bodily changes from muscles, tendons, and the like. They are part of a complete inner sensory system that regulates our internal organs, which some physiologists describe as "interoception." The first interoceptions of our lone self feed the capacity to be alone. The total interoceptive system includes "our conscious feelings of, and unconscious monitoring of, bodily processes." [20] In the womb, receptors begin to signal the fetal brain so that homeostasis, an inner regulation, can be maintained. Once the child is born, there are types of postural tests, balance situations, mirror experiences, and auditory-visual examinations that can show an active, alert neonate able to differentiate self as perpetrator and manipulator of the environment and perhaps delineate boundaries between what is me and what is not me. [21] Babies use receptor information to self-adjust and regulate.

Eye gaze is central to the way babies self-regulate. It is biologically adaptive for babies, when it facilitates their comfort, to look away from an interaction. Like the consummate actor whose every small gesture conveys a fluctuation in mood, a baby's signals often operate in slow motion. To expand the sense of the baby as a lone as well as a connected being—have you ever watched infants announcing hunger? They do not typically begin by crying. Usually, they begin by being alert and active. Their movements are searching. When they are lying down, their hands begin to reach out and their heads turn to one side. Their mouths open and close, or their lips purse and their tongues show between the lips. As the feeling grows, the mouth opens wider, or the fingers explore the mouth and sucking motions begin. Only after this goes on for several minutes without food dispensed do babies become seriously agitated. First a whimper or two is heard, and then the loud wail. In our interviews with parents and in observations of videotapes,[22] the general expectation is that when a baby wants something he or she cries. Babies are varied in their ability to communicate, and most mothers and fathers are surprised by this. Crying is vital, but watching babies for long periods indicates that crying is one of a large repertoire of signals, and even a last resort for some newborns, used to being self-satisfied in the womb.

Self-regulation in an infant means more than the baby being able to suck, sleep, and eliminate, although that is part of the definition. Most important, self-regulation implies that babies teach a parent what type care is needed, through their catalogue of sounds and gestures. Giving babies alonetime and watching infants begin to understand their environment is what I teach to my parenthood and school psychology students, who will ultimately counsel parents. Parents have difficulty with the idea of letting children fall asleep on their own or not jumping to respond as soon as a baby lets out a sigh or opens one eye. One mother in my research was so overly conscientious that the second her baby blinked she was holding him. When he fell asleep in her arms she had to lift his eyelid and ask, "What are you doing?" If he was gazing into space at two weeks old she promptly put a black-and-white object or a mirror in front of him. When he turned from these toys she covered his face with kisses and kept moving his head to ensure his eyes met hers. Each time, he was able to duck away. In psychological circles, this game is called "chase and dodge."[23] But, alas, the baby couldn't find alonetime in dodging; the eager mother was always right up close. And this most adaptable child, who for twenty or more minutes was able to deflect the intrusions, finally cried in protest. "Albert, tell me what you want. Talk to me," the distraught mother said in frustration. The truth is, he *was* talking, but the message had nothing to do with wanting attention. Fortunately, over time, this mother became more responsive to her baby's cues for disengagement.

Watching and talking to parents such as this young mother inform me that most are unaware of infants' prelearning, which enables them to strive for, or to diminish, stimulating conditions. This unawareness is not surprising, as many have argued that without nonstop, immediate, personalized caregiving, the baby won't survive.[24] A favorite observation occurred in the nonscientific setting of a child's baby-naming celebration. In this instance, the week-old baby was being introduced left and right to important family members and friends. He tried to disengage by turning away but was never too successful, as people were closing in on his adorable face. Finally, when the baby was passed to one well-wisher too many, he let out a howl and his mother came to the rescue. I looked on in interest to see if the baby calmed himself and how much help he would need from Mom, whom people were noisily engaging in conversation. The baby did well at first, resting quietly in his mother's cradling arms, alert and open eyed. This lasted until several relatives began speaking at once. At first he squirmed, squeaked, and squealed to little avail. Suddenly, with the calm of a Buddhist monk he clasped his hands—fingers to fingers—and lay very still. Within five minutes his eyes drooped closed and he was asleep. His alone skills prevailed through self-touch.[25]

Human Adaptiveness: The Promotion of Attachment, or of Alonetime?

A baby controls through both self-touch and parental contact.[26] The Victorian parent controlled the child's sensuality and sensory discovery. But contemporary attempts at staving off stimulation are compromised by an overactive, constantly stimulating world. On the other hand, what happens when life casts the child into too much alonetime, with blindness or deafness? Evidently, even the blind child is sent into a tantrum if too much guidance is imposed on how to creep or walk.[27] Attachment under stress awakened us to the perils of abandonment and confirmed the essential need we all have for stable, loving relationships. Similar, yet less noticed, examples of the search for solitude under duress—as demonstrated by children in hospitals or stricken with polio or blindness—substantiate the basic need and desire for alonetime.

Touch is probably the first sense we experience—in the womb, of course—and the last to leave us. Touch and determination are probably what drew Helen Keller out of a life of restless, painful dullness. Ms. Keller, who navigated the loss of both hearing and sight, felt her deafness the far greater obstacle. One might suspect that, with her inquiring mind, she would have hated all alone experiences, having been dealt a far greater dose than average. Born in Tuscumbia, Alabama, in 1880, Ms. Keller had no visual or hearing problems. In fact, she was described as precocious and self-assertive, speaking at six months, walking at a year. But at nineteen months she was stricken with what was described as "acute congestion of the stomach and brain" and never saw or heard afterward. Her great urge to express herself, as noted in her early speech, manifested itself throughout her life. Ms. Keller's heroic story has much to teach us, as will the lives of others in extremis, in a later chapter. She says, "Gradually I got used to the silence and darkness that surrounded me and forgot that it had ever been different."[28]

We have two significant pathways for development—one through alonetime needs, the other through attachment. Miss Sullivan, Helen Keller's teacher, capitalized on the second. But the survival story of Ms. Keller before the advent of her teacher affirms the first pathway, and examples of self-teaching from her adult life emphasize her need for knowledge and subsequent self-sufficiency above all else:

> I had a French grammar in raised print . . . I often amused myself by composing in my head short exercises, using the new words as I came across them, and ignoring rules . . . as much as possible. I even tried, without aid, to master the French pronunciation, as I found all the letters and sounds described in the book. Of course this was taking slender powers for great ends, but it gave me something to do on a rainy day.[29]

Rainy-day activities are important in Ms. Keller's story, and she describes knitting, crocheting, and reading. Equally, she talks of her playful alonetime: "If I happen to be all alone and in an idle mood, I play a game of solitaire, of which I'm very fond."[30]

Some, in suggesting the loss of "primitive," Rousseau-like naturalism, confuse being in touch with our senses (as was Ms. Keller) with the glamorizing of hunting-gathering and agricultural societies at the expense of technologically sophisticated cultures. The close contact and affectionate relationships of such societies (as we explored in Chapter 2) are held as beacons of human adaptedness. But the adaptation is to their needs and times. The !Kung, frequently cited hunters and gatherers, are a long-suckling tribe. They nurse children for as many as five years. This serves purposes beyond child care as lactation and attachment, since poorly nourished groups stave off fertility while providing food for the young. This works differently in our culture.

A child patient of eight had problems separating to attend school and going to sleep at night. It turned out she was nursed (mostly at night) until five years old. At that time her mother stopped feeding her by breast. At age fourteen months, according to the mother, Abbie wanted to stop nursing. At five years of age, she wished to continue. The gratification established a new norm, overriding her own self-determination. Psychoanalytic therapy revealed the many fantasies Abbie associated with this loss, including the inability to tend to herself away from her mother: "What if I asked for a cracker and no one had any? What if my stomach starts to ache; how will it ever get better? I could fall down. Would anyone notice? What if I never fall asleep?" The initiative gained at fourteen months, when she was ready to go to bed on her own, was undermined by the mother's belief that she was shortchanging her daughter.

◆   ◆   ◆

Our culture is not set up for that degree of mutual regulation, nor do the incidents of starvation necessitate it. We need to feel both assured of our own skills for self-care and able to depend on others. For example, the Efe were another group of foragers, who lived in a forest in Zaire, in a community where all members of the group were physically and visually available to one another most of the time. The social contact was intense. Contact with mothers was not high, but when combined with that of other tribe members, contact exceeded the degree of touch between American mothers and babies. Physical contact facilitated thermal regulation and other growth, which made it essential for normal functioning, in contrast to standards for other cultures.[31] The principal field researcher of mother-infant interaction among the Efe is Harvard Medical School and Boston Children's Hospital researcher Dr. Edward Z. Tronick. This time reporting on primates as well as human mothers, he adds to this discussion:

> Motherhood has never been as straightforward as just turning on the milk and affection. Although the word mammal derives from the mammary glands and thus connects all warm-blooded, hairy, viviparous vertebrate animals together (including humans, according to Linnaeus' 1758 edition of *Systema Naturae*), for many centuries tens of thousands of babies in Europe were deposited in surrounding homes or shipped to middlemen who contracted for a lactating woman to suckle them.[32]

Again, I state my belief that these babies survived because alone skills compensated to some degree for the loss of attachment.

The work of infant researchers and clinical observers[33] documents periods of the baby's disinterest in the mother as well as times the mother is less involved with her infant. These moments, while noticed by all observers, are interpreted in different ways. Common parlance sees them as a need for open spaces for self-exploration, but as part of a two-person connection. Daniel Stern, a New York City–born clinical researcher now living in Switzerland, emphasizes the word "attunement" to describe the action of the mother who correctly reads her baby's signals. "Intrusiveness," by contrast, is the mother overreading a baby's needs. "Synchrony" is the harmony between mother's and baby's needs. "Matching" and "disruption"—so well described by Stern, Beatrice Beebe, and Frank Lachmann—synchronize the interactive rhythms between mother and child. Sometimes a baby follows the mother's cues. Other times it's vice versa. Disruptions are normal. But when disruptions are too frequent, either mother or baby or both are mismatching signals.

This dialogue is not different for fathers. Indeed, as you can tell by the names I have referred to here, men have great interest in observing and understanding the nitty-gritty of a baby's actions. Yet, from another concern, my students—many of whom are feminists—have asked me a bewildering question: "Why are fathers so often more idealized than mothers, and why is the affection of the father given greater value?" First, we need to wonder if this is true. As in most such questions, the answer is yes and no. This much seems correct: In recent history, fathers have played a far less consistent role in raising children. Yet mothers are given the greatest blame by both patients and nonpatients in terms of what goes wrong in a child's life. Fathers, by distancing themselves, offer children alonetime and give them greater choice in decision making. In certain cases, if fathers haven't retreated too far, they have ended up as the heroes. From the Victorian age to the last few decades, fathers were not involved in day-to-day home activities. Children may have been annoyed at fathers sleeping behind the daily newspapers, but they would not complain of too much father—only too little. The old-style Dagwood Bumstead father would often return from work and escape into the alonetime of sleep, TV, or newspaper. Society now demands more.

One interested father, a California-based researcher and psychoanalyst named Louis Sander, was the first person to see sleep as a psychological dimension of alonetime. A series of ingenious studies were set up by Sander, in which he wired a baby's crib so that he could observe asleep and awake patterns. Through his work he has documented the early personhood of infants, and has demonstrated infants' abilities to elicit reactions as well as to disengage, which for a baby means turning the head or rotating the body away from the caretaker, or sleeping. We hear a lot about sleep problems of infants; but most, by two months, have adapted their sleep behaviors. Moreover, they influence the responses of their caretakers as well. For example, it took baby Albert (from my research) until he was four weeks old to communicate through fussing to his mother when he preferred being placed in an infant seat to being held. Later in a baby's life, as skills develop, other wishes will inevitably compete with needs both for sleep and for alonetime. Then children need another to more actively intervene in order to effectively regulate sleep. To be enjoyed, sleep has to become a ritual of gradually leaving an exciting world. Unless sleep disturbances occur, the need to have alone, self-regulating periods of sleep prevails throughout life.

Self-Regulation and Uncomfortable Attachments

Let us recapitulate the importance of self-regulation. The ability to self-regulate is essential to one's initial experience of aloneness and vital to the continuing development of the capacity to be alone. It allows us to feel in charge of our body and somewhat in control of our emotions. We know when we are cold, sexually excited, hungry, or tired, and if we do not learn how to regulate these needs ourselves, we feel out of control. As babies, we experience the illusion of being in charge of bodily functions. As long as parents are fairly well attuned, babies continue to feel contented and self-regulating. But when children reach the age of two, they begin to realize the strength of another's will and needs. By this time, children have learned the joys of companionship, but the will to do the things one wants prevails, and the self-regulating battles begin. The "terrible twos" will not seem quite as horrendous if we realize that children are fighting to feel in charge of themselves so that they can increase their skills at handling life. Obviously, at age two, this cannot happen entirely. Any activity—from toilet training to brushing teeth, washing hands, or putting on gloves—can become a battle zone. The resolving of such potential wars means that parents have to grow accustomed to setting limits and to stepping back. Both pave the way for self-desired and self-motivated accomplishments.

Some fairly accomplished children—like Todd, a patient of mine—remain afraid to be all alone.

Todd was bright, a good saxophone player, and well liked. His mother, however, felt that she had to guide him in every decision. His father concurred to the point that every morning he requested his son to report his dreams, notwithstanding that every night he was asked to reveal to his parents his slightest anxiety so that they could talk things out. Todd wasn't allowed a private feeling. Any frown, down expression, or tilt of an eyebrow was reason for a family discussion. Todd himself requested therapy as he felt uncomfortable away from home when his elementary school had an overnight outing.

◆   ◆   ◆

I see Todd as having lost the meaning of his inner body signals, unable and perhaps disallowed to respond to sensory cues. Children like Todd also may have learned too well to have another person step in, and they substitute the other for self-control. Their parents might have always made sure that they went to the bathroom before leaving the house and that their clothes matched perfectly. Fathers abound who still insist that their daughter take their arm when walking down the street or check if their son's face is clean well into the child's adolescent years. A mother might transfer her own physical pain onto the child and make the child an extension of herself, such as the mother who said to her nine-year-old daughter, "Lie down, I have a headache."

Conflicts of individual goals often create obstacles to balancing the alone and relationship needs required by children. Children in their middle years usually don't iterate their needs easily, especially a need for alonetime, except indirectly, much as babies signal the need for quiet, detached time. But they do speak of lack of privacy. A homeless boy seen in therapy by one of my students lamented that the very worst thing about community living was not the shared food, lack of toys, or changing faces. It was giving up his privacy. Never being able to find any separate space was something he said he would never get used to.

An example of parent-child conflict is apparent in observations of Charles and Molly, two seven-year-old children.[34] Charles's parents needed Charles to be "true Charles," strong and independent, whereas Molly's family was concerned with limit setting and "good girl" behavior. In the unfolding of the observational material, it became clear that the children were responding paradoxically. At seven years of age, Charles was described in school as a crybaby, a student who always needed to hold the teacher's hand. His need for aloneness appeared as reserve toward others and a melancholy introspectiveness. In her infancy and toddlerhood, Molly rebelled against the intrusive caretaking and showed her need to march to her own drummer. She had great joy in locomotion at one year of age and reacted positively to a punishment of time outs alone in her room. Using filmed observations to watch Molly and her mother, the researchers saw that Molly's need for self-assertiveness and aloneness was ever-present. Molly moved into her own space well before the "typical" developmental phase, and she showed what could be called "engulfment anxiety,"[35] a fear of being overly connected, at two years of age.

I often see children like Charles and Molly whose needs for selfhood and aloneness are either precociously fostered or thwarted by over-zealous limit setting. They may be too eagerly or rarely given the emotional responsibility of calming fears. Instead of developing comfortable attachments and solitude, such children attain these needs with varying degrees of success. Psychoanalytic literature has described them in a variety of ways, including "intellectually precocious,"[36] "overly anxious about separation,"[37] or "overprotected."[38] A number of interesting parent-child constellations interrupt a child's growing capacity to be alone, ranging from the overcontrolling, overly intrusive, protective parent to the overly indulgent parent. Having lost a child or experienced a child ill from birth—or even in response to an earlier loss of parent, lover, sibling, or friend—parents may become overly protective. Other parents have control and intrusiveness as characteristically ingrained. Exceptionally narcissistic caretakers, who can see and function only with children joined at the hip, have difficulty allowing their offspring space to be who they are, especially if it does not confirm the parents' character or adjustment to life.[39] "The joys of detachment," as Vivian Gornick notes, are hard for parent and child to come by.[40] We learn through the boundaries of disengagement that others also require time on their own. Moreover, accomplishments arise from boundaries, both naturally imposed and imposed by parents and society. Setting boundaries, like setting limits on connectedness, forces us to struggle on our own, which increases the ability to survive on our own.

Boundaries disappeared for identical twins Jennifer and June. In the story of these silent sisters, Marjorie Wallace tells an eerie tale of attachment and alonetime needs.[41] Until an enforced separation, June and Jennifer spent most of their time together in their bedroom, talking almost exclusively to each other. Nevertheless, by age seventeen, at the time of their conviction for theft and arson and subsequent commitment to a special hospital for the criminally insane, they had written a novel and dozens of poems, short stories, and essays. Jennifer and June kept minute diaries of their love-hate relationship, depicting how they could neither live together nor separately. They were continuously devising games, strategies, and rules to ensure that they would come too close together or drift apart. For each time the two sisters lost what D. H. Lawrence referred to as "star equilibrium"—being neither too close nor too far—they risked their own destruction.[42] Wallace's story is of bizarre bondage "by which the extremes of good and evil, which both June and Jennifer personify, have led to the possession of [each] twin by the other. It is about the waging of a silent war which neither could win: the struggle for individuality [quality alonetime?] . . . the power struggle in which . . . Romulus killed Remus."[43]

What Jennifer and June did, however, is isolate themselves from the outside world in their silences and secret affairs. Instead of fulfillment, they found a dark side to creativity. Crime became an answer to ennui. An early stay in prison led them to another period of creativity; during this time, June actually had a novel published. But after their sentencing to Broadmoor, the hospital for the insane, they were finally forced to separate and conform through use of drugs and discipline. Their playful spirits were gone as their struggles for independence, recognition of their creativity, and normalcy in alonetime seemed to have dissolved. The seduction of their savage attachment and cruel dependencies was annihilated in the equally damaging cure.

In the act of playing, children begin to objectify and try to work out their wishes, dreams, and fantasies. It is a pity when fantasy life takes over in gruesome ways—as in the case of Jennifer and June—because the use of symbolism is both an intellectual leap and an expression of our unique self. Symbolic play springs from the solitude of the self as originator of complex and powerful hopes, fears, and destructive wishes.

Developmental Glimpses at Alonetime

The fantasizing self is, metaphorically speaking, the womb that prevents a collision between the all-powerful wish and the real-world smallness of the wisher.[44] Along with Clark Moustakas, that pioneer in the study of positive lone experiences, I see in children's fantasy play ways of resolving normal developmental crises. Child analysts enter the sphere of the child as friends of fantasy, the healer of any rift between the child and his or her own place of inner solitude and creativity. Little Jeffrey, two years old with a new baby brother, moves himself in and out from under his easel and takes a truck—his brother?—back and forth through a tunnel until he emphatically decides to not let it come out. The next morning he returns to his play space and tells the truck, "You can come out now." Once the play and fantasy space is available to a child patient, the relief that ensues allows for numerous transferences, all of which seem as powerful as those we encounter in adult analyses.

To illustrate, five-and-a-half-year-old Louise invents a play scenario.

She invites the analyst to be a naughty child; she is the parent. As parent, Louise orders the child about: Louise interrupts the analyst's television watching, denies her requests for food, alternately orders her to bed and wakes her to feed her or asks for her help with the cooking. The analyst reflects through the play Louise's feelings that the analyst, in the little-girl role, is confused and feels bossed. Louise breaks out of the fantasy play and says, "Sssh! No talking—be patient!"

◆   ◆   ◆

Louise is not bossing the therapist but pleading for a play space where she can feel alone with her fantasy for a while. It seems to me that Louise is also saying, "Please don't let me know anything exists outside of me for a while. I need you as this extension of me so that I can allow room for both attachment and aloneness to grow."

School-age children continue to meet their aloneness needs through fantasy. Imaginary companions, I believe, have always been a child's way of re-creating and adjusting feelings of aloneness and attachment. Changeling fantasies, such as "The Frog Prince" and "Beauty and the Beast," comfort children disillusioned and humiliated by parents.[45] Not uncommonly, children fantasize exile or banishment from the adult world. Fiction that particularly appeals to children, such as *Swiss Family Robinson* or the *Narnia Chronicles,* suggests that children and other like-minded people or creatures may bond together to secede from the world of ordinary events. Recent examples of children's popular culture, such as the Teenage Mutant Ninja Turtles, are dropouts and exiles from the structured world of parents and their taboos. The "ick" of the child-oriented meal of monkey brains, scorpions, and floating eyeball soup in the Spielberg film *Indiana Jones and the Temple of Doom* fills the youngster, hoping the adult is disgusted, with glee. Other adventures that separate child from parent or solo journeys deeper into alone space have always been possible and fulfill the need for growing on one's own. Leaving family society by reading or reflecting is a time-honored custom of childhood, according to most reports received from our culture. Nothing is as complete to a child as to escape through imagination.

As adolescence approaches, cries of "Leave me alone!" accompanied by the slamming of doors may loudly pronounce the need to be alone. In *Rebel Without a Cause*, James Dean became the 1950s poster boy for alienated youth with his cry of "You're tearing me apart!" to his coddling and ineffectual parents. Adolescents often escape from friends into diaries, quiet days, and periods of sullen silence—self-exiles that Erikson described as useful.[46] Middle-school children and adolescents, when queried about aloneness and loneliness, see them as different concepts. Within our study,[47] adolescents and junior high school students viewed aloneness as a temporary, neutral state; loneliness, on the other hand, was colored by unpleasant and unwanted emotions. The shutting of the door against parents is the avenue that most reliably leads to selfhood and identity formation. The necessary secrecy of private ideas— from thoughts of coveting a friend's sweetheart to erotic masturbatory fantasies—and the absolute need for privacy carry the risk of complete isolation. Adolescents, whose intensity dictates an all-or-nothing approach, find themselves pulled alternately inward into fantasy of great and glorious achievements and outward, sometimes indiscriminately, toward others. The resulting confusion is often held responsible for the symptoms of psychotic breakdown. The hallmark of adolescent fantasy, whether it concerns sexual aims and wishes or a heroic scenario— whether it be spiritual, moral, artistic, political, or entrepreneurial—is its urgency. Parents of an adolescent are people who must reliably survive exposure to this storm of confusion and searching.

A young patient of mine found her own way around an unsettling conflict.

Heather, who came into treatment for help in overcoming a family trauma, gave her analyst the opportunity to see the need for aloneness in normal adolescent development. She came to her session after hearing *Meistersinger* performed over the weekend. Heather described the beauty of the opera and the devotion of the operagoers to the music. Then she described how she had trouble listening to Wagner, despite appreciating his music and theatrical gifts, because of his fascistic philosophy. This fifteen-year-old student of music needed to find a way to attend a performance and maintain her beliefs. She described how she dressed totally in black and wore a hat with a veil, in mourning for all the non-Aryans who died as a result of Nazism.

◆   ◆   ◆

This was her secret, and this kept her alone in her thoughts as she shared the magnificence of the performance with the others attending. A simple act of dress empowered her and helped her maintain her integrity.

Although adolescence as a focus was invented at the turn of the century, the goal of youth to be individualistic has always been in conflict with the aims of society. By contrast, in *Habits of the Heart,* Robert Bellah and his colleagues maintain that modernity is further fragmenting a society that already prides itself on separation, destruction of traditions, and an emphasis on individual growth and development.[48] With this in mind, the authors focus on reestablishing ties and commitment—not in a vacuum, but as a necessary accompaniment to individualism. I'm suggesting more. Individualism is as much a part of attachment and commitment as it may be of isolation. Even as adolescents strive for individualism, they commit themselves to groupie philosophies and go to often ludicrous lengths to follow trends. Emancipation from family ties is helped by joining a new family—the clique. But whereas the first blush of conforming to peer pressure brings security, after a while one's need for singularity emerges, as expressed by a sixteen-year-old who writes: "I now feel the need to find my true personality, if that is possible, and to define myself."[49]

Adolescent females seem to be particularly attuned to solitude. It is natural for young women to identify with the myth of Psyche and Psyche's freedom from adulation and idealization. She is carried away by the wind, and left to awaken blissfully alone in a bed of flowers—and only after this alonetime does she experience true sexual desire for Cupid.[50] Similarly, after a degree of separation, an adolescent—male or female—reunites once again with family members as a grown-up, usually insisting on different parameters within the relationship. Alone experiences are often seen as alien to family and commitment and, therefore, something to eschew.

Current and deep-seated myths fed to parents about infants', children's, and adults' *social* needs superseding all others are part of what I am looking at anew. And among the cultural myths is the idea that it is primarily the adolescent male—such as young Luther, Siddhartha, or

Gandhi—who feels that he is entitled to a moratorium in order to go off and rediscover his alone self. As Romain Rolland writes of his young hero in his novel *Jean-Christophe,*

> Free! He felt that he was free! . . . free of others, and of himself! . . . He looked at the wintry sky, the town covered with snow, the people struggling alone past him; he looked about him, into himself; he was no longer bound. He was alone! . . . Alone! How happy to be alone, to be his own! . . . what joy at last, to live, without being the prey of life, to have become his own master![51]

But transformations and resolutions in female adolescence are equally common, as clearly depicted in two novels of youth, Carson McCullers's *The Member of the Wedding* and Muriel Spark's *The Prime of Miss Jean Brodie.* These stories share neither theme, mood, nor purpose, but they both are psychologically true portrayals of female adolescent change and struggles. When Frankie, McCullers's heroine, is struggling with accepting moving on and growing up, her brother's love for his bride, and her own regressive wishes for inclusion as a member of their wedding (by symbolically remaining their child), she faces another death in her family and confronts her own possible end:

> It makes me shiver too, to think about how many dead people I already know. "Seven in all," she said. "And now Uncle Charles." . . . [She] put her fingers in her ears and closed her eyes, but it was not death. She could feel the heat from the store and smell the dinner. She could feel a rumble in her stomach . . . And the dead feel nothing, hear nothing, see nothing—only black. "It would be terrible to be dead."[52]

Unlike Tom Sawyer's viewing his own funeral as a way to glorify himself, Frankie's death fantasies are attempts to reconcile her deep passion to grow up and her tremendous fear of the consequences of loneliness. Moreover, they are a way to gain courage and learn to face dying and possibly a wish to join her dead mother. Her mother's dying in childbirth is also an unchangeable link between sexuality—which she is beginning to experience—and death. McCullers's story resolves fears of facing the alonetime of growing up in a typical pre- and early-adolescent fashion: Frankie—now Frances—finds a same-sex chum.

The Prime of Miss Jean Brodie offers a range of solutions to the crème de la crème of the Marcia Blaine School for Girls, but not before, in fairly typical adolescent style, her students forge a connection between sexuality and death. The reading of Alfred, Lord Tennyson's poem "The Lady of Shalott" induces in them fears that they will cease to be and thoughts of love. Dazzled by the potential love of Lancelot, the Lady of Shalott leaves her steady weaving and alone contentment, and in turning away from the mirror—symbol of alone self-sufficiency—she yields to a gloomy fate. All the girls glorify or run from this myth in their own style, but it is the rather aptly named Sandy Stranger, one of Miss Brodie's students, who faces this battle between alone and relational needs most obviously. Her identification with the mothering Miss Brodie is hardest to resolve, and nothing will destroy this suffocating relationship except estrangement from society. She converts to Catholicism, the religion disdained by her mentor, and actually becomes a nun. Finally, Sandy has the outward bars of the visitors' grille to protect her from herself and sexual longings.

Unprotected adolescent girls' longing to become pregnant is not merely indicative of a failure in family values—whatever that term means. Often, it is the dream of finally receiving requited love or the imagined escape from bondage to one's family by fast achieving womanhood and a family of one's own. Hardly a moratorium in reality, for many girls it still feels like an escape from the old, encumbering ties. Reviewing adolescent behavior[53] showed that not only negative reasons are behind youthful pregnancies. Cultural, developmental, and even positive survival motivations affect some pregnancy decisions in adolescence. Individual differences need to be taken into account, not just statistics.

While the self develops both in alone space and through validation by and experiences with others, heartfelt commitment can arise only from inner dialogue and ultimate conviction free from undue societal pressures and family cruelty and neglect. When the brutality of life takes over, as depicted in such films as *Hoop Dreams* or *Kids*, where (in the first) children are damaged by society's insensitivity or (in the second) are injured by the unruled clique, the self-sufficient adolescent's alone moments are not always restorative. Beaten down by raging against a dispassionate society or misattuned parents, the adolescent faces crises that can be irreparable.

I wonder about the so-called breakdown of family values. In everyday life, significant numbers of people are fighting to make a living and maintain homes. When they fail, does it reflect a collapse of family values, or does it reflect society's inability to come to grips with its own serious flaws? It is only in the twentieth century that culture has been able to lay the blame for all social ills at the parental doorstep. The fact that children and adults escape life through drugs or gambling is not just a family matter, especially considering how selling drugs and operating casinos are big business. Considering interrelationships between parent and child is a step forward, but let us stop sidestepping societal responsibilities. Families have been the mainstay of society. When families succeed, they offer time for alone growth and connectedness, and friends do the same. That leads to a productive population. But equally, since those close to us are most attuned, family members and friends can deliver the most painful blows to a psyche. Respites from close-knit ties can be enhancing, as the biographies of a Paul Gauguin or a W. Somerset Maugham have portrayed. I suggest that society is paying no more than lip service to family values, because everyone knows that we will not be seriously valuing families until we share resources in such a way that shows we hold dear all children and individuals.

The alonetime need identifies our separateness and gives impetus to individuation, but they are not the same process. Alonetime is not a way to escape from bonding. Frequently enough, we find our way back to someone else during alone contemplation and certainly forge commitments, while at the same time we reaffirm an understanding of ourselves. Young adulthood, in Eriksonian terms,[54] is the time of the quest for identity and mature love. I return to the actions of Patrick, the young patient with a history of learning disabilities, in order to illustrate how the obstacles of handicapping circumstances can cause conflict between attachment and alonetime needs and inhibit erotic development as well.

As a youngster, Patrick leaned heavily on others, especially his mother, as alter egos. Although he made constant demands for others' help and company and balked at independent activities, he was frequently rebellious and took needless risks on his own—some leading to destructive outcomes. He admired his mother and feared her disapproval. Nevertheless, from babyhood he was loath to allow her to be affectionate, except when putting him to bed. He was afraid of the dark, but even then he allowed only a perfunctory kiss. Neediness, coupled with rebellious distancing for self-preservation, was going to make it hard for Patrick to feel safe and approach closeness.

On a return visit to an analyst of many years, Patrick said, "Now that I finally finished college and have my own life and girlfriend, I can tell my mother when she comes to see me that I love her and even hug her close to me. Before, when we were living together, before I mastered doing things on my own, I needed her too much."

◆ ◆ ◆

We see, through Patrick's dilemma, that mature love has a better chance when parental ties don't overly bind us. As the great poet Rainer Maria Rilke wrote, "Only in this sense, as the task of working at themselves ('to hearken and to hammer day and night') might young people use the love that is given them." [55]

What Parenting Books Don't Discuss

A group of my graduate students undertook the task of reading the many parenthood books available. They were looking for four topics: (1) mention of infants' and toddlers' need to be alone; (2) the numbers of pages devoted to bonding, attachment, and relationships; (3) the interconnecting of time to be by oneself with time to be engaged; and (4) the importance placed on the caretakers' need for solitude. Most parenthood books, it was found, neglect the idea of time to oneself. Infants are not described as needing time apart—despite behaviors to the contrary. Aloneness receives attention from some authors, but usually in terms of how to avoid separation trauma. In some of the books parents are viewed as requiring time off from the task of parenting, but again this is mentioned in cursory fashion. In contrast, when parents are asked what they most miss in their new role, the answer is swift and straightforward: "Sleep and time to myself." In The Maternal Physician,[56] a book written in the early 1800s by an anonymous American matron, the author questions, "Who but a mother can possibly find interest in a helpless newborn babe to pay it the unwearied, uninterrupted attention[?]" It has been pointed out[57] that it wasn't unusual for seventeenth- and eighteenth-century mothers to seek relief from their duties of child care through family members, older children, or servants. The most radical suggestion for parental relief, especially for poor families, comes from Irish minister, politician, and satirist Jonathan Swift. Disgusted with societal neglect of children, he wrote "A Modest Proposal," in which he advocated that large Irish families sell infants or serve them as meat, and even offered recipes and cooking suggestions. He thought that his satire would shock people from procreating, or at least encourage government to assist in the arduous task of child care. Strangely enough, some, it is said, took him seriously.[58] Even the intense physical labor of housework seems to have afforded more gratifying alonetime than tending to a baby's pressing needs. Caretakers in those years readily doped their babies (and sometimes themselves as well) to increase hours of listlessness and sleep. Alcohol-based medicines were used to treat infant and adult patients alike; patent medicines—"soothing syrups"—contained such ingredients as syrup of white poppies, cordials, paregoric, catnip teas, and morphine, to name a few.[59] Even in the twentieth century, health food stores sell echinacea (with and without alcohol). A father in my parenthood class was warned by his daughter's pediatrician against applying a known folk remedy, gripe water, to her gums or for colic, saying, "One small dose was like serving a child a martini." The current overuse of Ritalin to sedate the controversially diagnosed hyperactive child could very well be a continuation of an age-old cry of distraught parents: "Keep out of my hair!"

The unrealistic expectations born from emphasis on attachment and relationships in turn make us lose respect for parents who fail to fulfill us and for lovers who do not answer our romantic dreams. Sometimes customs of the past rescue a child from such a difficult family situation.

> For my teaching fellow Edi, learning self-reliance and solitude replaced traditional family life. Her parents decided to divorce when she was eleven. Her mother was continuing in medical school, and they decided that a boarding school would be the solution for their children. From Edi's perspective it was a saving grace. North Country School had and has strong values—values of individual strength, love of nature, responsibility, hard work. Pain in separating from family occurred, but the school's message and structure offered its own balm. Edi especially remembers the ability to sign out a pair of skis and cross-country ski across the property. Without the experience of long walks alone, she believes, she would never be her contemplative, thoughtful self. Her creativity was born in her solitude, as was her resiliency.[60]

◆   ◆   ◆

Cultures change in their definition of "child" and of who are most in need of protection, but every society projects some image of childhood and old age, their nature and duration. Popular notions of correct parent-child interactions flourish only temporarily, just like the tools considered necessary to raise a child. According to Karin Lee Fishbeck Calvert's study of the artifacts of early childhood from the colonial era to the early twentieth century, "Visually no child-related objects have remained in continuous use in America."[61] By looking at changing designs in children's furniture, we can see interesting shifts in how parents conceived of children's attachment and aloneness needs, their ability to move, and moral standards: "Most children's furniture of the seventeenth century was designed to stand babies up and propel them forward, whereas most nineteenth century furniture was meant to hold infants down and contain them in one spot."[62] Very few objects before the mid–eighteenth century were designed for child use. Mainly, they were geared toward physical correction, such as the stand-up and walking stools that forced children to stand up straight and walk erect. The goal was uprightness in body and, consequently, in mind. The furniture of the mid–nineteenth century —crib, swing carriage, and high chair—promoted barriers between the worlds of child and adult. Ultimately they contain and restrain the child. Whereas self-sufficiency was once anticipated, now children are thought to need more protection and prolonged innocence. Car seats, Snuglis, backpacks, and movable feeding chairs are in vogue today.

This chapter has afforded another opportunity to capture the need for alonetime throughout development, but especially in infancy, toddlerhood, and the middle and adolescent years of childhood. Even though time alone contributes to a child's growth and development, children are the least likely to voice their need. Undisguised fears of aloneness pose an obstacle, while the equal dread of engulfment is masked for children in the form of witches, giants, Darth Vaders, and mean stepparents. The very best children's fiction captures the alone spirit in all of us. I began this chapter with a writer who understood alonetime. I conclude with the vision of another such tale spinner, Dr. Seuss, and this time thoughts are geared equally to us as adults. He did not shy away from the idea of being on his own or having to decide where he was going in life. In his poem "Oh, The Places You'll Go!" the things he warns against are not confusion, loneliness, being alone a lot, feeling scared, or foul weather. Only playing a waiting game, being stuck in one spot, is to be totally avoided. He instructs us all to take brave, lone steps, albeit carefully, for "Life's a Great Balancing Act."[63]

Reconstructing alonetime makes the balancing act less precarious.

PART THREE

The Reconstruction

of Alonetime

CHAPTER 8

Trances, Computers, and

Private Spaces

From the earliest glimmering of human consciousness we find an introvert view of life accompanying and complementing this extrovert view.

Aristotle's definition of man as a "social animal" is not sufficiently comprehensive.

ERNST CASSIRER, *An Essay on Man*[1]

Maybe it was not this summer when I first heard the voices, but I think it was, because I know it was before I played with bows and arrows or rode a horse (4 years old), and I was out playing alone when I heard them. It was like somebody calling me, and I thought it was my mother but there was nobody there. This happened more than once and always made me afraid, so that I ran home.

JOHN GNEISENAU NEIHARDT, *Black Elk Speaks*[2]

M Y CALLING CAME at a relatively young age—thirteen—in Miss Cameron's English literature class at Erasmus Hall High School. Never one to volunteer answers, I surprised myself by literally jumping from my seat and furiously waving my hand to announce what motivated Hamlet to hate his uncle and reject his mother and Ophelia. No academic question had ever excited me to that degree. In the passion of that response lay my future profession, even though to me, at the time, the field that explored the whys of human nature had no name. At fifteen, my world widened when a psychoanalyst cousin came to live with my mother and me.[3] On long walks together, my didactic training began. Later, when I attended college as an undergraduate, I was deter-

[167]

mined to enter the field of psychology. But the empirical study of psychology did not fully address my burning questions about motivation. For instance, what made people who hungered for love and affection behave so often in such distancing, even alienating, ways? At first opportunity, in search for the influences of biology and the environs on humankind, I chose a split minor in physiology and anthropology. With that change, I was following my calling, a desire to know what motivates people.

For someone with a wish to understand human motivation, anthropology proved more inspirational than undergraduate psychology courses. The adventures of Ruth Benedict and Margaret Mead, for example, made vivid an interplay between personality and culture, as here, too, were explanations of behavior. Being a mother as well as a college student, I had ideas on what created emotionally healthy children. It seemed odd, although plausible, that there were remarkable differences in how children were raised across the globe. Through thinking anthropologically and psychologically, I was drawn to questions about human choices in parenting, as each field complements the other in addressing these concerns. Both give us clues to our past and present, albeit in varying ways. Therefore, by examining alonetime's roots and contours in various cultures, we discover that not only is it universally apparent as a deep-seated motivation, but so is the clever adaptiveness of human nature in satisfying a basic want. In this vein, I see our society's far-reaching and witty embrace of the computer and the Internet as our modern way to fulfill needs to explore being alone and interrelating.

Sometime in college I first observed that many societies that emphasized close-knit family patterns also provided built-in loopholes that offered individual escape, acceptable ways to dissociate from society. Of course, ritualized times for alone moments in meditation existed, but what about times of solo pleasure in the midst of others, such as in tai chi, trance practices, or spaces for uninterrupted gazing? Western travelers to Japan in particular are impressed by the niches set aside in public spaces, such as shopping malls, in which individuals sit and stare. Clarissa Pinkola Estes[4] looks at ritual as a way to gain perspective on life and provide transitions between unlike but equally important activities. Alonetime and together time require smooth segues in order to avoid conflict. In this context, the image of Margaret Mead's extraordinary photographic journey with Ken Heyman, *Family*,[5] comes to mind. Within this book on relationships she made room for the child alone, quoting from Walt Whitman's poem "There Was a Child Went Forth":

There was a child went forth every day,
And the first object he look'd upon,
    that object he became,
And that object became part of him
    for the day or a certain part of the day,
Or for many years or stretching cycles of years.[6]

Cultures press their offerings on the young, as Whitman knew so well. Nevertheless, children in large part determine which adopted rituals they absorb and then what will become part of them. We hesitate to embrace rituals today, yet we find comfort in remembering the childhood routines for bedtime, cleanup time, and dressing for school. Whether in short, simple ceremony or in more complex traditions and structures, avenues to an aloneness experience are visible even in the midst of social contact.

In the high-ceilinged catacombs of the Museum of Natural History in New York, I invariably find a separate corner in which to contemplate. Architecture critic Paul Goldberger quotes Luis Barragan who says that "all architecture which does not express serenity fails in its spiritual mission."[7] At the turn of the century, the Western world's grand and ornate public architecture offered nooks and crannies for private thought. One day in the inspiring museum I asked, Would I see evidence of psychological and physical space in the give-and-take of people and culture, as I believe that both psychic and external space contribute satisfaction to the individual need to be alone? Is this a question that can be answered, given the theoretical debates within anthropology today on whether universals of human nature are visible cross-culturally? And what if a culture blocks expression of the alone need? I had to look into ills of culture and the individual in order to reconceptualize alonetime. I would think back to Hamlet, who, brooding about his destiny and cultural pressures, gave himself too much solitude.

Then, too, a fair amount of attention is given to what the infamous Unabomber called the "social and psychological problems of modern society." What viewpoints explain this and other grievances against technology? Journalist Richard Wright puts his finger on some of the problems, saying that at times we "get the feeling that modern life isn't what we were designed for."[8] But after acknowledgment of contemporary confusion and the rapidity of change, Mr. Wright and I quickly part company. He states that humans neither have evolved nor were designed for life in the jarring concrete jungle. Citing evolutionary psychologists' "mismatch" theory, he uses the example of hunting-and-gathering societies as our "original," and thus rightful, environment, advocating that once upon a time we *all* lived happily and socially. Isn't it dangerous, though—and perhaps impossible—to extrapolate psychologically from prehistoric times? Moreover, if we do that, then we must also consider our nomadic ancestry, in which individuals had periods of isolation. The ordeals of wandering interfere with connections to places and persons. In the film *The Gods Must Be Crazy,* the !Kung seemed an idyllic people living in a preindustrial innocence devoid of street crime, bureaucracy, technological glut, and Coca-Cola. But actually the !Kung and other Bushman tribes, no longer truly isolated, are not an exact replica of past societies. They were *relegated* to a dry area of their territory because their freed lands were put to other use.[9] Countless visitors studying them have had an influence as well. We cannot assume that so-called more primitive societies have it better or are closer to a more satisfying existence. Hunting-and-gathering societies are not pure models for brotherly love, and we shall see that within the tight interpersonal networks a private escape is possible in a variety of ways, including trance rituals.

Certainly, attention needs to be paid to the changes arising from the technological tailspin. Before we all don fig leaves or leopard skins, however, and commit ourselves to the belief that our ancestors enjoyed fulfilling bonds of neighborly interdependence, we will need to take a closer look at the evidence. Can it be true that those who live outside of the communication superhighway avoid burnout? While evolutionary biologists might deflect Freud's viewpoint that the restraint on sexual and aggressive drives is the principal cause of neurosis in life,[10] I equally dispute any portrayal of humans as totally innocent bystanders in the race toward computer heaven. Without a doubt, cultural traditions and social practices regulate and perhaps even transform the human psyche, the result being mental and emotional cross-cultural diversity. Equally significant, however, is that culture and individual "are interdependent; neither side . . . can be defined without borrowing from the specifications of the other."[11] Technology may swing a baton that possibly leads in a march toward overload. If so, we need to know why so many of us willingly join the parade.

Moreover, it is the pace of change more than the type of changes that could be overwhelming, even blinding. Notwithstanding a readiness to try anything, including the sci-fi brave-new-world approach, our systems may not entirely be keeping up with the assaults of perpetual change. As did Charlie Chaplin in his parody of modernization and mechanization, *Modern Times,* I, too, wonder about our information glut. In the classic silent film, Charlie Chaplin's "modern" man runs around in circles tightening screws and bolting bolts in mad precision. Even lunchtime has him chomping on ever-rotating corncobs. Today, Chaplin's postmodern equivalent punches the keyboard, moves from chat room to E-mail to game screen, and sails into virtual reality with an earnestness that can cause equal delirium. Ultimately, how will culture and the individual be sustained amidst the additional stimulations of faxes, cellular phones, interactive TVs, and computer networks—with temperance, or with frenzy? I anticipate adjustment, since people are so adaptable. But are the adjustments occurring within awareness and in people's best interests? Already psychologists and others are labeling a new neurosis—Internet addiction.[12]

Stephen Jay Gould points out that, in the hundreds of thousands of years of planet history, the human species has jumped from a few groups of individuals using stone and then iron implements to billions with cars, airplanes, cities, satellites, frozen foods, nuclear families, and computers —all without significant genetic changes.[13] The chameleonlike nature of the human species confirms my belief that evidence of the dual needs for bonding and aloneness manifests itself in varied ways in societies and individuals.

Alonetime's Place in Egocentric and Sociocentric Societies

Broadly speaking, recognizing these are comparative rather than absolute differences,[14] the relation between the individual and society can be divided into two categories—egocentric and sociocentric. In sociocentric societies, group and individual roles and rights are apportioned interdependently. The egocentric society, in contrast, places greatest value on a personalized self. Both types of culture make room for alonetime.

If one glances at the friendly and very socialized people of some cultures—for example, the sociocentric agricultural society of Bali—the quick thought is that in their communal way of life, no universal need for alonetime exists.[15] According to one anthropologist, the idea of Balinese people as contented in their ritualized powerlessness is misleading. Hidden behind happy facades are jarring fears of malevolent spirits. A strong hope among the people is for a special spiritual power, *sakti*—a force that can prevent anyone from harming you. *Sakti* gives one the ability to secure an enveloping safety.[16] Then, too, visitors who stay in Bali awhile comment on the artistic nature[17] of each individual, the regularity of dance, including that of trance dancing, and then on inhabitants who at least twice a day enter alone, for the most part, into their private chapels to meditate and pray. In these small "churches" connected to homes, people offer tokens to their god. "What do you ask for?" a colleague of mine questioned during her stay. The man she witnessed repeatedly visiting his shrine replied: "I don't ask for. I mostly just sit there and think my thoughts."

Sociocentric societies subordinate individual interests to the good of the group and do not conceive of looking at an inner person in order to explain human behavior, because often they do not believe that person exists. Nevertheless, in nations such as India where the familial self is emphasized, social privacy limited, and a competitive individualism severely frowned upon, great importance is also placed on a "richly developed inner world of feelings, thoughts, and fantasies, and an unusual ability to create an inner private space."[18] Let us not forget that monastic practices, probably, and Buddhism had their origins in that nation.

Privacy, according to most anthropologists, is a Western anomaly. Despite the previous examples, in some sociocentric cultures, the idea of a room to oneself is unlikely. From early on the young are subject to constant intrusions of personal space. In the summer of 1995, my son Gary, an archaeologist,[19] wrote me a letter from Oaxaca, Mexico:

> Mom, I was thinking this week about your book topic. The Oaxacans (at least in the village) have a rather different view of aloneness and privacy. For example, at Rinaldo's [his Mexican helper and friend] seven people (he, his wife, their two sons, their wives, and grandmother) share a single house lot with one bathroom and one shower area. Other people (grandchildren, people who work in the family's weaving compound, etc.) are constantly wandering in and out as well. Rinaldo has a relatively ample house lot with several rooms, but it is not uncommon to see 5–6 people crammed into single room house lots. Yet, to close one's door is almost insulting to others. It seems that people rarely have any privacy or are alone. Pablo's [another worker and friend] wife says that they do not like to be alone, and even when people go to Mitla or to the fields, they generally go with someone else.
>
> An American friend of ours, who lives in Oaxaca and heads a teenage exchange program between Oaxaca and Ontario, told us of a Oaxacan boy who went to Canada. His host was a Canadian boy and his mother. Each person had his or her own room, and the Canadians would frequently close their doors

for privacy. As the story was told, the Oaxaca lad was socially miserable there, as he was used to much greater interaction.

At times, though, you do see farmers, shepherds, hunters, young boys, old men or even old women walking far to the community store, taking goats to pasture or ambling alone in the fields or woods. Interestingly as well is that in Mitla, a bigger and slightly more "cosmopolitan" town than where Rinaldo lives, I am beginning to see a handful of solitary joggers in the morning when we drive off to the field. I am not sure what this means?

In answer to the last question, Gary is observing rules of privacy changing in parallel to the growing economy. One aspect of alonetime depends on obtaining privacy from others. But in certain centuries and different cultures where neither the individual nor the private self is overtly recognized, we can still find evidence in living space for private and social needs historically and culturally. In his book *Home,* Canadian professor of architecture Witold Rybczynski briefly charts the role of privacy.[20] He believes that what we consider privacy was unknown until the 1600s. Others argue that well-to-do people have always provided themselves with unused space, small private rooms and side chambers.[21] Often the Hispanic house, while open to family, is closed to neighbors. Built around a patio, it can be hidden from outsiders behind a wall. In Mexico and Spain, I have seen people waiting interminably for entry through the gate of a walled home. Compare this to a suburban neighbor dropping by to borrow a cup of sugar. But I have to agree with Rybczynski that privacy took on different meanings in earlier times. In the ancient city of Ephesus, for instance, I viewed a lineup of marble keyhole-shaped privies that men seemingly unself-consciously used side by side.

Rybczynski helps us to understand the change from confined living, especially for the poor, to the expectations of privacy in the modern Western world. Certainly, in thinking about the public homes of medieval times, we must also remember that family life and its intimacy (as we know it) were uncommon. Children were not sentimentalized and frequently sent away to work by age seven. Homes, as compared to the hovels of the very poor, served to entertain, transact business, and house the immediate family, which included employees, servants, apprentices, friends, and protégés—all in one or two rooms. Only hermits and scholars had the luxury of solitude—so, perhaps here is another reason for the popularity of monasteries in the Middle Ages.

People of the Middle Ages—insulated like Rinaldo's family—were unaware of separate living and did not consciously miss it. Gary would say, however, that the intimate family of Mexican life is very different from the impersonal closeness of medieval parent-child relationships. How, then, is the balance between alonetime and connection played out in Oaxaca or similar rural communities? Individuals in these communities gain great satisfaction from intense family connections, but also have long stretches of sleep to compensate. Even so, the price of this compromise seems far too high—diminished curiosity and exploratory activity, and a loss of reflective solitude.

Just because people have the need to be alone, it doesn't mean that family custom and tradition will not infringe on that need. A Mexican woman, when visiting Gary and Linda in their modest three-room rented space, asked, "Aren't you afraid, solo in these big rooms?" She associated the space with sadness. Little wonder the Mexican woman was afraid.[22] According to Octavio Paz, the Nobel Prize–winning author who understood Mexican culture from its very core, women have submitted to the culture and become open and vulnerable at all times: "The Spanish attitude toward women is very simple. It is expressed quite brutally and concisely . . . woman's place is in the home, with a broken leg? . . . Or, to put it more exactly, she is an incarnation of the life force, which is essentially impersonal. Thus it is impossible for her to have a personal, private life."[23]

Mexican men, on the other hand, he sees as lost in their solitude—not necessarily a solitude that includes hope and that is part of a greater whole and harmony, but one more akin to the ubiquitous solitude portrayed brilliantly in the breathtaking writing of Gabriel García Marquez.[24] This particular solitude is isolating and distancing and constitutes a fortress despite the mask of sociability. Paz says, "The Mexican *macho*—the male—is a hermetic being, closed up in himself, capable of guarding both himself and whatever has been confided to him."[25] Paz explores the many faces of solitude—for good and evil. His descriptions of the place of the family in Mexico and in society's protection of the family clear up some of the mysteries of alonetime implicit in Gary's letter: "Society denies the nature of love by conceiving of it as a stable unit whose purpose [through marriage] is to beget and raise children . . . with no other object but the reproducing of that same society."[26] Modern society, he continues, defeats love by ignoring the need for solitude. The cry for constant intimacy in relationships often closes rather than breeds connections that, after all, can arise only from contradiction, exceptions, and the oneness of opposites.

On a more everyday level, I explored with Gary the ways in which Mexican people compensate for their unfulfilled alonetime needs. Gary, having spent more than eleven summers in Oaxaca, assured me the rural people are outwardly happy, with few expectations—TV had not yet influenced the community. Nor are there cars, indoor plumbing, or running water. Despite lack of privacy, they have long hours of darkness and rest. Moreover, few feel pressure to achieve intellectually or even much desire to explore new terrain. Creative bursts and adventuresome urges that spring from solo contemplation are not part of their personality. Life moves at a leisurely pace.

Discussing Gary's letter with Juan, a Hispanic psychologist, uncovered boundaries: "But," he told me, "I know from my family and friends whom I visit in rural communities that when they are engaged in a task they are totally absorbed and oblivious to all else around them. In work they do not allow themselves to be intruded upon." My Peruvian friend Lee used to laugh at her grandmother, who emphatically said, "I am the kitchen." This reminded me of my own grandmother, who when baking became totally lost in the task. Even beloved grandchildren intruding in this reverie were scolded. Gary also makes note of alonetimes, beyond siestas and early bedtimes:

> Rinaldo's family are Adventists and both men and women spend a large amount of time in church praying. They also go to sleep very early as there is little inside light. Maybe they are in bed by eight or nine o'clock and on average don't arise until six in the morning. Among the men who are not Adventists there is a lot of drinking. Distilled cactus juice (Mescal) is popular in the rural villages. It is not uncommon to find men on the street dead drunk. They are not thought of as bums derogatorily. They may have just sold something and they probably will drink up half their money and stay drunk for a couple of days before going back to their family. Perhaps, mom, fiestas and rituals like the Day of the Dead incorporate a cult of life and death that displays these dual longings.

We can get fooled by descriptions that in a blanket way compare egocentric and sociocentric societies. Cassirer aptly describes an ebb and flow within cultures regarding needs related to individual growth and the preservation of the society as a whole.[27] At all stages of culture, he sees in human nature both the force of tribal custom (sociocentric) and a self-empowering and liberating impetus (egocentric). It is the egocentric side of humankind that results in most creative expression. Recent findings of magnificent cave paintings bring to mind that as long ago as the Ice Age people had the liberating impetus to produce art, which suggests that people even then were seeking creative expression. The finest Paleolithic art showed a perceptiveness of observation that rivals all achieved since. Animals are the typical subjects, but human forms and abstract designs were also depicted. The breathtaking compositions, especially those at the newly found Chauvet cave and well-known Lascaux caves in France, are thought to have symbolic value. Ian Tattersall—curator of the American Museum of Natural History, geologist, and anthropologist —hypothesizes on the human spirit behind Ice Age art:

> We can only guess at the exact motivations that impelled Upper Paleolithic artists to penetrate into pitch-dark dangerous and uncomfortable recesses deep within the earth by the light of flickering lamps made from juniper wicks stuck into lumps of animal fat, but we can be sure that they were profound and powerful indeed.[28]

The discovery of the power to paint decoratively goes back forty thousand years. Cave art is about twelve thousand to twenty thousand years old. It seems that art, as well as music and notation, is not a recent development in human history. Instead they are all part and parcel of what is meant by being behaviorally fully human, and this unifying factor seems to capture the breadth of the human spirit. Anthony Storr, however, who has written extensively on solitude as essential to creativity, sees cave paintings as more an expression of a group enterprise and rote human behavior than an individual endeavor. In contrast, I see cave paintings as similar to music and mathematics in their role in ancient times. All share pathways that satisfy an appetite: "Now Man could be awed not only by the moving, menacing mammoths, humpbacked bison, reindeer, and wild pig (external images). He had the power to awe himself by . . . his newly discovered power as creator."[29] These early visionaries are not all that different from Einstein, Mozart, or Picasso in exploring their feelings and thoughts and laying them before others. Faith in one's alone thoughts and feelings leads to astounding creations. I believe that cave paintings are expressive of the inner being's dignity, whether or not that expression represents a well-formulated self. From personal experiences of painting in a group setting, I have found the act of drawing and painting to be an individual enterprise that leaves enormous latitude for solo flight and images from inner egocentric space.

Altered States of Consciousness: Seeking Alonetimes

Indeed, there are many spaces in culture that are not cognitively, logically, or verbally dominated. A case in point is an altered state of consciousness. Many of these are trance behaviors, a person's way of gaining separateness. The universality of altered states of consciousness is understandable not only from the perspective of a consciousness born from sensory experiences, but also from the need to maintain balance between an over- and understimulating sensory world. Altered states of consciousness produced by both increases and decreases in stimulation can result in heightened alertness and activity or the opposite. They modify the individual in relation to self and other, the inner and the outer environments. The altered state may be "up" or "down," and the contradictory aims often reflect emotional regulation of pleasure or pain, excitement or calm, connectedness or disengagement.

Altered states of consciousness, intuitively familiar but virtually unstudied, exploded into Western awareness in the 1960s as fallout from the drug revolution and attraction to meditative practices. Cultural adoption of altered states—whether induced by group hypnosis, music, medicines, isolation, fasting, or charismatic leadership—is interpreted as anything from ritualized pathology to institutionalized religion. Proselytizers of the New Age said: "This is the zenith of experience." Others witnessed terrible consequences, even addictions, and said: "This is the nadir of despair." With us from birth, altered states are everyday occurrences, including the free-associative, partially conscious (hypnagogic) dream states, reading, and watching TV. They are incorporated into innumerable religious, magical, and healing philosophies that even are translated into modern techniques, as in Harvard professor of medicine Herbert Benson's "relaxation response," biofeedback, and, of course, alternative medicine.

A scientifically primed society such as ours may not take kindly to healing rituals grounded in fundamental, non-medicine-based alonetime impressions. Yet certain altered states seem a direct link to that earliest sensory state of aloneness in the womb, whether in their cocooning of individuals in the midst of others or in their allowing a person to drift into a private world despite what is happening all around. Similarly, because ritualistic chants and music, like repetitive environmental sounds outside the womb, are absorbed without conscious notations, the distant past and present are reunited.

When cultural anthropologist Marjorie Shostak lived for two years among the !Kung, she noticed that during dry periods, small economically self-sufficient groups begin to band together for as long as three to five months around a permanent spring, and wrote: "The large aggregations of people that result—sometimes more than two hundred—intensify the ritual life of the community as well as the social life of individuals. Trance dances occur more frequently (up to two or three times a week)."[30] In other words, when tribes are forced to live in unusually close proximity, compensatory behaviors ensue that offer relief, in this case the disengagement of going into a trance state.

Tribes, mainly sociocentric cultures, create customs and rituals that allow for both socially removed and connected behaviors, which suggests an innate necessity for counterbalance of the two needs. In cultures that promote freedom of choice, the ways are typically not ritualized. Yet, as the social life of the !Kung presses on them, modern life is crowding us. Maybe that is why almost all the technological inventions for pleasure, beginning with the automobile and the radio, offer individual reverie— because we have no other prescribed way to escape from the masses.

I began to wonder about the escalating marketability of products like Walkmans and Nintendos in the last twenty years. A friend of mine wishes he could be lost in the woods with a cellular phone; that way, there could be utter silence with the opportunity to connect if he so desired. Manufacturers capitalize on unrequited needs. Commercials might picture people watching television together. In reality, in many families children have rooms with their own TV set. These gadgets for zoning out, however, backfire as they do not automatically allow for productive or satisfying alonetime any more than they promote intimacy. Most tend to be quite stimulating in their own right, which further cultivates the need for the protective elements of alonetime to kick in. A neurosurgeon told me that after a hectic day he tuned into TV to achieve some respite. He watched one of the magazine news shows and spent hours attempting to fall asleep, overstimulated by the subject matter.

Jennifer, a young patient, has five hours of homework every night after prep school. Saturday nights, she attends house dances—her means of escape. She tried to explain what house music is. The idea eluded me until, strolling on a busy boardwalk at Baltimore's Inner Harbor, I found a vivid illustration and the final clue needed to think through the connections between trance, altered states, the technological blitz, and alonetime. The pavement was alive with boom boxes playing loud music, and a young man began to gyrate to the sounds. Every part of his body moved in synchrony. His small group of older friends chanted, "Go, Melvin. Go, Melvin. Make yourself busy, make yourself busy. Go, Melvin. Go, Melvin. Make yourself dizzy, make yourself dizzy." Melvin was danc-ing himself into a trance. His eyes glazed over, his movements quickened; he was down on the floor and quickly up again, pulling the reins of an imaginary horse, cantering, turning around. At first Melvin followed the instructions of the chanters, but before long he was in his own world, setting the pace, choosing his moves, until he collapsed in exhaustion. Trance dancing is a favorite type of house music and in Melvin it had a captive. The role of trance dancing in our culture is minor compared to the fact that 90 percent of 488 societies studied cross-culturally have ingrained forms of altered states of consciousness.[31] Trance behavior is one of the extreme versions of this. "The potential for trance which, in any case, includes a broad and ill-defined range of behavioral changes, may be said safely to be biologically inherent, or 'natural' in humans."[32]

If we attempt to understand the meanings of trance behavior—the symbols conveyed, the conventions behind it, the significance of it—in connection to our society, then we may be at "cultural zero."[33] If, how-ever, we look at spiritual possession as a commonplace way to be both engaged and disengaged from one's social connections and conventions —if we look at the process of trance—then we can entertain it as among the clever ways devised to regulate the individual's role in society and the cultural position held for alonetime and attachment. Though faith healing, some evangelistic practices, and the mass trembling at a Shaker meeting relate to trance as altered states, none have been incorporated into our general culture, perhaps because even industrialized societies automatically provided space and undiluted time in the past. We shall discover, after we delve into trance society, that now it is the computer— with its own steady beats—that is mesmerizing and transforming us.

In the well-structured Mayotte society, spirits are said to rise precisely in order to change and influence interactions with people. Let us picture this tiny island, 250 kilometers from the northwest coast of Madagascar in the Indian Ocean. The Comoro archipelago, of which this is the south-ernmost island, is off the mainland of East Africa. Varied languages and cultures intermingle. Despite intermarriage and bilingualism, social unity is maintained by the Islamic religion and by island loyalty. These were the conditions at the time of an intense study in the 1970s of a people who for centuries maintained trance behavior.[34]

Women can own property in this dynamic society, and often have equal control with husbands over crops. In return for sexual favors, they receive money and goods. Women are free to make friends outside of the marriage and maintain cash income independently, yet their authority is limited—they usually cannot control the budget, expect public power, or obtain any position of leadership. Islam further weakens women's authority and control. Thus, women resent male privilege. In turn, most spiritual ghosts in this country are male, and more females fall into trance.

The spirits are not part of the Islamic religion; in fact, they must be kept apart from religious ritual. Spirits are, like humans, created by God, but their powers at times exceed those of mortals. On any given day, a person may awake in the night no longer familiar to friends and family, transformed in character and possessed by a spirit who will still manage to eat, sleep, calculate, and learn like other humans. Taken for granted by the society, the spirit replaces the person and instead talks, dances, emotes, quarrels or cooperates, remains sullen, or thrashes about in a new way. When these Jekylls turn into Hydes, or, more surprisingly, when Lois Lanes turn into Supermen, responsive individuals join and go in and out of trance as well. Although not worshiped, the spirit moves people from their sociocentric focus to a new and separate plane. Actually a transformation of regular society, spirit society touches most inhabitants one way or another.

Spirit belief is not a manifestation of pathology. At times, it seems a self-possessed ritual of abandon, a medium used to exert power and assert ownership. Specialists who have studied cultures in order to test whether visionary and pathological states are comparable find important distinctions between the two states. Invariably such societies, with separate words for the insane, note that in contrast to the psychotic person, the shamans and the visionaries show control.[35] The spirits serve as a *model* for how not to behave socially. In fact, inappropriate, abnormal thinking or acting is constrained. For example, if the possessed would be likely to expose herself, someone will step forward to hold her skirts down.

In general, trances provide a medium for expression of the idiosyncratic. Spirits seem to function in societies that highly structure human relationships, breaking down sociocentric codes. To achieve these aims, some cultures rely solely on chemical substances; others use masks, seclusion, and the reversal of established role relations. Mayotte trance behavior is supported only in part by these means. Trance behavior is equivalent to any number of private retreats that provide a way to break conventions and relieve tensions. Seen in this light, metaphysical practices provide measures for individuals to gain distance from sociocentric tribal structure. Vodun (or vodoun), the ancient religion of West Africa, which includes the rites of trance, teaches "that one must take time to sit quietly rather than rush through life."[36]

Levels of Awareness

An altered state is a different level of awareness. Permutations of awareness and lack of awareness are associated to being alone or relating, altered or unaltered consciousness. For example, one can be inwardly and outwardly aware in meditation, or outwardly aware and inwardly self-absorbed in heated conversation. One can also be oblivious when lost in a lover's arms or in a trance. Obviously, even in dreaming (an altered state) there is some consciousness. How else would one remember dreams? Awareness of and intentional attunement with another, alert mutual gaze, and keenness of purpose are considered unaltered states of consciousness. Newborns are capable of a wonderful E.T.-like focused gaze, and, of course, they are also known for the faraway stare.

Princeton psychologist Julian Jaynes's depiction of the bicameral mind and consciousness as a relatively recent behavior of our species may be illuminating. I am struck by his idea that modern human minds are vestigial glimpses of the way things were, neurologically speaking. He portrays illusion, hallucination, and even imagination as remnants from an evolutionary past way of action and reaction. In a review of several books by eminent Swiss psychologist Jean Piaget, who also concerned himself with unconscious actions,[37] I cited Jaynes's brilliant thesis because I agree that a good deal of what people do is done outside of awareness. Learning and even reasoning may prevail outside of conscious experience. To me (unlike Jaynes), however, a shifting awareness as well as visions and trances are not mere traces from early man's split mind. Like any powerful computer, our brain processes a lot of information without constant screening. This pattern of processing probably occurs even in the early prenatal and postnatal alone state. Piaget has documented such functioning in toddlers. In different ways throughout development we reenact metaphorically that most alone of private places (the womb), in which we first gain precision in privacy and establish learning patterns, while reestablishing and reenergizing ourselves.

"Spacing out" seems a natural state, if we recall the baby's peaceful blank gaze. Have you ever observed toddlers suddenly leave the flow of action and, by temporarily entering their imaginary world, turn inward?

Or have you seen youngsters watching TV? You can pass something briefly in front of their eyes and they'll not blink or notice. They are entranced. Similarly, in day-to-day life, people space out while driving cars, walking, listening to music, and punching computer keyboards. People often say, "I thought I'd just check my E-mail, but it was four hours later when I turned the darned thing off." The way in which the computer eats time surprises us all. Colleagues routinely ask, "What does this immersion signal?" To me, this clinging to a computer (as cultural artifact) is a disguised attempt to balance needs for bonding and alonetime.

The Computer "Trance"

Are we just now becoming like trance societies, routinely using the computer and sometimes TV to find alonetime without realizing the unfulfilled alone need? However, the explorer of the Internet, tuned in to electronic information, is inundated with knowledge, and he or she is never completely freed from the world. I believe that this generation is becoming more and more incapable of living in the moment or losing itself (without the aid of drugs), except in technological time outs like the computer, which fluctuate between alone and invasive interludes.

Computer immersion, as in the behavior of the computer nerd, began as a quirky way of breaking from society. Now losing oneself in the computer is commonplace as Web site ways to waste time become increasingly inviting. What can be expected when virtual reality comes completely on board and we take lunch breaks on some island paradise? However, given the predilection in our society to embrace an abstract vision of mental health as the norm, an important group of doctors has included those who day and night are hunched over their computers in a list of oddballs suffering from subthreshold disorders.[38] Whether this behavior is a mild form of a mental problem or not depends a good deal upon whether the person literally suffers from such conditions and how society tolerates these deviations. But given the sheer numbers of people who play endless games on the computer and interconnect around the clock with their PC, the craze is hardly limited to those with personality problems.

I am not the first to argue that a variety of altered states of consciousness may be ubiquitous expressions of one underlying process.[39] In our society, where high activity and even hyperactivity seem typical, people either look for ways to escape domination from overstimulation or grasp ways to stimulate themselves in order to keep up with the crowd. While hardly blaming all social ills on our lack of alonetime, I agree with Jaynes that we are paying the price for the current frenetic demands in today's culture through being unwittingly led by technology into stupors. We are confused over whether to become more inwardly or more outwardly directed. In societies such as the United States in which people lead crowded lives, always on call, I see confusion and frantic methods for avoidance emerging. The guilt factor contributes as well, prompting professionals to add to already overcrowded schedules. Ritualized means to deflect the invasion of private time do not exist, and so people become helpless in the face of all the choices when insufficient time is given to pondering and reflecting. A narcissistic stance may be a cry for help out of the dilemma that our rich and overstocked culture presents. Our senses are overwhelmed, deafened and dumbfounded, by abundance and a flooded open market. As sociologist and social commentator Anthony Giddens states, "In a post-traditional order . . . an indefinite range of possibilities present themselves not just in respect to options for behavior, but in respect also of the 'openness of the world' to the individual."[40]

The idea of computer cyberspace—the ability to push a button and tune out—worries media expert Neil Postman because he sees on the horizon an end to direct social contact. If we are embracing some new technology, says Postman, we need to ask the question "What problem is this solving?" Computer life *is*, I believe, an attempt to solve a problem. It tries to address the problem of balancing our social needs with our alonetime needs in a culture that no longer provides wilderness (even national parks are overcrowded), stretches of time, or long distances separating people and events. Unfortunately, if we are not aware of why computer technology is attracting us, we cannot use it to our best advantage. Even Alvin and Heidi Toffler,[41] in their enthusiasm for the great technological revolution of modern times—the Third Wave—recognize that individuals are engaged in a superstruggle, an attempt to make sense of the outpouring of stimulation from every direction of their lives. Progress, according to the Tofflers, should not be measured in terms of technology or material standards of living. An advanced society must be morally, esthetically, politically, and environmentally sound. Otherwise, despite riches or being technically sophisticated, it has not made progress.

A catch-22 of the lack of alonetime is that, without it, people do not have the opportunity to recognize missing time alone or to think through philosophical dilemmas. Futurists like the Tofflers are recognizing an urgency in providing time for needs equal to those for stimulation, goods, and interconnection. All people require a lot of time to step back, not as a cure-all but because the requirement is part of human nature. Can we pause to appreciate the internal price we may be paying in leaping into the technological fray or holding back? Ever alert to change, the Tofflers state that the emerging society brings with it a new "psycho-sphere that will ultimately alter our character."[42] If this evolution is happening, might we not be better prepared by knowing about a fundamental need that, when honored, guards against sensory bombardment? I think that this need is being hastily usurped by our automatic overimmersion in computer use or by more self-destructive means for spacing out, such as alcohol or drug use. With awareness, however, the new technologies could be less threatening and reemployed to greater advantage. We will return at the end of this chapter to the computer as technoculture's solution to our dual needs after achieving a better understanding of cultural ills.

One Thing or Another — Each Culture Has Its Own Price

Is mental illness less prevalent in less technologically sophisticated societies? If technology is the real reason behind our alienation and emotional distress, because we are unable to adapt to a high-tech world, then it would not be an imbalance between alone and connected time that should be society's concern. Rather, we should immediately halt technological advances, as the Unabomber tried to warn us. However, according to what we know about mental health, this is not the case. In hunter-gatherer villages and societies that exist without the social isolation that industrialization brings, some suggest there was and is zero mental illness, almost no anxiety, and total lack of depression. On two counts this is not entirely true. First, it is important to note more than a tad of evidence of aggression and warfare recorded in the bones of our forefathers and that every culture has names for syndromes that connote when people run amok. Second, as Giddens tells us, current society precludes social isolation—instead, globalization is the rule, allowing for immediate contact with others no matter where they might be. But most of all, significant evidence gives reason to believe all is not harmonious even in such natural settings. According to Tattersall, rather than violence being low among hunting-and-gathering peoples, "research on skeletons found in ancient cemeteries of such peoples have revealed that half or more of the occupants may have died violent deaths."[43] Then, too, some of the highest rates of schizophrenia are found in ostensibly peaceful communities like rural southern Ireland.[44] Rural Ireland offers little relief and comfort to a stifled existence but liquor and the church. These are the root of a problem exacerbated by lack of gainful employment, prolonged living with parents, and guilt from religion and family.

All cultures, rural or urban, struggle with when not to withdraw from society and when withdrawal is part of a more healthy response to stress. Psychologist Lois Barclay Murphy noted an overriding tendency to regard withdrawal as a poor way of coping, when in fact strategic withdrawal in situations of limited choice can be quite positive.[45] Magic and myth, trance and vision quests, may not be the first choices as means to restore balance between social demands and the inner need for alonetime, but they, like dreams, may be self-empowering. Obvious last resorts are illnesses when the immediate environment or the culture ignores the pressing requirement for creative, restorative alonetime. Therefore, I reexamine suffering in order to further my case for the universality of an aloneness need and to open another doorway for reconstruction of priorities vis-à-vis time alone.

It's Being So Miserable As Keeps Me Happy[46]

Happiness in either the social or solitary sphere is ephemeral. The fact that inwardly, through solitude and its compensations, one can transform suffering and bleak childhood into happiness does not necessarily mean that the person is settling for second best.[47] Rather, they are making greatest use of one of two avenues humans have for creative happiness, social support and alone pursuits. Giddens views a culture that binds and gags creativity and self-expression—perhaps such as that of the rural Irish—as preventing emotional growth and courting ill health in its people: "[When] people cannot live creatively either because of the compulsive enactment of routines, or because they have been unable to attribute full 'solidity' to persons and objects around them, chronic melancholic or schizophrenic tendencies are likely to result."[48] For other writers and thinkers, it is our spiritual side that offers relief. Philosopher and religious scholar Houston Smith calls suffering one of the great limitations of human life. He looks to the Hindu religion to understand strictures on joy, seeing in psychological pain the frustration of achieving our desires, the greatest suffering. These personal expectations of the individual ego can stand in the way of wholeness. "Under the aspect of eternity," according to Smith, people can accept difficulties in life by loving and being alone.[49] Then failure is as natural as success and devoid of painful consequences. But for this to occur, one needs a certain detachment from everyday ego involvement, and factors sometimes stand in the way.

Suffering may be defined as the experience of distressful and unwanted subjective changes, including feelings, perceptions, sensations, and thoughts. In our day and age, when suffering disrupts functioning, we focus on a biomedical explanation as the cause and relate the problem to chemical changes. In that context, the classical problem of Job would be treated with Prozac. We know already that there are no miracle drugs. People who take antidepressants certainly may be helped, but many people grow to tolerate them and they lose their effectiveness. Most do best when these medications are combined with some form of talk therapy. Medications have been compared to ingested spirit healers, and conceivably "efficacious ingested substances might turn out to be a kind of broad-spectrum anesthesia (or opium of the people) for psychic, spiritual, and physical pain," and thus they would be nonspecific as to etiology.[50]

To understand the connection between suffering, the human psyche, society, and alonetime, I turn first to a theory of individual suffering from a psychodynamic perspective.[51] Robert Fulghum, author of *All I Really Needed to Know I Learned in Kindergarten*, tells the story of the man who complained daily of the lunch that he brought to work. Finally, one of his coworkers dares the unspoken question: "Well, who makes your sandwich?" The man replies: "I do." This joke suggests that people may hold on to pain and continue to suffer, as in depressions, even when circumstances could easily change. There may be an unconscious clinging to painful events in the lives of depressed people. Under such circumstances there is the fear of letting go of a lost or unavailable object, and an inability to even contemplate the void that absence of suffering might bring.

Unlike what is generally referred to in child psychology as a "holding environment"—the comfortable, emotionally safe space provided for babies by caretakers who give them room to be who they are—the *negative* holding environment is filled with both vague and sharply disturbing memories. It can be as empty as a black hole or as stabbing as a slap on the face. It can convey a sense of worthlessness, helplessness, or frightening nothingness, or the rage and revenge fantasy of an overly attached, bitterly disappointed, or abused child. It is all one may have left of a parent who died too soon or a caretaker who was too bonded or—the opposite—too lost in self-absorption. Perhaps it translates into the existential angst of being totally alone in the world—the living death, point of no return of nonbeing.

The blessing in being able to readily bond and adjust to others is mixed, as some attachments deter smooth sailing in life. To explain how problems arise from being unable to loosen the shackles of the past, it is necessary to understand the *illusion* that on no occasion are we ever totally alone. Author and psychoanalyst Louise Kaplan says: "The child's game of peek-a-boo is a dialogue that speaks of a never-ending human existence. . . . The regularity of the reappearing face is the infant's first essence of what it means to be part of a trustworthy universe."[52] Infants and toddlers squeal with delight playing peekaboo and later love the disappearing and finding of hide-and-seek. The illusion of lost things returning and remaining the same is a source of hope, renewal, and optimism to a young child. We continue to carry this illusion. Recalling a return to a familiar place or person provides strength and courage in unpleasant isolated moments. Hope of things to come or to be restored adds to the capacity to be alone, to create, pursue truth, or find spiritual fulfillment. For some adults, though, as Kaplan further states, "the fantasy of eternal return is a manic denial of separation and loss."[53] When the pendulum swings so that sorrow from loss is completely denied, the individual is alienated from common culture and fate. People engaged in a belief that they have no separate alonetime or any pain from loss forfeit the ability to empathize with others' grief and mourning. They live in a past that never disappears, without either an ongoing need for self-reflection or the recognition of another's plight. If one remains the little child who can still claim the right to protection from Mommy or Daddy, the illusion is that no one else is necessary.

Whatever a negative hold is, no matter how cruel, frightening, or stupefying, at least it is not complete severance of connection. Ending suffering feels like the end of memory, or going into a state of amnesia. For if we eliminate the unsatisfying, bad, and sad past, there may be nothing. Yet, this is what some individuals need to brave before reexperiencing soothing alonetime. The sufferer who gives up the autonomy of the alonetime experience clutches to a state of pain without realizing that the helplessness of the negative holding environment is based on a truncated and stubborn internalization of themselves as a permanent child. The loss of self-perpetuated suffering may be the gain of adulthood.

The commonality in descriptions of and explanations for suffering is that withdrawal in suffering both connects and disconnects the person from others. Hamlet, in his embittered heartbroken solitude, cannot get his mother, father, or even Ophelia out of his mind: he is both alone and not alone. So, too, the depressed. Their suffering epitomizes the paradox of modern life.[54] Defeated by the pressures of culture or their inner demands, people who are depressed withdraw into their own space. Few are as emotionally removed from others as the depressed, but, simultaneously, they are at the mercy of others, refusing to eat or sometimes even to bathe—hence, they return to a dependent state. Emotional suffering, though insufficient mental housekeeping, addresses the paradox, as for a time it did for a friend of mine.

Janine, a brilliant East Indian woman—designer, mother of two, socially adept, and married into a wealthy family—hates her life. She is suicidal, angry, unhappy, and unable to move from her bed. Her friends feed her and take turns accompanying her to several shrinks. Medication isn't working, nor is additional therapy with a senior person in a situation with cotherapists—male and female. All therapy over a period of eight months brought little change. Ultimately, however, her cure was instant and revelatory.

One morning, her husband, who had professed his undying love and concern, became fed up. He took their two children back to Asia and began divorce proceedings. I was with Janine when she read the letter from her husband. As a friend, I had been forewarned to be with her that morning and to expect the worst. While she read his words, Janine's sullen face changed and broke into a total smile. She laughed as she hadn't for months. I thought she might be on her way to a psychotic break, as the smile and laughter continued for several minutes without her saying a word. Then she said quite calmly: "That was a very good idea of his. I think he'll be much better off without me, as will the children." Immediately after that Janine jumped out of bed, showered, dressed, called a cab, and went back to work. The decision to be on her own was countercultural and had been too painful to make. She was relieved when her husband took the initiative.

◆　◆　◆

Desperation led Janine to extreme measures. She was listening to her inner self, but she did not know how to respond, because her feelings violated the social norm. Janine could not find a creative way to respond to, examine, and overcome what is described elsewhere as the struggle between the "over eye" of others and the "I" of self.[55]

The Creation of Private Space

Today, people in the United States comment on invasions of personal space by an "over eye," as a signal of an unreadiness to engage. Czech author Milan Kundera is more violent in his grief over the loss of privacy by what he calls the "universal orgy" of looking.[56] Attacking the camera as a replacement for God's omniscience, he believes that an individual, in the flick of a shutter, becomes another's property. Who in a large city doesn't identify with *New Yorker* writer Richard Stengel?

> The phrase "personal space" has a quaint, seventies ring to it ("You're invading my space, man"), but it is one of those gratifying expressions that is intuitively understood by all human beings. Like the twelve-mile limit around our national shores, personal space is our individual border beyond which no stranger can penetrate without making us uneasy. Lately, I've found that my personal space is being violated more than ever before.[57]

Anthropologist and scientist Edward T. Hall[58] calls space part of a culture's silent language. To paraphrase Hall: culture itself is a form of communication that is frequently carved out of awareness. Since individual and culture are interdependent and intertwined, the dual needs and manifestations of alonetime and togetherness are communicated in very subtle ways. Space talks. But what does it tell us? Here are some depictions from student interviews:

A sister from the suburbs (country mouse?) comes to visit her big (city mouse?) sister and is astonished at the way she and her neighbors ignore one another's existence in the elevator and lobby of the big apartment building. The New York City "mouse" goes to another big city, Rome, and is charmed and delighted by the way the Romans make eye contact and greet one another, seemingly for the pleasure of it.

A young Turkish woman tells of her close family ties. Besides the immediate family of parents and siblings, her aunts, uncles, and cousins were always in and out of her home. She reflects that, in self-defense, she sought daily refuge in a closet, where she kept hidden a favorite teddy bear. No one ever found her secret hiding place.

◆   ◆   ◆

The lost gentility of period pieces from the "Age of Innocence" must be appealing, as few laugh when Jane Austen's characters apologize for intruding upon a friend's solitude. But it would be funny to hear coworker or pal knocking at our door and automatically begging forgiveness for interrupting our quiet times. On the other hand, some professions, like architecture, take special note of the significance of private space and secret places to hide.[59] Under certain conditions, so will a culture.

Cultural patterns of alonetime and relatedness within the home can influence school success and failure, as is seen in a comparison of preschool children of Chinese, Japanese, and American parents. The Asian parents seem to have lower expectations for self-assertiveness and playing with peers, and greater expectations for social maturity (good manners).[60] Study space is considered essential to scholarly achievement and, as was found in explorations of parental practices in urban Chinatowns, is often provided at great sacrifice.[61] "Homes and apartments in Japan, Taiwan and Chinatown are much smaller than those in the United States, and allocation of any space within the home for activities of a single individual occurs at a cost to the total family."[62] Nevertheless, families provide their children with quiet places to study. Motivation has to be unusually strong for Asian parents to make such accommodations. What stands out is that families in a society that promotes connections between people understand the link between learning and solitude and respect the need for long hours of study in a separate space.

Few in our society respect the sanctity of chosen alonetime. Even in a saucy book dedicated to fellow solitaires on how to make oneself company enough, author Barbara Holland mocks Henry David Thoreau's time to himself because he was never that far from human community.[63] The point missed, however, is that, for a while, Thoreau chose to reverse the typical priority of people over solitude, *not* to abandon attachments. On July 4, 1845, Thoreau made his famous autonomous move to what he hoped would be the quiet of Walden Pond in Concord, Massachusetts. "Every morning was a cheerful invitation to make my life of equal simplicity and I may say innocence, with nature, herself."[64] He went there to examine his life and to seek protection from the contamination of industrial civilization. Thoreau and his friend Ralph Waldo Emerson believed in nature's healing powers and feared social demands as impositions that took people away from their true course in life. Yet neither man was antisocial or selfish. For example, both concerned themselves with the pursuit of people's rights and were against slavery. Walden Pond stands for a successful romantic retreat from the vicissitudes of everyday life perhaps because Thoreau also responded to his needs for engagement. Choosing alonetime in lieu of social pleasures was a morally superior decision to Thoreau, much as it was to the monks of old. Thus, it also meant giving up many of the benefits of civilization and accepting the constraints of nature.

The technological innovation that purports to duplicate Walden Pond is the "electronic cottage."[65] This highly equipped homestead for work, play, and sleep is chock full of the artifacts of media saturation. Those who follow that more recent venture do not want to find useful vistas and forgo familiar levels of income or urban comforts. As Jorge R. Schement and Terry Curtis convincingly state:

> By escaping that coercion, the electronic cottage dweller can flee pollution, crime, and congestion—even living beyond the suburbs—while still staying connected to an industrial income . . . to [Alvin] Toffler and others like him, information technology retrieves Walden Pond. But unlike Thoreau, electronic cottage dwellers pursue the pastoral past by pushing into the electronic future.[66]

This new lifestyle is nevertheless an attempt to blend our need for alonetime with our needs to connect, although it is also a try at having the best—or most materialistically satisfying—of all possible worlds. In the late eighteenth century, work began to shift from the home to industrial cities. At this time, only a small percentage of people earned their total income out of their homes. Moreover, the craftspeople of days gone by were self-sufficient in terms of farming, supplying themselves with the needed staples, and making a personal investment in the quality of products. By contrast, today's home workers, in their attempts to differentiate between work and leisure (relaxation), face the greatest struggle in cultivating peace of mind. A case in point is the reported story of Noble Gunn by Schement and Curtis:

> Mr. Gunn, a management tax director in his own firm, works mostly at home in one room in his spacious apartment.

He has a desk, an IBM PC connected to a PS2 network unit, a modem, extra hard disk, letter quality printer, photo copier, fax machine, postage meter, scales, typewriter, calculators, adding machines and four full size filing cabinets filling the space. Additionally, he installed six telephone lines and several telephones with answering tapes, call forwarding, call waiting, call relay and connection to his PC in his Manhattan office. He feels in control of his time and enjoys great flexibility. Yet, he had to work hard to ensure boundaries between his social and work spheres and to separate work from friends and family. He still finds it far easier to gravitate to work at home and to allow work to monopolize him. In order not to work, he has to specifically make leisure time. When he works at home he maintains silence. Music is his favorite leisure activity because of the isolation it affords. He also flies airplanes as a way to isolate himself from the distraction of the phone and fax machine. Vacations in the Caribbean with his family isolate him further. Interestingly, he will drive into Manhattan—an hour from where he lives—merely for the solitude of the experience. The leisure activities of reading magazines and listening to radio and TV news are clearly pseudo as they involve the consumption of information which is part of his work. Although he touts his position as the model for the future he sees that the "scales can tip very quickly."[67]

There is real danger in blurring the boundaries between work and leisure. Maybe this shift foretells societal role reversals and other transformations. The noisy competitiveness of the commercial society has interestingly enough infiltrated religious space; some churches have adopted a new stance, expanding their social role through megachurches. Joining the twenty-first century, independent sects erect complexes for gatherings and events. Churches may once again become the social centers of society, only this time they will provide secular amusement, as we see our culture become increasingly isolated by the computer revolution.

As with the church changing from a place for retreat to a place for social activity, Gunn pursues quiet and leisure more frequently in the public sphere than at home. Leisure for Gunn is not always recuperative time, as he is frequently information gathering, unless far removed from home. He feels some sense of relaxation in his work, but lives in dread of the fax machine, which can disturb him anytime, night or day. Unlike the farmer or craftsperson of old, Gunn is dependent upon the society at large. He is, as are most professionals who rely on information, tied to the existing American and international power structures. As an individual he does not exert his own sphere of influence, and though disconnected from office routine, he is mightily dependent on electronic services. More and more, people are getting annoyed by the accessibility of modem hookups and the prevalence of telephones (on airplanes and in cars) because it makes them feel like they must work. The domains of workplace are disseminating into every part of our lives. Significantly, space between public and private areas needs reclarification so that what constitutes rewarding social interaction and refreshing alonetime is less confusing.

But whether a culture is inner or outer directed, egocentric or sociocentric, industrialized or technology-free, does not in itself cause or deter emotional dysfunction. At no other time in history, however, have people's minds and bodies been so accessible. When, in the film *Sleeper*, Woody Allen is stimulated and finds ecstasy in the orgasmatron box (a takeoff on psychoanalyst Wilhelm Reich's controversial device to treat neurotics by freeing "orgastic" energy), he satirized a futuristic world in which desires are instantly and mechanically satisfied. Was he clairvoyant in envisioning technology that would put complete gratification within our grasp? Certainly, there are times when the computer seems directly plugged into people's needs to be private and connected simultaneously.

Seeing how other cultures address the needs for both alonetime and attachment opens up possibilities in ours. Anthropology offers as many cogent answers to an individual's means of regulating these important needs as does psychology. Altered states, art, and seclusion are certain solutions, while being on-line seems the Western way to these complementary needs. But the solution brings its own dilemmas. Suffering may be culturally and individually a way to self-regulate, dissociate, and achieve some of alonetime's blessings, but at what cost? Keeping silent about the pleasures of alonetime causes us to remain unaware of why the draw of computer software marvels is so compelling. When an experience is altering our consciousness and we do not discriminate either *how* or *why*, then the experience is regulating us, rather than vice versa. In terms of life's unpredictable nature, we may not be complete masters of our fates, but we can be aware of how we use time and what is motivating our choices—especially when, next, we come to rethinking relationships.

CHAPTER 9

Relationships, Romance,

and Resistance

But in that casket—safe, dark, motionless, airless—[your heart]
will change. It will not be broken; it will become unbreakable,
impenetrable, irredeemable. The alternative to tragedy, or at least
to the risk of tragedy, is damnation. The only place outside Heaven
where you can be perfectly safe from all the dangers and perturba-
tions of love is Hell.

C. S. LEWIS, *The Four Loves* [1]

Now the whole dizzying and delirious range of several possibilities has been boiled down to that one big, boring, bulimic word.
RELATIONSHIP.

JULIE BURCHILL, "The Dead Zone" [2]

A lot of couples shower together. It's supposed to be romantic and
sensual. Truth? It's not all it's cracked up to be. Because one of
you is not getting water. One of you, therefore, is not taking a
shower.

PAUL REISER, *Couplehood* [3]

THOUGHTS ABOUT RELATIONSHIPS run the gamut. "It's hell with them
or without them" is the wrap-up phrase often used to describe life
with another—male or female. But are long-term relationships possible?
I believe so, if only we stop carrying around the unrealistic idea that
we're entitled to some perfect mate, or the belief that because we lost out
having Mr. and Mrs. Brady as parents, we should certainly be entitled to
constant fun and security from relationships as adults. Volumes leap from
the shelves of bookstores about couple and marriage strategies. [4] But, of
course, my blueprint, if one would call it that, has to do with reconstruc-

tion of and acquaintance with alonetime needs. And in discussing this other side to human desire, I am explaining why slogans, warnings on the demise of family values, and even guides on how to become a better mate or lover don't always do the trick or work as well as they sound. A student I interviewed sums it up: "If I go too long without finding private time, it is as if I am uprooted."

A great surprise and even disappointment to parents comes when children of all ages prefer time away from family activities. From the baby who turns his or her cheek to the adolescent who doesn't want to spend next weekend in the country with the family, parents interpret signs of rejection in these normal behavioral rhythms. My grandson Benjamin handled time alone as a wee baby with his many self-regulatory skills. Then he became caught up in the pleasure of company. At two years of age, he began to rework his alone skills alongside his newly formed relationships. Building his repertoire of alone skills as a complement to his love of his parents and their attention, Benjamin chose not to be downstairs with his mother, Jeanne, and friends. He wanted to continue to "read" his books. Within ten minutes he called for her and she went upstairs; he had dropped his books and asked if she would retrieve them (an age-old method of reassuring oneself of a parent's availability). She gave him the books that he dropped and several more and he amused himself alone for another half hour. Cultivating alonetime is difficult in this day and age, since relationships take center stage, with helpful how-to authors working diligently to spell out nonthreatening dialogues between partners.

Balance in Relationships — Love and Liberty

History has varied lessons in balancing alonetime and relationships. To a wandering Ulysses, Penelope was an unusually unperturbed and faithful wife by any standards. Perhaps she loved her alonetime? Certainly, she knew how to amuse herself while waiting and weaving as Ulysses was fighting against Troy. Contrast her with the anxious Trojan Cressida, who after being taken from her solitude by the love of Troilus, gives way to fear of loneliness and is unfaithful to her absent lover.[5] But in fact, historically, time together was often punctuated by long separations in a couple's life. The intensity of contemporary Western relationships seems to call for elaborate machinations and declarations between partners. Mainstream rituals of marriage from earlier times or other cultures often followed protocols relevant to economic rather than romantic needs. Oscar

Lans, who studied the Blackfoot tribe in the early 1940s, interviewed a Blackfoot chief about the advantage of having eight wives over one. Working together, the chief explained, eight wives could produce and dress 150 bison hides a year. A single wife alone could produce only four hides.[6]

Romantic love and a stable relationship were once seen as antithetical to each other. According to one study on couples, "Now the two are supposed to exist in harmony. Partners are supposed to be able to switch from lawn-mowing and diapers to torrid sex at the drop of a hat; from long hours at work to sweet moments in the sun."[7] The strain on couples to be all things to each other is no less than the general strain on people in all areas of society. What in the workplace is an injunction to produce more translates in the family or at home into high-level sex and total relationships. Can all this be accomplished without one of the partners calling for time out? Obviously not, for it seems as the push grows for greater and greater intimacy between people, so has the number of couples seeking separations and divorce.

With the divorce rate hovering around the 50 percent mark, many in this country believe divorce has gotten out of hand. Expectations of marriage may be too great because people feel entitled to instant happiness. But what zealous advocates for the emotionally attuned nuclear family overlook is its very short history and the added burdens it places on each family member. In Japan, where divorce statistics are relatively low and romantic love the exception, "toughing it out"[8] in a relationship is a given; aloneness, however, is very much part of the routine in Japanese marriages. But many Americans do endure hardship when choosing to be sole parents, either initially or through separation. Though many a couple will stay in an unloving union rather than *have* to face separation or divorce, when love is the reason for marriage significant numbers seem to take their chances with alonetime in preference to maintaining a stale union.

At least, women do. Strange, perhaps, are the statistics that repeatedly show that in the later years women fare better than men physically and emotionally (although not financially) after divorce. This is despite John Gray's popular formulation that men are the Martians, who focus on efficiency and succeeding on their own, and that women are the Venusians, who value communication, love, and relationships.[9] Is this because women have set up a better support network of friends than men, or express their feelings and needs more openly? At certain times that may be the case. More generally, I believe that by post–middle age, women have learned how to apply the Golden Rule in the emotional sphere: Do unto others as you would have others do unto you. A post-fifty woman who sheds the responsibility of being the caretaker can be responsive to her own needs—and not devastated by being alone. Once married, men, on the other hand, put their emotional needs on the back burner or, for the most part, expect them to be met by the women in their lives. Thus, aloneness for a man in his later years (other than a perennial bachelor) may be overwhelmingly solitary—and feel like desertion. By contrast, actress Lauren Bacall has had a love/hate relationship with being alone for quite a while, especially when in public places. In her generation, women seen alone were to be pitied: "So imagine my shock when I realized, at the tender age of sixty-five, that ... the final truth is this: I live alone ... (I enjoy my nights in; I enjoy the quiet and the aimlessness of them) ... I travel alone." [10] Descriptions of men's turning inward and escaping emotional ties, however, take on an inanimate quality. Nathanael West's sardonic and eloquent novel *Miss Lonelyhearts* captures with relentless pessimism an unpleasantness in human relations. His protagonist is as lonely, angry, and guilty as Camus's stranger or Dostoyevsky's Raskolnikov, though somewhat less violent. The male who hardens himself as he pushes everyone from his life allows emotional overload to force him into a retreat so complete it renders him impotent in the face of human misery. [11]

Though vestiges of these gender stereotypes, like West's character, are still visible, they are declining. A cultural and personal demand for better and happier unions is entirely understandable. But the construct of two-adult, two-children, one-pet families ignores a large segment of the populace. Many individuals have a tradition of single parenthood in their families, but for most the social teachings and circumstances dictate otherwise.

> The single-parent family, including divorced parents and those who were never married, is one of the more common variants in the United States. This type of family grew 300 percent from 1970 to total 9.7 million families headed by a single parent. Despite sitcom shows like *Murphy Brown* or popular films such as *Kramer vs. Kramer*—one emphasizing a woman's decision to parent a child without a mate, the other showing a man surviving divorce and solo custodial child-care—single mothers or fathers experience role strain increased by social teachings and censure. What seems newly acceptable to society and backed by research is the idea that men can successfully raise children without causing them harm. The role of father as primary parent, however, is still contrary to the bias of the courts. [12]

When I was nine years old, I received a lesson that truly set me wondering about my role as a "woman." A best friend, Inez, gave a Halloween party. We played spin-the-bottle, and Ronnie and I believed ourselves in love. To prove our loyalty, we exchanged good luck pennies. Obviously, I did not realize the extent of my obligations, because I found myself refusing play dates with him to do my own thing. Unbeknownst to me, Inez volunteered to take my place and keep him company. One day in school she delivered a letter from him saying that I was no longer his girlfriend, being too unavailable and too tall. He returned my penny, to boot. The lesson implied, so I thought, was not to leave your boyfriend alone too much—he might decide to replace you. Fortunately, I was young enough not to be very hurt by such misfortune or to interpret its message as gospel. As a thirteen-year-old, I was as practical and sensible as a Jane Austen character. No guy would automatically steal *my* heart. I had plans for my life. Companionship and dating were fine, but I had no trouble turning down fourteen-year-old Anthony, who wanted me to pledge absolute fidelity. The risk of losing him loomed small, and sticking to him felt suffocating. A tragic change was soon to occur, which altered my self-confidence and for me is proof of how insecurity fuels attachments, though not always at optimal times. With my father's sudden death went some of my pioneer spirit. In retrospect, I realize that I unconsciously went from being a girl who was exploratory, curious, and self-motivated to being an adolescent uncertain of her next steps. As my courage dampened, there came a great need to have a steady beau. Though from the outside this transition would seem age appropriate, I know now what intuitively I only sensed then: My new style of clinging behavior was not a symptom of deep, growing affections. It was not a sudden fear of being alone, or even my naturally increasing sexuality. I chose a relationship as a way to anchor myself during a time of great loss, when I was floundering as to whether I could make the dreams I had for myself come true.

Simone de Beauvoir flamed the twentieth century's feminist movement; Jean-Paul Sartre gave passionate voice to existentialism. They met at the French University in 1928, noticed each other's brilliance at once, but did not speak to one another for almost a year. When they finally did connect, they struggled most publicly between affairs of the heart and freedom of spirit. After their graduation, without invitation, Sartre, always an iconoclast, defied de Beauvoir's bourgeois roots by showing up in her home village unannounced. Despite obvious parental disapproval, he camped outside, a distance from the house. He spent his nights in the fields so that they might spend their days in concentrated and heated dialogue. De Beauvoir secretly met him each day, and her relationship with Sartre paved the way for her to escape from what she felt was a demoralizing family that hardly understood her.[13] To avoid the dependencies of love, which both philosophers thought disabling, they, for most of their many years of intimacy, slept separately. Writing at a time when women were economically dependent, de Beauvoir saw females as not trying to recapture their father's love in their willingness to enslave themselves to men, but rather attempting to find economic freedom:

> [A woman] chooses to desire her enslavement so ardently that it will seem to her the expression of her liberty; she will try to rise above her situation as inessential object by fully accepting it[14] . . . Genuine love ought to be founded on the mutual recognition of two liberties; the lovers would then experience themselves both as self and as other; neither would give up transcendence, neither would be mutilated.[15]

Sartre was not a faithful lover to de Beauvoir. When unrecognized, the need for self-regulation—de Beauvoir's "transcendence"—is negatively reconstructed in attempts to overcontrol the partner. The unfaithful Sartre postulated that sadism is present in all forms of love, but especially in acts of desire.[16] Having escaped his own past, he lived determined never to allow falling in love to entrap him so completely. In the less dramatic bindings of everyday life, people regularly put the brakes on closeness. Often the stopper is an argument.

Many times anger, if not carried too far, is simply the alone need asserting itself the only way it can. After the first phase, of ecstatic inseparableness, lovers feel a need to find themselves. Each may experience aloneness needs as narcissistic injuries, as below-the-belt punches when the other's statements are no longer reflective of shared feelings. The decline in synchrony between partners is rarely understood as part of the process of carrying a love relationship past the initial stage. When we look at them through an alonetime lens, our understanding of the dynamics of relationships can change. For example, picking a fight is multidetermined. It may be just what's needed to clear the air and gain breathing space and distance from your mate. Don't you remember as a young child playing happily with friends but getting into a fight moments before parting, which thus made it easier to say good-bye? For adolescents, among other things, a fight or disparaging comment may be a way to tell parents that they shouldn't be so intrusive. When lovers or parents, in turn, respond very angrily, what message about their wish for alone space are they conveying? Can love in the end conquer all?

Who's Number One? — Rivalry, Romantic Love, and Bonding

For almost five centuries, the story of Romeo and Juliet has fostered Euro-American society's belief in the prospect of passion. Both men and women are known to have spent lifetimes searching for a person with whom they can fall in love and live happily ever after. This obsession with romantic love is so ingrained in our psyches that it manifests itself in everything from classical literature to current movies and pop songs. Even in psychological literature, most research has focused on romantic love over companionate (friendship) or altruistic love.[17]

Contrary to popular belief, however, the idea of romantic love between men and women did not develop between the eleventh and fourteenth centuries, with the concept of courtly love. Recently, anthropologists such as Helen Fisher[18] cite evidence of romantic love existing in 87 percent of all cultures and throughout history.[19] She gives the example of Vatsyayana,[20] the author of the Kama Sutra, who lived in India between the first and sixth centuries A.D., who not only described romantic love between men and women, but also gave detailed instructions on how to court and copulate. Tales of star-crossed lovers who are torn between obedience to their elders and romantic passion for a loved one date back to seventh-century China. And we can't forget David and Bathsheba and Jacob and Rachel in the Old Testament, stories of love at first sight.

The mythology surrounding romantic love that developed in the United States did so with a fever that no other civilization embraced. Nor has any other ever tried to reassure its populace that love and marriage go together like ham and eggs. From the legend of John Smith and Pocahontas to Richard Burton and Elizabeth Taylor, our faith in romance survives because it offers escape from the conventional and the preordained, as a means to return to a personal self. It is a way to combine the needs for aloneness and togetherness. As one example, the sharing of the heart in nineteenth-century romantic prose often transpires between solitary couples distanced from each other, as is made clear in countless love letters. "One thing rest assured of, Dearest—distance does not weaken my affection for you," wrote John North in the 1800s to his wife of thirteen years.[21] Denis de Rougemont, in his book Love in the Western World, asserts that romantic love is more a myth than a realistic goal, and further states that *"the partings of the lovers are dictated by their passion itself."*[22] Romantic love, he continues, thrives in absences and multiplies when obstructed. Lovers in their joint dreams in truth remain solitary.

Nevertheless, Karen Lystra, student and author in American studies, gives great power to America's interest in romantic love: "Romantic love shaped the contours of American history as surely as technology and finance. Not only gender and sexuality but basic conceptions of what it meant to be a person grew and were nurtured by the romantic ethos. Romantic love changed individual feelings, perceptions, and behavior."[23]

So then, what is romantic love? One can look to both folklore and fact for the answer. One pupil of Socrates, Aristophanes, refers to the famous myth[24] that captures the desire for union that lovers experience. According to the ancient myth, humans were originally round hermaphrodites, spheres with four arms, four legs, and two genders. These individuals felt whole and were so full of pride that they had no need for love. Zeus and the other gods decided that the race of man was too strong and probably able to function without the gods (another dictum against alonetime?), and they chose to weaken them by cutting each human being into male and female halves. However, once each person was split, each half had an overwhelming need to reunite with the half from which it had been severed. Taking pity on them, Zeus moved their sexual organs so that people could periodically come together in a sexual embrace. The urge to merge and feel whole again on a spiritual and emotional level transcended the physical. Thoughts of merger are alive in Stendhal's *On Love*—love transforms and "crystallizes" the beloved into perfection—as well as in Walter Pater's description of comradeship in his novel of Christian sacrifice and homosexual relationship, *Marius the Epicurean*.[25]

From the perspective of fear of risk taking and of idealizing a mate, psychoanalyst and writer Stephen A. Mitchell discusses why romantic love fades. The trouble with taking a chance on love for the long haul and thinking of another as perfect is not that the other doesn't have these exceptional traits but that we expect Mr. or Ms. Wonderful to guarantee us against disappointment and solitude.[26] Mitchell thus questions what he calls popular culture's degraded form of romance, which establishes death and distance as necessary for establishing passion in a realm of safety. Authentic romance, he argues, is not separate from longings for security but a dialectic with it. In that sense, he is asking for a search for balance between not only safety and desire, but men's and women's alone and relational needs. Carol Gilligan aroused attention in 1982 with her groundbreaking theories on gender differences in every aspect of relating to life and the world.[27] She proclaims through her Harvard-based studies that females are oriented toward caring and relationships, while men are oriented toward the celebration of freedom. Without weighing either in value to society, Gilligan does see the social voice as female, and speaking out for autonomy as male.

Continuously fascinating to modern society is why men and women approach relationships so differently. In 1976, I conducted a study on the differences between boys and girls in their need and desire to form relationships, reemphasizing the Freudian perspective that girls in a nuclear family setting shift feelings toward their parents.[28] First, especially if their adjustment to life is heterosexual, they turn from mother to father as their primary love, always realizing that they have a rival to father's affections who preceded them—mother. The boys' position is different from the girls' if their gender choice is heterosexual. As one ten-year-old boy with his mother in consultation said: "Why aren't I your number one love? You will always be my first and best love." But Freud did not fully acknowledge that with a female's initial search for romantic connection with her father, she faces an emotional distancing from her mother, who may leave her more emotionally alone than she wishes to be. Males, for the most part, are in the position to feel they have more than they want of mothering, as they are not driven away either psychologically or hormonally.

In the debate as to how to distinguish the developmental pathways of love ties to parents, the varied mating choices of heterosexual compared to homosexual individuals provoke questions about attachment and alonetime needs. If men seek a same-sex lover, does that mean they relinquish rivalry with Dad? Not necessarily, if you want to be number one to Mom. If women say "Ho-hum" to Dad as a romantic image, does that mean they can put aside all jealousies of Mom? I wouldn't say so, because Mom might have other enviable perks. Besides, a lot of these meanderings are unconscious, and more than one exact route to grown-up relationships is available. Nor are gender decisions totally clear-cut and one-sided. Indeed, gay partnerships face the exact same pitfalls in terms of sanctioning alonetime as heterosexual relationships. The great success of Terrence McNally's play *Love! Valor! Compassion!* rests at least partially on the fact that gay men are portrayed with the same fears and wishes for aloneness, individuality, attachment, and empathy as the general public, not as an alien group. In terms of relationships and aloneness, each individual has to seek and decide what balance suits one's personality.

Alonetime needs may surface as flights to freedom. Often, physical distance is used as the means to decrease a sense of being caught in another's clutches, and gender affects the means of escape. Some new research on children suggests that, next to aggression, physical intrusion is the most-often-cited reason for disliking a peer.[29] In my day and age, at elementary school, kids did not feel so burdened by intrusive friends, and we could get away with leaning heavily on the shoulders of pals, pushing against them, saying "P.L.P.—public leaning post."

In the aforementioned study, reasons for liking and disliking did not differ by gender. Men, however, are more likely, especially in their younger years, to fear the complications of attachment. Women have a harder time being alone in the nuclear family as they struggle to secure relationships as ties to both mother and father undergo unsettling transformations. This is true whether the mother is rival for the father's affection (as described in the Freudian constellation) or friend rather than parent (as part of the reconstructed sisterhood). When patients, male or female, speak of a desire to break away from their loved ones, I hear an enormous longing to be alone coupled with an anguish about separating. The men seem able to enact the alone wishes more frequently in taking walks, going out singly, and extending business trips. The women think about fleeing but protest separation. Within the female dilemma is the question of maintaining equilibrium between two powerful magnets: caretaker mom and romantic-hero dad. In order to navigate this most challenging terrain, females improve their relationship skills. The stress —this time of switching allegiances—is bound to increase attachment need. Males emphasize their alonetime skills to enhance the capacity to fend for oneself.

Several psychoanalysts have written popular books that explore adult relationships in the light of childhood experience. In particular, Ethel Spector Person's[30] book on romantic love pictures an early phase of mother-child attachment as leaving a nostalgia for a merger with another. She also reinterprets the Oedipus complex in a way similar to mine in my 1976 study. She adheres to the idea of male-female differences and suggests that women's vulnerability in relationships and fear of loss of love evolve from the fact that the woman who has given them life becomes their rival. When children like Oedipus and Electra experience brutal childhoods, revenge escalates and sends them on pathological routes. Infamous deeds of revenge, betrayal, and murder in both ancient and modern history often stem from soured expectations of what others should and can give us.

Some of these embittered views arise from the idea honed by Margaret Mahler that falling in love is a reenactment of the symbiotic stage of development, and adults long to lose their sense of self in another. My perspective reinterprets this notion.[31] I suggest, instead, that romantic love is not experienced by partners as a relief from separateness, but rather as absence of conflict between people's separate needs to relate and be alone. Stephanie Dowrick states a similar perspective in her book about intimacy and solitude, but still implies the return to mother and a dyadic relationship: "What has been called a longing for merging or symbiosis may be rather more like a longing to be free of conflict . . . to have our needs recognized and met *as they were* in the pre-verbal period, *through mother 'knowing'* what we could not express" (italics mine).[32] Dowrick believes that the falling-in-love stage entails being attuned to each other's inner state, which echoes the early mother-child interaction, wherein the lucky infant is responded to with joy, pride, and admiration. The elation felt during the early stages of romantic love is primarily due to the temporary abatement of conflict and ambivalence. I agree with this, but I would say that knowledge of fulfillment can precede knowledge of being satisfied by another and go back to womb time, when we feel the least need to work hard to achieve contentment.

The recapitulation of the parent-child relationship, whether in deed or theory, stands in the way of satisfactory love. Not that we don't all play out child fantasies and even find comfort in parenting or being parented by our lover-mate. But child bride imagery leads to a dead end when the spouse awakens to a separate will. Certain views of modern intimacy can become unrealistic and, according to one author,[33] even vicious. If—as depicted in the films *Breaking Away* and Jane Campion's version of *Portrait of a Lady*—all we are worrying about is being threatened, being abandoned, or gaining control, love becomes a struggle. Here is where attachment based on anxiety, stress, and insecurity finds root. "Intimate terrorism" is when one uses knowledge of one's partner to intimidate, undermine, and exploit the partner, rather than incorporating that knowledge for admiration or pleasure. These methods can lead to infuriated rebellions and catastrophic deeds to escape or perpetrate the tyranny. While many wish for magical protection, in the long run few feel happy going back to being a child under the domination of another, no matter how safe it appears.[34]

Why, if people so dread being consumed, would the need for aloneness become eclipsed in an atmosphere of intense focus on attachment? Because of confused beliefs, we are much more likely to feel that we will be understood in our pain if we complain to a therapist or friend, "I have problems with intimacy," than if we say, "I need to be alone more often." Friends typically don't want to do things without company, even when they have a good time, because then they wonder if by having fun alone they are unfaithful to their friend or spouse. One young woman was in awe of her therapist, who designated a single day of her vacation time as a day apart from her lover. Maybe that does it for some, but it is not what alonetime is about. A day to do one's thing, just like a night out with the boys or the girls, creates diversity, but it does not cover the full spectrum of the need. I suggest learning to view solitude as part of ordinary experience rather than as an artificial barrier against involvement with the world.

Let's listen to some newly involved couples who have begun to feel uncomfortable about negotiating time apart.

She: "I don't understand why I worry so much if he doesn't return my call right away."

He: "When she didn't respond to my sexual advances right away, I found myself preoccupied with a list of all the things I don't like about her. I began to criticize her. Why did I do that?"

Although these people feel they have difficulty with relationships—a difficulty with intimacy—couldn't we also see their problem coming from a lack of understanding the parallel need within each for aloneness?

Aloneness can also be a prism through which to view other aspects of relationships. For example, if the need for aloneness takes its place on the stage along with the desire for intimacy, the following exchange between the partners might be easier to understand:

She: "I feel suffocated with him. Despite what he says, I know he wants me to fill a traditional feminine role. He'll say, 'I need to do some reading; you make dinner, OK?' "

He: "I can't change the demands of my work schedule, yet I think she's withdrawing from me because I've had to cancel our plans so often."

Was the male's search for some regulation in the cycle of togetherness clumsily expressed in asking her to cook their dinner? Was he using compulsivity about work as a way to create separation—and might his real need have been for time away from her and career? And perhaps she isn't really reacting to his involvement with work by being unavailable. Maybe she is responding to her own need for some alonetime. It is very rare today for couples or friends to be able to comfortably use the language of an alone need. Many of us would feel impolite using an alone vocabulary to ask for time off or to be left alone. After all, expressions such as "I need space" sting because they are so often disguised rejections. We can explain the need for alonetime without threatening others. But a lot depends upon people's perceptions, and therefore pat tactics won't cover all the bases. Besides, experiences with loneliness have to be considered. Yet I can picture one significant change. People meet. They probe each other's likes and dislikes. The questions get serious: "Where do you want to live? Do you want children? How would you raise them?" Add a few more: "Do you like to be alone? How frequently? Let me tell you what alonetime means to me." Of course, both partners will learn a lot about each other from these questions and feel closer to who they are. But more than that, these breezy dialogues may enable us to freshly air and even at long last blow away compulsive statements formulated to ensure saying the right thing.

The Bleak Side

To judge from abundant evidence yielded by surveys, the consulting room, and popular culture, many of the country's adolescent and adult population—single or attached—suffer from the great aching complaint of alienation.[35] Wanting to explore geographical and regional differences in the meaning of loneliness, the *New York Times*–commissioned freelance writer Louise Bernikow traveled around America and questioned couples and individuals about those feelings. Alone and lonely are different, she writes, and many people like to be alone and are happy that way. Then what brings people to a state where they feel that no one cares about them? Having no one to take care of them for a little while is different from yearning and having no one there at all. Writer Barbara Holland makes clear the differences between chosen and forced alonetime.[36] Many of the lonely feel that they cannot make friends; although this is a resolvable problem, the remedy is very likely to be linked to the individual circumstances of a person's life.

Longing for a lover, relative, or friend is not the cause of loneliness, nor is finding someone necessarily the cure. The human species, like many others, runs the gamut from self-centeredness—as in the case of the "red kangaroo, who may toss the larger of her joeys out of her pouch if she is too closely pursued"—to the altruistic, as when a Gombe chimp, Sniff, collected fruit for a researcher who had been unsuccessful in his attempt to knock fruit from a tree.[37] Not being lonely, as Bernikow found out in her travels, relates to a caring type of involvement. She focuses on involvement with community, but it could be involvement with God, with pets, or with work. Helping us to differentiate between love and security needs, as both are important to us, is what is implied by much of John Bowlby's writing on attachment: the person who matters most to another is neither the feeder nor the sexual partner, but the one who stays near and offers protection against danger, the unknown, and loneliness.[38] People handle the distress of loneliness in different ways. Some ride piggyback and let a friend, lover, spouse, or child shoulder the problem.

I know that the answer to the dire and devastating circumstances of loneliness is not universal. While the need for alonetime can sometimes bring one to loneliness, so, too, the smothering potential of the tight-knit nuclear family makes it clear that loneliness is not going to be cured within its bonds, because people in such circumstances can be just as unknown and lonely. Living closely with others is an art, or perhaps, as Reiser says, a business: "The problem is when two people live together, there is no more Business of Your Own. Your Own Business is closed . . . You have to run everything by the partners. And if there are too many conflicts of interest, the business may go under."[39] Conflicts of interest underlie flights into loneliness. Having one's own way can become a life struggle. To relate, as well as to be alone, depends upon people feeling able to self-regulate. Claustrophobia stems from feeling imprisoned or hemmed in by others.[40] What happens when you love your family, yet you have your own ideas and feelings overlooked? Not only the rebellious have to deal with these pulls to stay within the secure bonds of family as well as to go out alone. Sometimes such circumstances make one overly guilty and immobile. Under such conditions, escape is one resolution, as with a patient, Eva.

> Eva grew up with a loving but inadequate mother, whose awkward presence embarrassed her children when she visited teachers on open school day. Consequently, Eva and her two sisters substituted in one another's lives as parental figures. The father lost that option because he was too much the disciplinarian. These problems, however, bound the family together and they continued to be extraordinarily close emotionally and physically for most of Eva's grown-up years. Since all her concern was about family interactions, Eva could not find the energy to seek friendships or sustained romantic relationships. She sought treatment because she was so often lonely. To substitute for an external private life

she constructed a fantasy world as complex as any daytime soap opera, which provided romance, friendships, and alonetime. She played these inner videos wherever family obligations seemed large. Ultimately, she sought a position as a foreign correspondent on assignment for periodicals, and the time out of the country was a partial resolution to her problem. Away from home she was happy. She became close to people in three different Asian countries, learning the languages and customs. Then she fell in love with a Frenchman, also away from his homeland. Back in the States, she devoted time to her family with less intensity and no longer felt her fantasy world the one source of comfort.

◆　◆　◆

For many people who suffer loneliness, the capacity to sufficiently integrate a need for family with being one's own person eludes them. But doing one's own thing can also reach selfish limits, as defensive dependency can block both feelings of loneliness and needs for alonetime. What is defensive dependency? We see it in Helmut.

Helmut was stubborn, strong, and self-involved. Nevertheless, he could not pull himself away from a comfortable existence with his mother. She devoted herself to his every need, and he in turn kept her company. In his twenties, he spoke of leaving home and earning his own way, although he never came to do this. One job after another proved unpleasant. In time, going to the theater, to dinner, on trips, and the like with Mom seemed comfort enough. His youthful stubbornness translated into occasional sulks. Mom became his life and he stopped looking for other distractions. She was there to take care of him, and vice versa. Motivation for independence and alonetime was subsumed with the growing experience that anxious loneliness was no longer consciously discernible.

◆　◆　◆

Most people will not settle for this trade-off and will go on to seek a balance through finding someone or something that will keep them in the world with peers and alone in contentment.

Attachments, as Helmut's experience shows, are not automatically fulfilling relationships. Nor are relationships per se attachments. Attachment is at times remaining close even under instances of extreme personal compromise. Being held by ball and chain, being shackled and held hostage in a relationship are not uncommon analogies. In a stimulating analysis of the dwindling pleasures of intimacy everyone faces, psychotherapist and writer Michael Vincent Miller tells of the downside of love, which, though more present in everyday life, is masked in the confusion of love and power.[41] Marriages are now based on equality, so with time for love lessened in the busy world, the commodities that relationships offer are more scarce than ever before, for children as well as adults. This makes for a rivalry over the goods of love. According to Miller, a dark force that always played its part in close ties—power—has come out of hiding, causing "intimate terrorism." People fear losing love, so they are ready to fight hard for its wares. War has infiltrated domesticity so that family abuse and violence, in our culture's transition to allowing women equal privileges, pervades every aspect of people's thinking and expectations. These are fears that may be cultivated in family.

People in touch only with self or family members may be more positioned for loneliness than others. But often that very lonely time allows us freedom from self. I do not believe that loneliness can be totally banished from life, nor should it be. Like anxiety or guilt, it is a part of the human condition. It tells us that we are not being understood and are perhaps too isolated from community. Or it can be a signal that we are not taking time to be in contact with our inner selves. Of all the creative geniuses who examine relationships and struggle with the dual longings for others and time apart, playwright August Strindberg and artist Edvard Munch personally and in their art clearly depict the dilemmas. As a writer, Strindberg reaches for the jugular, exploring every nook and cranny filled with competition, hatred, envy, devotion, and ineptitude. What James Thurber comically portrayed as the "battle of the sexes," Strindberg depicts as "nuclear" warfare, toxic explosions of unfulfilled love.

As we look at the prominence of alonetime and relationships, we sometimes must turn typical conclusions and insights upside down. Situations occur in which maintaining a separate and esteemed self and experiencing the connection of love are doomed. Take for example what is referred to as the *Liebestod,* or love-death fantasies, of romantic love, in which the mates so dread living without each other that, like Tristan and Isolde, they choose death. The fatal attraction of the *Liebestod* motif reaches its most perverse in Richard Strauss's opera *Salome,* based on the Oscar Wilde play.[42] Two forbidden longings drive the music and story forward: fourteen-year-old Salome's infatuation with Johanaan and the passion of her stepfather, Herod, to see her half-naked body in dance.

She makes a bargain with Herod; she will perform the dance of the seven veils if he will deliver to her the head of the longed-for Johanaan, who refused her kiss. It is the cannibalistic imagery in these last scenes of the opera that I call to your attention. In this degenerative and devouring relationship, touch and distorted self-determination interweave throughout the monologue that Salome delivers to Johanaan's head. Oral-incorporation fantasies, as bizarre as they seem, are inevitable to all of us, especially in the breast fed, who have suckled on their mother's skin. But even in those bottle fed, usually held close to the caretaker's skin, it is easy to see why harboring such images of devouring occurs. Doting parents and grandparents are always mouthing to adored children, "I could eat you all up." At times the allusions to cannibalism are religious, as the eating of the sacrament is absorbing the body of Christ. Sometimes the imagery is loving and sensual: "drinking one in," "looking good enough to eat," "a feast for the eyes," "sweet as sugar candy." Other times the implications are "I'll eat you alive," as in the desperate words of Strindberg's captain in *The Father:* "You see, I'm a cannibal, and I want to eat you. Your mother wanted to eat me, but she couldn't. I am Saturn, who ate his children because it had been prophesied that otherwise they would eat him. To eat or be eaten—that is the question."[43]

To merge in this holistic way goes beyond Bertolt Brecht's satiric lines from the ballad sung by Macheath in Kurt Weill's *The Threepenny Opera.* The question is, "What keeps a man alive?" The answer is that he eats his brother, "every hour torturing, stripping, attacking, throttling and devouring his fellow men."[44] Examples of cannibalism are found in ancient and not so ancient cultures' modes of human sacrifice: "Homovores are a stable ingredient, so to speak, of narratives as diverse as *The Thousand and One Nights* . . . [and] the memoirs of Marco Polo."[45] Claude Levi-Strauss refers to cannibalism as a form of alimentary incest, and the small group of serial killers who are flesh eaters bear that truth in mind. Yet these isolated people maintain their separateness and closeness in the most extreme, concrete manner. Perhaps in the terrifying isolation of a Hannibal Lector, boundaries need to be blurred: "What motivates people like Dahmer is a catastrophic failure of the imagination, an inability to think metaphorically which compels them to act out the symbolic order regardless of the cost to themselves and others, in horror and degradation."[46] But it is more than imagination that fails cannibals. They suffer a distortion in the empathic process. Strindberg's father typically believes, just as individuals in societies that practice cannibalism do, that the victim is serving a better purpose through the sacrificial death. This voracious attachment allows no room for empathy toward another's separate and individual life.

Strindberg suffered from lack of an empathic environment. Besides having a sensitive temperament, primary is the fact that at ages four and thirteen his life changed drastically. First, his father went bankrupt, leaving him with memories of bailiffs removing the furniture.[47] Then his mother died. Though he observed that he was an Ishmael from a family with "the wanderlust lay[ing] in our blood,"[48] he sought home, family, and children. However, unlike his compatriot Ibsen, Strindberg could not break with family or withstand an intense longing for his unloving mother. His wish for mother seems to stem from insecurity even beyond his early loss. Strindberg is the writer, in an article on Ibsen's *Rosmersholm*, who coined the term "soul murder," a kind of killing in which the victim's spirit dies through constant hostile and cruel yet subtle attacks. Leonard Shengold[49] took the term "soul murder" and extended it to describe children who lose faith in life when neglectful or punishing parents continue, even so, to be idealized by the dependent child. In these situations there is a mind-splitting operation that interprets and registers negative deeds as their opposite or as performed for the child's well-being, cutting the child off from acknowledging what is really experienced. According to critics and biographers, Strindberg must have felt under such threat and duress. He was not his mother's favorite; she had betrayed him to his strict father for discipline and she neither encouraged nor expressed joy over his growing accomplishments at school. Therefore, to keep her prominent, his image of her was overly idealized. This idolatry and sense of loss spoiled him for future relationships and his own joy in his creativity.

Edvard Munch's life also brought him to a head-on collision with alonetime and relationship struggles. Unlike Strindberg, Munch—who lost his mother at age four and suffered the untimely death of a beloved sister in his teens—was somewhat able to feel restored by the powerful visual and written expression given to these painful experiences and moods.[50] By all accounts he seemed to come to grips with the anxiety and inner turmoil of his life. During his own bouts with mental despair he explored the depths of "the other side of the eye"[51] and found a creative solution to the meaning of life. Munch symbolized both positive and negative ties between men and women with undulating lives; in his pictures, he contrasted crowds with the lonely individual. In different versions of *The Scream*—such as the lone person on the bridge, or the screamer alone in his agony as people face away from him—one sees the ability of friends to ignore or be unaware of another's inner desperation.[52] But Munch painted hundreds more pictures than that one, including images of love, and found a way to clarify his own life's meaning through his alone struggles: "When I paint illness and vice it is . . . a healthy release. It is a healthy reaction from which one can learn and live."[53]

Life Full of Passion

A loss occurred in my life that made me question whether everything I have to say about relationships and alonetime will change. Chapter 9 began in relative quiet—by that I mean harmony among friends and family. For my life is like yours, still one that is frequently caught in the whirlwind of contemporary times. I am picking up the threads of this chapter now that I have returned home after weeks spent watching my sister, Vida, battle to stay alive in the intensive care unit at Torrance Memorial Hospital, in southern California. Thinking of our childhood, I realize that many of my attachments were attachments made under stress, since from as far back as I can remember, my older and only sister had asthmatic attacks. Despite her condition, sibling rivalry did not elude us. My favorite memory is of her making me walk home limping with one foot in the gutter and one on the curb in order to receive the pleasure of her company. At twelve, I turned the tables and, limping like the villain in a Peter Lorre film, I scared her to distraction. We both happily escaped from those tortuous times, but also happily returned to closeness. First we needed distance and alonetime to sort things through. The recent time spent with her and my nieces, uncle, aunt, cousins, and brother-in-law demonstrated the power of family. As I try to digest the experience of my sister's death and my changed position, as the last of the immediate family, alonetime seems no less integral to life. Watching death, I could not help but see my sister's readiness to leave life. When I came home I had to face the fact that, even though sustained by all whom I love and who love me, I felt relief when I gained privacy to grieve, to integrate my experiences, and to enjoy freedom.

For some it is only in death that one attains freedom. De Beauvoir saw as one meaning of the *Liebestod* myth the message that absolute passion leads to the end of liberty so that death is the only solution: "Two lovers destined solely for each other are already dead; they die of ennui, of the slow agony of a love that feeds on itself."[54] In such fantasies, well-captured by poets, writers, and artists, despair and misery rule. Is death a way toward a lover, or an escape from the stronghold of requited love? Sylvia Plath struggled for a very long time with this dilemma until suicide seemed the only way to reunite not only with her departed father but with herself and remain separate.[55] In Plath's writings the starkness of death usually seems more attractive than love, which could be smothering. This type of love, states psychoanalyst Helen Gediman, makes death a preferable alternative to the

> blur of losing one's sense of identity through merger with a . . . loved other. The strains of craved death from sexual passion emerge out of anxieties about the annihilation of one's sense of being a self existing separately from an enamored other. It is as though actual death and implied resurrection of the self were preferable to the love-death and implied annihilation of the self through merger and dying together.[56]

In Gediman's emphasis on a dual orientation in life in which the individual must follow an autonomous stance as well as a feeling of community with others, excesses in either direction lead to, on the one hand, excessive self-love and, on the other, to excessive fusion. Even if, as Freud said, the human being has "originally two sexual objects—himself and the woman who nurses him,"[57] then to construct good relationships one must have the alonetime to acknowledge the self and the together moments to discover the comforts from another.

In the pursuit of alonetime and its meaningfulness in people's lives, I continue to step into dangerous territory. Even as we explore sexuality we are again reminded of death and love being readily coupled, this time in passionate orgasms labeled *le petit mort*. Freud set us straight (no pun intended) on sex being part of the life force and as basic a part of our nature as the desire to eat and drink. And like eating and drinking, sex can be disciplined or convoluted. Sex can propel intimacy into ecstasy. Yet even today in the age of AIDS, sex is often casual. Throughout the ages we have assumed that people have a hard time controlling their sexual appetite or that the devil makes us lustful. Could it be more than body heat and body chemistry that pushes for sex at any cost? Writer Vivian Gornick has one answer: "It's not me he loves . . . it's the sensation I arose in him."[58] People need to and want to make contact, but do not always consider that those contacts will become deep and everlasting. Accepting brief sexual intimacies as legitimate goes against almost all doctrines of morality and perhaps species survival as well. But if we are going to establish moral values, then we first need to consider the truth of human nature. Sex cannot be thought of only in terms of establishing a relationship or releasing sexual tension. Sex is sometimes to the adult what contact sports is to the child, a means to feel touched and massaged and self-reliant. Adultery is not always finding a more perfect lover than one's mate, or even giving in to uncontrollable passion. It is used as a means for securing a relationship as well as for breaking the bonds of intimacy. And masturbation is often just reassurance that one can make it on one's own. Sometimes it is absence that makes the heart grow fonder, and at other times it is out of sight, out of mind.

Attachments are vital, but sexual encounters like those above are not always long-entrenched relationships. Blanche DuBois ends the Tennessee Williams play *A Streetcar Named Desire* with the memorable sentence "I've always depended on the kindness of strangers." This statement— uttered by a sad, disillusioned woman graceful in her pain on her way to a mental asylum—is possibly true, for how else could we care for those beyond our family circle? Once again, our alone skills, along with the relational, allow us to brave new and forbidding social ties. If one didn't feel confidence or at least strength in being on one's own, one would not dare converse with an unknown person. Kids who grow up as only children find things out about alonetime somewhat earlier than most. They have to deal with the power of parents without the potential of peer support from brothers and sisters.[59] Thus, they quickly learn versatility in connecting and disengaging.

Only Children

Few studies are available on the inner life of only children. The only children that I meet tell me that when they're sent to play they spend more time in solo play space relating to make-believe characters. One adult related a memory of looking out her bedroom window, longing to participate in a grown-up party. Soon, however, her tears changed to glee when she imagined each fringe of the window shade as a separate character. At the same time, play dates and school friendships may be highly coveted. But one interesting look at affiliation patterns of only and firstborn children shows them to seek attachments more often during times of stress than later-born children do. Usually, onlies and first-born infants would receive quicker responses upon crying than would later-born children. This is probably because only children, self-sufficient at other times of their lives, need to make the extra effort to connect when distressed. Achievement seems highest in only children, and a disproportionate number of only and firstborn children are found among the eminent.[60] The typical explanations for this are that the adultlike relationships that evolve early on tend to add to maturation and achievement motivation. But remember that such children probably also have more alonetime. Despite the commitment and concern for only children, parents sensing their quickness to mature give them solitude. Only children have a strong tendency to be more inner directed than externally oriented. As they mature they seem to spend more time committed to solitary, intellectual, and artistic activities than group-oriented and social ones. A precocious four-year-old in therapy told his father who was offering him a choice of activities: "Sometimes I just like to be my lone." Of course, parents also have their reasons for having only one child; the opportunity for the parents' alonetime decreases as the number of siblings increases. Sometimes a different interplay arises, in which a parent makes a sole child an obsession and the child loses independence.

One dimension left over from childhood is a feeling of stifling dependency. Friendships can become competitive and dissolve, or build through cooperation. What makes the difference? Anger is often the tool we use to negotiate from dependency to necessary alonetime. At times it seems disruptive and at others it is a relief. In distorted relationships, abuse becomes the destructive antidote for dependency. This is when individuals' fear of both closeness and alonetime is profound. To expand on this, let's meet a patient of mine who was too doted upon as an only child.

Hector grew up feeling dependent upon his mother. Neither his culture nor his ideas on masculinity permitted this need to be evident. He spent long hours in a gym with the guys building his muscles and little else. By the time he was seventeen, he was strong and handsome. However, he hardly spent a moment alone, and despite his strength he never felt secure on his own. To compensate, he became a security guard at a hospital for the mentally disturbed. He handled weapons to impress "the girls."

At age twenty, still living at home, he got Felicia pregnant by forcing sex and persuaded her to marry him. Even after marriage and fatherhood, his dependency needs and efforts to counter them were incentive for extramarital relations, during lunch breaks and after work. When his wife wanted to talk things over about their child or their life together, he never had the time. When his girlfriends wanted to get serious, he had to go home to his wife. He had lots of company and what he thought was freedom of choice. But, in truth, he was a driven man without intimacy or alonetime as compensation.

Despite his attempts to juggle his life to avoid awareness of his deep yearnings for closeness and independence, the pressure mounted. One day his wife announced she'd like to go to college. He toyed with this notion, but it kept bothering him. He didn't know why. The day she called to tell him she was accepted, he left work early, came home, and beat her up. Felicia was a determined woman. She took her child and walked out the door to a friend's house. Hector was distraught—for the first time in his life he faced head-on the consequences of his behaviors and being left alone. Too embarrassed to seek forgiveness, he sulked and showed all the outward signs of severe depression.

One of the psychiatrists at his workplace directed him to psychotherapy. At first he was humiliated in doing this. It matched neither his image nor his professional stance. When the question was asked as to what did make him feel secure, he could not find an answer. This tough man was so tightly watched over as a child that he hardly ever did anything for himself. He described being hungry as a nine-year-old, marching to the kitchen, and his mother arriving in front of the refrigerator door to help him before he had time to open it. As strong as he was, he wasn't sure of his ability to survive on his own. Living alone was a prescription he filled for a year, and it changed his perspective on everything.

◆　◆　◆

Hector, in a way, was still living out his childhood, but realizing that he could survive on his own helped him to evolve and saved his marriage. This story has a happy resolution because Hector and Felicia cared for each other enough to tolerate the past and appreciate changes. Felicia felt a bit at fault, too, for continuing to overindulge him and not insisting they confront what they knew was wrong in the marriage. When the dialogue became direct, the marriage could establish new rules, which allowed them to change the nature of their expectations.

Incorporative Attachments, or Friendly Relationships?

In Woody Allen's *Annie Hall,* Alvy Singer tells Annie, "A relationship, I think, is like a shark, you know? It has to constantly move forward or it dies. And I think what we got on our hands is a dead shark."[61] Certainly there are well-made marriages, but if we are primarily social animals, why would such bonding prove so arduous, even be described as frag-ile?[62] We are solitary creatures, too. Reiser calls this need for separate space "selfishness," but not in a pejorative fashion: "Theoretically, mar-riage is all about two people becoming as One. But in the real world—and let's be really clear about this—you ain't One. You're Two. And there's only so much two people can blend."[63]

A theory that hearkens back to ecology sees cohabitants as coevolving in cycles of relatedness.[64] Coevolution takes place between animal and nature, or between a plant and its surroundings, or between different people. As individuals coevolve, so does the couple itself in a relation-ship. People constantly transform one another, as is seen in couples who begin to look alike or finish each other's sentences, and in turn the rela-tionship alters. This can truly be for better or worse, since things in relationships do not stay the same. Sex is sometimes hit-and-run—some-times a union is so deep that it feels biological. On the other hand, com-mitment can seem like a chain around one's neck or a joyous sacrament. People also hold on for dear life to stagnation, fearing anything that could upset their stability, no matter how debilitating. The changes are, of course, important, but what I am emphasizing, however, is that any change can appear threatening to an individual's integrity, as is seen in Hector and Felicia's story. This is one of the reasons alonetime needs—time to reflect and sort things out—escalate in a relationship and become paramount. Divorce isn't the answer, since unresolved childhood dramas tend to repeat themselves and poor unions recapitulate. Recognizing the alone needs helps some.

A young woman decided to confide in me about her marriage, which she thought was good but did not follow the expected pat-tern. Her husband is a wonderful lover, she began, but unlike in other relationships she's had, she does not seek endless sex with him. On the other hand, she claims, she was never as intimate with her other partners—they all had been rather aloof. The intimacy between her and her husband is remarkable—conversations con-tinue while one of them is on the commode in the bathroom. During the day they might share time together at the drop of a hat, and weekends are intense. She feels herself changing from a person casual about relationships to one who depends on them, wondering if she is getting enough closeness. Looking at things that way, sex once a week or every other week is absolutely suffi-cient. Lately, they neither go to bed together nor wake up at the same time. This could be part of the problem, but she doesn't wish to break this habit—at night she is exhausted, goes to bed first, and is too tired to think of sex. In the morning he's still sleeping, and frankly that's her best time of day. No one is up at 5 or 6 A.M. —when she arises—and that's when she sips coffee and reads the paper. The streets are quiet and it's the only time she is truly alone. *She'd never give this up for sex.*

◆　　◆　　◆

We may be entering into a postsexual revolution, where a woman could believe that sex is quite secondary to her pressing need to be alone! Interestingly, this woman's dismissal of passion is not a singular act. The intense highs of romantic love are often followed by a more enduring, secure love called companionate love. It is this latter type of love that is thought to be the best type of love with which to raise children. Caring, intimacy, and commitment serve the function of keeping the parents together, thereby increasing the probability that their offspring will receive protection and nurturance. At some point most idealized lovers become ordinary human beings. I propose that with the reappearance of this reality, a restlessness born from too little alonetime also becomes apparent. Now each partner has to return to their individual concerns in life, no longer able to rely on their new love to fight their battles. Couples who successfully handle this impasse in their relationship do so usually through a renegotiation of the amount and condition of time spent together. This is, of course, a tricky balance because it sets one's emotions free to fall in love passionately, perhaps with someone other than the spouse this time.

Another advocated way around these struggles for balance is choosing companionate love over passionate love to form the basis for selecting a marriage partner. Parent and couple counselor Sol Gordon advocates marrying a good friend.[65] He believes that sexual attraction and chemistry are greatly exaggerated as critical factors in a successful marriage. In fact, he ranks sex as number nine on his list of the ten most important factors in a good long-term relationship, which include intimacy, a sense of humor, honest communication, and shared experience. Gordon's definition of a successful marriage is one in which, after a number of years, the partners can still look at each other and say, "I like you." Friendship is key to a continuing relationship. Getting along as friends does not mean entering conflict-free comfort zones. The emphasis today on harmonious and reciprocal smooth interaction is a trend emanating from an attachment theory perspective. *Dyssynchrony* is just as much a part of relationships as *synchrony*.[66] However, no one pathway—companionship or romance—ensures survival of a relationship or the deepening of sexual intimacy.

Nowadays, the break from marital intimacy has found a new venue —cyberspace. As one reporter tells us, "Cyberflings are heating up the Internet."[67] Things have gotten even far more out of hand in real life than in Stephanie D. Fletcher's novel *E-Mail: A Love Story.* One New Jersey spouse is actually suing his wife for divorce on the grounds that she committed sexually explicit tête-à-têtes on-line. Love letters of the licentious type are not new, but the virtual reality and quick exchange of computer sex could become more commonplace and seemingly far more threatening. Nonetheless, as author Sherry Turkle tells us, without the physical body as part of the love equation, the issues are cloudy.[68] "Adultery" on-screen, without sex, is a number of steps beyond quietly lusting with the heart. But without visibility and touch between partners, whether pen or computer pals, you in part are floating in alonetime—a time of the imagination—as well as relationship time. It is exactly that strange mixture of intimacy and anonymity that keeps the sparks flying.

What was poet John Donne saying in his quest for mutuality with his lady love: "To teach you I am naked first"?[69] This great composer of love sonnets was claiming a need to know himself and then to take on the challenge of love. But can one know self or other through electrifying computer currents, and are they able to replace the thrill of a touch? In reviewing *Deeper,* John Seabrook's entertaining tale of his two-year love affair with his Mac and his full immersion in the computer world, *New York Times* writer Christopher Lehmann-Haupt says that Seabrook's discoveries give pause and make one reflect on the potential false worship of cyberspace. Lehmann-Haupt suggests that this exposé could just as well have been named *Shallower.*[70] So far, on-line engagements don't seem to be adding up to their promise, and thus relationships are perhaps as endangered as aloneness. Although for Seabrook himself, as stated in a television interview with Charlie Rose, the connections with his readers feel closer since he went on-line.

Whenever individual solace is hard to find, the preciousness of coupling increases. But without alone skills, no one would survive the loss of loved ones, hospital stays with tubes and tormenting tests, and the daily ordeals of love and work. Selfobjects, in the guise of people and attachments, that is, do not take care of all the contingencies. I have been in situations of great stress when relatives, friends, and other caregivers are trying their best to ease the pain and burdens. But the isolation that Munch depicts on the bridge is a part of most people's lives at one time or another. Without sustained and ongoing inner as well as outer connectedness to add fortitude, we do not get through those grueling, stressful times. Munch wanted to help people to overcome the vicissitudes of life and resistances—including his own to romance. He chose to do this with words and visual messages. A creative solution is what we all seek to life's problems. Alonetime, as we shall see in the following chapter, helps in that direction.

CHAPTER 10

Creativity, Curiosity, and Celibacy

It is testimony to Beethoven's strength and resiliency of character that he was able to withstand [the stresses of parental rejection]. Nevertheless . . . Beethoven largely withdrew from the society of his fellows and playmates, and from his parents as well . . . Beethoven's "happiest hours were those when he was free . . . when all the family were away and he was alone by himself. . . ." Cäcilia Fischer recalled Beethoven "leaning in the window with his head in both hands and staring fixedly at one spot."

MAYNARD SOLOMON, Beethoven[1]

Curiosity killed the cat.
OFFICIAL PROVERB, American Speech[2]

Sex has been domesticated, stripped of the promised mystery, added to the category of the merely expected. It's just what is done, mundane as hockey. It's celibacy these days that would raise eyebrows.

MARGARET ATWOOD, Wilderness Tips[3]

BEETHOVEN WAS UNUSUALLY creative and unusually emotionally forlorn, but he was not at all unusual in his search for solace. For example, Jack Benny writes:

When Mama went over to help in the store, I stopped practicing [the violin]. I'd watch the boats [from my window]. I'd watch the people by the docks. I'd fall into a trance and dream of running away to far off countries. I'd try to keep an eye out for Mama, crossing the street . . . I would get so dreamy that I would forget to watch out for her returning home.[4]

Benny, too, sought a place of comfort despite a stable upbringing, as he describes: "I should warn you now . . . I did not triumph over adversity.

[221]

I did not go through struggles and hardship. I come from a conventional, warmhearted Jewish family."[5] Daydreaming and creativity are solidly linked and vacantly gazing (spacing out) is a common memory for most of us. Everyone accepts that solo escapes are an important route to creativity. But less recognized is how for some the synergy of the group also inflames imagination. I will discuss the Brontë and Mozart families, in which this is exemplified. Even in terms of the creative spark, everyone strikes his or her own balance between these two needs to relate and to be alone—with muse or without. This does not deter from the fact that the artist in us, the part of the self seeking an individual solution to life's unknowns and hardships, must risk disconnection. Creative and long-lasting choices about who we want to be and how we want to live require quiet deliberation. In this chapter and the next we shall witness what may happen if alone needs overcompensate in the lives of alienated people, when creativity soars and when it backfires. For to reconstruct alonetime we need also to see just how far people will go when they feel their aloneness is being overly encroached upon.

I once saw in psychoanalysis a well-known artist who insisted his art depended upon his vow of celibacy. This was a strange turn in his life, since he was, prior to these new convictions, a bit of a ladies' man. I wondered, did he sculpt less well during the former, promiscuous days than he did now? He was convinced that his sexual drive consumed too much of his passion. Describing the relational demands he left behind, he realized that it was not the flow of semen that wore him out, but rather the continued desire for his time. This was dramatized by the fact that with the changes he imposed upon himself and his wife—the value of separate beds and renouncing of sex—came also a withdrawal of verbal and physical affection. Why this drastically new lifestyle? His treatment uncovered some reasons. For one, the celibacy vows followed the achievement of recognition and success among his peers. The renunciation was both a sacrifice and, as he put it, a way to "find my own way again. If I had kept up barhopping, sleeping around, and having passionate affairs on top of responding to reporters and art dealers who suddenly found me interesting, gradually I would be diminished to nothingness." Interestingly, though, the press and public courtship by the art world held little attraction for him, and automatically he completely avoided this. So we had to look deeper. One day he told me about a side of his lovemaking previously unrevealed: "When I lay in bed with a new woman it was to me like Balboa discovering the Pacific. The waves and undulations of her body translated to the movement in my sculptures. I was curious about every detail of her form. Each new acquaintance was not a conquest, but rather fresh knowledge. After a while, this curiosity about others wore thin. It was from the outside, and I seemed to be avoiding what was inside myself. Perhaps my divorcing the world is too complete, but it is the only way I can proceed for now."

◆ ◆ ◆

He was right—he had begun to move away from his own creative force while depending too much on inspiration from the outside. I think of how Cézanne or Matisse repainted the same fruit or landscape over and over as a clue to what was missing in him. My patient had forgotten his private thoughts, the good ideas from within.

Artists have not reached a consensus as to whether art is a public or private act or whether society, culture, and art should divorce from one another. Whether society is described as alienated, as ours sometimes is, or as caught up in traditions, artists and individuals still find themselves groping for a silent place in which to create. Artist, sculptor, designer, and builder James Hubbell, as one example, sees the "process [beginning within] the part of me that is empty . . . Art is learning how to be quiet."[6] The artist's dilemma is not confined only to those who make their way in the creative world. Is not living life creatively the task before all of us?

What keeps people from feeling in charge of their feelings, thoughts, and actions? Some say it's all biochemical. A study of conjoined (Siamese) twins with identical genes shows that they have strong dissimilarities, which suggests that physical makeup might not be solely responsible for personality. Six-year-old Abigail and Brittany Hennel are among the few, five hundred in all, babies born of an incompletely divided single egg known to survive their first year.[7] No more than four sets of these twins are believed to have shared an undivided torso and two legs, as they do. Yet they have learned to walk, ride a bike, and swim in their special world, which requires unusual coordination and cooperation. They are hardly duplicates, however, for they have separate heads, hearts, stomachs, and gallbladders, and three lungs. They also have two distinct personalities and, demonstrating the power of this first form of disengagement, avert their gaze through eye and head movements to gain alonetime. What explains the psychological distinctions? According to

J. David Smith, professor at the University of South Carolina and expert on the psychology of conjoined twins, "It isn't genes or the environment. People are actively involved in creating their personalities. They make different choices, pursue different directions." The development of conjoined twins, he says, "is a compelling study in human freedom."[8] If it is true that we create our personalities, and I believe to a good extent it is, then such creation demands fantasy time and exploration—alone and with others.[9]

The Creative Path—Life As Art

We all know about the lone and creative artist. Anthony Storr has expanded this definition of the artist considerably in his work, gently suggesting that *some* development of the capacity to be alone is necessary for the brain to function optimally.[10] But I know how hard it is to forge a happy and worthwhile life and do not psychologically distinguish between living creatively and creativity itself—the creative act. Having the sagacity to navigate life gracefully and fully, "floating upward" as Larry Morgan does in teacher and novelist Wallace Stegner's contemporary gem *Crossing to Safety*, compares well with works of art that require precious strokes and careful molding. So I ask, what happens from day one to a baby's contented time alone, to the creative eighteen-month-old child who pretends he is reading a book as he makes up his own story, or the two-year-old ballerina dancing before imaginary crowds? Many people continue in their chosen pathway to charm the world and brighten theirs and others' lives. Obviously, some grow up to be lawyers, businessmen, plumbers, shopkeepers, and so forth. Some maintain creative avocations or imaginations or both. But many don't grow up trusting or realizing their dreams, because the dual needs of being attached and being alone can come to be treated as antagonistic. When that happens, escaping the conflict may sour into an antisocial isolation. Some great geniuses manage to create in that atmosphere, but like others, the ordinary individual can get sidetracked into regressive fantasies. Similarly, when attachments become unyielding or obsessive, the creative stimulus is lost in an enervating monotony. Only detailed examination of a person's life can mark what has deterred someone from a creative path.[11]

While it is not only the poets and writers who recognize alonetime's fullness in life, Tillie Olsen is among those who realize that artists risk more than most as they frequently lead the way into free and creative silent space.[12] Strangely—as in the case of Beethoven, Virginia Woolf, and others—these escapades are treated as withdrawal, as an abnormal option that only genius-level intelligence excuses. Even rather recently a biographical essay on Woody Allen treats comic genius as an ability to create joy out of the morbidity of solitude.[13] Anthony Storr similarly demonstrates how the lonely pasts of writers may unexpectedly turn into productivity, suggesting that such creative solitude is primarily reserved for artists and writers.[14] But staring blankly into space is not only a habit of the gifted, as any grade-school teacher will confirm. The alonetime need permeates every pore in life, but in certain enterprises, such as artistic production, its presence is ever more palpable. Certainly, many authors have seen aloneness as a requirement for beginning serious creative work. And fortunately, we can all take lessons from those who describe the way.

Distinctive voices in the discussion of solitude and creativity, such as Virginia Woolf's in *A Room of One's Own*,[15] give a title to the idea that one's own room, a cocoon of privacy, signifies a person's stature as a discoverer of plans, narratives, magic, or ideas. Thoreau's time alone in a small cabin on Walden Pond allowed him to theorize about the fruits of solitude.[16] Poet May Sarton knew of the plenitude of solitude and how easily we can find restorative comfort in not having to struggle with another's moods and tastes. All the same, she forever sought to conquer via love another's soul. Sarton writes about cycles of intimacy and solitude, which she feels are essential to creative work.[17] Novelists Doris Grumbach and Alix Kate Shulman write of learning and growing in their lives and work while living alone for an extended time.[18]

To explain further, Grumbach experiments with a self-enforced solitude that many besides the literary have tried. Her journey teaches her austere lessons on ways to face death and more. She writes that by the end of her time alone she realized that she needed to live "with the top layer of my person known to the outside world and displayed for social purposes. But, close to the heart there had to be an inner sanctum, formed and cultivated in solitude."[19] What makes this contact with the essence of the self so important throughout aging? The rising numbers of robust elderly continue to want singular independent lives, like my mother-in-law, who fought until she was into her nineties to manage her apartment by herself. Similarly, a friend's mother of seventy-eight years angrily informs her son that she will furnish her new apartment without his help. In that stubborn resistance people find their creative and solitary acts as restorative. Alone states are absolutely essential to all for basic and extraordinary survival. My mother-in-law in her forties could not have had the sustained courage to escape from a preconcentration camp in France—a monthlong journey to and over the Alps by herself until she reached Switzerland—without aloneness being an ongoing force in her life.

Growing Up Creatively

The question of what in the personality elicits great creative works and energy catches the interest of psychologists.[20] Adolescents are known to seek and greet solitude as energetically as they do peers. Research on creative and talented teenagers suggests that the most talented young-sters are those who treasure their solitude.[21] For further clues, psychologist Dean Keith Simonton of the University of California at Davis dips deeply into the biographies of geniuses, artists, and leaders to understand what traits predispose people to create—whether scientists, writers, or painters. The profiles seem to match in one characteristic above all others: an extreme proclivity toward introversion, or what is called by R. B. Cattell "schizothymia"—a cool reserve, detachment, and introversion.[22] Nevertheless, reportedly some geniuses are creative extroverts, like Alexandre Dumas, who could presumably write a novel in his head while engaged in repartee. Such verbal swordplay is the exception to the rule. For although inspiration for creativity depends on relationships as well as solitary moments, the characteristic of dedicated preoccupation most fitting to creative production is hard solitary work. The attractions of the outside can indeed disrupt the creative process, as Charles Dickens discovered. On the one hand he protested against such distractions:

> "It is only half an hour"—"It is only an afternoon"—"It is only an evening," people say to me . . . but they don't know . . . that the mere consciousness of an engagement will sometimes worry a whole day. These are the penalties paid for writing books. Whoever is devoted to an art must be content to deliver himself wholly up to it.[23]

So said Dickens, and so he was able in his later years to neglect the home hearth to work, but he was also himself victim to a love of public. Eventually, his desire for admirers ruined his health and his art. It was a taste of control over audiences and hence obsessive readings onstage that became addictive and eventually fatal to his health.[24] Enjoying an audience may inflate to intoxication from the limelight. Being talented and creative does not exempt one from the same pitfall we all face when failing to figure out the right proportions of alone and engaged time, and early childhood experiences influence us to a degree in these decisions.

Sometimes parents' needs for children to be creative are actually displaced wishes for their own self-expression. One might think that women's returning to or entering the workforce is the best thing to happen to them and their children. Now women who have the energy to work can do so, and children will benefit from *satisfied*, high-powered moms. But women with drive who feel deprived of time to create outside of the household have been known to create havoc in kids' lives. Take the story of domestic life in Silver Spring, Maryland, a suburb of Washington, D.C., reported by Mark Singer in the recent women's issue of *The New Yorker*.[25] Singer reveals the tale of Sera, for example, who approaches each mothering task completely seriously: " 'I'm a designer,' she says. 'You have to design your children's future to a certain point . . . Sometimes I wake up at night and have an anxiety attack—that I've forgotten about this or that part of my child's brain.' "A new phenomenon for many a well-educated, professional woman is to come back to the home—to be a mother to her own children. To women still not cured of the supermom strivings, ambition today seems to take a different shape, however, from that of a Renaissance woman, a role in which many feminists saw themselves in the early 1970s. Now for some, work and parenthood is not the solution. Women put their all into being mothers.

Today's children frequently cannot escape the do-gooding, informed parents who think stimulation and attachment are everything. It is almost as if parents these days feel their children are all little Mozarts. Allowing children time to figure things out, ignoring mild bad habits, and providing unprogrammed moments are parts of a beneficial benign neglect. Contrast Sera's parenting style with that of Margaret Dean Daiss; the latter is the woman who wrote the pro-alonetime article sent to me by my anti-alonetime colleague, described in the Introduction.

> "Man, I'm bored," announced my six-year-old daughter . . . [on] Spring Break . . . I remind her that I am writing. She stomps off to her room. Bang! she slams the door shut. Later—much later—my daughter's humming seeps into my consciousness. I knock on her door. It cracks open, and a small girl with a pleased and gaping grin peers up at me . . . she has created a post office . . . For the rest of vacation, she is occupied with the business of running the post office.[26]

Neglecting children's education, social life, or dependency needs, we know is bad. But micromapping every free moment could be equally debilitating. We are potentially doing away with self-steering, ability to resolve times of boredom, independence of imagination, and most of all finding creative solutions on one's own. Daiss says that she regards "solitude as essential as air" and gives it to her children plentifully, both instinctively and with deliberation.[27] Not so for Mozart!

The retelling[28] of Mozart's life dispels the well-established myth perpetrated by his family, himself, and Peter Shaffer's play and film *Amadeus* that Mozart remained forever a little boy. Gifted as a child beyond the extraordinary, he found in music all to amuse him in life. And since this talent enabled his father to live out his own thwarted fantasies and pleased his mother to no end, he was indeed a mostly happy child, if not a bit overly compliant. His wishes and his parents' wishes for him were on the same track—alone, self-regulation, attachment, and relational needs found harmony. Or they almost did. Leopold Mozart was the superparent in this case, wanting to extract from his son the devotion, status, and wealth he felt had been denied him in his own quest for musical recognition at the expense of disinheritance by his mother. Even before Mozart reached age five, his father tasted in his son's musical genius what would quench all his own ambitions. Leopold Mozart's calling became the teaching, training, and molding of everything in young Mozart's life. Mozart found satisfaction in this, as his one wish was to play with music. The myth of Mozart as an impulsive, gullible, unserious youth was invoked over and again in Leopold's sermons to his son as a means to perpetuate subjugation. When Mozart first struck out on his own, his mother was forced to go with him. She in some ways encouraged Mozart's independent strivings and remained in their quarters whole days alone, giving him freedom in the music world. But even she, when Mozart began to show fondness for another family and love for a woman, impeded his separation. Mozart's wish, as a child, to be loved and to please others compelled him to endure bouts of sadness. His music and life in his later years were a constant struggle to regain his separate soul. In *Mozart: A Life,* Maynard Solomon tells us that

> Mozart wanted to leave childhood and its subjections behind, to shatter the frozen perfection of the little porcelain violinist and to put in his place a living man, one with sexual appetites, bodily functions, irreverent thoughts, and selfish impulses, one who needed to live for himself and his loved ones and not only for those who had given him life.[29]

If anyone tried to achieve the goal of harmony between alone and attachment needs, it was Mozart—not only in his music, but in seeking spiritual independence from his home through Freemasonry. Yet the hovering presence of his father was apparently too overshadowing for young Mozart to comfortably acknowledge his alone spirit. As recorded in his words upon hearing of his father's death, he saw the end of life as an existential pathway: "the true goal of our existence," "the best and truest friend of mankind," "the key which unlocks the door to our true happiness."[30] Separation anxiety, as seen from the perspective of Mozart's life, is certainly not a natural outcome or basic fear of leaving vital attachments; it is instead the painful consequence experienced in response to implanted warnings by overly zealous and controlling parental tactics. When caretakers or loved ones rail against one's striking out alone, pleading misery as Leopold did, those who are kind of heart, like Mozart, are stricken with ambivalence, considering their own need to be selfish as unworthy, blocking some of their spirit of adventure and natural curiosity, and fantasizing about death as a release.[31]

The Enhancement of Creativity: Curiosity and Being Left Alone

" 'Curiouser and curiouser!' cried Alice. She was so much surprised that for the moment she quite forget how to speak good English."[32] Outside Wonderland, no one better than H. A. Rey, in the adventures of the monkey Curious George, captures childhood's never-ending creative curiosity.[33] Curiosity has been called "the urge to knowledge."[34] Psychoanalytic literature contains tales, as does the Bible, of how this desire for information is linked to interest in sex, the origins of humankind, and unshared knowledge. Seeking novelty and nosiness, though laden with taboos, are from early on exciting. When we feel well-apprised of things it fortifies our will and ability to be alone. We are compelled to know; and because the answers are rarely totally satisfactory, we are equally compelled to fantasize and pursue answers on our own. As psychoanalyst and Freud scholar Herman Nunberg has written, "Curiosity and the need for causality are boundless. There are individuals whose urge to know is unlimited and whose ego seems to lose control over this urge and to become its prisoner. Individuals of this type may be utterly ruthless in their avidity for knowledge and totally unconcerned with the possible consequences of their search."[35] The destructiveness of certain intrusively enquiring, sensation-seeking tabloids is fairly apparent.

Curious George's activities stop just short of curiosity becoming a solo, all-consuming, invasive push for knowledge. In the beginning of George's captivity, the plan was to place him in a zoo, thwarting George's goal to be free to explore. This continuous battle between personal desire to savor information and society's need to capture and suppress individual curiosity, perhaps for protection but also due to fear of the unknown, gets played in each adventure. In one episode, George breaks away from the zoo and into a woman's apartment while it's being painted. He adds his creative touch and paints murals of trees and plants on the living room walls. Escaping when the painters return, he jumps out a window and breaks his leg. The apartment owner shouts—playing the role of society—"He got what he deserved!" And the elevator man says knowingly, "I told him he would get into trouble. He was too curious."[36]

Being a know-it-all, sticking one's nose in other people's business, and opening forbidden doors speak of keeping children out of mischief and maintaining boundaries between adult matters, such as sex, and children's free play space. The harmony of the family depends to a degree on conformity. This is not usually hard to achieve, as children by nature identify with those around them. And praise is typically given for behavior that consolidates family goals. If, in the quest for family unity, curiosity—exploring that which is unlike, unknown, and unpopular to the unit—is seriously dampened, the child may choose to become secretly rebellious or accept life as a Caspar Milquetoast. Of course, such destinies typify the extremes, and many who have their space to explore hampered find some compromise.

To my way of thinking, bold and brazen curiosity about the world—as exemplified in the *Books of Knowledge* that I avidly thumbed through as a child—is essential to learning. Psychologist and *New York Times* columnist Daniel Goleman informs us that curiosity is one of seven areas of "emotional intelligence" that predict success in kindergartners.[37] Curiosity would also come within the frame of eminent educator and Harvard professor Howard Gardner's breakdown of "multiple intelligences."[38] I focus on Gardner's idea of intrapersonal knowledge, that is, knowing oneself. Without the confidence that learning about ourselves is ultimately positive, we would find it difficult to gain the insights about our bodies and minds that give us mastery through self-regulation. If we do not take on self-regulation commensurate with our self-knowledge and general capacities, we begin to feel stuck, at a loss for creative solutions, and afraid of alonetime. Several stories come to mind.

The parents of a child patient, Hillery, divorced when she was three and her brother one year old. Hillery's mother, strapped for money, returned to work. First the children had substitute home care, but when my patient and her brother reached six and four years, respectively, they became latchkey kids. This responsibility was not taken lightly, and the little girl felt fearful all afternoon till her mother returned. The obligation was so overwhelming to her that during sing-alongs at school, when the last line of "Farmer in the Dell" was sung, she burst into tears, thinking of the cheese standing alone. At six, Hillery was hardly able to contain all her own needs, let alone her brother's. Only in therapy was she able to realize some of the benefits of this self-care system. Self-care, self-reliance, and self-control at age six is not a phenomenon exclusive to children in the era of working mothers, when house keys around children's necks became a typical sight.

◆ ◆ ◆

In 1903, at age seven, George Burns joined with a six-year-old bass player to perform as the Pee-Wee Quartet in saloons. He was obviously creatively ready for self-sustenance; my patient was not. What's the difference? This is an important question since, according to an 1987 Census Bureau report, over 7 percent of all five- to thirteen-year-olds are in self- or sibling care after school, and two and a quarter million children are unsupervised by an adult before school.[39] Home alone—or with a sibling—is not just a film fantasy. Readiness for self-care, to be alone, is not merely based on age or family needs. I think it is tied to a child's physical, emotional, social, and creative readiness. Without ignoring the necessary safety measures that need to be in place in terms of the community, an open communication line with a parental figure, and instructions about emergencies, my focus is on what readies a child emotionally to feel safe alone. And is it absolutely necessary for a child to be protected from all loneliness and fear? My sister and I were not latchkey children in the modern sense of the term. I did, however, sometimes come home to an empty house at age seven. I also rode the subway alone at that age. Occasionally I did feel incapable of being on my own, and sometimes I did wish for company. My subway memories, however, consist of the countless scenes that flashed before my eyes, the colors, the changing architecture, and the quick flashes into people's lives as I passed the different homes. The rides were soothing and fanciful.

To be psychologically equipped to handle being home alone, a child needs to be comfortable alone without *excessive* fear, have an acceptance of rules, and generally not be a withdrawn, hostile, or self-destructive person. Socially a child needs to feel at ease with neighbors and friends so as to solicit help if necessary and know the roles of community resources. Not too much data is available on the fear and loneliness quotient of children left to self-care as compared to children in day care or children under all-day parental care. So far, except for one study on inner-city ghetto children (in which the interviewer was presumably biased), the differences are not great, with latchkey children actually being ahead in positive characteristics such as good grades, strong friendships, and self-competence. They have also been rated as more headstrong.[40]

Being headstrong is rooted in the family dynamics of psychologist Margaret Cornelia Morgan, born in 1914 to a preacher father and teacher mother.[41] As her daughter Sara Lawrence Lightfoot tells the inspiring story, color lines kept Margaret and her brown father in one corner and her light-skinned mother alone.[42] Because of dissension between her mother and father she became a parentified child acutely attuned to her father's needs. But neither her allegiance to her father nor her recognition of her mother's independent dedication to teaching was enough to propel her to be a great healer of children. A lot depended upon her creative thoughts during alonetime:

> As an only child, Margaret spent long periods of time with no one to talk to but herself. "I walked to school, across town to the railroad tracks, up the railroad tracks to Cherry Street . . . a long way . . . at least three miles, probably more . . . thinking about everything under the sun." There were no brothers or sisters with whom she could test out her feelings, and there was no one to distract her from thought. Her mind turned back on itself and built elaborate, embellished narratives.[43]

Some might say that Margaret represents the only child who experienced too many alone moments, but who changed loneliness into strength. Unless people have just such time to dialogue with themselves, however, they do not build character. The isolation was a stepping-stone to her own self-analysis and later psychoanalysis. Learning about herself, she realized she desired a career in medicine. After much thought and discussion with her husband, Fred, she applied and became the first African-American to be accepted into Columbia's Psychiatric Institute in New York. Throughout Margaret's life grew two strong parallel lessons: to pursue independence and to pursue trust and intimacy. Both furthered personal achievement and brought her to a place where she could creatively grasp the opportunity to link with a dedicated feminist as a husband. Together they encouraged their three children's autonomy and appreciation for the familial bond.

Margaret was a child who studied herself, even though her parents, through their own unsettled lives, demanded considerable contemplation and concern on her part. For the successful individual like Margaret, or artists like Mozart or Beethoven, unhappy life events and even anger are absorbed creatively. Through the biographies of artists, we learn how they draw from negative feelings to power their work: "Henry James' 'secret wound' and Dostoevsky's 'holy disease,' even [Beethoven's] loss of hearing was in some obscure sense necessary (or at least useful) to the fulfillment of a creative quest."[44] Beethoven understood that a pursuit of idleness was energizing to his work. Beethoven also relegated romance to a back burner.

Celibacy

Thinking about the compulsivity with which some pursue romance and sex, I can understand the equal ferocity with which celibacy was sometimes favored, by Beethoven, my artist patient, and others. Letting go of one's sexual need for others leaves that aspect of self-regulation to only oneself. Sally Cline, writer and faculty member in social and political science at Cambridge University, makes an unusually strong appeal to women to favor that choice, raising the question in my mind whether sexual abstinence has to accompany creative solitude.[45] Following the history of the Shakers, who denounced sex, and a more radical group of females called the Sanctificationist Sisters, who viewed genital coupling as the primary misfortune and evil in America's culture, Cline elaborates on these groups' positions of social reform that offered an expansion of women's rights. It is clear from the writings of these women of the late 1800s that feeling in control of their own lives was most important to them: "It was no longer woman's duty to remain with a husband who bossed and controlled her," said one Sanctificationist. "God made man and woman equal."[46]

Cline emphasizes that solitude and living alone are increasingly seen as pejorative in American society. She states that sexual congress of whatever type—from heterosexuality and homosexuality to adultery and sadomasochism—is an activity pursued not out of love or perhaps even desire, but with mandatory consumerism. Thus, she questions what she calls a genital myth of sex leading to health. After interviewing various women over a period of two years, she instead recommends passionate celibacy for creative and spiritual growth—for females, a sexual singlehood. While she does not establish its relevancy to both genders, Cline is among a rare number of people who consciously claim aloneness as a personal need and is particularly clear in her definitions of aloneness, loneliness, and solitude:

> Solitude is the state of being alone, and is not to be confused with loneliness ... Loneliness *can* result from solitude, but it does not have to. There are times I have never felt more lonely than at a large noisy party. At other times I have felt a deep joy at being on my own ... Too much time spent with other people ensures my desperate need of a retreat ... It is as if with the coin of fun and companionship I let other people buy small pieces of my soul and I can only retrieve them by spending time alone.
>
> On these occasions I have a *need* to be on my own, which is different from the *capacity* to be alone. I have always had that need ... It is only in the last few years that I have developed the capacity to be alone.[47]

Celibates were set against marriage, and the dictionary still states its meaning, stemming from the Latin *caelebs*, as "not married." Common usage of the word "chastity," the avoidance of genital activity, varies from the idea of singleness.[48] Saint Jerome, whose appeal to women we already heard in Chapter 3, stated: "As long as a woman is for birth and children, she is different from man as body is from soul. But when she wishes to serve Christ more than the world, then she will cease to be a woman, and will be called man."[49] So the chaste woman was woman escaping defamation for her sexuality (even in marriage) or the woman as man. Choosing chastity is a complex decision. Yet it is a decision made by several societies of women in order primarily to rebel against traditional female roles and to "transform women's dependent and subordinate status into one of independence and self-determination," according to Sally L. Kitch, an authority on such organizations.[50] The Commonwealth of Sanctificationists, as they were called, were committed not only to celibacy but also, to some degree, to the more controversial principle of " 'giving up the flesh,' that is, ceasing to have particular feelings about family members. Like Jesus, the sanctified sisters believed they must abandon any relationships that might interfere with their spiritual commitment to the community, even among parents and children."[51]

Creative solitude does not necessitate celibacy for me, but I can understand why it might. For some people, only celibacy expresses a sense of being in control. Celibacy is an unhealthy extreme only when it is used as an escape. My artist patient was fooled in his quest for celibacy because his true quest was for greater alonetime in which to restore his artistic integrity. Everyone has to work out their own compromises between the needs for aloneness and relatedness. A gentler route to a balance between community and alonetime, self-sufficiency and a newfound status and respect in life, may be writing down one's thoughts.

Finding One's Muse

If we understand that, historically, men were more able than women to shape their futures and follow a solitudinous call—at sea, on horseback, or through wandering—then we realize why females traditionally put deep longings of self-determination on paper. Journal writing may be *the* symbol of the lone creative woman. At the same time the Commonwealth of Sanctificationists was at its strongest, in the nineteenth century, the idea of the unmarried woman became less reprehensible, and even a desirable option.[52] Young ladies and married women kept diaries, and certainly single women wrote copiously on evenings alone. The journals, though private, were also left open to share with others. One can find examples of celibate and noncelibate women who in their solitude and passionate chastity create lasting works. Then there are those who find motivation from relationships.

The Brontës represent many points on the spectrum; the siblings were competitive, passionate, solitary, and very attached.[53] Emily seemed to love her isolation and solitude, as exemplified in *Wuthering Heights* and the sentimental and melancholy Heathcliff, who roams the hills of heather alone. He demonstrates a dedicated if not sometimes dreary solitude, as does Emily's poetry.[54] Her sister Charlotte, bound by soothing solitude, also reveled in sibling company. Certainly, she loved her alone musing: "The human heart has hidden treasures, in secret kept, in silence sealed."[55] But with the death of her second sister, Anne, she lamented, "And now, benighted, tempest-tossed, Must bear alone the weary strife."[56] Charlotte did not prefer creating in solitude. Charlotte's best and preferred working space was at the round table, walking around reading aloud her manuscript or listening to those of her brother and sisters. After her first year of successful study in Brussels with Emily, she stayed on alone in 1843. She became homesick for all: "I am left during several hours quite alone with . . . great desolate school rooms at my disposition. I try to read, I try to write in vain."[57] The myth of the Brontës as innocent dreamers perpetuated by Charlotte herself has now been put to rest. They were savvy, hardworking, and disciplined writers.

By comparison, Emily Dickinson is renowned for the depth of her chastity and aloneness. Her poetic achievements are even more riveting than her life of isolation.

> Some keep the Sabbath going to Church—
> I keep it, staying at Home—
> with a Bobolink for a Chorister—
> And an Orchard, for a Dome—[58]

Queen Recluse, her neighbors called her, this poet who has been described in multiple ways ranging from descendant of Buddha to mad or clinically depressed to secretly homoerotic to spiritually married to her Rev. Charles Wadsworth. Whatever her "cracks," they were the space where "the light came through."[59] For most, the solitude of Dickinson would be too isolating. She even described herself as paying a high price for being able to capture the perfection of a moment and seeing all through her mind's eye. She used her poems to heal herself—the "balsam word" of poetry. Still, Dickinson was never lacking in humility, spirituality, and gratefulness, as some creative people are. In their solitude, they find an overbearing autonomy, as portrayed by William I. Thompson in this synthesis of Wagner's struggle:

> What artists are struggling with is how to be creative without all the trappings of the Wagnerian ego. The Wagnerian artist is really a pathology, the stage of individualism taken to its extreme . . . The Wagnerian phase is one of domination where the artist says: "I am more important than you. I am more important than nature. I am the most important thing."[60]

If the lone artist makes singularity and separateness a state of superiority or reason for specialness, he or she courts an unbalanced way of being. Even so, one might prefer to create in aloneness. In the art studio where I work, I see the pull between mutual desires for camaraderie and solitude in the artists who work there. There are those, like myself, who find a quiet corner and paint or sculpt. So absorbed am I in the act and aloneness, I feel almost shocked when someone approaches, and have jumped many a time when hearing my name called. If I could afford the space, I would paint alone. Others in the group love the interventions and indeed work together, pounding their stone and gabbing in one large room in the studio. Some move back and forth from hibernation to group activity.

Normal Human Work and Creativity—An Oxymoron?

How can we measure the value of alonetime to a creative work life? Abraham Maslow's concept of self-actualization provides a useful theoretical starting point.[61] Maslow writes, "A musician must make music, an artist must paint, a poet must write, if he is to be ultimately at peace with himself. What a man can be, he must be. He must be true to his own nature."[62] That might be part of what Freud thought about when he said that emotional health depended upon love and work. Work in Freud's time invited a solitary component, not just for writers and philosophers, but also the seamstress making and repairing garments, the farmer plowing his fields, the bookkeeper on his chair pondering the numbers, and the clerk in the deeds office doodling in the margins. Shrinking leisure, and mental and physical exhaustion following long workdays, after which all people want to do is sleep, are by-products of our accelerated work shifts. We all know people—if not ourselves—who cancel dates and say, "As soon as I'm home, I'm going to sleep." Week after week, such work fatigue causes sleep to go on overtime, as well as the canceling out of other lone activities and important social connections. People today, caught in a struggle to produce work at the rate demanded by society, never consider the lack of alone moments to think, create, and regroup.

The lack of creative professional alonetime embodies a true absence.[63] Without time to pause, with too many experiences devoid of depth and appropriate challenge, people face the danger of overload. That's not revelatory in itself, but I am surprised at how the popular long lunch hour has been replaced by a lunchtime muffin at the desk followed by dinner next to the computer. Perhaps outside work as a whole never did promote alonetimes or attachments, but some companies did offer breaks in the workday, which we all know are rapidly disappearing.[64] The idea that people can work on an assembly line, in a sweatshop, or nonstop grew in tandem with the Industrial Age, and once-outlawed practices are having a comeback in today's competitive marketplace. If one takes the position, as I do, however, that creativity is part of everyone's industry and life, then allowing time and space to be alone even during the heavily demanding workday is not seen as luxury or laxity, but as lenitive and learned. The idea of practice and discipline also needs to be addressed in this context. From the basketball player to the ballerina to the linguist to the lawyer, an eagerness and devotion to a task is a component of excellence. Mozart did not at first mind his father's strict routines, because music was his own way, but when he grew older he needed to strike a different balance. When one's work ethic is totally based on a father's or a company's needs instead of the individual's, either the finished product or the person's life is left wanting. Time for alone pursuits at work, along with time for relating, may be a way to resolve the impasse between the impersonal demands from the top of the organization and the conflicting needs of employees.[65]

By contrast, the healing aspects of alonetime have not gone wholly unnoticed in some of the current psychological literature on coping. For example, highlighted is the utility of time out[66] as a coping strategy for professionals involved in emotionally, mentally, or physically stressful work. The literature defines time out as an "emotional breather"[67] that allows an employee to engage in less stressful work, such as "paperwork, cleaning, or food preparation."[68] Time outs suggest that, in the theater of life, relating and stimulation are the important dramas and alonetime merely intermission.

The nature of alonetime in the workplace may vary, but the benefits are universal and consistent. Ask yourself how you best manage a busy day at home, or a sense of feeling crowded. Not only does passive achievement of solitude energize or perhaps reenergize one in the face of numerous daunting stressors; most of all, knowledge that the individual need for this time is respected creates confidence and comfort. Profound thought and inner peace,[69] fostering of creative thinking and freedom from restrictions imposed by social norms,[70] and fuller appreciation of life[71] comprise some of the other important potential gains. In this sense, gratification of the need for aloneness is viewed as having wide applications for creative coping. Rather than prescribing specific strategies to address specific stressors, I propose this more holistic approach. But if one wished to sample specific "downloading strategies," business journalist Amy Saltzman[72] offers ways of taking control of professional life: backtracking by self-demoting; "plateauing" by turning down promotion; career shifting by changing to a less-pressured field; employing oneself, for control over hours and location; and escaping the urban scene by opting for less-high-pressured environs. With an eye on the unused porch swing, whose emptiness speaks of a gone-by, quieter era, she sees leisure and work converging to the detriment of all. This loss is especially noticeable to what popular psychology calls the child within us, in this case the imaginative and free-spirited part of us.

In his classic work on education, Carl R. Rogers captures the raw creative power of the child's "wild, unusual thoughts and perceptions."[73] Rogers equates creativity with man's tendency to achieve in work and living his full potential.[74] His observations are compatible with contemporary reports on classrooms that frequently squash creative energy and in its place breed compliant, conformist learners. According to Rogers, as the child gradually transitions to adulthood, creativity optimally will maintain a central place in healthy growth. This cannot happen if young children's individual freedom to imagine is shackled and corralled. A natural inner trend toward maturation, development, and growth is viewed by Rogers as the primary motivation for creativity. I emphasize creativity because the creative adult is one who is sensitively open to new experiences, and is thus able to live harmoniously within the culture. Clearly, creativity in this formulation carries important implications for coping. Rogers, in fact, suggests that creativity plays an indispensable role in our efforts to adapt and survive in a changing world.

Creative Constellations — From Calm to Chaos

Why do creative solutions require alonetime? Because alonetime is requisite for the unconscious to process and unravel problems. Others inspire us, information feeds us, practice improves our performance; but we need quiet time to figure things out, to emerge with new discoveries, to unearth the answers. Not that the unconscious isn't working more or less full-time or that alonetime precludes being with others. Certainly practice —the steady pace of disciplined action—and even performing mindless tasks offer lone experiences. But some of us, myself included, may at times fill such moments with obsessive worrying, repetitive thoughts, nonstop tasks, or information gathering. Letting myself slide into reverie has proven far more productive when I'm stuck with a problem. It's a kind of openness one learns as a therapist. A patient presents a dilemma. Focusing head-on isn't what typically resolves it. More often the answer arises unexpectedly, when you're not searching for it. Novelist Leo Rosten tells the story of Captain Newman, M.D.,[75] who heads a "psycho" ward during World War II. One situation involves Coby Clay, who refuses to make his bed:

> Coby was an Alabama lad . . . [with] some inner reservoir of content. He walked around in a private cloud of delight . . . He was entirely at peace with the world and at home with himself —his body, his reveries, his Maker, his soul . . .
>
> Coby was [also] the only private in the United States Army who never made his bed, his sergeant [did] . . . Neither sergeants nor lieutenants nor captains nor majors nor colonels could prevail . . . They tried . . . command and cajolery, blandishment [and banishment] and bluster and threats of reprisal [including solitary confinement]. [Coby] would gravely consider the appeals to teamwork, to *esprit de corps*. Then all he would say, with the utmost kindliness, was " 'Taint fit for a grown man to make his own bed."[76]

But Coby was a fair-minded, nontroublemaking person, and it did not sit right with him that the sergeant was doing this work. Finally, after weeks of deliberation, he comes up with a remedy:

> "Well I been thinkin' out about this bed-makin' . . . I been thinking' an' scratchin' aroun' an' all, an' I don't see no right reason why a man cain't make up someone *else's* bed, like you been doin' for me . . ."
>
> From then on, until the whole contingent of brave men was flown into action overseas, while Sergeant Pulaski made Coby's bed each morning, Coby—humming of dark glades and promised lands—made Pulaski's.[77]

Coby allowed himself unsettling alonetime in order to think through an acceptable and humorously creative alternative. Moreover, although he empathized with others' feelings, he did not crave approval or attention from them.

Nothing is wrong with people trying to attract the positive notice of authority figures—many a creative person had that bent when they were children, fantasizing how they would show the world (or parents) how great they were. But children can become caught up in a rat race quite easily, unhappy, running around, well before the contest should properly begin. Some become so disgruntled by their failures to please out-of-step expectations that they completely stop trying. In fact, they reverse the whole game. They represent the dark side of creativity.

Think of creative energies turned to negative pursuits. The serial killer is also a solitary and at times weirdly creative individual. Master writer of malfunctioning lives Joyce Carol Oates dramatically illustrates this in her small but eerily accurate novel *Zombie*. Zombie is not the "hero" of the novel; it is the creative goal of the bizarre mind of Quentin P., who wallows in "unnatural" silences, those silences that dare not be shared. Quentin P., with an IQ of 121, an interest in boys, and awareness of the hypocrisy and lies in his family, is not the apple of his father's eye. From age twelve, when he is forced to hide his homosexuality, he begins to hide every other thought and feeling that could be in the least contrary. It is the burial of his real self to the point of referring to himself in the third person and an evil curiosity that separate him from others and continue to motivate his attempts to create an underground existence with a lobotomized slave to satisfy his sexual lusts. But he is not unlike others in his desires to control his bodily needs and gain personal mastery; only, he, through a sad past, has lost all ways to go about this except by overpowering someone else. Writer John Coston,[78] an expert on serial killers, says that their deepest motivation is to get someone else's life in their hands. All their attempts focus on gaining control and getting what they want. And the victim's fate is sealed once the murderer knows that task is accomplished. On a sympathetic note, Coston contends that serial killers try to relive what in childhood was abusive, reversing roles in order to reregulate the situation so that they are now in charge. Quentin's aloneness is a haunted madness as he is never freed from the internalized negative imprints of his family. Always fearful of his father's eyes or live contact with others, he aspires to make a sexually safe partner in a zombie so as not to have "awake eyes observing me at intimate quarters."[79] His connections are loveless, with only enough empathy to survive. Is time inside or outside him, he ponders, and decides, "If INSIDE you do what you want. Whatever, you create your own Time."[80] The paranoia in Quentin's character reinforces the angry element within, as all that is bad in him is projected outside of himself, justifying his rage-filled deeds. Is alonetime adding resonance to satanic voices? People controlled by negative messages receive them in and out of company. Alone, however, they have additional time to generate plans for acting demonically.

Beethoven, whose creativity spurred on his mental health, neverthe-less went further than Quentin P. He wanted to create his own family from start to finish—first as the hidden son of royalty and then by litigiously adopting his nephew.[81] He, too, felt driven angrily away from flesh and blood. Unlike Quentin, he found his music and positive recognition for his creative thoughts. I have heard people ask: "What might have happened to Hitler if the art academy had admitted him, or if he had had sufficient faith in his painting?" In like manner, futurist and queen of cyberspace Esther Dyson wonders what might have happened if suspected Unabomber Ted Kaczynksi had shared his thoughts on the Internet.[82] When one delves alone into oneself and creative energies feel unreachable or completely overshadowed by rage, do the heart and soul of an individual become stunted by destructive musings? In composing and living, Beethoven chose to face continuous challenges and made powerful music as a result of that perseverance. Creativity rings positive, but it is multifaceted, like all other traits: the genius in the darkened room or hidden in the basement could just as well be Edison inventing a lightbulb or Dr. Frankenstein creating his monster.

A new theoretical explanation of creativity is proposed by psychologist Howard Gardner.[83] Rather than conceptualizing one specific type of creativity, he views creativity as pluralistic. Just as there are multiple intelligences, according to Gardner, there are multiple creativities. Through his description of seven extraordinary achievers across diverse fields (Freud, Einstein, Picasso, Stravinsky, Eliot, Graham, and Gandhi), the author demonstrates how various types of creative ability have led to grand accomplishments. In his effort to find common traits or defining characteristics among creative individuals, Gardner turns to childhood as well. He suggests that creative persons are able to use childhood experiences and insights in a productive way. It is through a merger of adult understanding in a specific domain with the ability to draw on one's experience as a "wonder filled child"[84] that an individual is able to be creative. I think a major link to these earlier feelings lies in a person having time, courage, curiosity, and skill to be alone, without that experience being impaled by past negative attachments. "Great men feel and know everything that mean men feel, even more clearly, but they seem to have made some kind of an ascension, and those evil feelings, though they still understand them sympathetically, no longer exert any power over them."[85]

But until that ascension can occur, most people need to gradually learn about how to be free.

Ralph, a former patient, hardly let a session go by without debating the reasonableness of separating from his family of four. The cramped quarters of his two-bedroom apartment seemed prohibitive to his writing. While his wife worked as a set designer, he stayed home with his preschool son and daughter. After knowing him for several months, I asked, "Do you want to be a married man with children, or devote your whole self to writing? Or maybe you'd like both?" He didn't hesitate; he wanted both, but was he asking too much? And why did he feel so depressed and bitter and always as if he was tearing himself from his writing?

The creative struggle to work or be with family is a basic dilemma. Ralph was equally all mixed up about what was OK and not OK to do. Was it all right to want to create plays? His highly meticulous parents, consumed with dotting each *i* and improving his spelling errors, had critiqued all his early writings. Writing while holding on to those memories was not an act of joy or enthusiastically pursued. Each page was painfully produced. Composing poems for literary magazines and articles for popular journals brought him income, but not delight. Similarly, wiping his children's noses or changing diapers was fine in the doing, but after several hours of caring for them, he questioned his fate. No matter how much fun he had as a father, he felt something was wrong. After all, most of his college buddies weren't in this fix. Nothing he did offered calmness or serenity. He was caught up in pushing himself, whether to write, to parent, or to feel happy as a two-fisted general. The first gain Ralph made was to find space in his public library. At first appalled because he had found an alone corner to idle in, he soon found his play was actually being written, without guilt-inspired nasty injunctions left over in his mind.

◆ ◆ ◆

Once control over our own schedules is lost, it is harder to find solitude and creative times. Like others, Ralph found the dreamy idleness of his earliest childhood that had inspired him to be a writer in the first place.

The critical importance of individuality and the self is elaborated by Anthony Giddens.[86] He confirms the message of every practiced meditator by suggesting living each moment as a new moment, with greater sensitivity to one's thoughts, feelings, and physical sensations.[87] This is how one escapes the cultural message "Intimacy is all," which eclipses consideration of important potential implications of creative solitude and aloneness. Through continuous self-reflection and self-observation—

achieved by asking oneself introspective questions regarding the affective, cognitive, and sensory experience of the moment—a person becomes more self-aware and therefore better equipped to achieve change. In this formulation, self-actualization is linked to the presence of "zones of personal time" (similar to the concept of time in aloneness described above) distinct from universal standardized time, which is external to subjective self-experience.[88] Essential to Giddens's formulation is the belief that a person is motivated and guided by "reference points that are set from the inside."[89] On this same point, Clark Moustakas claims that "the creative life is always based on self-values, not on the values of the system."[90] Private Coby understood this. Perhaps the creative life is also possible when the values of the individual are accepted by the society so that person and system are in greater harmony.

Moustakas's poetic statement on creativity and solitude delivers a relevant and potent message: "In the spiritual and creative experience, there is often no other way but the lonely way."[91] It is hard to find role models for such alone behavior. How does one do more than give lip service to becoming less stressed, more self-actualized, and truer to one's own nature? When I read the memoirs of people great and small, I sometimes think this is the basic riddle that most of us spend our lifetimes trying to figure out. A level of calm is a necessary addition to this entire environment that sometimes seems headed out of control.

In Brenda Ueland's book on how to write, she tells the story of one of her pupils, an unself-confident woman whose attempts at writing improved so dramatically: "[She] had one advantage and that was that she has had such a sad and lonely life. But this just gave her a great deal of time to think, for her imagination to work, and the need to express it, to write it."[92]

The natural creativity in all of us—sudden and slow insights, helpful ideas, bursts and gentle bubbles of imagination—is found as a result of alonetimes. Often people become discouraged from their past experiences, "trying" to create or being told something wasn't up to par. Passion evolves in aloneness, as it does in celibacy, when chosen as a means toward self-regulation. Both creativity and curiosity are bred through idle contemplation, for our best thoughts usually arise unexpectedly, but not necessarily hurriedly. Looking at close-ups of artists' childhood struggles growing up, and their fight to transform their dreams into realities, I do not find great differences between them and my patients, my students, my friends, or even myself. Whether it is Mozart seeking his freedom, or a medical intern opting to enter business school, or Virginia Woolf searching for privacy, or a teacher friend demanding immersion in utter silence after spending a day with high school seniors, part of a creative resolution requires that alone side of ourselves to assert itself.

But what happens when alonetime is less in our control and foisted upon us due to circumstances? Where does the alonetime need fit into the picture of extreme conditions? Does the alonetime need contribute to pathology? I proceed to investigate these questions next in order to finally reinforce alonetime's rightful standing as a basic need.

CHAPTER 11

Autism, Abuse, and Asylum

The Normal is the rarest thing in the World.
SOMERSET MAUGHAM [1]

The issue of control—over our actions, our feelings, other people's behavior—is central to any compulsion. The lack of control is what compulsion seems to be about.
GENEEN ROTH, *When Food Is Love* [2]

But my conscious mind had begun to awaken to reality. I began to realize that only by reaching deeply within myself could I find the wellspring of strength that could help me to survive or even to endure whatever fate might be in store for me and so, I began to build a fortress around myself that no indignity, no humiliation, no cruel treatment could ever penetrate.
JOSEPH CICIPPIO, *Chains to Roses* [3]

JENNY ARRIVED SPINNING into my room, trailed by her bewildered mother. Like a whirling dervish, the four-year-old twirled, clutching a tiny porcelain doll to her chest. Every so often she paused, pointed her index finger, and spoke several words in a language totally indecipherable to me, but which, I was to learn, had a form and function of its own. This event, during my second internship experience in a hospital, was my first encounter with an autistic child, a child whose relentless desire to disengage set her apart from the world. In Chapter 1, I investigated emotional learning, fears, and societal expectations that prevent, disrupt, or distort direct expression of the alone need. Now we will see alonetime as a total refuge, an escape from too much stimulation.

Autism,[4] as we shall see, is one of those refuges, but difficult to define. How can a child so emotionally removed from her family sustain her actions, her world, and herself? Jenny, who tested at least of average intelligence on a nonverbal test—the Leiter International Performance Scale—certainly had a context for her life, with definite rules and regulations. In fact, outside of relationships with people, she was one of the most self-regulated[5] children I was ever to meet. Although it is not always the case for autistic children, where and when Jenny ate, what she ate, how she spent her time (barring a few parental demands), when and where she slept, and the clothes she wore had through tireless persistence come under her domain of control.

The opposite is true of many other types of children with troubled lives. Like Jenny, they are unable to navigate the external world. But regardless of how valiant their strivings to self-regulate and find asylum, children trapped in cycles of abuse, like their adult counterparts, lose the battle of attempting to control their bodily needs. The efforts of those abused—often guided by the very people who are hurtful to them— backfire. These busy children whom I meet through my students and in private practice are caught between trying to destimulate and restimulate themselves in ways comparable to the extremes with which they were brought up. Like Marilyn, a six-year-old sexually abused by a stepfather, they go from unhappily isolating themselves in a corner of the classroom while attempting to hide from classmates to exposing their bodies to fellow students recklessly or riskily confronting both those known to them and strangers.

Yet, reckless risk taking is also an appropriate way to describe aspects of the behavior of someone like Borge Ousland, the explorer who isolated himself for over fifty-two days while trekking from Siberia to the North Pole and has, indeed, now conquered the South Pole solo after two attempts. What is the difference between autistic children, the abused, and people like Ousland or Alaskan schoolteacher Hannah Breece,[6] who brave the wild and unknown? I believe that the latter are pioneers whose extreme alone needs are free to rise far above the status of a protective shield. For example, although lonely at times, Breece nevertheless finds her purpose in educating the needy. She flourishes on her alone skills and motivations. But what about people forced into isolation and held hostage against their will? Do those sensory-deprived experiences add insight into the capacity and need for time alone? Can we find a distinguishing factor that makes the straitjacketed asylum of a hospital for the insane different from self-selected asylum?

As zoologists inform us, extremes of behavior would not be possible unless the biological foundations for such behaviors were present in the general population. While this chapter's focus is on the outer limits of aloneness in people who inhabit a range of human mental endurance and social circumstances, I also explore what can be learned from varied examples of exaggerated aloneness and sometimes even attachment. Fetal experience and animal studies suggest that the ability and motivation to sustain periods of alonetime is innate. But only in viewing aloneness in the extreme can we fully appreciate the biological origins of this need, the abilities it strengthens, and the importance of restructuring its position in our lives.

Our endowment and skills to function alone are part of the natural protective and healing processes nature provides. Otto Rank speaks of will as the manifestation of the life force.[7] When we are struggling against too many stimuli or forced into isolation, believe it or not, the will to live takes us into the safe reservoirs of the alone dimensions. What I hope to demonstrate through viewing the extraordinary, such as children raised outside culture and civilization (feral children), is the ever-present developmental fuel of alonetime. The aloneness that in autism is the mark of disease, that in feral children makes them alien, and that in the overly independent invokes the label "loner" or, worse still, "antisocial" *is* the very quality that helps those thus labeled (as well as the rest of us) to function under conditions of deficit, deprivation, or abuse. Alonetime coping strategies save lives as basic survival mechanisms.

Language and Autism

Could anything in human nature be more remote than the child whose emotions are unreachable? Learning about such children over the years, and viewing nonautistic youngsters who twirl their bodies till they make themselves happily dizzy, I have to assume that there is self-soothing comfort in spinning and flapping the arms, or in becoming completely lost in activities with toy objects, or in the feel of flowing water. With the autistic child, however, the inordinate privacy of the developing self leads to growing vulnerability as the demands for social interactions, particularly in the form of language, become more intense. Often it is at this point, with intensified withdrawal and an increasing reliance on protective mechanisms, that the child's peculiarities become readily discernible and a diagnosis possible. Autistic infants socially retreat. Is it constitutional, or in fear, or in anger, or all three? Are mental retardation and autism one and the same? And if not, why can't autistic children engage in life and continue to adapt to people?

Specifically, it is the child's lack of language (sometimes following the precocious use of words) or idiosyncratic utterances that will trigger the concern of parents and the turn to professionals. Autistic children may be mute, which suggests a lack of preverbal context that makes communicating and sharing an experience impossible. Some articulate well, speaking clearly and even dramatically, but only echoing what they have heard previously, frequently in terms of slogans or whole excerpts they have picked up from the radio or television. One child patient was so adept at this that his voice changes ranged from a baby's wail to the quiver of an aging patient in a TV commercial listing *her* ailments. But it is not uncommon to see a child reverse pronouns, mispronounce words, or speak in a word salad, a proliferation of words strung together without meaning. The autistic child's language echoes and reverberates capacities as well as skewed development. For instance, some children sing like angels or draw to match a well-trained draughtsman. Others' imitative ability is evidenced in the replication of isolated actions long after they have seen them: "Perhaps of primary importance is the fact that these children do not appear to be using language to communicate to another . . . They seem to be speaking to themselves."[8]

Language is one key to understanding the emotional distancing of autism. Being left alone by lack of language, however, is not the sine qua non of asocial behavior. The remarkable story of a twenty-seven-year-old Mexican man, Ildefonso, deaf for all his life, makes that ever more apparent. Susan Schaller—as dedicatedly persistent, caring, and sensitive as Helen Keller's teacher, Anne Sullivan—brought this man without words to the realm of communication through the slow, painstaking teaching of sign language. What is so different about this accepting, resourceful, and cheerful man, who never learned to connect a name to himself, and others in the lone experience of deafness? Psychiatrist Frieda Fromm-Reichmann's own father committed suicide when he became stone deaf. And it is possible that her own encroaching complete deafness was inspiration to write a paper on loneliness (she died before completing it). Thinking about the difference between Ildefonso's state of mind and that of Fromm-Reichmann's father gives me some ideas about the different ways of experiencing an alone state. We will see in episodes of political imprisonment that enforced isolation of a certain kind is as painful as being locked in an abusive family relationship. Neither may be escapable, and in both, unutterable loneliness is the result. But not being lonely or needing people is one advantage to being autistic, according to Jim Sinclair,[9] who saw his disorder as having freeing as well as limiting aspects. Loneliness, as Frieda Fromm-Reichmann distinguished, is not the same as being alone or temporary aloneness, or the inner reality of subjective flights into fantasy. Well beyond lack of communication with others, the panic and dread she describes in a loss of reality and a fragmented, catastrophic world speaks of a broken-off communication with oneself. The autistic illusions of schizophrenics—her population of patients at Chestnut Hill—are a withdrawal, not just from relationships to a symbolic world, but from painful inner thoughts and feelings as well. Formulated to heal and shelter an aching soul, this is an isolation resistant to either inner or outer repair. A failure to initially develop relationships and a withdrawal from overstimulation better describes the autistic child. Ildefonso's deafness, like Beethoven's or Helen Keller's, did not accede to either category.

We who hear are accurate in projecting loneliness onto becoming deaf and cut off from a world we want and know.[10] Inner chaos often results when one is kept from regulating life in known ways. This fact is illustrated in the lives of abused children who finally are moved to stable surroundings or of individuals taught new means of adjustment. Even when changes are potentially for the better, once one has adjusted to a condition, fear and rebellion accompany change.

Ildefonso wholeheartedly wanted to acquire language late in life. His heroic metamorphosis begins when "he . . . enter[s] . . . humanity [by] discover[ing] the communication of minds. He now knew that he and a cat and a table all had names, and the fruit of his knowledge had opened his eyes to evil. He could see the prison where he had existed alone, shut out of the human race for twenty-seven years."[11] Is it the discovery of the connection to others through language, the shared meaningfulness of words, that brings that decisive shudder down the spine of a child destined to be autistic and precipitates total immersion into the private world? Or perhaps it is the opposite—knowledge that their inner world does not match the sensibilities of the unlike voices of others. Even Ildefonso, who wanted this connectedness, felt the pain of entering a new world. When sight or sound is an invasion of the senses, connectedness can be no less devastating to those pervious than aloneness is to the lonely. Donna Williams described her autism as "meaning deaf." She could speak three languages fluently, but as she says, "I can't always hear myself with meaning."[12] She felt in some ways lucky because she could "sleep-walk and sleep-talk."[13] Her luckiness related to being able to avoid the constant threat of the world outside herself. She had no concept that "a sense of 'self' and 'other' could exist at the same time."[14] Only when the gifted Williams began to create and place trust in a stable, self-regulated world for herself did she venture out to find means for a communication, which reconfirms an innate wish for balance of the two needs. This is not always what happens.

Autism — The Most Extreme of Alonetimes

Autism has been called among the most serious psychopathologies a family endures, yet its exact origins remain unknown. According to estimates of the Autism Society of America, approximately four hundred thousand children born in the United States will be diagnosed as living lives that rotate around extreme alonetime rather than relationships. Some of the most imaginative theories have been developed to explain autism's etiology. Over the years it has been changed from a problem of a child's early years to one spanning a lifetime. Although the symptoms have been sporadically described for at least two hundred years,[15] detailed diagnosis and classification has occurred only in the modern era of psychology. In keeping with the times, theories on autism—whether founded upon biological, genetic, behavioral, or early psychoanalytic views—were based on a one-person approach to human development. That is, they consider individuals as distinct from environment.[16] While old and new theories have given us a rich and varied picture, they also impart seemingly contradictory and fragmented explanations. A two-person psychology[17] that searches for meaning within a complex system of behaviors and circumstances provides an alternate framework with which to understand the development of autism. Here, the cause does not rest in infant or in mother, in nature or in nurture; rather, explanations lie somewhere in the total interactive universe. Maybe a lesson in this diagnostic multiple choice is to stop looking down a one-way street for cause or rehabilitation. I myself prefer scanning a wide terrain, viewing certain behaviors as coping methods for autistic individuals, which in turn place certain autistic behaviors on a continuum with the normal.[18]

Because autism manifests itself so early in infancy, the intrauterine landscape also adds to an understanding of the symptomatology of autistic children. Embryology describes the physiological state of the fetus and provides us with actual illustrations of beginning development, but a complementary need arises to extrapolate the psychological condition as well. The foundation of the pathology of autism rests on the belief that a balanced development depends on the ongoing interaction between caretaker and infant. Nothing less provides the necessary environment in which the infant's capacities are maximized. To my thinking, infant and caretakers contribute to the relationship as it unfolds, and the balance is always different, depending upon the nature of the participants. Therefore, vulnerabilities will impact the formation of mutual regulations. But before this, under typical circumstances it would be correct to expect the experience of total receptivity and nurturing in the giving surround of the womb. I have postulated that if all goes well, the fetus experiences a sense of containment in these tight first quarters. In this optimally stress-free environment, the fetus is soothed by physical sensations through contact between its body and the membranes and wall of the womb. This protected experience provides sensory metaphors for both comforting connectedness and self-satisfied aloneness. One might postulate the womb experience as too gratifying or the opposite, an already frightening experience that sends the fetus into flight behaviors.

Thinking about this, I remember the Divine Child, our fictional anti-hero in Chapter 6, put off by what lay in store for him outside the womb, where he was to become only one of many. For him certainly it was encounters with how and what language teaches and fails to teach that caused his final retreat. What about language may frighten the child who stays thus encapsulated outside the womb? Does a child seem capable of that precious understanding of just how enslaving words can be? Be the cause biochemical, structural and neurological, familial and genetic, psychological, environmental (as far back as the womb experience), or some complex combination that is not the same for every child who is autistic, phenomenologically *fear exhibited by retreat seems a constant element of autism.* Accompanying each turning away is a dread of conscious incorporation of a world outside that demands acknowledgment and participation. True, some autistic children seem never to have developed language, others have language very early on and later lose it, and others continue with their language skills, keeping them discreetly to themselves. But whatever the way, not sharing a common language may be that which enables an acutely sensitive child to remain in the fantasized safety of a self-perpetuating world.

With so many still-to-be-discovered answers, I do not dwell on pinning down the actual antecedents of autism.[19] What most compels me is that these behaviors, which taken together seem so removed from the world of people, are actually located on a continuum within human development. Margaret Mahler saw this connection. But while she gives credence to the repertoire of behaviors as part of a normal infant phase, she postulated that the child's maintenance of equilibrium through avoiding inner and outer stimulation and sustaining the "autistic orbit"[20] was not out of an awareness but reflexive, and an innate and automatic response. Thomas Ogden, in his reformulation of relational theories of Klein, Winnicott, and other British psychoanalysts, introduced a state of being in isolation as basic, and he relates it to an autistic realm of experience. His thesis rightly establishes this early neurological and behavioral organization as an integral aspect of normal development. Interestingly, though, he maintains the term "autistic" to label normal alone needs for the very reason I propose as necessary for dropping it:

> I have retained the word autistic in the designation . . . despite the fact that the term is usually associated with a pathologically closed technological system that I do not feel is characteristic of the normal autistic-contiguous mode. I have done so because I believe that pathological forms of autism involve hypertrophied versions of the types of defense, the method of attributing meaning to experience, and the mode of object relatedness characterizing the normal autistic contiguous organization.[21]

Here Ogden focuses on the pathology (self-containment as a defense) that grows from unheeded psychological needs, literally the terror inherent in coming to life among the unknown—in this case, human beings. Yet it is important to first acknowledge that these needs are natural. Using a different term—"alonetime" or the "alone state"—does this best. The physiologically and psychologically safe sensations the autistic child clings to are first and foremost normally embedded. Thus, in a newborn who through accident or design develops autistically, we see augmented a natural turning away from engagement in active encounters with people to a structured world in which he or she feels better prepared. This results in a skewed course of development and the set of behaviors usually associated with autism: withdrawal from human contact and the insistence on sameness.[22] Simplicity is optimal when individuals are running the world on their own. Even the nonautistic, when they feel put upon by life and obligations, often withdraw, pare down their lives, and seek uniformity. Autism just takes the withdrawal act to extremes.

In the autistic child, being with another does not transform an unsafe world into a safe one. The consequent difficulties in communicating and relating create barriers to the children and to those caring for them. Though extraordinary behaviors interrupt relationships, they do not deny those with autism some sense of self. No matter what the symptomatic picture (and characteristics of people so encapsulated and removed from the world vary), the family of an autistic child is in upheaval to the point of unbearable despair. An autistic child is immobile like dynamite before it explodes. These children suddenly and deliberately may claw when held, use feces for clay, scream, bellow nonstop, and painfully self-mutilate. But out of this chaos, autistic people do find calm through their concentration.

Because emotional perceptions of autistic children come to be questioned, it is important to emphasize that they do have an experience of another, and areas of interplay between self and other do develop. The outer environment is hardly formless. On the contrary, in many ways it is remarkably formalized because it becomes a protective mechanism. How does this fit with ideas of the interpersonal laying the foundation for self and intellectual development?[23] The very capacities that certain autistic children display—for example, organizational, memory, motoric, visual perceptual—attest to a structuralization that forms selfobjects and connections to things, not people. Thus, the autistic way of being can and does translate to a self-picture.

As Dustin Hoffman showed us in *Rain Man,* some autistic people, either especially high-functioning ones or so-called idiot savants, have unusual capacities and perform amazing feats. Deficit makes room for gain. Oliver Sacks, lover of the atypical and adventurer into autistic lands, weaves amazing stories of such remarkable individuals. His understanding captures the fact that many autistic individuals have shaped a cohesive self. He looks closely at a remarkable autistic woman named Temple Grandin, an inventor and university professor whose selfobjects originate not from relationships but from her exceptional visual abilities, which enable her to build thought from images.[24] Intriguingly, no matter how high autistic persons climb in their art or industry, like Grandin they still remain, often without deliberate intervention, socially hampered.[25]

My personal life has taught me the differences between the impaired autistic child and a child equally but differently impaired. My youngest son, Phillip, has severe learning disabilities that when he was a child sometimes resulted in behavior characteristic of autism. He could not contain his temper and would react with disorganization to overstimulation. A joke between us when he was running wild would be, "Shall I make you into a pretzel?" Then he would climb upon my lap and let me cross and fold his arms and wrap my legs around his until he settled down. Like an autistic child, he would repeat sentences in an attempt to process meaning. But unlike one, he longed for and sought personal ties and never was afraid to seek help from others. His troubles in life are not dissimilar to those of the autistic; he clings passionately to a need to solely regulate and control his life, but regulation by another was only a sore point if it encroached upon his perceived and unconscious needs or independence.

A Verbal Moratorium

But where does a child who has fine language skills and stays within society, but who refuses to communicate, fit on the aloneness continuum? The earliest descriptions of elective mutism are found in German literature, dating back to 1877, and they involved physically normal children who developed mutism in specific situations. At this time, the condition was called "aphasia voluntaria."[26] In 1934, the term "elective mutism" was coined to describe children who can speak but who do so only with very few people and/or in a small number of environments. This definition excludes all other forms of mutism, including hearing loss, aphasia, schizophrenia, and autism. The most common situation consists of a child who speaks to parents and siblings at home but refuses to talk to teachers or anyone but their most intimate peers at school.[27]

Indeed the current nomenclature replaces the word "elective" with the word "selective" in describing the disorder, as the individual selects to whom or whether he or she will talk. Selective mutism is so rare a disorder (there are far fewer instances than autism) that it is difficult to study. According to one count, only 0.4 per 1,000 children display this symptom;[28] thus an understanding of selective mutism is drawn from individual case studies or small studies with no control groups. The family of Ada, the erotic and self-willed heroine of Jane Campion's film *The Piano*, was lame in coaxing her to shed the mutism. Anyone who has seen *The Piano* knows that with mutism Ada's gain in self-regulation was astounding, especially under her situation of suppression. She also benefited by parentifying her child in allowing her daughter to be both her spokesperson, through sign language, and the bearer of Ada's moral burden in life. As psychoanalyst Isaac Tylim commented in a review of the film, "Unlike a classical fairy tale in which the handsome prince kisses the sleeping beauty and awakens her to love and eternal felicity, in *The Piano* sleeping beauty seems to take good care of herself."[29] In Ada's case, self-regulation reached narcissistic proportions, as her daughter's childhood was sacrificed.

Poet, writer, and humanist Maya Angelou halted her voice at eight years old for far more altruistic reasons—feeling terribly guilt ridden when the man who raped her was murdered. This trauma kept her silent until age thirteen. This is an amazing quiet for a woman who through strength of spirit is always talking back.[30] Yet she feared her tongue's wagging had caused the man's death.[31] Although Angelou's statement can be read as self-sacrificial, she used this period of mutism as a time to read and bolster her sense of self until she was ready to face life's problems again. Many reasons may push a child into the full silence of selective mutism, but we've all had days of withdrawal when through the quiet we were able to consolidate our psychic strength and restore integrity.

Trust

The difference between the autistic child and children with developmental disabilities, or the totally catatonic and those who for short or longer time spans choose to be mute, lies buried somewhere within the realm of trust. Trust of those outside ourselves won't take place if leaving the tight insulated space for very long spells catastrophe. The well-meaning efforts of caregivers—professional or not—require long periods of trial and error before anything resembling mutual regulation is attempted by those who gain self-regulation and safety in an asocial world. Autistic children typically pull themselves together through the use of objects rather than people. Before exploring nonhuman objects further, let us first become acquainted with Winnicott's explanation of the often-observed way special toys and objects are used by nonautistic children.

But long before Winnicott described the furry animals and favorite toys of children as "transitional objects,"[32] A. A. Milne was writing children's fiction about the fond attachment of his son, Christopher, to his bear.[33] According to Winnicott, the meaning behind Christopher Robin's affection for Winnie-the-Pooh, or that of the *Peanuts* character Linus for his blanket, emanates from their symbolizing the space between the internal and external. For Winnicott, toys get their special power from their relationship to caretaker; to me their magic rests in their connection to early nonpeopled comfort as well. Either way, as children begin to build a notion of the separation and boundaries between inner and outer worlds, they carry along objects that help them smooth out the rough journey.

In autism, the child's use of objects seems radically different. Descriptions of autistic children[34] highlight the fact that for these children, relationships with objects are stronger than relationships with people. Frances Tustin, a British psychoanalyst and prominent therapist for autistic children, describes fully these interactions:

> Unlike transitional objects . . . "autistic objects" are most often hard and interchangeable: the autistic child does not insist upon one particular object, but rather any object which can provide the same sensation . . . unlike the transitional object [in the Winnicottian sense], the autistic object continues to be used in a rigid way, indicating a lack of change in the child's experiential world.[35]

When Tustin pictures autism, she sees a frozen child who was prematurely ripped from an "illusion of oneness," in this instance a symbiotic oneness with the parent. Depression, withdrawal, and the building of protective barriers are the responses to a wrenching, overly alone psychological state. But this interpretation suggests that an autistic toddler is embracing what is presumably most terrifying—aloneness. True, an older child or adult who is rejected may adopt alone behaviors. But to me, for someone to go so completely into aloneness, the other (environment or person) has to represent the fearsome monsters and absolute disequilibrium.

Both transitional and autistic objects are manipulated by the child to reestablish *safety* via alone behavior. When Jenny first approached psychotherapy, she held her well-used doll close, but later she incorporated many objects into her stereotypical autistic play. Steering around me as if I were a piece of furniture, she would pick up Lego pieces out of a box, press them against her cheek, and place them in a line. She repeated this emptying and refilling the container. At first I tried to initiate change by placing the next piece, but she would react to my gesture by rocking in an agitated manner. Her use of the object in a routine, unchanging way reinforced her self-sufficiency. When really feeling intruded upon, Jenny would say in her high-pitched voice, "Nodon." I gradually realized the meaning of the word "nodon," as Jenny's command to keep things the same became apparent when I happened to put down something that I was holding and muttered, "All done." In excited singsong, Jenny started her refrain of "Nodon, nodon." "No done" had meaning! After many attempts to connect by playing, instead I began to mirror her behavior with my own similar actions nondisruptive to hers. I was then allowed to approach her more closely, particularly wondering if the world of the autistic child was such a miserable place despite being removed from normal interactions. One parent, Clara Claiborne Park, speaks soulfully through her knowledge of her autistic daughter:

> I knew that my fourth child was not like the others, who needed me and loved me, as I loved them. The fairies had stolen away the human baby and left one of their own. There she moved, every day, among us but not of us, acquiescent when we approached, untouched when we retreated, serene, detached in perfect equilibrium. Existing among us, she had her being elsewhere. As long as no demands were made upon her, she was content. If smiles and laughter mean happiness, she was happy inside the invisible walls that surrounded her. She dwelt in a solitary citadel, compelling and self made, complete and valid. Yet we could not leave her there. We must intrude, attack, invade, not because she was unhappy inside it, for she was not, but because the equilibrium she had found, perfect as it was, denied the possibility of growth . . . Which of ourselves could call ourselves as content as Elly was? The world we would tempt her into was the world of risk, failure and frustration, of unfulfilled desire, of pain as well as activity and love. There in nirvana, why should she ever come out? Yet she was ours as well as her own, and we wanted her with us . . . Confronted with a tiny child's refusal of life, all existential hesitations evaporate. We had no choice. We would use every stratagem we could invent to assail her fortress, to beguile, entice, seduce her into the human condition.[36]

Psychologically, autistic people rely primarily on their exquisite ability to self-regulate. But self-regulation is most effective when it is complemented by a capacity for social interaction at appropriate times, and vice versa. Most forms of therapies mainly relate to bringing the child out socially, and they range from the strictly behavioral[37] (with alerting bells and restrictions) to the psychoanalytic therapies. The search is for balance, and since generally cognition and survival improve with emotional connections, this is a logical quest. But just how is a therapist able to infiltrate the seemingly airtight armor of an alone autistic person? To surmount this wall, autistic children's teachers and therapists have to release any stakes in the battle and hand over both sides in the war to the child. Only too often, in trying to lure a child to "the world," people invade and mercilessly bombard a person's space. Or as Williams observes while working in a school for autistic children, "I got the feeling that if they could have used a tire jack to pry open her soul and pour 'the world' in they would have done so and never have noticed the patient had died on the operating table."[38]

The Three Davids

To enable you to envision the continuum from autism to extreme chosen aloneness, let me tell you something about three very different Davids. Autistic children can command or retreat. Sometimes, to further self-regulation, they use the analyst as a thing—for instance, to retrieve a toy out of reach or shut a cabinet. But when does that mechanistic exchange turn into true acknowledgment of another presence? Tustin[39] describes David as a boy patient who attempts to render her helpless and lifeless —a thing to manipulate in order to obtain gratification of his demands. He plucks the features from a self-made head of armor, calling it his father. She views this careless statement of disregard as a reenactment of the original illusion of oneness, and lack of differentiation or feeling for another human being. While agreeing with Tustin's mode of treatment, I see the dynamics differently. From my perspective, David's manipulation of the head of armor (father) is connecting a missing link in his development. He is using a compromise position; by treating the father image (a source of strength, as denoted by armor) carelessly, he is declaring himself unafraid. Figuratively, David is making the protective coat of armor his to build or destroy; he can deepen his ties with others as he, too, is beginning to feel in charge.

In the brain of an autistic child, no memory of a helpful adult resides, since those interactions either cannot be taken in or are refused admission. No division of labor exists; the child's language is not the parents'. Arousal, excitement, noise, and displeasure are not leveled out by contact with somebody, but through self-regulatory functions. Speech is not experienced as helpful; it only adds to the confusion. And as Tustin points out, the world outside the body has no importance, since learning takes place independent of the social. Why Tustin's painstaking, very engaged, and long hours of therapy work so successfully, I think, is that her treatment does not intrude upon or insist on social connections (despite her belief that their loss is basic to autism). She begins by making sure the child continues to experience a relatively safe self through the "normal autistic" position, unlike the probing and insistence on communication that Williams described in the treatment center in which she worked.

Gradually, Tustin introduces the other in the guise of herself and her thoughts and feelings. When children with autism are no longer as worried about self-regulation and losing their alonetime, they may take at least minor steps to venture out into an interactive world. In a similar vein, as proof, some of the children who develop a recognizable and accepted talent will afterward at last acquire language.

Another David, a delinquent, was diagnosed by his therapist as an autistic boy.[40] In today's vernacular he would probably be seen as borderline with many autistic features. Thus his "autism" is not to the extreme, as he continues to relate to the outside world. His particular isolation was maintained by strict control of his body, obscuring communication, and identifying with machines as transitional objects. Even in the following short extract from the brilliant work of the psychoanalyst Beulah Parker we see how she deciphers David's code to promote *his* self-regulation and establish human communication. Parker's responses to David's statements are in parentheses.

> I'm thinking of a geometry problem. How many times you divide an angle (depends on your goal . . .). I'm thinking of a friend's cycle. He has put a heavy motor into a light frame. He may have to change it over into a heavier frame or the motor will shake the frame apart. It may be too heavy anyway. (I suspect you are talking about the transition from boy to man. You seem to have the feeling that the strength of your impulses has outweighed the capabilities of a boy . . . This might extend into the sexual area.) That's it exactly.[41]

Parker's David uses language in an autistic pattern for protection from people, but he is not totally shielding himself from sensory stimulation in the way of children who are autistic from infancy. The same issues are at stake, however: whether privacy is protected and whether he is strong enough to regulate his emotions in the social arena. Psychoanalyst and author Bruno Bettelheim, who worked with autistic children, describes these defenses similarly: "After all, the patient knows his old prison, as terrible as it is, and somehow has learned to protect himself against its most painful features through his symptoms."[42]

Perhaps a third David, who first made the news in April of 1996, can finally differentiate the autistic child from those whose retreats are reclusive or antisocial and thus foster stale thoughts. Those in anger and fury disengage from society. Speculation on the details of his history that are available adds explanation to differences in need for alonetime among those whose lives are marked by seclusion from society, from the shy to the autistic and even the socially disillusioned. David is one of two brothers—the brothers Kaczynski, as they are referred to now.[43] Though separated by fourteen hundred miles, they undertook seemingly similar lifestyles for about eleven years but were emotionally as different as chalk and cheese. David's love of the solitary was not retreat from the world or a pseudoindependence. Neither excessive fear, rejection, nor hatred of others seems the prime motivator; perhaps admiration of his older brother and sibling rivalry were the cause. And maybe a necessary self-reliance and philosophy emanating from yet-unveiled family dynamics and a rapidly changing world brought both of them to sparsely populated territories. To understand this David, we must contrast his brother, Theodore Kaczynski, suspected of being the Unabomber, who has a greater grievance against modernity, technology, and current affairs. The brother's life is more hidden, as he leaves few personal traces, but his anger may begin at home. Although his mother reputedly devoted herself to educating him, he is reported referring to her as a "dog." Wanda Kaczynski was for a long while not very welcome in Theodore's life. He seems to have refused contact with his parents, not even attending his father's funeral. The older Kaczynski's distrust of family, if we can call it that, is echoed in the paranoid writings discovered by his brother, filled with diatribes against technology. The self-chosen solitude is not autistic; the sullen aloneness that separates Ted Kaczynski from an autistic person takes on other characteristics. Unlike autistic geniuses who become expert to the last detail in drawings and unlike Grandin in her engineering feats, Kaczynski's homemade bombs are far from productions of great craftsmanship. Detonating explosives in fields and garbage cans, having an active bomb in his home, mailing weapons of destruction, and looking for public notoriety turned the loner into a miscreant, a political paranoid, and a power-hungry person. Traits associated with intentionally doing damage are not a fixed feature of autism or living alone.[44]

The psychologist in me responds to two small events reported about Ted Kaczynski. As a baby, he had to bear hospitalization while his family was kept away, a cruel practice most children's wards now have abolished. Then, when his brother was born, again the medical staff did not let him visit his mother, something hospitals now allow. This time he was left waiting in the lobby. Whether these were traumatic separations or not, they certainly could have upset Ted Kaczynski's sense of privilege in his mother's heart, and he in retaliation could seek distance.

Most likely autism does not arise from a terrible fear of separation; rather, everything points to a fear of contact. Some children are marked by devastating wounds in the attachment process. These are symbiotic characters[45]—children whose wills get crushed and for whom adventure and agency are no-no's. But pseudoindependent aloneness could arise out of having been rejected by parents. It stands to reason that there must be capacities that would allow for survival and self-development under conditions of abandonment psychologically or physically. Without the alone skills alternative, wouldn't all rejected children remain overly dependent, infantile personalities, unlike autistic children, who insist on their independent will? Alone needs would become so forbidden that they would submerge along with any vestige of an autonomous self. This is descriptive neither of Ted Kaczynski nor of autistic individuals.

Bruno Bettelheim, who housed autistic children at the Orthogenic School (under the rubric of the University of Chicago), refers to his residents' state of being as an "empty fortress," yet his written work illustrates understanding of their rich dreams and fantasy life.[46] Despite all the controversy surrounding this man of ambivalences, Bettelheim seems to clearly depict the plight of an autistic child as disconnected and living

> in a deep, dark hole without exit, imprisoned there both by his anxieties and by the insensitivities of others which he views as inimical designs. We have to invent and construct a way out for him—let's say a ladder . . . To bring this about, it must be possible for him to watch us work long and hard putting together this ladder, which must be very different from all others that have existed before. The patient will try to destroy the ladder convinced . . . that we do not fashion it to help him climb to liberty, but only to induce him to move into a worse prison . . . that will benefit us more than him.[47]

David Kaczynski helped others to build a ladder to his hole dwelling in the area of Texas labeled *despoblado*, or unpopulated. However, this escape was not quite as remote as his brother's settlement below the vastest stretch of wilderness in the United States outside of Alaska. David seems not so afraid, writing Western novels instead of manifestos, allowing his parents to visit, attending his dad's funeral, and seeking assistance to learn how to dance and compose love letters. The three Davids seem to live up to their namesake of the giant fighter, as all three wrestle with their individual demons, maintain strong needs for alonetime, but work to connect to others. David Kaczynski's life was not a counterpart to an autistic existence, nor was Theodore's. Unlike many who are truly autistic, Theodore in his self-imprisonment was unsettled and restless. I wonder why the Unabomber targeted people rather than machines and the system itself, since his rage was supposedly against technology. Unfortunately, though gifted with words, Theodore seems even less adept than many autistic individuals, and he had no one who worked unremittingly for his return to an inclusive life. One brother knew how to reach a balance between his solitary needs and those for friendship; the other didn't have a clue. The best he could do was try to insulate himself by escaping into the alone dimension, but the protection wasn't sufficient to keep him from having vengeful thoughts against the "madding crowd."

Pseudoindependent Alonetime

Maybe Theodore Kaczynski, like others, became self-reliant out of fear before he had developed a repertoire of skills to securely and satisfactorily be on his own. The young child seeking independence fantasizes about being adopted. Teenagers hurt by a best friend decide that they no longer need any friends. These autisticlike solutions may be short lived or become a part of a person's style of life. They do not, however, have to exclude the person from the world at large. Although these positions stem from an individual's need to be alone, they are primarily reactive—pseudoindependent aloneness. Most of the time such defensive states are fleeting. When, however, the feelings become constant reactions to extreme rejection, the capacity to be alone develops precociously. Recently, a new interest has emerged in precocious ego development and in what is called by some the "pathology of self-sufficiency."[48] I question linking pathology to self-sufficiency, even though I know those who out of great hurt and disappointment brush people aside and claim they need none other than themselves. The self-sufficiency side of that equation is, however, hard earned. My work with people who are removed from their dependency needs focuses on both an appreciation of their alone skills as healthy and the constant reminder that those alone skills are not everything they need in life. The difference between alone states that may have anger at their core and healthy alone states is similar to the distinctions between relationships of mutuality and ones ruled by domination or abuse.

Extreme Attachments — Abuse and Aloneness

Abuse is on everyone's minds. The key word for the traumas of our times, it comes in several guises—in the form not only of sexual or physical wrath but also of self-harm. Abuse is so prevalent in daily life that I do not enter this arena happily or attempt to perform quick therapy. I am interested in the ways alonetime plays a part. For one, people who abuse substances seek a relief that they have not been able to achieve with others or on their own. When we looked at trance societies it became apparent that the altered states drugs provide are age-old pursuits. In this era, however, most things used for pleasure and escape have proven to have dangerous side effects.

All forms of abuse share one commonality: once begun, they become addictive. We are aware of the physiological reasons, but why else? I have already discussed one reason in Chapter 8, called the "negative" holding environment experience. People become afraid to let go of what's unfavorable when associations are connected to something desired. They continue abusive behaviors, thoughts, and feelings despite restricting and negative aspects, fearing a void from their absence. Also, violence is a stimulant that requires increasing doses with time. That is why the excitement of an old Hitchcock movie is diluted when compared to those of Martin Scorsese, Oliver Stone, Brian DePalma, or Wes Craven.

Abusers believe that their actions will give them control. Drug abusers believe that alcohol will calm them, or that the pill will be a quick fix. Brutalizers believe the beaten child will succumb to their will, or stop crying out his or her need, or act normal, as defined by the perpetrator. Threatening, "Behave, or I'll beat you within an inch of your life," may change some people into robots, but for the most part it sends them underground. Rapists and molesters think the child or adult is powerless to resist them. The overeater, sometimes described as substituting food for love, is trying to self-soothe. But the disassociated, out-of-touch, lost-in-space, fugue state of bingeing or starving is actually the opposite of relating to others. The bingers and purgers are resisting others but trying to provide all things to themselves. Yet abusers are controlled by their perverse needs far more than they are in charge of them. Each inhalation has them sniffing for more. In the mind of the abuser is: I am in charge of regulating myself and others.

A false belief among mental health providers is that an abuser's primary goal is to gain, improve, or restore a sense of relatedness. Can that point be true? If we act like Saturn, the Titan forefather of the Roman gods, who devoured his children to protect his sovereignty (which seems to be the resolution to many world problems as well), will anyone be left to whom we can relate? The abuser really wants *self-control*. In the case of abusing another, domination is believed to be the way to restore an inner control. Abusers are actually caught in feelings of helplessness, searching not for a relationship but for an undemanding supporter and even confidant in the child they sometimes see as self-reliant. Quickly they learn this is not the case and they interpret the cries and whimpers as the voice of their own critical and demanding parents. Embitterment and shame turned to rage and intimidation distort the caretaking role. Usually enmeshed in a failure to parent is an individual's own dual loss of bonds and alonetime. Fortunately, not all abused people become abusers, but many do battle against such an onset.

My day-to-day experiences are witness to savagery, self-damage, and extreme abandonment, but also to the resiliency of children and adults who rely on themselves and find a way to new relationships. But if society or individuals think that they can beat and punish people into obedience, let me reinforce what we all see and know from everyday life: that method is not reliable. Because we all have inborn means for survival by ourselves, corporal punishments and totalitarian regimes, while cowing some individuals, just as frequently awaken alone skills and a retreat from others.

A Pseudo Cry to Relate: Aloneness and Substance Abuse

Wordsworth realized that "we have given our hearts away, a sordid boon!"[49] This laying waste of our powers requires replenishment, but not through misguided attempts at reregulation by alcohol or the like. And Shakespeare saw that abusers under the influence have to deal with far more aggression. As Othello exclaims, with reference to Iago, "O thou invisible spirit of mind, if thou hast no name to be known by, let us call thee devil! . . . O God, that men should put an enemy in their mouths to steal away their brains! . . . and transform . . . [themselves] into beasts!"[50] A psychologist decided to test Shakespeare's claim to see if alcohol and a host of drugs actually increased depression and aggression.[51] The study I'm referring to covered all the literature on low doses of various drugs and their effects on aggression. The author combed publications through computer from 1974 to 1992, studied recent journal issues from 1991 to 1993, and directly questioned experimental researchers who had previously published their work or that of colleagues. Strong evidence existed to suggest that even low doses of central nervous system (CNS) depressants cause humans to act aggressively. The idea that depressants, like music, soothe the savage in us is untrue. Another fake premise that children of alcoholics are bound to hear is a message of their parents, "I love you so much." That, however, turns into a lie once drinking commences. What is the truth: caring, or violence? And can individuals regulate their own signals after being misdirected by caretakers? [52]

The relationship between self-regulatory deficits and substance abuse is well documented. [53] Generally, however, the literature seems split. Though most researchers seem to support the notion that self-regulation difficulties can lead to substance abuse, ideas about why individuals turn to alcohol, food, or drugs differ. The premise here is that people use substances as attempts to cope and to regulate themselves when their natural mechanisms break down.

What are these natural mechanisms? Some are properties relating to alonetime. As endorphins work to numb us from physical pain, dissociation eases psychic trauma. In the late nineteenth century, Freud first explained symptoms of amnesia, paralysis, memory lapses, fugue states, and the like as seen in patients with hysteria as a defense against actual trauma. [54] This theory of dissociation as a defense was dropped—as Jeffrey Masson, temporary archivist for the Freud papers, has pointed out —when the veracity of patients' stories was displaced by Freud's theory that they were fantasizing their own abuse. [55] Now dissociation has regained its validity as a defensive and adaptive function. [56] Dissociation, an unconscious device, is a defense mechanism that allows the individual to remove himself or herself from a commotional event either by numbing feelings or splitting off the intellectual from the feeling state. Anyone who has seen *Annie Hall* will remember Diane Keaton disassociating as a ghostly double image, sitting in a chair, smoking, and watching her corporeal self in bed having sex with Woody Allen. It can be a manifestation of the quest for separation from others. Akin to denial, it is another aspect of people's ability to tune out, to move away from debilitating situations or emotions that put the mind and body on overload. While medications and psychotherapies can be used to provide protection, and self-drugging has always been a choice for some, we must remember people's inner resources. Dissociation temporarily can be an escape route now and again until healing in terms of others' empathy and positive self-regard step in.

When people flee to drugs, they are attempting to restore emotional balance to a system that isn't maintaining homeostasis. All too frequently, the results are not positive, but the temporary relief gives the illusion of a solution to pain, anxiety, or disequilibrium. Substances take on a life of their own. At first they can start off as a "container," to give the individual the sense of emotional integrity, or they are used as attempts to balance the effects of one of the many symptomological reactions to being emotionally out of control. In short order, the relief diminishes and the person is faced with the same—or a worse—degree of anxiety and depression. Most addictive substances taken repeatedly raise the rate of desire for dosage within a short while.

Food can take on similar meanings. Overeating is not a moral problem, but undereating can be a moral protest. Though related, the two are seen separately. I have helped people who struggle with food and fat through understanding the alone need. Some children learn that the stakes are high and their power can prevail when it comes to food, so little boys and little girls both spit out their food and refuse meals. Anthony Giddens, among others, sees anorexia nervosa—Western society's strange illness of starvation in a land of overstocked supermarkets—replacing hysteria as the symbolic illness of a postmodern age. Working from the same position, Maud Ellmann, a fellow in English at King's College, Cambridge, extends Franz Kafka's metaphor to understand "hunger artists" of all dimensions. She sees anorexic women in a "self-defeating protest; [as] they collude in their oppression by relinquishing the perilous demands of freedom in favor of the cozy compensations of infantilism."[57] In other words, they give up the alone fight to be themselves and stay in the power of their caretakers, while at the same time defying the authorities secretly and self-destructively. Actually eating themselves up, they reach a state of disembodiment or, not infrequently, death. Not unlike depression, anorexia is an attempt through misguided self-regulation to balance what have become strict polarities—to attach and to be alone. Ellmann uses writing to understand the private protest of those who transform starvations beyond the family dynamic to renouncement of worldly values. Both writing and starvation are interpreted as circumventing body boundaries:

> Hunger strikers . . . refuse to be influenced by the authorities
> or to swallow the values that their captors are ramming down
> their throats. Yet . . . this denial of the other necessarily entails
> the isolation and annihilation of the self. To fast is to create a
> dungeon of the body by rejecting any influx from the outer
> world; and writing also insulates the body . . . it is possible to

write even if one's ears are stopped and lips are sealed . . .
writing, like starvation, fortresses the self against the world,
perfecting its calamitous autonomy.[58]

Eating too much rather than too little also has to do with caretaking.
I eat when I'm tired. I learned this as a young mother, rising in the dead
of night to nurse my eldest son and unable to stay awake. I can remember
the taste of the apple pie and its quick solution to my worry about
remaining alert enough to care for Gary. From this experience and my
patients' varying stories of why they eat, I searched for a common theme
and found one. People mistakenly assume that eating is taking care of
something, regulating, giving time to ourselves in an important way,
restoring control. A lot of eating takes place compulsively, which means
it's outside of awareness, or dissociated. Although the compulsive eater
may obsess about food, the amounts taken in and the act of eating are
typically performed without full consciousness. Geneen Roth's thoughts
embody this dynamic:

> The drive to eat compulsively is not about food. It is about
> hungers . . . something in you—the voice of your hungers—
> does not want you to die without having realized your own
> uniqueness, so it calls to you. When you don't listen, it screams
> at you. Trying to escape from it is like trying to escape from
> your own shadow.[59]

The only way to know what the escape is about, what food means to you,
is to sit with the hunger and not fill it. If food is the symbol of control
over one's life, which hunger receives top priority? Is it the wish for an
improved self-image, reduction of anxiety, rest, love—or a hot fudge
sundae? Thus, truly taking care of oneself becomes confused with giving
oneself a treat. Many of the reasons for eating are linked either to insufficient or too much time with oneself, for oneself, and by oneself or to an
imbalance in a relationship. Besides the vicious psychological cycles of
abuse, a person's system becomes fixated biochemically. Drugs present
obvious changes, but foods, too, will elevate and lower our equilibrium
with chemicals like tryptophan, which affects serotonin production. We
are what we eat, as the saying goes, but also what we think, feel, and
take in from others. Abuse behavior tells us that many people feel barely
in charge of themselves. Alonetimes help to restore that balance. But
individuals have to work far harder to delve into their own alone resources when alonetime is forced upon them.

The Loss of Trust — Sanctuary in Aloneness

Former film star Frances Farmer wrote about her ordeal in a mental institution and dispels any illusions about the soothing effects of hydrotherapy:

> The first crash of icy water hit my ankles and slipped rapidly up my legs. I began to shake from the shock of it, screaming and thrashing my body under the sheet, but the more I struggled, the more I realized that I was helplessly restricted in a frozen hell . . . Hydro was a violent and crushing method of shock treatment, even though it was intended to relax the patient. What it really did was assault the body and horrify the mind until both withered with exhaustion.[60]

What Frances Farmer is describing with her words "withered with exhaustion" is the extreme alone capacities taking over, leaving the person depersonalized from her own self. Hydrotherapy, like the padded cell, has to do with depriving the senses of ongoing stimulation.

Storr reminds us that immersion in water—for that was part of the sensory deprivation experience—has a complex history, as it was employed presumably as a "relaxing change" in asylums for the insane.[61] It was not that long ago—twenty to twenty-five years or so—that one could walk in any large city and spot a store featuring asylum through sensory deprivation. These strange shops with their darkened windows were never as popular as the locations that followed their demise, featuring hot tubs and Jacuzzis, but they had their moment. Today, the relaxation method of choice vended in retail is simpler to undertake and less time consuming: one doesn't even have to strip to receive an eight-minute massage. Isolation chambers in their heyday—the late 1960s and early 1970s—were also used experimentally and in preparation for astronauts, who were going to face long periods of confinement in outer space. Their popularity grew in conjunction with the drug revolution and fitted the mottoes of that time, "Cool off" and "Tune out."

One of the chief proponents of work in understanding sensory deprivation is Jay Shurley, former head of adult psychiatry at the National Institute for Mental Health. In off-duty hours he developed with others the *warm*-water sensory-deprivation chambers.[62] He was his own best user, and what he hoped to simulate was the hallucinatory state of a disembodied mind. These dissociative dream places, "break-offs," were already well known to pilots who flew above the clouds faster than the speed of sound. But how do we reconcile this seeking of total sensory blindness to the dreaded torture of enforced isolation? In effect, sensory isolation is different from social isolation. Being held against the will involves far more than being alone.

Prisoners, or abused children, are not isolated from all that is social. What they do experience is society in its worst form. The isolation that they manage to achieve on their own is ultimately the only saving grace. Violent attachments have much in common with absence of people to relate to; both are without emotional comfort. The ability to exist devoid of active emotional help from others is a necessary system for feral children's survival as well as for those abused, taken hostage, and confined against their will.[63] The girl Genie reflects all the above negative attachment that leaves one little choice but to be extremely alone, and alone endurance that persists despite devastating circumstances. Born to an inhumane father and emotionally crippled mother, Genie was raised without responsiveness or kindness. She came under hospital care at age thirteen, a modern-day feral child: silent, severely abused, unsocialized, without the ability to stand erect and without control over salivating, urinating, or defecating. The scientific community had not had a feral child to consider since Victor, the Wild Boy of Aveyron, came to the attention of Dr. Jean-Marc Gaspard Itard. And even at this late stage of her life, Genie at first benefited from the caring hands of these modern scientists working in a fine pediatric hospital. But circumstances intervened, and now Genie is institutionalized under sanitary conditions.[64] Though no fairy tale ending of a sleeping beauty transcending her past, Genie's story does astound us with the strength of the human spirit to fight on even within the unspeakable horrors of abusive imprisonment.

The strange thing is that despite the humiliations, filth, isolation, and countless terrors of this life, in the end realization of freedom becomes scary. "The thought of being thrown back into a world where money and ambition created a pressure pot terrified me," admitted Frances Farmer, who had grown accustomed to her confinement.[65] Paradoxically, so it seems, the same techniques used to achieve rest and calm are what criminals, prisoners of war, and hostages are asked to endure as extreme punishment. Solitary confinement for a prisoner in jail is a respite and not always the terror it is intended to be. In fact, these additional alonetimes, for some, lead to the quickly dissipated jailhouse religion, a reform of the soul that disappears soon after discharge. Yet others, like Malcolm X, are able to shed destructive patterns of the past in their alonetime contemplations and move away from lessons of hatred and alienation to achieve transformation.[66] Asylum against one's will changes the very nature of alonetime, as Harvey Weinstein intimated to me in a telephone conversation after his horrendous ordeal underground. Weinstein's twelve days (in August 1993 in New York City) of captivity in a dark, six-by-four-foot cramped pit were all the worse because among his kidnappers was a so-called loyal employee who worked for Weinstein's company, Lord West Formal Wear, for eight years. As they should and must be, parts of his alone experiences will remain private.

Unmistaken, however, in what we know of Weinstein's captivity and that of others, like Winnie Mandela, is that alone skills are operative. Being an ex-marine was probably helpful, as Weinstein, in Houdini-like fashion, freed himself of chains, enabling himself to stand up straight. Among the mental games he played was narrating the story of his life to himself. Winnie Mandela accounts her days imprisoned, mostly in solitary confinement, and her need to keep alert so that her interrogators would not break her down. Many times she recalled fainting as nature's way to give her relief. The combined memories of her past, plus her endurance and lone bravery, helped her to survive.[67] So inured was she from 491 days in solitary confinement that when she was acquitted, she turned to go back to her cell, dazed and like a zombie. As Frances Farmer relates after her eight years of state "asylum": "During those years I passed through such unbearable terror that I deteriorated into a wild, frightened creature intent only on survival."[68] She describes her prison as "a steel trap, and . . . I crawled out mutilated, whimpering and terribly alone. But I did survive."[69]

Survival, perhaps some are thinking, doesn't seem that satisfying a goal. But the will to live, in struggles to overcome torture, is a triumph in and of itself. Imprisonment makes a travesty of privacy. Since every day in captivity increases the empowerment of the captor, the alone self of the captive is hard won, if that happens at all. Frightening, life-threatening, painful, and disorienting punishment in captivity forces people to marshal every resource to stay sane and unified.

Examples from hostage and prisoner experiences suggest the ways people cope and adapt on the outer edge of the alone continuum. In the mid-1980s, the confusion of Middle East politics led to a series of captures of American civilians. An administrator, a teacher, and a journalist chose to tell their stories of abuse and mental torture, and contained in these personal tales, along with courage and resourcefulness, are factors that allowed them to triumph over incarceration. Joseph Cicippio, comptroller of the American University in Beirut, became a hostage on September 12, 1986, and his first lessons in survival began when he dropped in and out of consciousness from a blow to the head, followed by the fortress he built around his mind and soul.[70] Naturally, not all times can be equally endured, yet somehow Cicippio always sounded inwardly prepared. Again and again, in recitals of death and castration threats and humiliation, it is the inside person that defies defeat. Brian Keenan, a Belfast-born teacher of English literature, was held against his will for four and a half years and coined the most descriptive term for this attempt to dehumanize: "evil cradling." Yet he emerged from the worst of it, a chamber of isolation, with himself intact. Keenan describes how alone skills took over his survival:

> We exhaust the strategies of denial . . . as we move further into awareness of our new reality. The new conditions about us have the effect of reconditioning us. We move into a process of acceptance, but this acceptance should not be seen as a defeat of our powers of resistance and of maintaining the integrity of the self. It is simply that in a situation of total confinement one has to learn to unhook from the past in order to live for the present.[71]

Rather than on mechanisms for alone survival, a good deal of emphasis has been placed on the odd and surprising relationships that form in prison from an exchange of a blink of the eye through cell windows or a prison guard's kindness. Chief Middle East correspondent of the Associated Press, Terry Anderson was held up at gunpoint off a street in West Beirut on March 16, 1985. Not only isolated and tortured, he was kept blindfolded for weeks on end. Anderson's struggle was to conquer the time of incarceration and reach a place of sanctuary: "But at the bottom in surrender . . . there is no coherent thought, no real pain, no feeling, just exhaustion, just waiting, there is something else. Warmth/light/softness. Acceptance, by me, of me. Rest. After a while, some strength. Enough, for now."[72] As Anderson demonstrates, alonetime fears are not as inborn as is suggested by existentialism. If they were, then the imprisoned, constantly beleaguered by death, would not be experiencing the regaining of a peaceful alone state that transcends the fear.

In this age of abuse, marriage and family are not the only institutions that have confounded our expectations of where to find safety. Religion and education, too, are not the symbols for refuge that they once seemed. With religious workers, day care workers, and teachers violating ethical codes of protection, society (like the autistic child) seems ready to fall back on its own means of asylum—asylum in the solitude of aloneness.

Autistic individuals teach us about our self-protective alone reserve. They are versatile in using untapped sources for comfort and soothing, which we in our busy lives rarely bother knowing. Their silences, like those of the deaf and mute, seem unbearable handicaps. Certainly, being cut off from communication can be beyond fright, paralyzing. Yet journalist and essayist Lynda Morgenroth came to prefer silence in her travels to foreign lands and the altered state it provided. From her insights the links between the extreme of autism, the escape provided by dissociation, the contrasts between chosen and enforced asylum, and the pleasures in discovering our alone vocabulary are readily apparent:

> Not being able to speak the language generally means you can't understand what's being said to you, either . . . [This] can be quite pleasant if you learn to stop struggling and proceed gently into the void. After a few days . . . you enter a salubrious quiet, a kind of spacious inner room . . . The calming of compulsory silence has taught me . . . to simmer down . . . I spent two weeks alone in Paris . . . In the beginning I felt depressed, lonely and isolated . . . But after the first few days of shattered ego, I was as comfortable in the silence as a bear in a cave. Silence became part of the soothing, soft fog that hung in the air that winter and of the pleasing strangeness of things . . . Perhaps in silence we become our essential selves. We approach the inner being that gets trampled by the gregarious, chameleonlike outer-directed self.[73]

Mother nature operates within the law of parsimony. All that we have seen in those extreme, paranormal experiences of the autistic, the abused, and the heroic prisoners reinforces the fact that sustenance is achieved through alonetime. If under extraordinary conditions our alone abilities, even when untutored by considerable experience, fill in and ensure survival, think of how they can help us if we reconstruct their meaning to us in plain and ordinary life experiences. To paraphrase W. Somerset Maugham, nothing is less typical than the normal. The normal perhaps is nonexistent and really only an ideal. The fact that one struggles for control—be it in excessive substance intake or even in the horrendous abuse of others—is not remote from our own consciousness. These deeds remind us of how we all struggle to take charge of ourselves. On the other hand, we all have imprisoned parts and hidden recesses wherein lie our spirit and fortitude. Protection indeed—but also miracles of survival, vital spiritual strength, seeds for courage, and integrity of being. The alone skills that accompany the asylum provided by our alonetime need keep us in touch with our pilgrim hearts and protect us from soul death. No less has been said of strong and positive relationships with others. Now, however, this same truth about chosen and unforced times alone can be similarly broadcast.

CHAPTER 12

Reclaiming Courage and

Confidence: The Reconstruction

of Alonetime

From childhood's hour I have not been
As others were—I have not seen
As others saw—I could not bring
My passions from a common spring—
From the same source I have not taken
My sorrow I could not waken
My heart to joy at the same tone—
And all I loved—I loved alone.
    EDGAR ALLAN POE, "Alone"[1]

I have a house where I go
When there's too many people,
I have a house where I go
Where no one can be;
I have a house where I go
Where nobody ever says "No";
Where no one says anything—so
There is no one but me.
    A. A. MILNE, "Solitude"[2]

THROUGHOUT THE WRITING of this book, my husband and I had a deal.
Since my teaching and patient commitments forbade lengthy solitary
sojourns, he offered to do all the driving on long car trips, leaving me
free to sit, think, or write. As a longtime sufferer of motion sickness,
originally I thought the offer generous, sweet, and unreasonable. Surprisingly, however, times en route became favorite found moments for con-

solidating my thinking. I did not realize the depth of my concentration until, while seated next to my husband in the car one afternoon, he asked me about my ideas for a chapter. His innocent words, viscerally felt, became like knife wounds. I identified with what it must be like for the autistic person in withdrawal. Thus taken off guard, I answered sharply that I wasn't as yet prepared to talk to anyone about this chapter. Interruptions in alonetime are not consciously experienced, as are sudden deprivations in attachment. The strength of my reaction brought forth other associations, such as a baby's startled response to noise, a child not answering when her or his name is called, people's blank stares during conversations, and an ability I recognized since childhood—being focused on something to the point that I was oblivious to conditions of cold, heat, hunger, or thirst. These natural meditations are a part of the alonetimes of life. The quest is persistent and pervasive throughout human existence, but now, more than ever before, obtaining alonetimes requires active searching. Throughout the book, I have suggested some guideposts and shown examples of how people have restored alonetime in their lives, and I will continue to do so in this chapter.

The New Alonetime

Alonetime, like the solitude described by philosophical writer Philip Koch, has an "equal status with encounter."[3] Koch's focus is mainly on the grown-up dimensions of solitude. I have not placed solitude in a rarefied atmosphere. It is but one of various forms alonetime takes. The need and love for food is satisfied in many ways besides eating a gourmet meal; we are sated also by a snack, dieting, cooking lessons, reading recipes, "grazing," or a barbecue. Similarly, alonetime finds its place while we are with another, in crowds, with noise, in sleep, or in alert and chosen isolation. Alonetime does not always require quiet and stillness, an absence of outside or inside noise. The aware meditative state and other altered states of consciousness may use sound patterns to achieve their goals. But it is so much harder to experience this release when it goes against the grain of social mores. Because alonetime is not in our everyday vocabulary, it is more difficult to know the ins and outs of alonetime's pleasures, and desire for acceptance can even cause us to be sneaky in its pursuit. Yet if we realize that in the early womb environment we learned how to achieve the calm of aloneness, then the relaxation response, meditations, and retreats are not new skills but forgotten abilities restructured, relearned, and reclaimable as remedies to contemporary strife. Of course, these practices can reach extraordinary dimensions when—as they were for Moses, Buddha, Saint Anthony, and are for modern figures like the Dalai Lama, Deepak Chopra, Krishnamurti, and Thich Nhat Hanb—they become life's core. At these heights, alonetimes open one to enlightenment, but these paths are hardly necessary for everyone.

Alonetime is not a pursuit only of those initiated to spiritual practice. It is nonsegregational, wanted and needed by all. The advocates of such practice as well as the numbers of Americans now seeking solace through all forms of spirituality and asylum speak to a general crying need for alonetime. A danger I see in new allegiances to religious and philosophical sects is that rather than address the root of the need, each sect is only another attempt to gain mass appeal. Moreover, by establishing necessary rules and regulations, such practices lead to rote actions that may not be inner directed or fit with an individual's particular alone or spiritual needs. However, if philosophical psychoanalyst Erich Fromm is correct, scores of people prefer escapes from personal freedom and consequently forfeit self-regulation because following another's routine spares them the guilt, hard work, and potential alienation in striking their own chord.[4] Culture and civilization certainly do breed conformity in all of us to one degree or another. Now with technology and consumerism motivating society, planning daily living is getting out of hand for everyone. We are drowning in recommendations on how to escape stress and overwork— self-help through relaxation, religious practice, spiritual rebirth, exercise, and general caring for the mind and body—as well as on how to improve relationships, ameliorate abusive practices, and escape a dysfunctional legacy. Inward explorations are recommended to offset the unsettling cacophonous chaos of the outside world, while lessons in empathy and commitment are similarly marketed to restore relationships. Tools for obtaining individual balance are in front of us, but we cannot steadily hold on to them unless we grasp what is out of balance in our dual needs for alonetime and bonding.

Placing alonetime and attachment parallel, as givens that are equally necessary in maintaining equilibrium in mind, body, and life, leaves a lot up to the individual. Nevertheless, many within today's world, unlike Fromm's sheeplike individual of the 1930s and 1940s or cult followers of the late twentieth century, buy into self-gratification and development and could—by a slight shift toward looking inward instead of into the mirror—take stock and reflect more deeply on self-improvement. From this vantage point, control through inner regulation is reassuring, obtainable, and responsive to individual differences. This requires reconstructing one's thinking to be mindful of the alonetime need as far more than a resting spot for escaping traffic jams, satellite signals, pollution, or the many hazards of modern times. The aloneness that I have written about encircles all of our lives, and thus extends even further than melismas—the rhapsodic, long chants of monks. Alonetime is equivalent to all absolute needs and motivations, and therefore to face its fullness means taking strong notice of the crowding-in daily experiences and then reframing and regrouping priorities. A new openness and accessibility to the alone need is not like lifting the lid to Pandora's box. We are already versed in the grim fears associated with being alone. The well-kept secrets of alonetime will yield pleasures, not sorrow and regret.

The Ubiquitous Need

Alone needs are constant in one form or another, from wombhood through old age, helped to flourish but not encompassed in bite-sized meditations. Octavio Paz says, "Man is the only being who knows he is alone,"[5] but this aspect of that knowledge scares people into retreat from truth. Historian Arnold J. Toynbee speaks of the history of every people revealing the "two-fold motion of withdrawal—and return!"[6]

A restorer of energy, the stillness of alone experiences provides us with much-needed rest. One cannot overemphasize, for example, the importance of a good sleep. Given that we sleep more time in life than anything else, isn't that sufficient alonetime? But even slow-moving cultures supplement sleep with additional lone activities. Moreover, according to British Columbian psychologist and author Stanley Coren, we are surrounded by "sleep thieves."[7] Ever since Thomas Edison—a man who thought the elimination of sleep would increase productivity—gave us the lightbulb, not only work time but also playtime have steadily increased, and have become twenty-four-hour happenings. Coren feels that the effects of loss of sleep can, if not kill us outright, cause a gradual but specific deterioration in health.[8] This is especially disconcerting when I note that it is during wee hours that some people leave messages on answering machines or send E-mail. Besides reducing irritability and giving us energy and verve, getting sufficient shut-eye promotes clear thinking. Problem solving can happen automatically in sleep time. Evolution provides a way to achieve alonetime naturally in sleep, in meditative states, and through stimulus barriers.

That is nature's way. Technology works both ways; it gives us time, but it kills it, too. The computer for some is like music or art. It provides a way into quiet self-absorption, but simultaneously, worldwide computer networks keep us in touch day and night. My response to the question of why software is gaining in allure over face-to-face encounters is that the computer is the one machine that seemingly offers it all—stimulation, knowledge, news, varied alone pursuits, relationships, and even sex. The computer allows for laid-back or active interactions with sound effects and no arguments. One might say it has universal appeal. Will it eventually be the first serious challenge to religion? Bestowing it with omnipotence and giving it dominion in our lives naturally has drawbacks.

Were the editors of the *New York Times* aware that they were making a statement when they put the headlines "Longing for a New Lone Genius" and "@ Wit's End: Coping with E-mail Overload?" back-to-back?[9] How many of us these days have the courage to lessen technological connections and stay with ourselves alone? Perhaps Albert Einstein's or Charles Darwin's theories would have arisen with equal potency in the culture if they had been shared over worldwide broadcasts. Or, more likely, if "Al" or "Charlie" were posting their work on a bulletin board, it would not take more than one of their exciting statements to electrify the Internet. Thus, when I imagine these great men inundated with upwards of one hundred E-mail messages per day—not counting responses to friends asking about tickets to the opera or soccer games—I see their progress fizzling. Figures of genius with original thoughts and heroic posture may be obliterated by a society that allows as the norm intrusions into creative time and space.[10] And even though, as I have shown, alone needs pop up in one way or another in the nooks and crannies of history, culture, and present-day life, there exists a general unwillingness to accept the need openly as a psychological axiom.

No one except perhaps the poets knows alonetime's psychological origins and gives full voice to the need. Let us rely on them to create a new language to free aloneness linguistically and conceptually. Stephen Spender is one poet who realizes that the etymological, symbolic, and perhaps even death-challenging roots of solitude lie in the soul, as do seeds of greatness: "I think continually of those who were truly great. Who, from the womb, remembered the soul's history?"[11] First, unshackle aloneness from its negative position as kith and kin to loneliness. Remove it from battles with bonding, attachment, and relationships. Make its message part of the social norm! Then uplift it from its lowly place on the mental health shelf. Psychologist and scholar Arnold Modell rightly argues, as I and others have, that the self is hardly exclusively a social self.[12] The relief of solitude, reverie, contemplation, alone and private times is typically chosen and primarily isolated from communicative exchanges.[13]

We should not fool ourselves by saying that human contact is lessened in the age of machines. It is only face-to-face connections that we are losing. Whereas, in olden times, three or four letters were written in a day, now we can compose dozens of E-mail messages and respond to as many voice mail messages within twenty-four hours. Distanced and distancing communication is well illustrated in contemporary life with countless examples of overconnected men and women attempting to live in the fast lane. They may have good intentions to deepen and pare down their commitments but they despair when their answering machine tells them, "No new messages." These great-at-friendship, lousy-at-intimacy people on the move often can't be alone, unable to bear any quiet moments and caught up in achieving fame and money.

Attachments under stress or to ward off loneliness—as it frequently seems with those trapped by the lure of success—are adhesive bonds, although not necessarily the most fruitful. As my friend Jill reports, we can unlearn the lesson that separations are prima facie life threatening and go back to an ability to balance both needs comfortably. She wrote to me:

> When I was ten and my mother first went back to work, I was very afraid to be alone. However, I soon got used to it and then found it was a state familiar to me and that I had to have it. If I don't get enough, I find myself edgy and crabby. My husband and son go away for some weekends camping. I always have mental plans of seeing old friends or having a weekend guest, but I never do. I stay home, rarely watch TV or even listen to music. I love the tranquility and silence. I read voraciously, daydream like I did when I was a kid and sleep late. It is heaven. I am refreshed when they return and yes, eager to see them. Unfortunately, I sometimes allow the American guilt factor to seep in and fret about all the projects I should have done around the house.

Jill is uncommon in that she has actively considered her need to be alone in the context of her equal need for relationships. While what Jill writes about could serve as a template for some, others search religion for the space to be alone and connected.

— ə ʃɪɛɪɪɪɪɪɪɪ̯ —

The Tie of Organized Religion to the Alonetime Need

A well-read friend of mine was surprised about the comeback religion has made throughout the world, as well as in Western civilization. This no longer startles me. Religion ranks as one of culture's most successful inventions. Why now, when scientific truths seem preeminent, is New Age spiritualism, along with traditional or alternative practices, taking hold? Arguments from refound nationalism to humankind-as-mythmaker provide plausible explanations, some given in this book. While religion often enough falls short of providing for the individual or common good, its relevance is profound. Not only does it service spiritual and ethnic needs and give moral guidance; it is also perhaps the best harmonizer of the needs to attach and detach. Whether viewing voodoo, other African-derived religions, trance behavior, Hinduism, Judaeo-Christian traditions, Islam, individual prayer, or the repeated refrains of cult practices, one sees in each serious act of devotion room for calming connectedness and disengagement. The sweetness of that resolution and encounter has proven to many people over the centuries to be worth the sacrifices, suffering, and even evil that accompany some of these beliefs. It is perhaps in the knowledge that community and aloneness were sufficiently incorporated in the spiritual message that monasticism gave up its attempts to balance the labor of the secular world with the pace of the spiritual. This embracing statement is not meant in disregard of the great and fruitful studies of myth and religion. Nor do I mean to ignore the transforming power of belief in God—or even to suggest God doesn't exist, since God's existence obviously does not depend upon religion. The gift of aloneness with which religion provides the individual achieves acceptance because it appears in the construction of a union with God. Therefore, with the exception of the religiously devout, such as monks and nuns, one rarely notes how much this offering satisfies the interior desire for a more absolute alonetime. Suppose we follow innermost thoughts a bit further before returning to religion and alonetime.

Possibly a lost art from the so-called Dark Ages is the interior dialogue. In our time of illumination, perchance the Neon-bright Age, talking to oneself spells insanity. Yet only through an inner communication system can we self-regulate. My former assistant Charlotte has a theory about why so many otherwise normal people talk to themselves in the streets and subways of metropolitan New York. She attributes it to the fact that people in the city have less privacy (a lot of them use public transportation and have roommates in order to save money) in which to engage in these little monologues. New Yorkers sing to themselves all the time out in public, which they might do in the privacy of a car if they had one, for example. Talking to oneself is not the same as hallucinating voices; in psychosis, the private self is not at peace, and inner exchanges reflect unhappy conflicts.

When internal dialogues lead to destructive acts—murders and suicides—from lonely, antisocial lives, people are quick to associate the lack of friendships negatively with aloneness. One can be sure, however, that it is not only the amount of alonetime that is out of whack; it is the quality of relationships as well, and often even the environment at large. Those who perpetrate violence have not just been fed overdoses of alonetime. They have been victims of, and seen too much, bad relating and abuse. And if such outcasts plot their revenge in solitude, the numbers are far fewer than those who plot murder and pillage in gangs. When the internal dialogue goes haywire, it is regulated primarily by others' voices and mechanistic beliefs. For the psychologist, however, there are lessons to be learned in patients hearing voices.

Colleen Murphy was one of my first patients when I began practice in a psychotherapy clinic. She was raised in New York by Irish-born grandparents. She was gifted with a magnificent voice and sang for an opera company. She sought treatment with me when she could no longer perform. She was filled with terror of "the devil and his banshees," whose voices she occasionally heard in her mind. One day, she told me a dream. She was in the garden, a large flowering space with anemones and roses and flowers of every color. It was an unusual assortment, but beautiful in the way the flowers interlaced with one another. She had just finished weeding and trimming the dead leaves when she looked down at her hand to see that she had grown an enormous, bright green thumb. She screamed and awakened. No less terrified as she recounted the dream, she began sobbing forcefully. All the while, she mumbled indistinguishably about someone, a doctor, being right. Undaunted, I plunged into trying to unravel the dream.

I started questioning the color and appearance of her thumb. It turned out to be a kelly green and not in and of itself grotesque. The size was disturbing. The color led us to Ireland and the fact that her grandfather couldn't resist fanciful storytelling every time she visited. He believed in all the fairy spirits of Ireland and had a tale for every event in a person's life. I laughed about this, exclaiming my allegiance to anyone with such a vivid imagination. Colleen looked somber. She said my reaction was so different from that of someone whom she'd seen before me. He had responded to a dream in which she talked to "little people" as if it were an ominous sign and suggested that she might feel better taking thorazine (an antipsychotic medication). She felt like never seeing him again after that, but that week she had a concert and didn't want to disrupt her routine. It was at that performance that she first experienced unusual stage fright.

When Colleen brought her adaptive "regressive" dream images into treatment, the doctor may have felt threatened by the unreality of her dream. I was lucky to have had an African friend and colleague who told me about how she gained restorative calm through bridging the world of her family, their spirit practices, and her hectic adopted culture. Having worked with hospitalized schizophrenic patients, I felt comfortable distinguishing between a consciousness sufficiently fluent to employ the imaginative and a consciousness trapped in the whirlpool of distorted thinking. The garden was of Colleen's own design and a meditative place. With this interpretation of her dream, she changed the tentative "My former therapist was right" to an assertive statement: *"He was wrong."* Colleen went back to singing.

◆　　◆　　◆

Talking to oneself in prayer serves a purpose not unlike Colleen's discussions with the "little people." Midway in my teaching and practice, I noticed how compelling other aspects of religion were when a very bright and outspokenly feminist Christian student decided to live with her Iranian husband in the Khomeini-dominated country of his birth. Everyone wondered how she would accept living in purdah. Was she rationalizing, bravely accepting her desire to be with her husband, resigning herself to her fate in cowardly submission, or did she see something different in her determination to accept this devout practice? Indeed, she felt the garb gave her enormous liberty. Reporter Judith Miller, in her opus on the militant Middle East, *God Has Ninety-Nine Names*, supports my student's claim.[14] She notices that Islamic modesty serves as a social buffer. Women behind the veil no longer feel like sexual objects or the need to dress up as such. The sameness of the cultural costume serves as an analgesic to one's surroundings, as do school uniforms. I want to point out another paradox: something that to one person appears hypercritical or intemperate feels like relief to another. In this sense, I hope to further illustrate the importance of stepping aside to contemplate one's own personal way to ensure time alone—and not only that, but the fact that at different times or at another stage of life, the choices vary. As an example, Emerson—who realized the route of religion to the transcendental—advocated full consciousness of experience and objected vociferously to employing the paraphernalia of the church. Addressing the alone desires of individuals who like himself sought freedom of expression, he felt that sedating spiritual fountains could be achieved essentially through solitary inner contemplation, all the while insisting that dogma and ritual hindered the discovery of an unfettered divine spark within us all.

In what is cited as Joseph Campbell's most prophetic book, *The Hero with a Thousand Faces*, he traces the similarities of the human psyche and spirituality through underlying common myths, despite variations of race and religion. And in explicating these similarities, Campbell carves out the basic function of mythology and rite as "to supply the symbols that carry the human spirit forward, in counteraction to those other constant human fantasies that tend to tie it back."[15] Campbell thinks it is basically the work of the hero to retreat from the secular to the inner springs, whether soothing or fearful. I think this is an ongoing task craved by all, and everyone finds ways to obtain seas of calm and wells of courage. To me, the mightiest and most universal force of religion is its potential path to this calm and confidence, despite the "God" in whose name people have slaughtered each other ad infinitum. That same intellectual friend who was surprised at religion's comeback believed that scientific changes wrought in society would render religion meaningless, as technological ways would dispense with the myths through which gods and goddesses gained power. The computer may take over part of religion's role, but not because myths become defunct. Medicines for healing and the answers provided by science and technology have not necessarily led to a disenchanted society or slowed the quest for renewed power or the spiritual, as defined here as an escape from the everyday. The social value of a religious identity, the longing for community, and the stability of sameness contribute to the continuity of belonging to a religious group,[16] but so do individual silent rituals.

Resiliency and Courage Through Private Contemplation

Robert Coles has talked to children of different cultures to find out their soulful ways. He believes that spirituality has its roots in childhood: not just because children seek out representations of their mother or father in God, but because children are thoughtful and intrinsically philosophical. For him, religion is more than the submission and dependence that Freud and Marx describe. Coles interviewed Tony, a boy forced by illness to isolation in an iron lung. Tony's ordeal helped him find a way to silence and privacy. Attached to his religion, he still preferred meditation and solo ruminations, exemplifying the personal nature of spiritual life. One might suspect that eleven-year-old Tony, scared of dying, traveling alone through the time and space of his illness, would accept the all-day comfort his mother offered to him. Rather, he sent her home. Tony also sent his priest away, risking alienation for the sake of privacy. He needed to ask and answer his own questions about death, morality, and the purpose of life. As Coles puts it, Tony basically needed no help. It was ultimately his private struggle "to gain control of what life he had, to master a machine which might well, he knew, be his last 'home' before he died."[17] Discussing childhood secrets, intimacy, and privacy, M. Van Manen and B. Levering state:

> The right to privacy is more than the right to certain liberties, to ownership ... or simply to be left alone. Privacy may also be seen as a necessary condition of human life without which personal morality and dignity would be hard to imagine. The experiences of secrecy, reserve and intimacy may ultimately find their genesis in the fundamental condition of privacy [alonetime]. The possibility of privacy, of separating oneself from others makes possible secrecy, reserve *and intimacy* [italics mine].[18]

Is Privacy Doomed?

Psychoanalysis and psychotherapy (with their rules of confidentiality), religious confessionals, and the once-quiet space of hospitals recognized early the need for privacy as part of a healing process. Quiet has been rendered obsolete. If coping and healing require the help of a private self and privacy is slipping away from us, shouldn't we be treating privacy as an endangered state? Privacy may be doomed, with computer and beamed-in satellite data generating enough information to keep all spies busy for life. One doesn't even have to be spying to invade privacy. My husband, a physician, stumbled upon the fact that any doctor in the hospital could key into the computer screen for information on the medication and blood chemistry of any patient being treated, his or others. Apparently, medicine today does not widely subscribe to the Hippocratic Oath, which was once considered the eleventh commandment to physicians: "Whatsoever things I see or hear concerning the life of men . . . I will keep silence thereon, counting such as sacred secrets." So while the Supreme Court recently upheld the virtues of confidentiality in psychotherapy, managed care, which adds a middle person to confidential records, is but one example of the invasion of private space. New hospital rules, genetic testing, computerized records, and attempts to change laws on confidentiality all might spell good-bye to the personal self as an inner resource.

Perhaps a reverse of this antiprivacy revolution will naturally occur. Right now our personal diaries, even when they expose colossal flaws in ourselves, are the media's and the public's delight. Maureen Dowd quips about the gush in memoir writing in her *New York Times* op-ed column entitled "Banks for the Memory."[19] But even TV talk-show hosts may soon tire of the can-you-top-this quality of their guests' true confessions. "Been there, done that" and "ho hum" could soon be the responses of an I've-seen-and-heard-everything audience. My psychology training suggests that after the fun of self-disclosure wears thin, people's need for privacy will hold sway. But in that hope there is also a fear that if we reverse direction automatically, obfuscation, concealment, and cover-up will again dominate.

Awareness of the reasons behind these cultural waves may supply us with a steadier course of action. Recently, I saw *Time* magazine editor Henry Grunwald on *The Lehrer Report*, discussing his book *One Man's America* and his belief in action through secular crusades.[20] His comments made me think of the actions of Lena, the sister of a patient of mine.

Lena was an elementary-school teacher in a small town out West. Her brother was pastor in a community many miles away. He called on his sister for help in a most unusual situation. Two high-school girls had been impregnated by a convicted rapist. He asked his sister if she could house them during the last few months of their pregnancies to protect them from further gossip and mean attention. They were both very creative youngsters looking for a place where they could be alone in their thoughts and have privacy. Their babies had been promised already for adoption, and the adolescents themselves were looking for sanctuary.

After housing one of the girls, seeing her through the adoption process, and then having the second girl move in, Lena received a phone call from a neighbor who accused her of running an illegal adoption agency. Next, the local paper called her for an interview on the topic and said that they were preparing a story for the next edition. Lena asked them to hold the story and promised to reply to them in a week. The next day, Lena called all the parents in her first-grade class and had a conference. She announced that she was being accused of something that was not true, that she did not want to reveal the story behind her actions, and she hoped that they would, in their trust of her, fight for her privacy in this matter. The parent community responded with letters about Lena's right to privacy. Lena herself spoke to the editor of the newspaper, telling him the basis for the accusation. The editor squashed the false reports.

◆   ◆   ◆

Perhaps secular crusades for both privacy (without interfering with the First Amendment) and creative reduction of pressure in all walks of life will be set in motion before making money and the desire to know supplant all else.

Self-Regulating: Knowledge, Stimulation, Quiet, and Love

The right to know, while most important, has now superseded privacy, without serious forethought to what we stand to lose from gains in knowledge and information. Take a couple I treat in marriage counseling, Emma and Jake.

They live in small, cramped quarters and work as restaurateurs in a pressure tank of public service by day. Private time is being eroded from their lives at work, and at home both tear into their laptops to get on the Internet. Emma, when she started therapy, had retreated to sullen anger in the relationship. Jake found that angry outbursts relieved his feelings of always being encroached upon and overrun. On the other hand, they were so used to attention from each other that if one openly read a book and wished for quiet, or expressed tiredness and a need to be uncommunicative, it was experienced as a rejection and threat. As a hostile attachment was building, both were finding more and more excuses for separate, lone activities. Their best times were becoming those when away from each other. As Dan Hicks and his Hot Licks sang in the seventies, "How can I miss you when you don't go away?"

◆　◆　◆

Decoding what was underneath Emma and Jake's actions took time, but once it was accomplished, they began to develop a new way of communicating that took into account their exhaustion from too much world *and* their love for each other.

But all the external pushes for more togetherness may be at saturation point. An increasing dependency on drugs, a rise in cases of intrafamily abuse, and people's cynicism about sentiment must connote a certain restlessness about close relationships. Not to mention that, these days, relationships seem harder to make and easier to break. Mary Karr, author of *The Liars' Club*, was stunned by the numbers who respond to her memoir of family life with shock of recognition. It led her to a new definition of the dysfunctional family: "any family with more than one person in it."[21] The flow of alcohol kept up myths of fun and harmony in the Cheever household but didn't actually help Susan Cheever's family to get on:

> We laughed while alcohol twined itself around our family like a choking, deadly invisible vine. No one talked about it. No one saw what was happening. And all that time we had no idea why my mother was crying upstairs in her room, or why my father was always on the way to the hospital, or why I had to marry the wrong man—and then marry the wrong man again and again.[22]

The mixed messages in the psychotherapy world are as rampant and complex as in the social world. I could not ever totally take in one ideology in psychoanalysis because I myself found inner exceptions to the tenets. The value and power of psychoanalysis and psychotherapy are enormous, but to me, not so much just because they improve relationships. Here I agree with Alfred Kazin, who states that he "know[s] for sure that the disorder in my soul is not altogether covered by the deficiency in 'interpersonal relationships' I hear about three times a week."[23]

Now, I find the influence of infant research has brought psychoanalytic theory closer to recognizing the equal importance of self to mutual regulation and of disengagement to engagement.[24] But I do worry about the unconscious and aggressive and sexual motivation becoming underrated, the movement to hurry treatment into what could be called instant, or "microwave," therapy, and that society and the individual will find another way to push aside complexity. Alone needs gain impetus from one of Freud's persuasive positions at the heart of early psychoanalytic theory. He understood that human beings "are not [only] gentle creatures who want to be loved."[25] Our alonetimes give us respite from being perfect parents, productive workers, and ideal mates. We can even find through creative and energetic use of this time ways to give our beasts an airing without becoming stuck in negative obsessions.

Throughout this book, aspects of the lives of other people were detailed. Some were not at all attuned to alonetime needs. One patient, Isabel, has a relevant story:

Isabel entered treatment amiss about the "lousy" love affairs in her life and begging for help in relating. After six or seven long and short unsuccessful couplings, including marriage and motherhood, she was now living with a man, Edward, and pretty sure things would be coming to a finale with him, too.

Initially, I thought that she must be choosing the wrong people and needed lessons in forming and keeping relationships. Or perhaps she just required a good therapeutic relationship in which to develop new ways of interaction. Even though living alongside all these men, Isabel had never committed to them in any deliberate fashion. Each man filled some specific need, as required by her current life. He could be her banker, sex partner, companion for a trip, a man to father children, or a protector with whom to walk the dog at night. Mostly, her men were people to go places with, as the day-to-day routine was boring for her, except in the company of a friend. At her office, she had the reputation as the gal with the juiciest gossip and was always at the hub of a group of coworkers. Weekends were whirlwinds of activities, sometimes involving six or seven different social events.

During one session, I asked her if she ever wished she were a politician, as she had enormous social stamina. She broke down in tears. The jet propulsion motivating her life stemmed from enormous anxiety. As a little girl she viewed the glamorous life of stars and jet-setters with envy, thinking that they never worry about being friendless as she did. Grown up, she clung to the men to whom she attached, fearing if they were left on their own they'd find someone better than she. If someone sat listening to music, it was the sonata she envied and she would interrupt the sounds with nonstop talk about her day. When her companion brought work home, she would tease him about being a workaholic. Then, when her husband left her for a man, her worst fear was realized.

Yet there had been times she lived alone. But she totally discounted those times as nonexistent. She viewed being alone as abject misery, as a mark of failure, and anyone alone as an object for ridicule. I said that although it was true that her relationships did not last as long as she wished, it was her being alone that she needed help in achieving. Right now, failing to recognize that need was pushing away the people she cared most about.

She started crying in response to that as well. Her son had told her something very similar. "Mom," he yelled, "you insist that I stay home with you because of all the risky things outside, but when you start complaining about why I should stay in, you make me want to leave all the more." Isabel heard her son through me. She remembered the intense sorrow with which both her mother and father pointed out all the "lonely" people living in the apartment building of her youth. During childhood, one of her greatest terrors was to end up like one of them. However, she also remembered that one of them was an opera singer, happy and successful in life.

Isabel eventually ended up far more happy and successful herself. By cutting down on office gossip, she had sufficient time and energy to go to a gym. She began taking solo vacations and writing, and actually ended up marrying Edward.

◆   ◆   ◆

Still thinking from within a child's framework, Isabel had become caught up in the either/ors of life. Isabel believed that she must live a social merry-go-round or she would become lonely and ignored. She did not realize consciously that she was not blue when all alone. Isabel taught me to be somewhat suspicious of those who plead poverty in relationships and to consider rehabilitating and nourishing alonetime needs as a productive form of therapy. In fact, here is where self-regulating again comes into the picture. Patients, friends, students, and couples inform me that most often they know when they are adjusting themselves to the point of discomfort in order to keep a relationship from falling apart or a partner from becoming angry, or as a means to seduce or manipulate their lover. Inevitably these relationships either explode and require rene-gotiating or hit rock bottom. Clues like lack of interest in sex, disinclina-tion to join a partner in fun, stubborn refusals, excessive tiredness, and irritability are indicators that our thermostats are out of whack. "Spend time alone seeing what is maladjusted" is my most current dictum. We cannot make our partners reform or conform to our needs, but we can set our own limits before the urge to run away takes over, as it did for Delia, an Isabelesque character in Anne Tyler's *Ladder of Years*.

Married and a mother of two almost-grown kids, Delia takes a walk on the beach one day during a family vacation and keeps on walking. Living her life half aware of her romanticized version of relationships, she starts a new life in a bathing suit, her husband's beach robe, sun-glasses, and sandals! Taking downsizing to its extreme, she rents a barely furnished room in another town with only a bought dress and underwear on her back. Purposefully, she doesn't buy anything to fix up her room because she now prefers "no-things" in her life. While her tale could have had dire consequences, it ends with her finding new friends, a job, and a kitten—and realizing she might as well go back to her family. Delia is not the epitome of pioneer women, who faced long alone treks, or even of a Margaret Cornelia Morgan, healer to the poor. Yet Delia's "woman quest" for alonetime seems to illuminate how society shapes the female's posi-tion. When Delia hitches a ride with an unknown repairman, we worry that she's in the hands of a serial killer. Because she is fed up with her social pulls, escaping half in fantasy seems the only way she can divorce herself from her "womanly tasks." When one thinks that Edna Pontellier, almost one hundred years before Delia, in Kate Chopin's novel *The Awak-ening* also struggled to leave her family and wanted to be let alone, one acknowledges that feminism may not have made woman's cultivation of alonetimes necessarily easier, since the movement stresses women's value as experts in and healers of relationships.[26] This makes alone and asocial pursuits more self-regulatory and possibly courageous and admirable, but also contrary to what is suggested as the basic nature of woman. Tyler demonstrates that Delia's need to relate (or to be alone) is no differ-ent from that of her husband, Sam, and her time trip is a self-reliant lone adventure that somehow works to straighten things out.

Indeed, Delia's fictional adventures end quite differently from those of the nonfictive Bob, who lives in abandoned subway tunnels and other

spaces underneath the streets of New York City and takes privacy seriously. As chronicled by journalist Jennifer Toth, Bob set off one day in his
car to go grocery shopping and never returned, leaving a "nagging" wife
and a daughter behind. "I like the way my life is now," he says.[27] And
his only friend, Bernard, feels they both have found the secret to life.
Thirty-something Bernard graduated from the University of Maryland,
earning a B.A. degree in journalism with a minor in philosophy. He
worked at CBS and as a model. But after he stumbled into the tunnel one
night, he never left, despite pleas from his brother and an offer of $10,000
to return above ground. Bernard believes this is the best life for him now
and he says without a sense of inferiority: "I don't pity us and they
shouldn't either. Everyone is responsible for his own life . . . I sit here at
night at the fire with a pot of tea and just the solitude of the tunnel. I
think what I've discovered down here is that what one really seeks in life
is peace of mind."[28] Peace is what philosophy and religion promote. This
shared secret is unavailable in the buzz of ordinary life and is mostly
discoverable by tunneling deep within ourselves. Psychoanalysis started
out as an entry into the private soul, searching for what was concealed
and forbidden.[29] Now it seems far more focused on curing the ills and
proving the boundlessness of relationships.

Reconnecting Alonetime to Life

I can see why there is objection to the notion of a need of alonetime for
the dependent infant, which seems almost cruel and inhuman. While the
exaggerated alone stance, described in the preceding chapters, of the
angry and distrustful of society proves the inherent capacity to be alone
and survive, it is harder to portray the invidious aspects of too much
togetherness, fear of engulfment, and why an individual's personal integrity simultaneously depends on an alone persona. Author Vivian Gornick
manages to capture such a transaction in her memoirs:

> When the space is wide and I occupy it fully, I taste the air, feel
> the light, I breathe evenly and slowly. I am peaceful and ex-
> acted, beyond influence or treat. Nothing can touch me. I'm
> safe. I'm free. I'm thinking. I go to meet my mother. I'm flying.
> Flying! I want to give her some of this shiningness bursting in
> me, siphon into her my immense happiness at being alone . . .
> "Oh Ma! What a day I've had," I say. "Tell me," she says, "do
> you have the rent this month?" "Ma, listen," I say. "That review

you wrote for the *Times*," she says. "It's for sure they'll pay you?" "Ma, stop it. Let me tell you what I've been feeling," I say. "Why aren't you wearing something warmer?" she cries. "It's nearly winter." The space inside begins to shimmer. The walls collapse inward. I feel breathless. Swallow slowly, I say to myself.[30]

But why do we stay so attuned to parental attitudes as grown-ups? Suppose people important to us leave us, desert us, or simply no longer want our company. If we were to begin to imagine that only those people had what we want, love, and need, maybe we'd become desperately helpless or brutally self-sufficient and antisocial. Then we have become enslaved and imprisoned by them even outside of their presence. If we then escalate the thinking to a belief that no other in the universe will ever care for us, we are back to babyhood—totally dependent on individual caretakers. Only, in this adult scenario, a parent figure is absent. We cannot breathe or fly in this frightened atmosphere. Do you ever consider why we prefer that our friends, sons, daughters, and lovers are like us? Not only would life be easier without having to understand the ins and outs of someone else, but we can feel that we are our own person at the same time that we are attached to another. *If he's like me, and me's like he, then I will always be myself.* Differences, however, are the rule, not the exception. We do not achieve either intimacy or solitude before discerning ways to allow ourselves and others the space to be separate individuals. My mother used to say that it's the challenges that make life interesting. Maintaining our integrity and accepting someone else's is one challenge.

Philosophers pose another. It was Socrates, I believe, who gave us this warning: "Beware the barrenness of a busy life." Saint Theresa long ago suggested another, with equal caution, that keeping busy is the one sure way to offset severe depression and a sense of uselessness. Society is poised on the horns of this dilemma, and unless we let into our sense of being the full realization of aloneness as a vital claim, we will have no comfortable way out of this position and will find ourselves constantly seesawing between the two forces.

But a last chapter could leave things like that and state: "We all lived happily ever after, newly alert to a basic need, and thus able to balance our lives with alonetime and attachment." An ending, however, is also the last opportunity for an author to express a vision and wishes for the future. Mine are based on the aspects of life that I've witnessed and some bold resolutions by friends and patients that I've told you about. Now I'll add another.

No one would deny creativity at work in the artistic gardens of Frederick and Claske Franck in Warwick, New York, dedicated to world peace —Pacem in Terris. Entering their environment of a couple of acres is like entering a wilderness of unending serenity. They offer a world of music and art created by toil born from desire. Their work revives the inherent capacity to create and its relation to nature. They cause one to think of any creative work and the true heroes of imagination (large or small), the vision within that has to arise from attempts to unify the dual needs within ourselves. This may be a happy task, but from all reports it takes hard work. The motivation for hard work comes from within, measured by the joy of alone accomplishment, for how else could we engage in the excruciating process of making anything? Art, music, and literature are obviously difficult works to produce, but a garden, a learning environment in a school or at home, and developing our way of life are equal to those creations.

The Francks have added a gentle and protective moral overcoat to the human need to achieve and engage solitude. Walking through their special sanctuary, where nature and art interweave, even reading their chatty newsletters and anticipating their park concerts, soothe because they bring us back to the true essentials in life. So, Mrs. Geisel, think of the Francks as you contemplate enshrining the memory of your husband with a theme park; keep in mind that the commercial highway is programmed for speed. Therefore, why not build next to it acres and acres for a child's exploration, with miniature mazes, large doodling pads, real sculptures as in the Francks' garden, and lots of flat rocks to toss into a running stream where children watched over by their caretakers could get lost in inwardly inspired dreams? Isn't that in best keeping with Theodore (Dr. Seuss) Geisel's love of privacy?

Academia now also pursues business practices for survival and secular recognition, and to promote health and industry it has given up old pathways to the privacy of the ivory tower. Being in touch with education at all levels, I have my own ideas on reform and standards, culled from past orators such as Socrates and John Dewey, and the current mess in many of the big-city schools. Let's begin with alonetime. All of the quiet moments in schools—prayer, meditation, study time, lunch break, bathrooms!—have been eroded. I do not believe in prayer in schools, because it is alienating for nonbelievers or those whose worship is out of the mainstream. However, I remember the relaxed feelings from clasping one's hands in school, or from the true quiet of study halls. One could think and *mentally* do anything that one wanted. Realistically, we cannot automatically reinaugurate such bliss in a chaotic environment. But what I propose for school change is radical and would leave room for disengagement. We have taken neither new understandings about intelligence nor individual differences into account in elementary schools, which might be the place to begin to reteach old habits of quiet times. We cannot apply high standards to learning if we are trying to fit everyone into the same mold. Learning to read, write, and understand numbers is important. But there are many children for whom mere exposure teaches those skills, and they need to be challenged differently, through complex projects. For the relatively small population who need direct coaching to learn, tutorials have to be established. Then, in general, besides the basics, young children have enormous energy to incorporate knowledge about dance, music, language, art, feelings, and cultures. Some elementary, middle, and high schools and teachers do combine the arts and sciences with academics quite successfully—the key being an excellent principal.[31] But in a sufficient number of schools, these essential programs are thought of as auxiliary to the three R's. We conceive of children finding their own niche in learning as special education, apart from other teaching. Actually, all education is special. In every case, whether it's standard learning for those needing assistance to catch on, or far-reaching learning for those with high learning curves, or creative and athletic instruction in a school that combines every facet, a child's strength and energy will find an outlet. And in that engaged and engaging environment, which gives children a chance to learn according to their best potentials, productive rest times will be welcomed.

Probably closer on the horizon than a revolution in elementary school education is adding augmented and virtual reality to our lives. Michael L. Dertouzos, the head of the Massachusetts Institute of Technology's Laboratory for Computer Sciences, believes that these new technologies are responsive to and incorporate old motivations of humans and thus will not radically change us. While I agree that new technology is driven by individual as well as corporate aims, I do not think we are aware of what motivates us and where we might be headed.

These new realities are beautifully explained by Dertouzos.[32] An augmented image lines up an external field with an internal one, as in the operating room where computerized devices overlap the operating site and act as guides to the surgeon's knife. Virtual imagery appears when one uses a computer with a tracking helmet and goggles. These gadgets tell where one is and in what direction one is gazing, and they project to the senses a programmed, imaginary world or even aspects of the real world such as one's home or a faraway place. With the added gear of a three-dimensional bodysuit one can actually sense oneself in the visual semi-make-believe world to the extent that even from afar one can seem to be alongside and touching another person.

Nothing to fear? Not only neurotics or Walter Mittys abandon the real world for one of fantasy. Evidence from our proclivity to daydream as well as from spiritual and computer trances suggests that this is so. Virtual reality will lessen a person's need to outlay mental energy for these sojourns. TV already affords such an opportunity. Can we completely discount the possibility that further immersion in the virtual world may forecast the end to real relationships and real alonetime—when beguiling fantasy scripts supplied through software become easily accessible? Our delight in watching a magician's sleight of hand already informs us that we enjoy being fooled. How deeply we are prepared to plunge into a prepackaged, pretend world of gratification, which I would call virtual unreality, remains to be seen.

This brings me to the further question of reality and alonetime as representative of the inner world as opposed to the outer, public one of the physical. Modern society prides itself on its scientific, pragmatic, and technological prowess. But steadily incorporated by other societies are the dream images of the West—Hollywood films, *Baywatch*, pop music, and advertising. Parts of the Asian world, with its emphasis on spiritual enlightenment and integration of philosophical wisdom within the social order, excel in productivity and technical wizardry. How very strange. And yet doesn't this also illustrate a balance, the return of the repressed? People want both to produce and to dream, but frequently a culture emphasizes only one or the other. Thus, what is often on the surface as a society's philosophy may not be its true belief. Perhaps the society that stresses speed, logic, and practical solutions to everything, with small interest paid to the wear and tear of such attitudes, will be a population that pays highest notice and gives first priority to the entertainers who can relieve the pressures of life. In his 1963 study, *The Self in Transformation*, Herbert Fingarette writes: "All of us in the West are so in bondage to the public, physical orientation that we can only allow ourselves to come to terms with the 'inner' world . . . by indirection; we do so on various levels of awareness through art, play, or dream, conscious fantasy, neurosis, or psychosis."[33]

And of course we need to add substance abuse and cyberspace to his list of altered states or awareness levels. Are imaginative alone pursuits and subjective inner states fundamentally more powerful than shared objective, external, or empirical experiences? At times. My firm suggestion is to know to what degree you require personal contemplation, public or private space. But perhaps we are all past a state of dehydration—in other words, we are dried out from overexposure and cannot figure out the extent of these needs for ourselves. The sleep doctors say that if we stay in a quiet place with no alarms to wake us up and sleep three hours or more past our usual time span for rest (barring being depressed), then we are sorely lacking in sleep. Maybe we should apply similar litmus tests to other aspects of life. For example, a television personality whom I know, whose workday surrounds him with people, never wants to socialize—diagnosis: a requirement for time alone. The patient Maureen used alcohol as a means to prove she was in charge and could resist external controls—diagnosis: a need to reestablish lone self-regulation. A young working mother bombarded with family and household responsibilities including two nursery-age children finds herself reluctant to go out with her new baby, as all the streets and parks seem overly active and too noisy—diagnosis: a lack of still space. A ten-year-old child balks at being tickled by his dad, prefers doing homework by himself, and turns down his parents' offer to play a game or watch TV together—diagnosis: overstimulation and too little privacy.

Once upon a time—actually not *that* long ago; 1938, to be exact—Gregory Zilboorg wrote in the *Atlantic Monthly* what was descriptive of those times:

> For reasons which appear obvious to many . . . it is not considered *comme il faut* to talk about one's self. One's private life is supposed to stay private and we don't like those who make an exhibition of themselves. We consider our feelings, concerns and emotions as things which, like some of our physiological needs, ought to remain enshrouded in total privacy.[34]

This is certainly in opposition to our current instructions to constantly "tell all" and "relate-relate-relate."

A part of the world is feeling, instead, "Retreat-retreat-retreat." "There is not sufficient time in the day to do all that is needed to be done," said my mother, even many years ago when I was a child. And she would plea for the impossible: "I wish I had three hands." Some of her friends would go shopping just to kill time until their husbands or children returned home. The current middle-aged among us more commonly comment on time flying and wish for days of old when hours leisurely drifted by. I can recall, even in my busy schedule as mother, student, housewife, tutor, and bookkeeper at age twenty-two, that I sensed and remarked on the slowness of passing time. My students today of twenty-plus have different sensations. They say that things seem to be happening almost before they occur. Grabbing on to events or keeping up with the world feels a lost cause. I can accept that as the ultraconsequence of global news in our face nonstop and the rapidity with which earth-shattering new stories are relegated to back pages in days, minutes, and seconds, overshadowed by equally momentous events. But what about the eight-year-old I overheard in the elevator telling his mother, "These days go so quickly; it was just Christmas and now it's Easter tomorrow"? Or how to explain what is going on to my elementary-school-teacher patient who talks about her small ones being upset about time marching on too quickly? It is difficult to understand why this is happening. The laws of time in outer space are also baffling and beguiling. Speed does change the rate of time. Relativistic effects on time during space shuttle travel are referred to as the Lorentz transformation. Up to a point, speed in outer space slows the inner clock and decreases the aging process. In the context of life speeding up, why aren't our internal clocks similarly slowing down, as they do on rocket ships? Unfortunately, we are not in space time. Instead, the frantic pace is closer to the rate of time in manic-depressive conditions. Speed and locomotion in the manic stage of the disorder are quickened. Thoughts and actions race. Even time perception tests have shown in mania a fast internal clock ticking away as compared to judgments of time during periods of normalcy. The accelerated internal rates change future time perspectives and manic people burst with plans and overextend themselves with their diverse ideas. Sometimes as I watch people's lives I think everyone is in this hypermanic state of extreme euphoria and nonstop rhythms. Certainly too many of our children are diagnosed as ill equipped to sit still, as having attention deficit disorders. "Every living organism is a clockshop of billions of clocks,"[35] and the pace of occurrences gives people a sense that their clocks are on speed. In Shakespeare's As You Like It, Rosalind says to Orlando, "Time travels in divers paces with divers persons. I will tell you who time ambles withal, who time trots withal, who time gallops withal, and who he stands still withal."[36] Few amble now, and all seem running at a gallop. As critic and essayist Michiko Kakutani[37] comments in a review of Milan Kundera's novel Slowness, a "failure of our speed-obsessed age

[is] to appreciate the delights of slowness (in lovemaking, in travel, in the rituals of daily life)." I see this in myself as well, this desire to rush to the finish line, the quickened pace of academe, and the need to do it all. But I have my own version of the Lorentz transformation.[38] That is, I learned to change my motion relative to inner instructions. When I have too much to do and feel particularly short of time, rather than hurrying through the tasks, I begin to slow my actions. When the pressure feels hot, I cool down. If the pace feels dizzying, I step back and take in a slow breath. Moving at a snail's pace is what one can learn by viewing the other side of the manic-depressive state. The depressed person's movements are slow—even retarded as compared to the typical. That ultimately corrects the mania, but unfortunately to the other extreme. Yet one doesn't have to live in extremes and reach disturbing levels to realize the need for internal reregulation—you just have to have an inner alone dialogue. Slowing down works for me and allows my work to get done.

The Balance—Attachment and Alonetime

During the summer of 1995, before I put pen to paper to write this book about my thoughts, research, and clinical work on alonetime, I painted a picture of a flower. The long narrow canvas holds an agapanthus with a long stalk. Only three-quarters of the flowering part is on canvas. The rest is left to the imagination. The background of muted colors is suggestive of many forms. Two absolute shapes, a triangle and an obelisk, are clearly depicted. The triangle is colored as the background, the obelisk is devoid of color—negative space. Nevertheless, that so-called negative space is white. White is the repository and source of all color on the spectrum, a combination of all the wavelengths of visible light. A flower is considered independent of the plant, yet it is not to be questioned that the stalk is the peduncle supporting it. The space of my picture dominates and cooperates with the other form. My painting is named *Alonetime,* but only now do I realize the meaning of the imagery. The surrounds of the plant, except for the white obelisk, represent the environment. Alonetime, like the flower on this canvas, stretches beyond the frame. Like this particular flower with its multiple stamens, seeds, and strong stem—and all flowers —alonetime blooms and pollinates our lives and often is the best and choicest part of what we experience. As is suggested by Susanne Langer in *Mind: An Essay on Human Feeling,* the visual arts are closer to displaying the "living stillness" of a plant.[39] With similar alive stillness, alonetime will thrive, evolve, and mature successfully. Such is the essence of alonetime, but other aspects of its nature were addressed and need to be faced before receiving the fullness of a flower's power. Alonetime is a great protector of the self and the human spirit. Many in society have railed against it. Some have overused its healing potential. Others have kept it as a special resource both knowingly and unknowingly. But the plant's name completes the aloneness imagery on my canvas. Agapanthus comes from the Greek word *agapē*, meaning love, openness, curiosity. The only way we shall achieve this ideal love is if we are allowed to flower in the due course and pace of our inner life. Whether or not we were fortunate in our growing up to blossom this way, plenty of time—alonetimes—awaits us now to make the necessary readjustments.

Attachments have positive names—platonic, companionate, peer, romantic, brotherly, motherly—and negative ones—dysfunctional, abusive, passive-aggressive, sadomasochistic. Alonetime has no identification that isn't somewhat tainted pejoratively, even solitaire. If you're in actuality a nun or monk, your aloneness is acceptable. But for one outside of the church to be called such is a put-down. Ask Hamlet if you doubt me. Relatively few would see role models in reserved, isolated, introvert types, although the computer nerd (thanks to Bill Gates) has found new respect these days. I am not addressing terms such as "uncaring," "selfish," "self-absorbed," or "self-centered" (although we might as well admit here that even the most philanthropic and loving among us are like that occasionally). Most private people are considered snobs, and only recently have females living alone lost the stigma of "spinster" or "old maid." But if alonetime assumes its rightful place in the hierarchy of needs, then maybe we will adopt "soloist"[40] rather than "loner" as a positive term for those who prefer, more than most, unescorted and unaided sojourns through life.

An aspect of the unifying principle in Chinese philosophy is helpful in understanding the coexistence of alone and together states. In Chinese thinking, nothing is solely yin or solely yang. Everything is complementary, composed of both tendencies in varying degrees. The *Tao Te Ching* captures the duality of which we speak poetically:

> We join spokes
> Together in a wheel,
> But it is the center hole
> That makes the wagon move.
>
> We shape clay into a pot,
> But it is the emptiness inside
> That holds whatever we want.[41]

Little in life is our own. Alonetime *is,* and, more than that, it offers equal opportunity to leave the limbo of living in the past or being a slave to modernity. Yet it does not have to be only dissidence. As in musical compositions, alonetime and attachment needs function together as point and counterpoint. Within this new structure, there is a true liberty in tranquillity, and harmony in being is no longer a balancing act.[42] The reconstruction of aloneness informs us that the process for developing sound and wholesome independence and dependency indeed resides within both attachment and alonetime, and that the needs are equal and concomitant with each other. The idea that from reconstruing our world we can reconstruct it is not new. But no one formula provides the ingredients to match each specific person's claim to be alone. For me to prescribe exactly what you should do to achieve alonetime not only would be counterproductive, but would rob you of the solitude necessary to contemplate your life and tap into your own self-regulatory skills. The seeking of solutions is just as important as the finding, because the journey *is* alonetime. With the superabundance of information, everyone is expected to come up with answers quickly and remove fears associated with not knowing. But once we all existed in the heavenly peace of alone, quiet, and empty reverie. It was a part of us then; it is an essential piece of us now.

NOTES

Introduction

1. Hall, L. (1986), *The Solitary* (New York: Charles Scribner's Sons), 11, 36.
2. Ibid., 38. I found that Elyse Eidman-Aadahl also wrote about Hall's novel in Chapter 12 of *The Center of the Web: Women and Solitude*, ed. Delese Wear, 1993, State University of New York.
3. *The Complete Poems of Emily Dickinson (1831–1886)* (1960), ed. Thomas H. Johnson (Boston: Little, Brown), no. 1116.
4. William Wordsworth (1770–1850), in the first verse of the poem "Daffodils," wrote:

> I wander'd lonely as a cloud
> That floats on high o'er vales and hills.
> When all at once I saw a crowd,
> A host, of golden daffodils;
> Beside the lake, beneath the trees,
> Fluttering and dancing in the breeze.

See *The Oxford Book of English Verse 1250–1918* (1961), ed. Sir Arthur Quiller-Couch (London: Oxford University Press), 621.

5. In the Oct. 25, 1993, issue of *U.S. News and World Report,* in "Beyond 1993" (pp. 70–80), Neil Postman speculated on the state of the world in 2053:

> Public life will have disappeared because we did not see, in time to reverse the process, that our dazzling technologies were privatizing almost all social activities. It became first possible, then necessary, to vote at home . . . We replaced schools with home computers and television. We replaced meeting friends with the video telephone and electronic mail . . . We became afraid of real people and eventually forgot how to behave in public places.

6. *The Independent* (London), May 20, 1995, reported on predictions of Prof. Peter Cochrane, futurologist and technologist. He sees the silicon chip in 2020 linking directly to the brain. "The link would create a physical connection between the carbon-based memory of the human brain to the silicon memory of the computer chip." Quoted in the Princess Cruise Line's newsletter, June 1995, 1.
7. Goleman, D. (1997), "Laugh and Your Computer May Laugh with You, Someday," *New York Times,* Jan. 7.

8. Editorial, *New York Times,* June 14, 1994.

9. Markoff, J. (1994), *New York Times,* Sept. 19, 1994, op-ed page.

10. During World War I, Wittgenstein joined the army and recorded thoughts for his *Tractacus* while on the battlefront. Wittgenstein was renowned also for separating from public life for long periods of time in Norway. See A. H. Modell (1993), *The Private Self* (Cambridge: Harvard University Press).

11. Gould, G., in 32 *Short Films About Glenn Gould* (1993).

Chapter 1: Fear, Helplessness, and Loneliness

1. Krishnamurti, J. (1981), *On Fear* (San Francisco: Harper), 37.

2. Hobsbawm, E. (1994), *The Age of Extremes* (New York: Pantheon).

3. *The Oxford Universal Dictionary* (1964; London: Oxford University Press).

4. *Random House Webster Dictionary College Edition* (1991; New York: Random House).

5. Koch, P. (1994), *Solitude: A Philosophical Encounter* (Chicago: Open Court), 49.

6. For more information, see E. Buchholz and C. Chinlund (1994), "En Route to a Harmony of Being: Viewing Aloneness As a Need in Development and Child Analytic Work," *Psychoanalytic Psychology* 11 (3): 357–74.

7. Clark, H. H., and E. V. Clark (1977), *Psychology and Language: An Introduction to Psychoanalysis* (New York: Harcourt Brace). When I say loneliness is the negative opposite, I do not mean it as bad; rather, it is an uncomfortable state of aloneness. Loneliness is a natural feeling and sometimes felt as warranted, as in the World War II song "I'll Walk Alone":

> I'll walk alone
> Because to tell you the truth
> I feel lonely
> But I don't mind being lonely

8. As in church sermons against reclusing oneself: "No man is an island, entire of it self"—J. Donne (1624), "Devotions upon Emergent Occasions," Meditation 17, in *The Columbia Dictionary of Quotations,* ed. R. Andrews (New York: Columbia University Press), 473.

9. Teicholz, J. (1980), "Is It Natural to Want to Be a Mother?" *Harvard University Gazette* 75, no. 41 (July 18): 3.

10. The National Alliance for Optional Parenthood used to counsel people deciding whether or not to parent. They published a paper called "Am I Parent Material?"

11. Teicholz (1980).

12. Ibid.

13. Fisher, H. (1992), *The Anatomy of Love* (New York: W. W. Norton).

14. Ousland, B., and K. Ovestorvik (1994), "Alone to the North Pole," *The Sciences,* July / Aug., 14.

15. Bloch, D. (1978), *"So the Witch Won't Eat Me": Fantasy and the Child's Fear of Infanticide* (Boston: Houghton Mifflin).

16. Fromm, Erich (1969), *Escape from Freedom* (New York: Holt, Rinehart and Winston). Fromm discusses how devastatingly frightening this sense of our aloneness is. In fact, writing at a time when so much of the world had been caught up with Nazism and other isms, his thought-provoking book explained how people are willing to follow demagogues and cult leaders in order to avoid problems of identity, death, and alienation alone.

17. Alvarez, A. (1995), *Night, Night Life, Night Language, Sleep and Dreams* (New York: W. W. Norton).

18. Coren, S. (1996), *Sleep Thieves* (New York: The Free Press).

19. Field, E. (1889), "Seeing Things at Night," in *The Eugene Field Reader*, ed. M. E. Buth and M. B. Cable (New York: Charles Scribner's Sons).

20. Levin, R., and M. S. Hurvich (1995), "Nightmares and Annihilation Anxiety," *Psychoanalytic Psychology* 12 (2): 247–58.

21. "For infants born with particular types of deficits . . . we could speculate that increased postnatal stresses, one form of which may be intermittent rather than continuous contact with the caregiver during sleep, may exacerbate those deficiencies"—J. J. McKenne, E. B. Thoman, T. F. Anders, A. Sadeh, V. I. Schectman, and S. F. Glotzbach (1993), "Infant-Parent Co-sleeping in an Evolutionary Perspective: Implications for Understanding Infant Sleep Development and the Sudden Infant Death Syndrome," *Sleep* 16 (3): 263–82. On the other hand, T. Berry Brazelton indicates, "In our society, at least, to be able to sleep alone in childhood is part of being an independent person"— T. B. Brazelton (1992), *Touchpoints: Your Child's Emotional and Behavioral Development* (Reading, Mass.: Addison-Wesley), 385.

22. Kaplan, H. I., B. J. Sadock, and J. A. Grebb (1994), *Synopsis of Psychiatry*, 7th ed. (Baltimore: Williams & Wilkins).

23. Tobler, I. (1988), "Evolution and Comparative Physiology of Sleep in Animals," in *Clinical Physiology of Sleep*, ed. R. Lydic and J. F. Biebayck (Bethesda: American Physiological Society). Sleep deprivation coincides with a broad spectrum of physiological and psychological changes—all negative, such as fatigue, loss of concentration, and irritability. The non-REM sleep has been seen as critical to tissue restoration, and, conversely, deprivation may be linked to alterations in the immune system. Slow-brain-wave sleep seems to enhance immune function. See M. J. Sateia and P. M. Silberfarb, (1993), "Sleep in Palliative Care," in *Oxford Textbook of Palliative Medicine*, ed. D. Doyle, G. W. C. Hanks, and N. MacDonald (Oxford: Oxford University Press).

24. Hobson, J. A. (1988), "Homeostases and Heteroplasticity: Functional Significance of Behavioral State Sequences," in *Clinical Physiology of Sleep* (see n. 23).

25. Hobson, J. A. (1995), *Sleep* (New York: Scientific American Library).

26. These ideas on the absolute privacy of dreams and other dream meanings can be explored further in C. Rycroff (1979), *The Innocence of Dreams* (New York: Pantheon Books) and B. D. Lewin (1958), *Dreams and the Uses of Regression* (New York: International Univ. Press).

27. Potter, D. E. (1990), *Existentialism* (Oxford: Blackwell Publishers).

28. Moustakas, C. (1961), *Loneliness* (New York: Prentice Hall). "Loneliness is a condition of existence which leads to deeper perception, greater awareness and sensitivity, and insights into one's own being" (p. 50).

29. Burton, R. (1965), *The Anatomy of Melancholy: A Selection*, ed. L. Babb (Detroit: Michigan State University Press), 379.

30. Spacks, P. M. (1995), *Boredom* (Chicago: University of Chicago Press).

31. Ibid.

32. Storr, A. (1988), *Solitude* (New York: Ballantine Books).

33. Friedman, M., and R. H. Rosenman (1974), *Type A Behavior and Your Heart* (New York: Knopf).

34. Coleridge, S. T. (1992), "Rime of the Ancient Mariner," part IV, lines 9–12, in *The Rime of the Ancient Mariner and Other Poems* (New York: Dover Publications):

> Alone, alone all, all alone
> Alone on a wide wide sea!
> And never a saint took pity on
> My soul in agony.

35. Potter (1990), 29.

36. Saunders, C. (1993), Foreword, *Oxford Textbook of Palliative Medicine* (see n. 23).

37. Ariès, P. (1944), *Western Attitudes Toward Death from the Middle Ages to the Present* (Baltimore: Johns Hopkins Univ. Press).

38. Armstrong, K. (1993), *A History of God* (New York: Ballantine Books). This book echoes Ariès in locating a sharp rise in fear of death at the time of the Renaissance, as preachers added the horrors of hell to their sermons and authors such as Dante implicated individuals, even high officials in the clergy, as responsible for evil deeds.

39. Elisabeth Kübler-Ross has devoted herself to establishing death and dying as a natural passage. Sherwin B. Nuland has recently tried to make death more familiar in a frank manner. See S. Nuland (1993), *How We Die: Reflections on Life's Final Chapter* (New York: Vintage Books).

40. Corr, C. A. (1993), "Death in Modern Society," in *Oxford Textbook of Palliative Medicine* (see n. 23).

41. Becker, E. (1973), *The Denial of Death* (New York: The Free Press), 70.

42. Peplau, F. A., and D. Perlman (1982), *Loneliness: A Source Book of Current Theory, Research and Therapy* (New York: John Wiley & Sons).

43. Zilboorg, G. (1938), "Loneliness," *Atlantic Monthly*, Jan., 48.

44. Hall, R. (1990), *The Well of Loneliness* (New York: Doubleday Books), 32.

45. Riesman, D., N. Glazer, and R. Renny (1961), *The Lonely Crowd: A Study of the Changing American Character* (Connecticut: Yale Univ. Press), 22.

46. Slater, P. (1990), *The Pursuit of Loneliness* (Boston: Beacon Press).

47. Paz, O. (1985), *The Labyrinth of Solitude* (New York: Grove Press), 9.

48. Current research, in fact, on people and animals now suggests two profiles

related to brain excitability in the amygdala. Highly reactive normal babies are more fearful than low-reactive types. And the high-reactive profile in infancy seems to relate to greater social inhibitions in later childhood and shyness.

49. A link is suggested between loneliness, shyness, and the inhibition of social risk taking: "It is important to differentiate, however, between two types of shy children. Some shy children acquire their shy profile primarily as a result of experience alone (e.g., peer or parental rejection)"—M. Putallaz (1987), "Maternal Behavior and Children's Sociometric Status," *Child Development* 58: 324–70. These children are shy with people, but they are less likely to avoid most unfamiliar places and objects. Shy children of the second type are born with a physiology that biases them to acquire an avoidant style to many unfamiliar events—people as well as nonsocial stimulus events. These latter children differ from the former in autonomic functioning, affect, and physical features. See J. Kagan, J. S. Reznick, and N. Snidman (1988), "Biological Bases of Childhood Shyness," *Science*, no. 240, 167–73.

"The physiology is not deterministic, however; both behavioral profiles require actualizing environments . . . It is important to appreciate that the referential meanings of inhibited/uninhibited in our research are based on direct observations of children, rather than parental descriptions derived from interviews or questionnaires. The correlations between parental reports of shy or sociable behavior and behavioral observations that define each of the two categories are positive, but not high, averaging between .2 and .4"— J. Kagan, N. Snidman, and D. M. Arcus (1992), "Initial Reactions to Unfamiliarity," *Current Directions in Psychological Science* 1, no. 6 (Dec. 1992): 171–74.

Philip Zimbardo suggests that shy people need to develop more adequate general response styles in addition to specific social skills. Group therapy is the preferred treatment for shyness as a means to gradually encourage socializing. See C. G. Lord and P. G. Zimbardo (1985), "Actor-Observer Differences in the Perceived Stability of Shyness," *Social Cognition* 3 (3): 250–65.

50. Becker, E. (1973), 284–85.
51. Estes, C. P. (1992), *Women Who Run with the Wolves* (New York: Ballantine Books), 131.

Chapter 2: Wilderness, Wanderlust, and "Wild" Animals

1. Stevenson, J. (1990), *Mr. Hacker* (New York: Greenwillow Books), 4.
2. Emerson, R. W. (1941), "The Method of Nature: Nature Addresses," in *Nature Abounding*, ed. E. L. G. Watson (London: Faber and Faber), 127.
3. Schopenhauer, A., "On Noise," *Studies in Pessimism* (New York: The Modern Library).
4. Bequette, F. (1994), "Defeating Decibels," *Greenwatch: The Unesco Courier*, June, issue 6, 23–25.

5. Ibid.

6. Hochfield, G., ed. (1966), *Selected Writings of the American Transcendentalists* (New York: The New American Library).

7. Cronon, W. (1995), *Uncommon Nature* (New York: W. W. Norton).

8. In addressing the fundamental appeal in wildernesses that cures that longing, I need to acknowledge what environmentalists, historians, and theologians call the problem with wilderness. The insight we have today about preserving nature, and the absolute rights of all races and ethnic groups to own property and inhabit land, was not accepted by our forefathers. Political historian, author, and professor of environmental studies Kenneth C. Davis makes no bones about the amnesia in the United States about our own blatantly ruthless policies established in order to take over all the land possible in North and Central America. See K. C. Davis (1995), "Ethnic Cleansing Didn't Start in Bosnia," *New York Times*, Week in Review, Sept. 3, sec. 4, pp. 1, 6. Theologian William Cronon and ethnologist Hansford C. Vest similarly disperse any lingering romantic notions we might have about the early settlers and citizens of the United States. Manifest Destiny was a land-grabbing policy reserved to the "white with might" and requires all to think carefully about these yearnings. Both Vest and Cronon warn of dangers in investing too wholeheartedly in the peaceful isolation of wilderness. This guideline is understandable, given our history. But does fully acknowledging our striving for alonetime in the open wild have to end in abandonment of others? I think not, and I am trying to show how such feelings spring from origins other than greed and selfishness. No need exists that cannot be corrupted by excess.

9. MacLeish, A. (1968), "The Great American Frustration," *Saturday Review of Literature*, July 13, 1968, 13–17.

10. Less convincingly, Hansford C. Vest etymologically divides the origins of "solitude" into "solus" and "soul-mood," splitting hairs, I believe, between the root in the first case and the root and suffix in the second. "Alone" as in "alone by oneself" he describes in terms of Platonic ideals too abstract for modernity. Most confusingly, "alone qua alone," a so-called negative solitude, seems related to what he labels good solitude, or soul-mood. Nevertheless, his division of solitude allows him to take the leap from "solus," which is a good "nonalone" solitude, into a puritanical notion of loneliness, which is alone, withdrawal, retreat, or an excuse for people's possessive desires. Was it lonely isolation from people that made empty land a negative concept? It is confusing to draw a parallel between what was then called "lonely" (meaning unused land) and people's need for alonetime. No doubt the Manifest Destiny policy gained unjust capital by equating the sanctification of land with inadequate use. But clarity is lost on both sides of the political argument in relating the personal requirement for solitude to policies of Manifest Destiny. Moreover, solitude means different things to different people. Complete isolation is certainly balm to some souls and actually restores many to community. See H. C. Vest (1987), in *Environmental Ethics* 9(4): 303–30.

11. Krakauer, J. (1996), *Into the Wild* (New York: Villard Books), 142–43.

12. Ibid., 106.

13. Hillary, P. (1996), "Everest Is Mighty, We Are Fragile," *New York Times*, May 25, op-ed section, 19.
14. Berne, Betsy (1995), "Tired Chronicles," *New Yorker*, Aug. 2.
15. Melville, H. (1944), *Moby-Dick* (New York: The Modern Library), 72.
16. Nabhan, G. P., and S. Trimble (1994), *The Geography of Childhood: Why Children Need Wild Places* (Boston: Beacon Press).
17. Burnett, F. G. (1987), *The Secret Garden* (New York: Harper Collins).
18. Sendak, M. (1963), *Where the Wild Things Are* (New York: Harper Collins).
19. Twain, M. (1980), *The Adventures of Tom Sawyer* (Berkeley: University of California Press), 46.
20. Markoff, J. (1994), "The Lost Art of Getting Lost," *New York Times*, Sept. 18, sec. 4, pp. 1, 6.
21. Bronowski, J. (1973), *The Ascent of Man* (Boston: Little, Brown), 60.
22. Ibid., 64.
23. Ondaatje, M. (1992), *The English Patient* (New York: Vintage Books), 154–55.
24. Humphrey, H. (1966), speech at the University of Chicago, Jan. 14.
25. Estes, R. D. (1991), *The Behavior Guide to African Mammals* (Berkeley: University of California Press), 370.
26. London, J. (1960), *The Call of the Wild* (New York: Platt and Monk), 53.
27. Ibid., 124.
28. Thomas, E. M. (1993), *The Hidden Life of Dogs* (New York: Houghton Mifflin).
29. Steinbeck, J. (1962), *Travels with Charley: In Search of America* (New York: Viking Press).
30. Thomas (1993), 121.
31. Harlow, H. (1958), "The Nature of Love," *American Psychologist* 13: 673–85; Harlow (1959), "Love in Infant Monkeys," *Scientific American* 200 (6): 68–74.
32. Masson, J. M., and S. McCarthy (1995), *When Elephants Weep: The Emotional Lives of Animals* (New York: Delacorte Press). The authors point out the tortuousness of such experimentation but ask an important question addressed in the next chapter: how can experimental conditions of extreme stress teach about natural human emotion? What we learn has to be skewed to conditions of emotional pain. Harlow's experiments may have had humanistic goals. On the other hand, one does not have to be an animal lover to see the cruelty—unintentional or not—perpetrated. Not only were monkey babies separated from mothers (for "health purposes"); some were later exposed to "evil mothers"—surrogate mothers in those cases might suddenly blast a baby with compressed air, or have a mechanism that shook babies off, or a catapult that could send an infant flying, or even concealed brass spikes that might emerge on call. All this occurred, including Harlow's "rape rack" for impregnating adult monkeys that never learned to connect or mate in their stress-induced youth, in the name of science. For more information, see H. Harlow, M. Harlow, and S. Suomi (1971), "From Thought to Therapy: Lessons from a Primate Laboratory," *American Scientist* 659: 538–49.
33. de Waal, F. B. M. (1995), "Reflection of Eden," *New York Times Book Review*, Feb. 26, 31.
34. Gould, S. J. (1987), *An Urchin in the Storm* (New York: W. W. Norton), 66.

Chapter 3: Hermits, Monks, and Philosophers

1. Cutting, R. (1992), "Inner Peace," *Parabola* 17, no. 1 (Spring): 69.
2. Armstrong, K. (1993), *A History of God* (New York: Ballantine Books).
3. Merton, T. (1956), *Thoughts on Solitude* (New York: The Noonday Press), 103.
4. Wishart, A. R. (1900), *Monks and Monasteries* (Trenton: Albert Brandf).
5. Ibid., 114.
6. Ibid., 17.
7. Merton, T. (1992), "Between Work and Prayer, Prayer and Work," *Parabola* 17 (Feb.): 34–36.
8. Green, A., ed. (1994), *Jewish Spirituality (From the Sixteenth Century Revival to the Present)*, vol. 14 of *World Spirituality: An Encyclopedic History of the Religious Quest* (New York: Crossroad).
9. Melville, H., *Moby-Dick*, in D. J. Boorstin, *The Creators: A History of Heroes of the Imagination* (New York: Random House), 641.
10. "The Benedictine *Rule*, composed in the sixth century, mingled labor and prayer . . . In the following centuries monasticism struggled to keep the balance between spirituality and economic self-sufficiency. In the course of time, Benedictine Monasteries became the victims of their own success, as they grew wealthy from rents, church revenues, gifts, titles, and other fees, and labor ceased to be performed by the monks but was delegated to peasants and servants"—F. and J. Gies (1994), *Cathedral, Forge, and Waterwheel Technology and Invention in the Middle Ages* (New York: Harper Collins), 4, 9.
11. Chaucer, G. (1946), Prologue, *The Canterbury Tales*, trans. Frank E. Hill (New York: The Heritage Press), 5–6.
12. The philosophy of Karl Marx preaches an ascetic existence but leaves little room for imaginative introspection. See K. Armstrong (1993), *History of God* (New York: Ballantine Books). After this chapter was almost completed, I came across a biography of Thomas Merton that described his interest as well as the Dalai Lama's in the social and economic side of Marxism. Merton thought there were similarities in the asceticism and was fond of quoting a French Marxist who said, "We are monks also." See M. Furlong (1981), *Merton: A Biography* (New York: Bantam Books).
13. Russell, B. (1960), *A History of Western Philosophy* (New York: Simon & Schuster).
14. Marcus Aurelius, in *The Harvard Classics*, vol. 6 (Cambridge: Harvard University Press), 211–12.
15. Delbanco, A., and T. Delbanco (1995), "Annals of Addiction: AA at the Crossroads," *New Yorker*, March 20, 50–63.
16. Ibrahim, Y. M. (1997), "Finland: Improbable Land for the Universal Use of Technology," *New York Times*, Jan. 20, D1, D6.
17. The bibliography on this theme is extensive, as philosophers and theologians have for centuries debated this fundamental question: is the individual's private self or social self primary? Before Copernicus revolutionized cosmology the arguments could be resolved through the close connection of man

with God—after all, man was the center of the universe. In the movement away from an anthropomorphic system, the search for the fundamental nature of man delves into whether people are rational or emotional, spiritual or scientific, objective or subjective. Are they motivated by instincts and passions, or money and power? Are they essentially sinful or good, animal or human? Are the answers to be found in logic and mathematics, or mysticism and symbolism?

Surprisingly, these questions overlap with whether the aim of an individual is for a separatist self-containment and individuation or a connected social unity and wholeness through integration with the group. From my perspective the underlying dualism is a result of the biological and psychological givens of the human condition. Since we are born with experiential and physical qualities that establish our readiness to attach and to be alone, from the beginning our direction is twofold. For those interested in pursuing the specific philosophical and religious questions, see E. Cassirer (1944), *An Essay on Man* (New York: Doubleday); H. Frankfort, Mrs. H. Frankfort, J. A. Wilson, and T. Jacobsen (1951), *Before Philosophy* (Middlesex: Penguin Books); O. Rank (1989), *Art and Artist: Creative Urge and Personality Development* (New York: W. W. Norton); E. Becker (1973), *The Denial of Death* (New York: The Free Press); K. Armstrong (1993), *A History of God* (New York: Ballantine Books); B. Russell (1960), *A History of Western Philosophy* (New York: Simon & Schuster); B. Hannah (1994), *Subjectivity and Reduction: An Introduction to the Mind-Body Problem* (Boulder: Westview Press).

18. Cassirer (1944).
19. Thilly, F. (1950), *A History of Philosophy* (New York: Henry Holt).
20. Arendt, H. (1994), *Essays in Understanding* (New York: Harcourt Press).
21. Watts, A. (1995), *The Philosophies of Asia* (Boston: Charles E. Tuttle), 16.
22. For example, writer Jack Hitt gave up his position as editor of *Harper's* magazine, his apartment, and his friends for "a season of walking"—a two-month pilgrimage—at age thirty-five. See Jack Hitt (1994), *Off the Road* (New York: Simon & Schuster).
23. Merton, T. (1956), 222.
24. Attributed to Gordon Allport in A. R. Fuller (1994), *Psychology and Religion: Eight Points of View* (Lanham, Md.: Littlefield Adams).
25. Becker (1973), 152–53.
26. Guisinger, S., and S. J. Blatt (1994), "Individuality and Relatedness. Evolution of a Fundamental Dialectic," *American Psychologist* 49 (2): 104–11.
27. McFall, L. (1993), "Solitude, Suffering and Personality Authority," *The Center of the Web: Woman and Solitude* (New York: State University Press), 13–24.
28. Kleinman, A. (1992), "Pain and Resistance," in *Pain As Human Experience: An Anthropological Perspective*, ed. M. D. Del Vecchio, P. E. Brodwin, B. C. Good, and A. Kleinman (Berkeley: University of California Press), 187.
29. Kundera, M. (1991), *Immortality* (New York: Grove Press).

Chapter 4: Abandonment, Attachment, and Theory

1. Gibbons, K. (1995), *Sights Unseen* (New York: G. P. Putnam's Sons).
2. Throughout this book, most of the time I have used the term "bonding" as synonymous with "attachment." Ainsworth, along with Klaus and Kennel, differentiated attachment and bonding. Technically, the two terms are understood differently. In ethology and psychology, bonding is the initial connection of a parent to her offspring. Attachment comes later and represents the outcome of the child's need for the parent and the parent's connection to the child. But bonding is a large part of everyday parlance—mothers and daughters, brothers and sisters, and family circles in general bond. Therefore, I shall continue *not* to make this distinction except if discussing specific studies on bonding. See M. D. S. Ainsworth (1982), "Attachment: Retrospective and Prospects," in *The Place of Attachment in Human Behavior*, ed. C. M. Parkes and J. Stevenson-Hinde (New York: Basic Books), 24.
3. I first learned of this fact during my postdoctoral analytic training. My friend and colleague Esther Menaker later informed me that it was Paul Roazen, in *Brother Animal* (Vintage, 1971), who made public what was only private to Freud's inner circle. Menaker and Roazen are currently writing a book on the topic of Anna Freud's analysis by her father.
4. For a further critique of the attachment literature see M. Rutter (1974), *The Qualities of Mothering: Maternal Deprivation Reassessed* (New York: Jason Aronson); D. E. Eyer (1992), *Maternal-Infant Bonding: A Scientific Fiction* (New Haven: Yale University Press); E. Burman (1994), *Deconstructing Developmental Psychology* (London: Routledge).
5. A. Freud made another less well known but personal contribution to attachment theory. Her boiler man in the Hampstead Residential Nursery for homeless children, James Robertson, became assistant in naturalistic observation to psychoanalyst and attachment theorist John Bowlby. Robertson had impeccable training as such, for A. Freud systematically required all her staff members to keep detailed notes of children's behavior that became part of weekly group discussions of the children. See I. Bretherton (1995), "The Origins of Attachment Theory," in *Attachment Theory: Social, Developmental and Clinical Perspectives*, ed. S. Goldberg, R. Muir, and J. Kerr (Hillsdale, N.J.: The Analytic Press), 45–85.
6. Ribble, M. (1943), *The Rights of Infants* (New York: Columbia University Press).
7. Zukerman, B., and E. R. Brown (1993), "Maternal Substance Abuse and Infant Development," in *Handbook of Infant Mental Health*, ed. C. H. Zeanah (New York: The Guilford Press). Furthermore, "failure to thrive," a condition in which a seemingly normal child does not grow, was no longer thought to be caused only by lack of maternal attachment. Although it is related to absence of physical contact (touch), statistical studies describe this lack of growth as primarily the result of maltreatment. "In approximately 70% of cases of failure to thrive, 50% of these are cases of neglect, while the other 20% are accidental (e.g. errors in formula preparation)" (p. 161). The main cause of failure to thrive, unlike in the earlier clinical reports, is linked to children's needs not

being sufficiently attended to, rather than lack of an actual bond to the caretaker. As substantiation of children's ability to survive with alone skills, once children are able to walk, "and especially after age 2, the situation improves because the children can obtain food for themselves" (p. 161). Obviously, such conditions are not optimal or even satisfactory. But they do illustrate that failure to thrive incorporates more than an attachment.

8. Holt, L. E. (1894), *The Care and Feeding of Children* (New York: D. Appleton).

9. "Hospitalism" is, by the way, currently used diagnostically to describe adults left in institutions and deprived of interaction and stimulation.

10. Spitz, R. (1972), "Hospitalism: An Inquiry into the Genesis of Psychiatric Conditions in Early Childhood," in U. Bronfenbrenner, ed., *Influences on Human Development* (Hillsdale, Ill.: Dryden Press), 212.

11. Quoted in Elizabeth M. R. Lomax in collaboration with Jerome Kagan and Barbara G. Rosenkrantz (1978), *Science and Patterns of Child Care* (San Francisco: W. H. Freeman).

12. Bowlby, J. (1977), "The Making and Breaking of Affectional Bonds," *British Journal of Psychiatry* 130: 201–10.

13. Bowlby, J. (1988), *A Secure Base* (New York: Basic Books), 26–27.

14. Bretherton, I. (1985), "Attachment Theory: Retrospect and Prospect," in *Growing Points of Attachment Theory and Research Monographs of the Society for Research in Child Development*, ed. I. Bretherton and E. Waters, serial number 209, vol. 50 (nos. 1–2), 4.

15. Currently, Penelope Leach and other authorities who speak out for the welfare of children have incurred the wrath of those who interpret the plea for children as restrictive of women's rights. In actuality, the two parallel needs of attachment and alonetime are not mutually exclusive. Indeed, Bowlby and Leach, if read carefully, do recognize both children's and parents' needs for separate time.

16. Holmes, J. (1995), " 'Something there is that doesn't love a wall': John Bowlby, Attachment Theory and Psychoanalysis," in Goldberg, Muir, and Kerr (see n. 5), 19–43.

17. Currently, Bowlby is accepted by developmental theorists. At the dawning of his contributions, however, he was a pariah to both camps. He was too interested in the internal (psychic) mechanisms of the mind for developmental psychologists. To psychoanalysts he seemed a traitor. Bowlby appeared to be neglecting the inner catacombs of feeling and thinking that analysts desperately were trying to prove existed to a resistant society. His ethological interests emphasize the environmental and cognitive sciences and view relationships in terms of regulation of security needs. This made his system one where control of safety outweighs the desire to relate. For traditional psychoanalysts, the realms of the outer world seemed far less important and certainly less compelling. With today's relational and subjective trend in psychoanalysis, in which not only the patient's external and internal life is important but also the analyst's, Bowlby returns to the analytic fold as a far-seeing hero. The public at large, while benefiting from this additional perspective, has also suffered. Because people were spared the complexity of

attachment theory (as they are of most basic theories), the prevailing message to them is that attachment is a dominant behavior rather than one of a group of behaviors necessary to promote health and well-being. Under this rubric, adults living singly could appear odd and lacking.

18. Ainsworth, M. D. S. (1972), "Variables Influencing the Development of Attachment," in *Readings in Child Behavior and Development*, ed. C. S. Lavatelli and F. Stender (New York: Harcourt Brace Jovanovich), 193–201.

19. Wylie, P. (1955), *Generation of Vipers* (New York: Rinehart), 203.

20. See also: R. Karen (1990), "Becoming Attached," *Atlantic* 265 (2), an excerpt from the book of the same title. Karen details the intricacy of the birth of attachment theory and many of its ramifications.

21. "Object relations" is the theoretical term for people relationships, both conscious and unconscious, but since this label is troublesome even to influential proponents of this theory, we shall mostly refer to interactions between people as just what they are. This awkward term adopted by psychoanalysis probably stems from grammatical usage, according to psychologist Esther Menaker. Grammatically speaking, people are both the subject and object of verbs. Unfortunately, that meaning stands in sharp contrast to common usage of the word "object." Many contributed to the development of object relations theory, from Ian Suttie to Henry Guntrip and, in particular, the current Kleinian school in England. My interest is in how those theories filtered down to the general public, as evidenced in aspects of Klein's life being incorporated into a popular drama, *Mrs. Klein.*

22. Sullivan was backed by the support and encouragement of a believer and fellow psychiatrist, William Alanson White.

23. Greenberg, J. R., and S. A. Mitchell (1983), *Object Relations in Psychoanalytic Theory* (Cambridge, Mass.: Harvard University Press).

24. In a similar fashion, psychologist Robert S. Weiss (1984) labeled loneliness as the "distress without redeeming features"—National Institute of Mental Health Monograph *Preventing the Harmful Consequences of Severe and Persistent Loneliness*, ed. Letitia A. Peplau and Stephen E. Goldston (U.S. Dept. of Health and Human Services).

25. Fromm, E. (1969), *Escape from Freedom* (New York: Holt, Rinehart, Winston).

26. Menaker, E. (1995), *The Freedom to Inquire* (Northvale, N.J.: Jason Aronson), 167. In a timely review of infant research, Beatrice Beebe, Frank Lachmann, and Joseph Jaffe argue for an integration of one- and two-person psychology (of which I am in favor). They say: "To view the dyadic interaction alone as the source of psychic structure formation omits the crucial contribution of the organism's own self-regulatory capacities." See B. Beebe, F. Lachmann, J. Jaffe (1997), "Mother-Infant Interaction Structures and Presymbolic Self and Object Representations," *Psychoanalytic Dialogues* 7 (2):133–82.

27. Dr. Caroline Chinlund, educator and psychoanalyst, added insight to the picture of the nursery-school space.

28. Mahler, M., A. Pine, and A. Bergman (1975), *Psychological Birth of the Human Infant* (New York: Basic Books).

29. Mahler indeed borrowed the term "hatching" to describe what she considered the baby's first stage of differentiation. Only after several months of extrauterine life did she endow the child with sufficient alertness to distinguish self from other and to "hatch."

30. Murphy, L. B., and A. E. Moriarty (1976), *Vulnerability, Coping & Growth: From Infancy to Adolescence* (New Haven: Yale University Press).

Chapter 5: Silence, Sharing Secrets, and Change

1. Foucault, M. (1988), *Politics, Philosophy, and Culture: Interviews and Other Writings 1977–1984*, trans. A. Sheridan, ed. L. D. Kritzman (New York: Routledge), 3, 4.

2. *Consumer Reports*, Sept. 1995, 734–39. This groundbreaking survey—"Mental Health: Does Therapy Help?"—reports perceived success in treatment for people with emotional problems. The article includes a short but accurate breakdown of types of therapies and therapists, insurance plans, the kinds of treatments that research suggests work for different problems, and an assay of medications. According to the article and those surveyed, a combination of medicine and therapy works better than pharmaceuticals alone, and psychotherapy has greater effectiveness alone than does medication. *Consumer Reports* didn't run control groups and thus we do not have the means to assess whether change would have occurred spontaneously. Although this study falls short in measuring effectiveness in a controlled way, it does tell us how the general public is reacting. Other research is available on behavioral methods of treatment within the psychology journals. A complex, sizable body of research on psychoanalysis as treatment and theory is also accumulating. Much research is qualitative (case studies and the like) but some is quantitative as well. Dennis G. Shulman and the Society for the Advancement of Quantitative Research in Psychoanalysis, Fordham University, have done the community a service in collecting this research, a fair amount of which, such as students' scholarly dissertations, never reaches either the scientists or the public. See D. G. Shulman (1992), "The Qualitative Investigation of Psychoanalytic Theory and Therapy: A Bibliography 1986–1992," *Psychoanalytic Psychology* 9 (4), 529–42. Nevertheless, psychoanalysis as theory and treatment has angered many groups. But the idea that there is more to human nature than one observes with the naked eye remains valid in thinking both before and since Freud. For a bold opening to this discussion, read Jonathan Lear, "The Shrink Is In," *New Republic*, Dec. 25, 1995, 18–25, and the subsequent letters to the editor in *New Republic*, Jan. 29, 1996, 4–5. Psychoanalysis is redefined by psychoanalyst Adam Phillips as a discipline that expands one's life while assisting one through the terrors of knowledge and introspection, thus maintaining its usefulness; see A. Phillips (1996), *Terrors and Experts* (Cambridge: Harvard University Press).

3. Artists, always sensitive to social climate, were noted in an exhibition curated

by Lynn Garnwell at the New York Academy of Sciences, Mar. 10–June 16, 1995, *A Century of Silence: Nonrepresentation and Withdrawal in Modern Art.*

4. I was heartened to see, however, a relatively recent (1996) discussion of solitude in the *International Journal of Psychoanalysis* 77: 367–71—"Panel Report: Psychic Reality and Solitude," chaired by Harvey Rich and reported by Julia Fabricius.

5. According to Robert Fancher (1995), *Cultures of Healing* (New York: W. H. Freeman), there are from fifty to five hundred different schools of therapy with the "full professional paraphernalia."

6. Crapanzano, V. (1995), "Dances with Myths," review of *The Story of Lynx,* by Claude Levi-Strauss, *New York Times Book Review,* Aug. 20, 1995, 12.

7. Self psychology is also in transition, and different supporters of these theories have varied from Kohut's original beliefs. For example, should a selfobject be personified? Early writing of Kohut and certain disciples suggests that in their descriptions. Others, specifically J. D. Lichtenberg, F. M. Lachmann, and J. L. Fosshage (1992), *Self and Motivational Systems Toward a Theory of Psychoanalytic Technique* (Hillsdale, N.J.: Analytic Press), downplay, in my opinion rightly so, the person's role as selfobject, rather discussing them as selfobject experiences.

8. Dalton was training in both self *and* intersubjective psychology. For a careful reading on this, see Robert D. Stolorow, George E. Atwood, and Bernard Brandchaft, eds. (1994), *The Intersubjective Perspective* (Northdale, N.J.: Jason Aronson).

9. In *The Romance of American Psychology: Political Culture in the Age of Experts* (Berkeley: University of California Press), Ellen Herman argues that "psychology sets the direction and texture of personal and public life" (p. 1).

10. West, Mrs. M., *Infant Care,* quoted in E. M. R. Lomax, ed. (1978), *Science and Patterns of Childcare* (San Francisco: W. H. Freeman), 77.

11. Quoted in E. M. R. Lomax, ibid., 60, from a 1914 issue of *Infant Care.*

12. There were other minor quakes as well, such as existential and humanistic psychology, both of which incorporated the notions of greater dialogue between analyst and patient and increased acceptance of the patient's truth. The encounter movement, as well as Campbell's theophilopsychology, told people to follow their bliss and gave back authority to the individual in the healing process. But these movements also had many people confusing "craziness" with alternative lifestyle and doing one's own thing.

For a fuller history of psychotherapy and changes and influences on the beginning of psychoanalysis, see James A. Barron, Morris N. Eagle, David L. Wolitzky, ed. (1992), *Interface of Psychoanalysis and Psychology* (Washington, D.C.: APA); Donald K. Freedheim, ed. (1992), *History of Psychotherapy: A Century of Change* (Washington, D.C.: APA); Peter Gay (1984–1995), *The Bourgeois Experience: Victoria to Freud,* 4 vols., including *The Naked Heart,* which recently completed the study (New York: Norton, 1995); M. S. Bergman (1993), "Reflections on the History of Psychoanalysis," *Journal of the American Psychoanalytic Association* 41 (4), 929–55; J. Sayers (1993), *Mothers of Psychoanalysis* (New

York: W. W. Norton); C. Yorke (1995), "Freud's Psychology: Can It Survive?" *The Psychoanalytic Study of the Child* 50 (New Haven: Yale University Press), 3–31.

13. These questions and the topic of the analyst's authority were explored in depth during a panel entitled "Times They Are A-Changing: Current Perspectives on the Analyst's Role in the Cross Cultural Arena" and a paper, "Countertransference? Counterculture? Where Is the Analyst's Authority?" (E. S. Buchholz and C. Chinlund), at the APA Division of Psychoanalysis meetings on April 16, 1994, in Washington, D.C.

14. Here, too, there is difference of opinion because Freud wrote about understanding mental processes as both scientist and romantic. In some works he divorced the idea of psychological science from hard-core science.

15. News stories about the rupture within psychoanalytic circles actually hit the press. Maya Pines was one of many authors who wrote several articles for the *New York Times* on that very subject.

16. Gill, M. (1994), *Psychoanalysis in Transition: A Personal View* (Hillsdale, N.J.: The Analytic Press), 53.

17. Nicholas Wright's play *Mrs. Klein,* in which Klein pushes her own daughter away, highlights how many in therapy long for a mother-child relationship.

18. Hillman, J., and M. Ventura (1993), *We've Had a Hundred Years of Psychotherapy and the World's Getting Worse* (San Francisco: Harper).

19. Ibid., 13.

20. See G. Blanck and R. Blanck (1974), *Ego Self: Theory and Practice* (New York: Columbia University Press), and K. Levy (1958), "Silence in the Analytic Session," part 1, *International Journal of Psychoanalysis* 39: 30–58 (one of the many examples of the era's theories).

21. See S. Ferenczi (1950), "On the Technique of Psychoanalysis and Silence Is Golden," *Further Contributions to the Theory and Technique of Psycho-analysis* (New York: Basic Books), 177–88, 250–51.

22. Weisman, A. (1955), "Silence and Psychotherapy," *Psychiatry* 18 (3): 241–60.

23. *King Lear,* act 1, scene 2.

24. Silences are not considered illegitimate in today's psychoanalytic climate; they are just rarer. For an example of how silence is considered, Darlene Ehrenberg, a relational psychoanalyst, writes in her timely book on the intricacies of therapeutic engagement, *The Intimate Edge: Extending the Reach of Psychoanalytic Interaction* (New York: W. W. Norton, 1992): "[A new patient] expressed her concern about whether this relationship could 'work,' and stated that she needed space and that what she wanted now was for me to be quiet and leave her alone. My first inclination was to respect her request for me to remain silent. Certainly there are times when any kind of comment by the analyst can interrupt a necessary experience or even foreclose it" (p. 74). In this instance, Ehrenberg felt silence was collusion in her patient's resistance, perhaps her patient's fear of "engaging in a process she felt she could not totally control" (p. 75). Thus, Ehrenberg handled the session by sharing her feelings and thoughts about the analytic relationship as it stood. Hers is

a wonderful example of process in treatment and the work of an analyst ready to push herself for the sake of the patient. My one additional thought would be to question why the patient's quest for silence was seen only as an attempt to control and mask fears and not viewed also as a necessary effort at self-mastery that could be relinquished with trust—something that is as valuable as the relationship about to be entered, but necessary to put aside for the sake of sharing problems and receiving help. See also Philip Bromberg, fellow of the William Alanson White Psychoanalytic Institute, in a profound and impassioned paper on the structure of therapy and the use of language, " 'Speak! That I may see you': Some Reflections on Dissociation, Reality, and Psychoanalytic Listening," *Psychoanalytic Dialogues* 4, no. 4 (1994): 517–47. He notes a patient proclaiming: "Only in my silence . . . do I feel real" (p. 526). Mark Epstein is ahead of all of us in integrating Buddha's teachings with Freud's. He shows immense respect for silence in treatment. See M. Epstein (1995), *Thoughts Without a Thinker* (New York: Basic Books).

25. Winnicott, D. W. (1958), "The Capacity to Be Alone," *International Journal of Psychoanalysis* 39: 416–20.

26. Ibid., 416.

27. Ogden, T. H. (1994), *Subjects of Analysis* (Northvale, N.J.: J. Aronson).

28. Ibid., 181.

29. Abrahamson, I., ed. (1985), *Against Silence: The Voice and Vision of Elie Wiesel*, vol. 11 (New York: Holocaust Library), 3. Wiesel, a Nobel Prize–winner, describes over and over again his experiences of living through the tempest of the Holocaust but also being able to take the flames away with him. He transforms that fire into positive energy. He thanks his teachers and he thanks his own dreams. In his writings I see a balance between his need for others and the solitary—that is the key to survival.

> Others taught me how to remember and not go mad. And still others taught me how to go mad and try not to turn madness into an act of vengeance, of punishment, of bitterness against man but, on the contrary, to turn it into something which would bring one closer to another, closer to man, and perhaps, on Shabbat, closer to God—but certainly closer to oneself . . . Who are my teachers? My teachers are my dreams. And whatever I give it is nothing more than what I have received [p. 20].

"My teachers are my dreams" suggests the poetic link between his inner separate self and all other important people in his life.

30. Helmreich, W. B. (1992), *Against All Odds: Holocaust Survivors and the Successful Lives They Made in America* (New York: Simon & Schuster).

31. Those with posttraumatic symptoms who seek or require treatment are not less able people. I am simply establishing choice in the decision to pursue therapy. Sometimes people make excellent adjustments to terrible occurrences without psychotherapeutic intervention and while psychotherapy works, it (no more than anything else) cannot save us from all pains, anxiety, and

unhappiness. Freud was very correct in stating that, once freed from neurotic anxiety and pain, the individual must face and deal with the unhappy, real moments of life.

32. I am hardly advocating an unexamined life, but when people have suffered extraordinary abuse, constantly repeating the past can become analogous to rubbing salt in an open wound.

33. Werner, E. E., and L. R. Smith (1982), *Vulnerable but Invincible* (New York: McGraw-Hill).

34. In a personal communication to Daniel Stern—see D. N. Stern (1985), *The Interpersonal World of the Infant* (New York: Basic Books)—Mahler said that she renamed the early-infancy phase "awakening." But that term, while descriptive of the relating of an infant to all in the environment, unfortunately also implies that the faraway gaze of a baby is part of "prebirth" rather than akin to an ongoing pertinent state of development.

35. Buchholz, E. S., H. Marben, and E. Tyson, "The Need for Aloneness: A Developmental Perspective," Aug. 11–15, 1995, APA Division of Psychoanalysis meeting, New York.

36. Daniel Stern, clinician, researcher, and writer, seriously challenged the use of the term "symbiosis." In Stern's thoughtful writing, he emphasizes the baby's separateness as well as interactiveness and sees merger as an uncomfortable rather than healthy state.

37. Another element to the individuation/attachment dynamic is added by Jacob Gewirtz, professor of psychology and chairman of the developmental psychology doctoral program at Florida International University, and Martha Pelaez-Noqueras, research assistant professor of pediatrics at the University of Miami Medical School. For a long time, Gewirtz has questioned aspects of attachment theory. See J. L. Gewirtz and E. Boyd (1977), "Does Maternal Non-Responding Imply Reduced Infant Caring?" *Child Development* 48: 200–207.

38. "Leaving Your Children Without Tears or Fuss," *Brown University Newsletter*, 1994, citing the Manisses Communications Group *Child and Adolescent Behavior Letter*.

39. Kagan, J. (1984), *The Nature of the Child* (New York: Basic Books).

40. Kagan, J. (1996), "Three Pleasing Ideas," *American Psychologist*, 51 (9): 901–08.

41. Kagan (1984), 91.

42. Storr, A. (1988), *Solitude* (New York: Ballantine), 13. Psychoanalysis has always recognized a polarity in personality development. Freud contrasted the "egotistic" urge with the desire for community. Although makers of theory describe these divisions as capacities that underlie two equal essentials, self-development and mature relationships, their formulations usually favor one or the other—striving toward a well-defined self and autonomy or seeking union with others. In my theory, self-definition and individualism grow from exchanges with others as well as from separate time; the alone state is a very basic need that motivates many of our actions.

43. Gibson, H. B. (1981), *Hans Eysenck: The Man and His Work* (London: Peter Owen).
44. Tiffany Field comes to the same conclusion. In a detailed study, cited in Chapter 7, she observed ninety-six neonates—half preterm and half full-term —using the Brazelton Assessment Scale, which includes studying infants' imitations of adults in close interactions, and reactions to stimuli, such as noise and pinpricks. The babies' reactions show the sensitivity of introverts and lack of reactions of extroverts.
45. Eysenck, H. J. (1967), *The Biological Basis of Personality* (Springfield, Ill.: C. C. Thomas). Eysenck describes facially expressive adults showing low-level physiological responses. In turn, such people rate themselves as extroverted and have higher thresholds to stimulation. By contrast, those less expressive physically, who have lower thresholds to stimulation and considerable physiological responsivity, are self-rated as introverts. Eysenck sees the propensity to introversion as an early-established, probably innate process.
46. Freud, S. (1920), *General Introduction to Psychoanalysis* (New York: Boni and Liveright).
47. Jung, C. G. (1971), *Psychological Types* (London: Routledge and Kegan Paul).
48. Gibson (1981). Also see H. S. Eysenck (1971), *Readings in Extroversion and Introversion*, 3 vols. (London: Staples Press). Recently researchers—J. M. Burger, R. W. Larson, and M. R. Leary, to name a few—are delving into the degree to which people choose to be alone and who these people are.
49. Meares, R. (1993), *The Metaphor of Play* (Northvale, N.J.: Jason Aronson), 14.
50. Modell, A. H. (1993), *The Private Self* (Cambridge: Harvard University Press).
51. Buechner, F. (1991), *Telling Secrets* (San Francisco: Harper).
52. *NBC News Report*, Nov. 4, 1995.
53. Scientific discovery is further eliminating boundaries between inner and outer "space." Genetic research is big science. Robert Cook-Deegan reports: "Genetics testing has the power to expose the body's most intimate secrets"— R. Cook-Deegan (1994), "Private Parts," *The Sciences*, March/April 1994, 18. Who gets the information? The article concerns itself with eugenics, racism, and serious misuses of information. My concern about this change in the information bank includes individual privacy and the loss of regulating what invades our person from the outside world. And what happens to self-esteem and self-knowledge when the touchstone of the self, the body, can be invaded in ways that give greatest knowledge about our functioning to others rather than ourselves?

People don't always want to see their lives laid out before them in tarot cards. Nancy Wexler, when appointed chairperson of a special permanent panel called the Working Group on Ethical, Legal and Social Issues for the U.S. Office of the Human Genome Project, considered her role in preparing people emotionally for genetic discoveries very seriously. Because she is a possible candidate for Huntington's chorea, she has a good sense of the problems that accompany disclosure of bodily secrets. She calls the dilemma this new technology produced the "Tiresias complex," after the blind seer who told Oedipus, "It is but sorrow to be wise when wisdom profits not." According to Wexler, "Most people are not equipped to know how and when and where they're going to die." The simple X ray that discovered tooth cavities and fluoroscopes that located gas bubbles in the stomach are now transformed through science into MRIs that can detect tissue change. In March of 1993, Nancy Wexler won a prestigious medical research award, the Lasker Prize, for work on Huntington's disease. See P. M. Rowe (1993), "Nancy Wexler Wins Lasker Medical Research Award," *APA Observer* 6, no. 6 (Nov.), 23, 31.

Until the latter part of the nineteenth century (1895), medical diagnosis was made with the hands, ears, eyes, and nose of the clinician. At the turn of the century, Wilhelm Roentgen's glowing rays began to be employed and added a new dimension to diagnosis. Crude at first, their use was limited to detecting fractures and bone diseases and, later, lung lesions. The advent of contrast media vastly increased the scope of radiology, as it was soon called. The stomach, intestines, kidneys, uterus, and fallopian tubes opened up their secrets. Just past the midcentury, soft tissue techniques became possible so that the female breast could be searched for early malignancy, and the computerized axial tomography (CT) scan was able to reveal details of internal organs. The most recent additions in imaging techniques do not even employ X rays. Rather, ultrasound delineates the inside of organs through ultrashort sound waves and magnetic resonance imaging (MRI) uses magnetic fields to delineate the organs and any pathology so that the exquisite details of tissues can be detected. What will be next? Apparently, a lot more. Scientists predict devices that will link directly to people's brains and determine unspoken thoughts. Will science invent the mechanisms that will betray our secrets, privacy, and silences?

54. Siegelman, E. (1990), *Metaphor and Meaning in Psychotherapy* (New York: The Guilford Press).

55. Ibid.

56. Ibid., 28.

57. Hall, G. S. (1907), *Youth: Its Education, Regimen and Hygiene* (New York: D. Appleton), 436. For an insightful interpretation of Hall, see G. Bederman (1995), *Manliness and Civilization: A Cultural History of Race and Gender in the United States, 1880–1917* (Chicago: University of Chicago Press).

58. Hall, ibid., 106.

59. One of the very helpful books stemming from the women's movement was *Our Bodies, Ourselves,* from the Boston Women's Health Collective (New York: Simon and Schuster, 1973).

60. The place of will in society is written about by Otto Rank (1945), *Will Therapy* (New York: A. A. Knopf); Otto Rank (1945), *Truth and Reality* (New York: A. A. Knopf); and in a biography of Rank by Esther Menaker (1993), *Otto Rank: A Rediscovered Legacy* (New York: Columbia University Press).

61. Melanie Beattie's book is quoted in *Simple Abundance: A Daybook of Comfort and Joy* by Sarah Ban Breathnach (New York: Warner Books, 1995).

62. *Gestalt* is a German word that roughly translates into "pattern" or "configuration." The approach of Gestalt therapy assumes people are made up of

a pattern of wholes that, when understood, opens them up to full, rich, holistic experience. See F. Perls, R. F. Hepperline, and P. Goodman (1977), *Gestalt Therapy* (New York: Bantam Books); and F. Perls (1993), *The Gestalt Approach: Eyewitness to Theory* (Washington, D.C.: Science and Behavior Books).

63. Skinner, B. F. (1962), *Walden Two* (New York: Macmillan).

64. Skinner, B. F. (1990), "Can Psychology Be a Science of Mind?" *American Psychologists* 45 (11), 1206–10.

65. Robert Jay Lifton (1993) expands this theme in terms of the fluidity of the self and human resiliency in *The Protean Self: Human Resiliency in an Age of Fragmentation* (New York: Basic Books).

66. Mithaug, D. E. (1993), *Self-Regulation Theory: How Optimal Adjustment Maximizes Gain* (Westport, Conn.: Praeger), 149.

Chapter 6: Rhythms, Sensations, and Womb Life

1. Paglia, C. (1990), *Sexual Personae* (New Haven: Yale University Press), Chapter One.

2. Beckett, S. (1982), "A Piece of Monologue," *Three Occasional Pieces* (London: Faber and Faber).

3. The Wisdom of Solomon, *The Apocrypha*, trans. W. O. E. Oesterly, D.D. (New York: Macmillan, 1918), 44.

4. Alice Adams uses that term in her book *Reproducing the Womb* (Ithaca: Cornell University Press, 1994), and Kathryn Allen Rabuzzi, in *Mother with Child* (Bloomington: Indiana University Press, 1994), voices a similar concern about society in the guise of technology, literature, science, and so forth, stealing childbirth from its maternal connections. Adams demonstrates the evolution of the technological takeover of conception from Aldous Huxley's *Brave New World* to Margaret Atwood's *The Handmaid's Tale*.

5. I am indebted to the thoughtful scholarship of obstetrician and gynecologist Leonard Wolf, M.D., for information on fetal development.

6. Preyer, W. (1885), *Specielle Physiologie des Embryo* (Leipzig).

7. Coren, S. (1996), *Sleep Thieves* (New York: The Free Press), 107.

8. Leboyer, F. (1975), *Birth Without Violence* (New York: Alfred A. Knopf).

9. Leboyer, F. (1975), interview in *New Age Journal* 8 (Oct.): 15–16.

10. Padel, R. (1992), *In and Out of the Mind* (Princeton: Princeton University Press), 100.

11. Elizabeth Sacks's research on Shakespeare's comedies and tragedies focuses on the impact of pregnancy on the bard's own creative force. See *Shakespeare's Images of Pregnancy* (New York: St. Martin's Press, 1980).

12. Grass, G. (1990), *The Tin Drum*, trans. Ralph Manheim (New York: Vintage Books), 46.

13. Rabuzzi, K. A. (1994), *Mother with Child: Transformations Through Childbirth* (Bloomington: Indiana University Press), xv.

14. Freud, S. (1920), "Beyond the Pleasure Principle," *The Standard Edition of the Complete Psychological Works of Sigmund Freud*, vol. 18 (London: Hogarth Press), 3–64.

15. Kaplan, L. J. (1995), *No Voice Is Ever Wholly Lost* (New York: Simon & Schuster). A further description of the personal connection of death instincts to Freud's life and description of *fort-da* (the peekaboo game) is in this significant book on loss in people's lives.

16. Ibid., 31.

17. Nicholas, M. W. (1994), *The Mystery of Goodness and the Positive Moral Consequences of Psychotherapy* (New York: W. W. Norton).

18. Piontelli, A. D. (1992), *From Fetus to Child: An Observational and Psychoanalytic Study* (London: Tavistock/Routledge). Study of fetal movements is a growing technology, with sophisticated equipment involving computer-assisted analysis of movement patterns available. The discovery of ultrasound, or sonar, emanating from its use during the Second World War and its application to obstetrics in the 1950s, has produced first a stream and then a rushing torrent of information on the movement and behavior of the human fetus.

19. Piontelli, A. (1996), "From Temperament to Character: Prenatal Origins of Individuality," Center for Modern Psychoanalytic Studies Conference, Nov. 16, New York City.

20. Gottfried, A. W. (1990), "Touch As an Organizer of Development and Learning," in *Touch: The Foundation of Experience*, ed. K. E. Barnard and T. B. Brazelton (Madison, Conn.: International Universities Press).

21. Weiss, S. J. (1990), "Parental Touching: Conclaves of a Child's Body Concept and Body Sentiment," in Barnard and Brazelton (see n. 20).

22. Freud, S. (1953), "Inhibitions, Symptoms and Anxiety," *The Standard Edition of the Complete Psychological Works of Sigmund Freud*, vol. 20 (London: Hogarth Press), 138.

23. Four types of MZ twins are possible. MZ twins result from an early division of the same fertilized egg. Identical twins can occur within a time period of fourteen days. If the division occurs very early, such as the first day after conception, the twins will have separate placentas, chorions, and amniotic sacs. If the division occurs within seven days of conception, the twins will share the same placenta and chorion, but not the same amniotic sac. As in the reported instance, if the division occurs later—the seventh to thirteenth day —the twins will share in addition the same amniotic sac. If on the thirteenth or fourteenth day, the result is conjointed, or Siamese, twins.

24. Write, L. (1995), "Double Mystery," *New Yorker*, Aug. 7, 49–62.

25. Piontelli, A. D. (1992), 46.

26. Amniotic fluid is 98 percent water and the remainder small quantities of salts, urea, uric acid, creatinine, lanugo, sebaceous material, and epithelial cells. This water isn't static and is actually replaced about every three hours. In the tenth edition of a standard obstetrical text, it is suggested in the wording that the idea of a fetus deliberately swallowing fluid was then rather sketchy: "The presence of amniotic fluid particles in the stomach and intestines indi-

cates that water and some food may be absorbed by the gastrointestinal tract"—E. S. Taylor (1976), *Beck's Obstetrical Practice and Fetal Medicine* (Baltimore: Williams & Wilkins), 77.

27. Piontelli, A. D. (1992), 47.

28. Birnholz, J. C. (1988), "On Observing the Human Fetus," in *Behavior of the Fetus,* ed. W. P. Smotherman and S. R. Robinson (Caldwell: The Teleford Press).

29. Ibid., 57.

30. Ibid.

31. Ibid., 58.

32. Hofer, M. A. (1988), "On the Nature and Function of Prenatal Function," in Smotherman and Robinson (see n. 28), 3. This book is one of a very few writings that combines the research and scholarship of psychologists, biologists, and zoologists in the neglected field of behavioral embryology.

33. Ibid.

34. Michael Trout, Ph.D., reporting in a videotape, *The Dance of Attachment.*

35. Bruckner, P. (1992), *The Divine Child: A Novel of Prenatal Rebellion* (New York: Little, Brown), 9.

36. Gesell, A. (1945), *The Embryology of Behavior: The Beginnings of the Human Mind* (New York: Harper & Brothers Publishers), 208.

37. Ibid., 225.

38. Preterm babies are not as attentive as their fully developed brethren. But overall, the musculature is in place for expressiveness, as well as the neuronal connections for making such discriminations. Moreover, not all preterm (or term) babies respond with the same intensity. Not only that, but primarily, late-stage fetuses feel and respond to environment on a broad scale. Varied patterns of high and low responsivity to stimuli are recordable, further reinforcing intrauterine individual differences, which probably influence temperament and personality in the long run.

39. Field, T. (1985), "Neonatal Perception of People: Maturational and Individual Differences," in *Social Perception in Infants,* ed. T. Field and N. Fox (Norwood, N.J.: Ablex Publishing), 31–52.

40. In another context, I have written about stimulus barriers, hypothesizing that neurologically impaired children may be deficient in the ability to self-regulate the input of stimuli or lacking in proprioceptive communication of internal stimuli, the result being understimulation. See E. S. Buchholz (1987), "The Legacy from Childhood: Considerations for Treatment of the Adult with Learning Disabilities," *Psychoanalytic Inquiry* 7 (3): 431–52.

41. Sidney S. Furst explores the stimulus barrier in relationship to traumatic experiences and gives a first-rate account of the history and relevant research related to this idea in "The Stimulus Barrier and the Pathogenicity of Trauma," *International Journal of Psychoanalysis* 59 (1978): 345–53.

42. Freud, S. (1920), "Beyond the Pleasure Principle," *The Standard Edition of the Complete Psychological Works of Sigmund Freud,* vol. 18 (London: Hogarth Press), 27.

43. Gediman, H. K. (1971), "The Concept of Stimulus Barrier: Its Review and Reformation As an Adaptive Ego Function," *International Journal of Psychoanalysis* 52: 243–57.

44. Emory, E. K., and K. A. Tomey (1988), "Environmental Stimulation and Human Fetal Responsivity in the Pregnancy," in Smotherman and Robinson (see n. 28), 141–61. Evidence of habituation—the waning of responsiveness to a repeated stimulus—is in the fetal change of responsiveness. Some see habituation as proof of consciousness, since memory and thought are interconnected. As the above study reports, when the stimulus changes, a renewal of responsiveness occurs (dishabituation).

45. Rushing, B. (1993), "When We're Together, I Feel So Alone: Solitude in the Midst of a Crowd," in *The Center of the Web: Women and Solitude,* ed. D. Wear (New York: New York State University Press), 76.

46. *Taber's Cyclopedic Medical Dictionary,* 10th ed. (Philadelphia: F. A. Davis, 1965), 108.

47. Tortora, G. J., and S. R. Grabowski (1993), *Principles of Anatomy and Physiology,* 7th ed. (New York: Harper Collins).

48. Thelen, E. (1988), "On the Nature of a Developing Motor System," in Smotherman and Robinson (see n. 28), 207–28.

49. Damasio, A. R. (1994), *Descartes' Error: Emotion, Reason, and the Human Brain* (New York: Grosset/Putnam).

50. Rolf, I. P. (1977), *Rolfing: The Integration of Human Structures* (New York: Harper and Row Publishers), 22.

51. Kuhlman, K. A. (1994), "Movement and Responses," in *Diagnostic Ultrasound Applied to Obstetrics and Gynecology,* ed. R. E. Sabbagha (Baltimore: Williams and Wilkins).

52. Chamberlain, D. B. (1987), "Consciousness at Birth: The Range of Empirical Evidence," in *Pre and Perinatal Psychology: An Introduction,* ed. T. Verhey (New York: Human Sciences Press), 78.

53. According to K. A. Rabuzzi (1994), rebirthing experiments date back to studies in hypnosis in the nineteenth century.

54. Bruckner (1992), 40, 42, 49.

55. Chamberlain (1987).

Chapter 7: The Baby, the Child, the Adolescent . . . Then Us

1. Stevenson, R. L. (1928), "The Land of Story Books," *A Child's Garden of Verses* (Philadelphia: John C. Winston), 78.

2. Ibid., "The Littlehand," 80.

3. Healy, J. (1990), *Endangered Minds: Why Our Children Don't Think* (New York: Simon & Schuster).

4. Hrdy, S. B. (1995), "Liquid Assets: A Brief History of Wet-Nursing," *Natural History* 104, no. 12 (December): 41.

5. Barker, P. (1993), *Regeneration* (New York: Plume), 107.

6. de Mause, L. (1970), "The Evolution of Childhood," in *The History of Childhood*, ed. L. de Mause (London: Souvenir Press), 1–74.

7. Calvert, K. (1992), *Children in the House: The Maternal Culture of Early Childhood 1600–1900* (Boston: Northeastern University Press).

8. Kendrick, W. (1995), "From Huck Finn to Calvin Klein's Billboard Nymphets," *New York Times Magazine*, Oct. 8, 84–87.

9. Psychoanalyst C. Yorke reminds us that Freud himself was an expert baby watcher. Father of six children (three boys, three girls), grandfather, and observer, Freud, too, produced a developmental theory. See C. Yorke (1995), "Freud's Psychology: Can It Survive?" *The Psychoanalytic Study of the Child*, vol. 50 (New Haven: Yale University Press), 3–31.

10. Beebe, B., and F. M. Lachmann (1988), "The Contribution of Mother-Infant Mutual Influence to the Origins of Self and Object Representations," *Psychoanalytic Psychology* 5: 305–57.

11. McFadyen, A. (1994), *Special Care Babies and Their Developing Relationships* (London: Routledge). My organization of babies' conscious states owes a lot to child adolescent psychiatrist Anne McFadyen. See also T. B. Brazelton and B. Cramer (1990), *The Earliest Relationship: Parents, Infants and the Drama of Early Attachment* (Reading, Mass.: Addison-Wesley), and A. MacFarlane (1977), *The Psychology of Childbirth* (Cambridge: Harvard University Press).

12. Moustakas, C. (1989), *Loneliness* (New York: Prentice Hall).

13. Another psychologist brilliantly researches loneliness with conclusions similar to Moustakas's. See R. W. Larson (1990), "The Solitary Side of Life: An Examination of the Time People Spend Alone from Childhood to Old Age," *Developmental Review* 10, no. 2 (June): 155–83.

14. Hoffert, M. B. (1995), "Weaving the Fabric of a Life: A Phenomenological Inquiry of Solitude Experienced by School Age Children," Ph.D. diss., University of Colorado Graduate School of Nursing.

15. Ibid., 87.

16. Phillips, A. (1993), *On Kissing, Tickling, and Being Bored: Psychoanalytic Essays on the Unexamined Life* (Cambridge, Mass.: Harvard University Press). Phillips also writes about how American psychoanalysis lost the drift of what Freud was saying by getting caught up in the cynicism of person bashing, noting that while facts about an individual's life help us to understand a theory, they do not either validate or invalidate the theory. His 1994 book, *On Flirtation: Psychoanalytic Essays on the Uncommitted Life* (Cambridge, Mass.: Harvard University Press), says it well:

> Freud-bashing, like any kind of bashing, frees one to have contact with something by creating the illusion that one is destroying it. To be a follower in psychoanalysis is to miss the point. Disciples are the people who haven't yet got the joke. And historically, in psychoanalysis disciples enact the catastrophe their leaders were trying to avert; Freudians become ascetic prigs, Winnicottians ridiculously spontaneous, Kleinians become enviously narrow-minded, Lacanians mirror the master, and so on [p. 149].

17. Hoffert (1995).

18. Ibid.

19. Porges, S. W. (1993), "The Infant's Sixth Sense: Awareness and Regulation of Bodily Processes," *Zero to Three*, Oct./Nov., 12–16.

20. Ibid., 12.

21. Butterworth, G. (1992), "Origins of Self Perception in Infancy," *Psychological Inquiry* 3 (2): 103–111.

22. Buchholz, E., H. Marben, and E. Tyson (1995), "The Need for Aloneness: A Developmental Perspective," presentation at APA meeting, Aug., New York City.

23. Beebe, B., and D. Stern (1977), "Engagement, Disengagement, and Early Object Experiences," in *Communicative Structures and Psychic Structures*, ed. N. Freedman and S. Grand (New York: Plenum), 137–54. See also D. Sorter (1996), "Chase and Dodge: An Organization of Experience," *Psychoanalysis and Psychotherapy* 13 (1): 68–75.

24. Arguing against the irreversible effects of lack of immediate attachment and bonding is the evidence of a renowned psychiatrist. Sir Michael Rutter, honorary director of the Social, Genetic and Developmental Psychiatry Research Center of the University of London's Institute of Psychiatry Reports, studied 166 children adopted from Romania. They were confined to cots, without playthings, verbal communication, or personalized caregiving. Feeding was entirely with gruel, with bottles propped up, and washing was by hosing with cold water. Some children were extraordinarily malnourished. The remarkable factor besides survival of all of these children is that those brought to London before six months of age completely caught up with other children socially and emotionally; the four-year-old mean IQ was "average." See M. Rutter (1996), "Romanian Orphans Adopted Early Overcome Deprivation," *The Brown University Child and Adolescent Behavior Letter* 12, no. 6 (June): 1–3.

25. Touch is, by many estimates, the need sine qua non of babies. See T. Field, ed. (1995), *Touch in Early Development* (Hillsdale, N.J.: Lawrence Erlbaum Associates). A rare addition to the parenthood literature is William A. H. Sammons's book *The Self-Calmed Baby* (St. Martin's Press, 1989). He discusses a baby's use of touch and disengagement to gain control (self-regulation skills).

26. Barnard, K. E., and T. B. Brazelton, eds. (1990), *Touch: The Foundation of Experience* (Madison, Conn.: International Universities Press), 6. Brazelton, ever the acutely sensitive observer of babies, emphasizes the importance of contact between mother and child but thoroughly recognizes how infants learn about themselves through touch. See also D. Ackerman (1990), *The Natural History of the Senses* (New York: Random House).

27. Fraiberg, S., with the collaboration of Louis Fraiberg (1977), *Insights from the Blind: Comparative Studies of Blind and Sighted Infants* (New York: Basic Books).

28. Keller, H. (1954), *The Story of My Life* (New York: Doubleday & Co.), 26.

29. Ibid., 72.

30. Ibid., 105.

31. Tronick, E. Z. (1995), "Touch in Mother-Infant Interaction," in Field (see n. 25), 59.

32. Ibid.

33. See, for example, J. D. Lichtenberg, F. M. Lachmann, and J. L. Fosshage (1992), *Self and Motivational Systems: Towards a Theory of Psychoanalytic Technique* (Hillsdale, N.J.: The Analytic Press); D. Stern (1995), *The Mother-Infant Constellation;* and B. Beebe and F. Lachmann (1992), "The Contribution of Mother-Infant Mutual Influence to the Origin of Self and Object Representation," in *Relational Perspectives in Psychoanalysis,* ed. N. Skolnick and S. Warshaw (Hillsdale, N.J.: The Analytic Press), 83–117.

34. H. N. Massie, A. Bronstein, J. Alterman, and B. K. Campbell (1988), "Inner Themes and Outer Behaviors in Early Childhood Development: A Longitudinal Study," *Psychoanalytic Study of the Child* 43: 213–42. This is a different focus from that of the researchers.

35. Mahler, M. S., F. Pine, and A. Bergman (1975), *The Psychological Birth of the Human Infant* (New York: Basic Books).

36. Wieder, H. (1966), "Intellectuality: Aspects of Its Development from the Analysis of a Precocious Four and a Half Year Old Boy," *Psychoanalytic Study of the Child* 21: 294–323.

37. Levinson, L. (1984), "Witches—Bad and Good Maternal Psychopathology As a Developmental Interference," *Psychoanalytic Study of the Child* 39: 371–92.

38. Levy, D. M. (1943), *Maternal Over-Protection* (New York: Columbia University Press). The idea that parental overstimulation may lead to faulty development, even psychotic withdrawal, is an old one—see L. B. Boyer (1956), "On Maternal Overstimulation and Ego Defects," *Psychoanalytic Study of the Child* 2: 236–42, 242–48.

39. Buchholz, E. S., and R. Haynes (1983), "Sometimes I Feel Like a Motherless Child," *Dynamic Psychotherapy* 1: 99–107.

40. Gornick, V. (1987), *Fierce Attachments* (New York: Farrar Straus Giroux), 199–200.

41. Wallace, M. (1986), *The Silent Twins* (New York: Prentice Hall).

42. Lawrence, D. H. (1992), *Women in Love* (New York: Alfred A. Knopf).

43. Wallace (1986), 7.

44. Some of the material in this section and the patient illustrations were written about in E. S. Buchholz and C. Chinlund (1994), "En Route to a Harmony of Being: Viewing Aloneness As a Need in Development and Child Analytic Work," *Psychoanalytic Psychology* 2: 357–74.

45. Freud, S. (1908), "Family Romances," *The Standard Edition of the Complete Psychological Works of Sigmund Freud,* vol. 9 (London: Hogarth Press), 237–41.

46. Erikson, E. (1968), *Identity: Youth and Crisis* (New York: Norton); E. Erikson (1959), *Identity and the Life Cycle* (New York: International Universities Press).

47. Catton, R., and E. S. Buchholz (1995), "Leave Me Alone: Preadolescent & Adolescent Perceptions of Aloneness and Loneliness," PCR Report 95, New York University.

48. Bellah, R. N., R. Madsen, W. M. Sullivan, A. Swidler, and S. M. Tipton (1985), *Habits of the Heart* (New York: Harper & Row).

49. Anna, as quoted in P. Barnes, ed. (1995), "Growth and Change in Adolescence," *Personal, Social and Emotional Development of Children* (Oxford, U.K.: The Open University), 30.

50. Benjamin, J. (1988), *The Bonds of Love: Psychoanalysis, Feminism, and the Problem of Domination* (New York: Pantheon Books).

51. Rolland, R. (1938), *Jean-Christophe*, trans. Gilbert Cannon (New York: Modern Library), 357.

52. McCullers, C. (1946), *The Member of the Wedding* (Boston: Houghton Mifflin). Aspects of this discussion of female adolescence are inspired by Katherine Dalsimer's evocative book (1986) *Female Adolescence: Psychoanalytic Reflections in Literature* (New Haven: Yale University Press).

53. Buchholz, E. S., and B. Gol (1986), "More Than Playing House: A Developmental Perspective on the Strengths in Teenage Motherhood," *American Journal of Orthopsychiatry* 56: 347–59.

54. Erikson, E. (1951), *Childhood and Society* (New York: Norton).

55. Rilke, R. M. (1954), *Letters to a Young Poet*, rev. ed., trans. M. D. Herter Norton (New York: W. W. Norton), 54.

56. *The Maternal Physician* (1818), author unknown, 7.

57. Calvert, K. (1992), *Children in the House: The Maternal Culture of Early Childhood 1600–1900* (Boston: Northeastern University Press).

58. Swift, J. (1948), "A Modest Proposal," *The Portable Swift*, ed. C. Van Doren (New York: Viking Press).

59. Calvert (1992).

60. I am grateful to Edi Tyson for allowing me to share her childhood experience.

61. Calvert (1992), 3.

62. Ibid., 6–7.

63. Seuss, (Dr.) T. G. (1990), *Oh, the Places You'll Go!* (New York: Random House).

Chapter 8: Trances, Computers, and Private Spaces

1. Cassirer, E. (1944), *An Essay on Man: An Introduction to a Philosophy of Human Culture* (New York : Doubleday Anchor Books), 17, 279. In writing this chapter, I returned to this classic essay, which I read in the 1960s, and found underlined passages related to the common origin of human activity, especially myth, language, art, religion, and man's need to self-generate and regulate above and beyond social imperatives.

2. Neihardt, J. G. (1975), *Black Elk Speaks: The Legendary "Book of Visions" of an American Indian* (New York: Washington Square Press), 15.

3. My cousin is psychoanalyst, group psychotherapy trainer, and author Dr. Louis Ormont.

4. Estes, C. P. (1992), *Women Who Run with the Wolves: Myths and Stories of the Wild Women Archetype* (New York: Ballantine Books).

5. Mead, M., and K. Heyman (1965), *Family* (New York: Macmillan).

6. Whitman, W., quoted ibid., 141.

7. Kenneth Frampton quoting Luis Barragan in "Bricks and Mortar," review of

Studies in Tectonic Culture by Paul Goldberger, *New York Times Book Review,*
Mar. 10, 1996, 5–6.

8. Wright, R. (1995), "The Evolution of Despair," *Time,* Aug. 28, 50.

9. Shostak, M. (1983), *Nisa: The Life and Words of a !Kung Woman* (New York: Vintage Books).

10. Freud, S. (1930), "Civilization and Its Discontents," *The Standard Edition of the Complete Psychological Works of Sigmund Freud,* vol. 21 (London: Hogarth Press), 59–151.

11. Shweder, R. A. (1991), *Thinking Through Culture: Expeditions in Cultural Psychology* (Cambridge: Harvard University Press), 73–74.

12. Belluck, P. (1996), "The Symptoms of Internet Addiction," *New York Times,* Dec. 1, Week in Review, 5.

13. Stephen Jay Gould, guru of evolutionary science, who teaches at Harvard, does not see people as limited in their ability to adapt to a changed and changing environment. He is hardly alone in stating that our large brains are probably underutilized anyway. The ability to adapt is not item specific. That is, as a group we are not preprogrammed to be nice or not nice to our spouse or computer friendly or not.

14. Levy, R. I., J. M. Mageo, and A. Howard (1996), "Gods, Spirits and History: A Theoretical Perspective," in Jeannette Marie Mageo and Alan Howard, eds., *Spirits in Culture, History and Mind* (New York: Routledge). This book provides interesting discussions on folk religions.

15. Sprague, S. (1970), *Bali, Island of Light* (Tokyo: Kodansha International, Ltd.).

16. Geertz, H. (1995), "Balinese Imaginings," *Natural History* 104, no. 2 (Feb.): 62–67.

17. An interesting story of Balinese painting is that it was initiated by two European artists living in Bali in the 1930s. Before then, making drawings with pen, paper, and brush was unheard of among Bali's traditional art forms. George Bateson and Margaret Mead, during a 1936 stay in Bali, collected paintings to make a study from them of inner feelings. For more of this story see H. Geertz, ibid.

18. Roland, A. (1988), *In Search of Self in India and Japan* (Princeton: Princeton University Press), 241.

19. Gary Feinman is a professor of archaeology/anthropology at the University of Wisconsin at Madison. He has written countless articles and many books in his field. His latest works include: T. D. Price and G. Feinman, eds. (1995), *Foundations of Social Inequality* (New York: Plenum Press), and T. D. Price and G. Feinman, eds. (1997), *Images of the Past,* 2nd ed. (Mountain View, Calif.: Mayfield Publishing Company). Linda M. Nicholas (who is Gary's wife) is codirector of many of their projects in southern Mexico, an honorary fellow of the Department of Anthropology at the University of Wisconsin in Madison, author and coauthor of numerous articles, a photographer, and cartographer.

20. Rybczynski, W. (1986), *Home: A Short History of an Idea* (New York: Viking Penguin).

21. Ariès, P., and G. Duby, eds. (1987), *A History of Private Life* (Cambridge: Belknap Press).

22. Levy, Mageo, and Howard (1996) suggest another reason for alone fears in sociocentric societies: people who are always in close proximity to others lose the capacity to be alone.

23. Paz, O. (1985), *The Labyrinth of Solitude* (New York: Grove Weidenfeld), 36.

24. García Marquez, G. (1970), *One Hundred Years of Solitude* (New York: Harper and Row). García Marquez has said that *One Hundred Years* is a political book on the oppression in Latin America with "one hundred years" as a metaphor for the continent. For a critique of García Marquez's writing, see *Plausible Prejudices* by Jacob Epstein (1981; New York: W. W. Norton).

25. Paz (1985), 31.

26. Ibid., 65, 199.

27. Cassirer (1944).

28. Tattersall, I. (1993), *The Human Odyssey: Four Million Years of Human Evolution* (New York: Prentice Hall), 160. When Anthony Storr discusses cave paintings, he does not include them as part of early humans' expression of an inner life, but merely ritualized magic. In any event, in keeping with Cassirer's philosophy, even if magic is behind the cave drawings, they would still be an expression of individual need.

29. Boorstin, D. J. (1992), *The Creators* (New York: Random House), 152–53.

30. Shostak (1983), 11.

31. Lambek, M. (1981), *Human Spirits: A Cultural Account of Trance in Mayotte* (London: Cambridge University Press), 5.

32. Ibid.

33. Ibid. "Cultural zero" is the term used to describe an absolute absence of cultural connection between a culture and a stranger to that particular culture.

34. Ibid.

35. Bourguignon, E. (1979), *Psychological Anthropology: An Introduction to Human Nature and Cultural Differences* (New York: Holt, Rinehart and Winston).

36. Blier, S. P. (1995), "The Place Where Vodun Was Born," *Natural History* 104, no. 10 (Oct.): 47.

37. Buchholz, E. S., and C. I. Saarni (1977), "Knowing About Knowing and Knowing: The Present State of the Field of Piagetian Education," *Review of Education* 3: 364–76.

38. Brody, J. (1997), "Quirks, Oddities May Be Illnesses," *New York Times*, Feb. 4, C1–2.

39. Berry, J. W., Y. H. Poortinga, M. H. Segall, and P. R. Daren (1992), *Cross-Cultural Psychology: Research and Applications* (Cambridge: Cambridge University Press).

Some go so far as to suggest a common psychological and biological state in which the parasympathetic-produced endocrines dominate. Most likely, psychological effects of alonetime and bonding are influenced by the neurological and hormonal systems and vice versa. At other times, being alone or bonded may influence our biology. Cultural practices implicitly correct for disparities between the need to bond and to withdraw alone. Anthropological evidence supports this, as does physiological corroboration from EEG studies of brain waves during trance states. Trance states, when tested physiologically, show parasympathetic activity. The energy-conserving function of that system confirms what I believe to be alonetime physiology of lowered heart rate, motor inhibition, and withdrawal from stimulation. I would hypothesize a potential common pathway as I emphasize several points: (1) Emotional expression is in general mediated by both the energy-conserving parasympathetic system and the energy-mobilizing sympathetic nervous system. (2) The neurotransmitter associated with the parasympathetic system plays a large role in behavioral adaptation and apparently puts our tissues (along with those of other animals) in better shape to withstand stress. Also see A. N. Shore (1994), *Affect Regulation and the Origin of the Self: The Neurobiology of Emotional Development* (Hillsdale, New Jersey: Lawrence Erlbaum Associates). (3) Alonetime, as a time of withdrawal from external connections, seems to be physiologically and psychologically demonstrated in trance states.

Jaynes has suggested a neuropsychological evolution of consciousness whereby changes in the connecting and integrative functions of the cortex cause people to be more alert today than in yesteryear.

40. Giddens, A. (1991), *Modernity and Self Identity* (Stanford: Stanford University Press), 189.

41. Toffler, A. (1980), *The Third Wave* (New York: William Morrow).

42. Ibid., 395.

43. Tattersall (1993), 137.

44. Scheper, N., and H. Saints (1979), *Scholars and Schizophrenics: Mental Illness in Rural Ireland* (Berkeley: University of California Press), 81. Numerous exotic mental disorders and culture-bound syndromes have been described in the literature, and both the interpretations and the names are indigenous to the culture. They range from running amok (a term adopted into our language) to the mild aggressive behavior identified in southeast Asia to *susto,* involving insomnia, apathy, depression, and anxiety, often among children. The symptoms among the people of the Andean highlands are believed to result from contact with supernatural forces.

Dr. Juan Mezzach, a psychiatrist at the Mount Sinai School of Medicine in New York City, is a leader of a movement recognizing the influence of culture on emotional problems. See D. Goleman (1995), "Making Room on the Couch for Culture," *New York Times,* Science section, Dec. 5, 1. At the Apr. 16, 1994, American Psychological Association psychoanalytic meeting in Washington, D.C., in a paper, "Countertransference? Counterculture? Where Is the Analyst's Authority?" (with C. Chinlund), we said, "Culture is like breathing, we don't notice it unless there comes a pause."

45. Murphy, L. M., and A. E. Moriarty (1976), *Vulnerability, Coping, and Growth from Infancy to Adolescence* (New Haven: Yale University Press).

46. Attributed to Nausea Bagwash, a character in the Tommy Handley radio show in England during the 1940s. She was described to me by my husband, Leonard Wolf.

47. Storr, A. (1988), *Solitude: A Return to the Self* (New York: Ballantine).

48. Giddens (1991), 41.

49. Smith, H. (1986), *The Religions of Man* (New York: Harper & Row).

50. The definition of suffering in this section of the book as well as the cross-cultural discussion on suffering with regard to depression were influenced by Richard A. Shweder's ideas as depicted in *Thinking Through Cultures: Expeditions in Cultural Psychology* (Cambridge: Harvard University Press, 1991), 326.

51. Buchholz, E. S., and E. Wolf (1991), "Tightening the Apron Strings: The 'Negative' Holding Environment," APA paper presentation, Division of Psychoanalysis, American Psychological Association, Eleventh Annual Spring Meeting, Apr. 13, Chicago.

52. Kaplan, L. J. (1995), *No Voice Is Ever Wholly Lost* (New York: Simon & Schuster), 240.

53. Ibid., 241.

54. What today is depression in earlier times might have been neurasthenia. Arthur Kleinman and Alex Cohen see neurasthenia as quite common in China with symptoms similar to both depressive and anxiety disorders. In general they believe that, in rural places all over the world, mental disorders are sharply increased and are poorly diagnosed. See A. Kleinman and A. Cohen (1997), "Psychiatry's Global Challenge," *Scientific American* 276, no. 3 (Mar.): 86–89.

55. Jack, D. C. (1991), *Silencing the Self: Women and Depression* (Cambridge: Harvard University Press).

56. Kundera, M. (1991), *Immortality* (New York: Grove Weidenfeld), 31.

57. Stengel, R. (1995), "Space Invaders," *New Yorker,* June 24, 90.

58. Hall, E. T. (1959), *The Silent Language* (New York: Doubleday).

59. Thanks to Norman Rosenfeld, fellow of the American Academy of Architects, for details on architectural planning.

60. Hess, R. D., K. Kashiwagi, H. Azuma, G. G. Price, and W. P. Dickson (1980), "Maternal Expectation for Mastery of Developmental Tasks in Japan and the United States," *International Journal of Psychology* 15: 259–91.

61. Hsu, C., and E. S. Buchholz, "What about Children in Chinatown: Looking at the School Success of Children in New York City's Chinatown in Light of Theories of Asian American Achievement," PCR #7-95-19, New York University, 1995.

62. Stevenson, H. W., S. Y. Lee, C. Chen, J. W. Stigler, C. Hsu, and S. Kitamora (1990), "Context of Achievement: A Study of American, Chinese and Japanese Children," Monographs of the Society for Research in Child Development, SS, serial #22, p. 47.

63. Holland, B. (1992), *One's Company: Reflections on Living Alone* (New York: Ballantine Books).

64. Thoreau, H. D. (1981), *Walden* (New York: AMS Press), 64.
65. Schement, J. R., and T. Curtis (1995), *Tendencies and Tensions of the Information Age: The Production and Distribution of Information in the United States* (New Brunswick, N.J.: Transaction Publishers).
66. Ibid., 234.
67. Ibid., 239–43.

Chapter 9: Relationships, Romance, and Resistance

1. Lewis, C. S. (1960), *The Four Loves* (New York: Harcourt, Brace), 21.
2. Burchill, J. (1988), "The Dead Zone," *Arena* (London).
3. Reiser, P. (1995), *Couplehood* (New York: Bantam Books), 161.
4. Wallerstein, J. S., and S. Blakeslee (1995), *The Good Marriage: How and Why Love Lasts* (Boston: Houghton Mifflin); M. V. Miller (1995), *Intimate Terrorism: The Deterioration of Erotic Life* (New York: W. W. Norton); M. Scarf (1995), *Intimate Worlds: Life Inside the Family* (New York: Random House); S. Goldbart and D. Wallin (1994), *Mapping the Terrain of the Heart: Passion, Tenderness and the Capacity to Love* (New York: Addison-Wesley).
5. This interpretation is based on the William Walton opera *Troilus and Cressida*.
6. A description from Oscar Lans's 1942 work on the Blackfoot tribe as furnished by Jane Fishburne Collier (1988) in *Marriage and Inequality in Classless Societies* (Stanford: Stanford University Press).
7. Dym, B., and M. L. Glenn (1993), *Couples: Exploring and Understanding the Cycles of Intimate Relationships* (New York: Harper Perennial).
8. Kristof, N. D. (1996), "Who Needs Love? In Japan, Many Couples Don't," *New York Times*, Feb. 11, sec. 1, pp. 1, 12.
9. Gray, J. (1992), *Men Are from Mars, Women Are from Venus* (New York: Harper Collins Publishers).
10. Bacall, L. (1994), *Now* (New York: Alfred A. Knopf), 46–47.
11. West, N. (1933), *Miss Lonelyhearts* (New York: New Directions Books).
12. Bigner, J. J. (1994), *Parent-Child Relations: An Introduction to Parenting*, 4th ed. (New York: Macmillan), 363.
13. Bair, D. (1990), "How Love Came to Simone de Beauvoir," *New York Times Book Review*, Apr. 8, 1.
14. Freud, S. (1920), "Beyond the Pleasure Principle," *The Standard Edition of the Complete Psychological Works of Sigmund Freud*, vol. 18 (London: Hogarth Press), 27.
15. de Beauvoir, S. (1971), "Dependent Love in Women" (from *The Second Sex*), in D. Norton and M. F. Kille, eds., *Philosophies of Love* (San Francisco: Chandler Publishing), 69.
16. Sartre, J. P. (1963), *Being and Nothingness*, in *The Philosophy of Jean Paul Sartre*, ed. R. D. Cumming (New York: Vintage Books).
17. This section of the chapter on romantic love draws a few thoughts from K. Rodman and E. S. Buchholz (1996), "The Impact of Cupid's Arrow: Compar-

ing Theories on Romantic and Companionate Love," Psychoeducation Center Report, New York University. Types of love have been delineated by many, but one of the first and most influential studies dates back to the 1950s, with Erich Fromm's book *The Art of Loving*. The types of love Fromm identifies range from erotic to spiritual to familial to fraternal models.

18. Fisher, H. (1992), *Anatomy of Love: The Natural History of Monogamy, Adultery, and Divorce* (New York: W. W. Norton).

19. Jankowiak, W. R., and E. F. Fischer (1992), "A Cross-Cultural Perspective on Romantic Love," *Ethnology* 31 (2): 149–55.

20. See Vatsyayana (1982), *Kama Sutra*, ed. M. R. Anand and L. Dare (Atlantic Heights, N.J.: New Delhi).

21. Lystra, K. (1989), *Searching the Heart: Women, Men and Romantic Love in the Nineteenth Century* (New York: Oxford University Press), 202.

22. de Rougemont, D. (1983), *Love in the Western World* (New York: Schocken Books), 42; italics in the original.

23. Lystra (1989).

24. In Norton and Kille's (1971) retelling of the age-old story, they point out that the origins of "better half" and "soul mate" rest on this myth.

25. Stendhal [Marie-Henri Beyle] (1947), *On Love*, trans. C.K. Scott-Moncrieff (New York: Liveright); W. Pater (1986), *Marius the Epicurean: His Sensations and Ideas*, ed. Ian Smalls (New York: Oxford University Press).

26. Mitchell, S. (1997), "Psychoanalysis and the Degradation of Romance," *Psychoanalytic Dialogues* 7 (1): 23–41.

27. Gilligan, C. (1982), *In a Different Voice: Psychological Theory and Women's Development* (Cambridge, Mass.: Harvard University Press).

28. Buchholz, E. S. (1975, 1976), "Developmental Differences Between Boys and Girls During the Oedipal Period," report of research funded by two Dean's Development Fund grants, New York University School of Education.

29. Albro, E. R. (1997), " 'I Bet He Didn't Know All About Girls': Gender and Children's Explanations for Interpersonal Preferences," biennial meeting of the Society for Research in Childhood Development, Washington, D.C.

30. Person, E. S. (1989), *Dreams of Love and Fateful Encounters* (New York: Penguin Books).

31. Dowrick, S. (1991), *Intimacy and Solitude* (London: W. W. Norton), and E. S. Buchholz and C. Chinlund (1994), "En Route to a Harmony of Being: Viewing Aloneness As a Need in Development and Child Analytic Work," *Psychoanalytic Psychology* 11 (3): 357–74.

32. Dowrick (1991), 41, 42.

33. Miller (1995).

34. Many psychoanalysts find that romantic love is related more to an enactment of the Oedipal phase. Psychiatrist and psychoanalyst Otto Kernberg believes that the idealization, longing, and sense of passionate fulfillment one feels when love is reciprocated all reflect the unconscious achievement of a union with the desired incestuous object. In this instance, however, one is victorious over the Oedipal rival without committing murder. See O. Kernberg (1980),

Internal World and External Reality (New York: Jason Aronson). He follows much of Freud's theories on love, which also derive from the Oedipal stage. And then he adds some. Kernberg emphasizes the necessity for a self with firm boundaries and an awareness of one's separateness from others as a condition for passionate love. Paradoxically, he states that there is also the need to be able to transcend the boundaries of the self so that one can occasionally have the experience of being one with the loved person. Kernberg believes that sexual passion integrates these contradictory features. Certainly, "the shared experience of sexual orgasm also includes . . . transcending the experience of the self and experiencing the fantasized union of the oedipal parents and . . . abandoning that union in a new object relation that reconfirms one's separate identity and autonomy" (292).

35. Quoted by L. Bernikow (1986) in *Alone in America: The Search for Companionship* (New York: Harper & Row), 6.

36. Holland, B. (1992), *One's Company: Reflections on Living Alone* (New York: Ballantine Books).

37. Masson, J. M., and S. McCarthy (1995), *When Elephants Weep: The Emotional Lives of Animals* (New York: Delacorte Press), 134, 163. The authors make a case against all animal behavior being motivated by survival instincts and the argument as depicted in Richard Dawkins's book *The Selfish Gene* (New York: Oxford University Press, 1976).

38. Bowlby, J. (1958), "The Nature of the Child's Tie to His Mother," *International Journal of Psychoanalysis* 39: 350–73; J. Bowlby (1973), *Separation: Anxiety and Anger*, vol. 2 of *Attachment and Loss* (London: Hogarth Press); J. Bowlby (1977), "The Making and Breaking of Affectional Bonds," *British Journal of Psychiatry* 130: 201–10, 421–31; J. Bowlby (1980), *Loss, Sadness and Depression*, vol. 3 of *Attachment and Loss* (London: Hogarth Press); J. Bowlby (1982), *Attachment*, 2nd ed. of vol. 1 of *Attachment and Loss* (London: Hogarth Press); J. Bowlby (1988), *A Secure Base: Parent-Child Attachment and Healthy Human Development* (New York: Basic Books).

39. Reiser (1995), 202.

40. Some of the ideas on dependency and loneliness that follow are in keeping with those of Melanie Klein (1963) as described in her article "On the Sense of Loneliness," *Our Adult World and Other Essays* (New York: Basic Books).

41. Miller (1995).

42. The Richard Strauss libretto is quoted in H. K. Gediman (1995), *Fantasies of Love and Death in Life and Art: A Psychoanalytic Study of the Normal and the Pathological* (New York: New York University Press), 71–72.

43. Strindberg, A. (1912), *The Father* (Brookline Village, Mass.: Branden).

44. Lyrics reproduced on a CD track by production supervisor Lotte Lenya for the Soloists Chorus Orchestra.

45. Smith, J. (1995), "People Eaters," *Granta* 52 (Winter): 69–84. Robert Louis Stevenson was disappointed by his encounter with one. Kooamua, whom Stevenson describes himself as meeting, took a bite from his enemy's arm, which he had slung across his shoulder, at one time of day, and later, dressed

in formal European-style clothes, paid his respects to French delegates. Stevenson had a hard time accepting this switchover.

46. Ibid., 84.

47. Meyer, M. (1985), *Strindberg: A Biography* (New York: Random House).

48. Ibid., 7.

49. Shengold, L. (1989), *Soul Murder* (New Haven, Conn.: Yale University Press).

50. Torjusen, B. (1986), *Words and Images of Edvard Munch* (Chelsea, Vt.: Chelsea Green Publishing). In fact, at the time of Strindberg's death, this kindred soul wrote a poetic description of the times the two gathered together, beginning with, "Strindberg is gone—a friend is gone."

51. Munch, quoted ibid., 43, n. 15.

52. Obviously, from the use of Munch's screaming figure in commercial design and entertainment, the symbolism is potent. In 1995, the National Academy of Design held an exhibition of Munch's art. The number of people standing fascinated by one of the several versions of *The Scream* attests to the meaningfulness of his image. It has become so familiar that it is part of the folk culture and even seen comically.

53. Munch, quoted ibid., 52.

54. de Beauvoir (1971), 67.

55. Plath, S. (1981), "I Am Vertical," *The Collected Poems of Sylvia Plath,* ed. T. Hughes (New York: Harper & Row Publishers), 143.

56. Gediman (1995). Helen Gediman has gently treaded on a terrain that psychoanalysts frequently avoid. Her insights are blessed with a profound knowledge of art and literature.

57. Freud, S. (1914), "On Narcissism: An Introduction," *The Standard Edition of the Complete Psychological Works of Sigmund Freud,* vol. 14 (London: Hogarth Press), 88.

58. Gornick, V. (1987), *Fierce Attachments* (New York: Farrar Straus Giroux), 167.

59. A recent book on siblings for those interested in reading about the great influence they have on families. See V. D. Volkan and G. Ast (1997), *Siblings in the Unconscious and Psychopathology* (Madison, Conn.: International Universities Press).

60. Falbo, T. (1984), "Only Children: A Review," in *The Single Child Family,* ed. T. Falbo (New York: Guilford Press), 1–24.

61. *Annie Hall* (1977).

62. Napier, A. Y. (1990), *The Fragile Bond: In Search of an Equal, Intimate and Enduring Marriage* (New York: Harper Perennial).

63. Reiser (1995), 207.

64. Dym, B., and M. L. Glenn (1993), *Couples: Exploring and Understanding the Cycles of Intimate Relationships* (New York: Harper Perennial).

65. Gordon, S. (1990), *Why Love Is Not Enough* (Boston, Mass.: Bob Adams).

66. Biringen, Z., R. N. Emde, and S. Pipp-Siegel (1997), "Dyssynchrony, Conflict, and Resolution: Positive Contributions to Infant Development," *American Journal of Orthopsychiatry* 67, no. 1 (Jan.): 4–19.

67. Miller, L. (1996), "On Line Adultery," *USA Today,* Feb. 6.

68. Turkle, S. (1996), *Life on the Screen* (New York: Simon & Schuster).

69. Donne, J. (1985), *The Complete English Poems* (New York: Alfred Knopf).

70. Lehmann-Haupt, C. (1997), "Getting Caught in the Web," *New York Times*, Feb. 13, C27.

Chapter 10: Creativity, Curiosity, and Celibacy

1. Solomon, M. (1977), *Beethoven* (New York: Schirmer Books), 19–20. Beethoven also shared the specific isolation of deafness. From his twenties to when he began to experience serious hearing loss, he removed himself from others, believing that if his loss was noticed his music would not be taken seriously. Without alone needs and skills being primary and available, this type of decision might not be possible.

2. *American Speech* 4, no. 1 (Oct. 1928).

3. Atwood, M. (1991), *Wilderness Tips* (New York: Doubleday).

4. Jack Benny, as transcribed by Benny and his daughter, Joan (1990), *Sunday Nights at Seven: The Jack Benny Story* (New York: Warner Books), 7.

5. Ibid., 7.

6. Interview with James Hubbell (1985), in *Lightworks: Explorations in Art, Culture, and Creativity*, ed. Milenko Matanovic (Issaquah, Wash.: Lorian Press), 16.

7. Waverka, S., K. Miller, and J. M. R. Doman (1996), "Together Forever," *Life*, Apr., 44–56.

8. As reported, ibid., 56.

9. Philosopher Susan Langer speaks of ways in which every individual transforms what they take in (and hence themselves): "Every fantasy is apt to have a hundred versions . . . embarrassed with [symbolic] riches"—S. Langer (1950), *Philosophy in a New Key: A Study on Symbolism of Reason, Rite and Art* (New York: New American Library), 68.

10. Storr, A. (1988), *Solitude: A Return to the Self* (New York: Ballantine), 25.

11. Winnicott stated, "We find either that individuals live creatively and feel that life is worth living or else that they cannot live creatively and are doubtful about the value of living"—D. Winnicott (1971), *Playing and Reality* (London: Tavistock), 71.

12. Olsen, T. (1978), *Silences: Classic Essays on the Art of Creating* (New York: Delta Publishing).

13. Lahr, J. (1996), "Profile: The Imperfectionist," *New Yorker*, Dec. 9, 71.

14. Storr (1988).

15. Woolf, V. (1957), *A Room of One's Own* (New York: Harcourt, Brace & Jovanovich).

16. Thoreau, H. D. (1981), *Walden* (New York: AMS Press).

17. Sarton, M. (1973), *Journal of a Solitude* (New York: Norton). See also M. Peters (1997), *May Sarton: A Biography* (New York: Alfred A. Knopf).

18. Grumbach, D. (1994), *Fifty Days of Solitude* (Boston: Beacon Press), and A. K. Shulman (1995), *Drinking the Rain* (New York: Farrar, Straus and Giroux).

19. Grumbach, ibid.

20. No one has completely answered this question, although Freud, Howard Gardner, Otto Rank, Charles Spezzano, Donald Woods Winnicott, and others have identified traits, emotional qualities, and parent-child interactions that seem to produce the will to create spontaneity, "interest-excitement," and imagination. See especially C. Spezzano (1993), *Affect in Psychoanalysis: A Clinical Synthesis* (Hillsdale, N.J.: The Analytic Press).

21. Csikszentmihalyi, M., K. Rathunde, and S. Whalen (1993), *Talented Teenagers: The Roots of Success and Failure* (New York: Cambridge University Press).

22. R. B. Cattell has performed the most detailed tests of people's personalities, both developing the Sixteen Personality Questionnaire (16 PF) and assessing individuals from all walks of life and determining profiles for all professions. Simonton reports on his work and others, in D. K. Simonton (1994), *Greatness: Who Makes History and Why* (New York: The Guilford Press).

23. Dickens quoted ibid., 269.

24. Boorstin, D. J. (1992), *The Creators* (New York: Random House), 376, 377.

25. Singer, M. (1996), "Domestic Life," *New Yorker*, Feb. 26–Mar. 4, 665–68.

26. Daiss, M. D. (1994), "Benign Neglect," *Mothering*, Winter, 38–41.

27. Ibid., 39.

28. Solomon, M. (1995), *Mozart: A Life* (New York: Harper Collins Publishers).

29. Ibid., 12.

30. Ibid., 493.

31. The punishing arm of Mozart's father stretched around Mozart's birthplace, Salzburg; for, interestingly, the whole city blamed Mozart for his self-exile. In Mozart's growing up and leaving, he was expunged from certain city records and Salzburg never honored his death with either concert or memorial gathering. Society sided with the father to repudiate an unruly son. No wonder Mozart, who as much wanted to give others pleasure as to please himself, saw death as a blessed escape from the dilemma and a means to finally give way to his creative self-directed adventuresomeness.

32. Carroll, L. (1963), *The Annotated Alice: Alice's Adventures in Wonderland & Through the Looking Glass* (Cleveland: World).

33. Rey, H. A. (1941), *Curious George* (Boston: Houghton Mifflin).

34. Nunberg, H. (1961), *Curiosity* (New York: International Universities Press).

35. Nunberg, H. (1961), *Practice and Theory of Psychoanalysis,* The Freud Anniversary Lecture Series, New York Psychoanalytic Institute (New York: International Universities Press), 78.

36. Rey, H. A. (1947), *Curious George Takes a Job* (Boston: Houghton Mifflin).

37. Goleman, D. (1995), *Emotional Intelligence* (New York: Bantam Books).

38. Gardner, H. (1983), *Frames of Mind: The Theory of Multiple Intelligences* (New York: Basic Books).

39. Hamner, T. J., and P. H. Turner (1996), *Parenting in Contemporary Society,* 3rd ed. (Boston: Allyn and Bacon).

40. Ibid.

41. This is but one of countless tales of survival over adversity that demonstrate

a person's self-contemplation, separateness, and alone skills as reinforcement against negativity.

42. Lightfoot, S. L. (1988), *Balm in Gilead: Journey of a Healer* (Reading, Mass.: Addison-Wesley).

43. Ibid., 58.

44. Solomon (1995), 124.

45. Cline, S. (1993), *Women, Passion and Celibacy* (New York: Carol Southern Books).

46. Ibid., 219.

47. Ibid., 230.

48. It is embracing a chaste life that raises eyebrows, unless one is part of a religious sect. Chastity and virginity gained prominence through embracing Mary, Jesus' mother, described as alone of all women. See M. Warner (1976), *Alone of All Her Sex: The Myth and the Cult of the Virgin Mary* (New York: Alfred A. Knopf). But for Mary to be the divine mother, maintain her virginity, and conceive asexually requires either spontaneous generation or the power of the Holy Ghost. Spontaneous divisions of the ovum apparently do take place, according to researchers—see Warner. Eve is the earth mother, cursed to bear children: "The whole of her bodily beauty is nothing less than phlegm, blood, bile, and the fluid of digested food" (58). Aquinas, citing Aristotle, carried forth the repugnancy of woman's inferiority and the misogyny in writings about women other than the virginal Mary.

49. Ibid., 73.

50. Kitch, S. L. (1993), *This Strange Society of Women: Reading the Letters and Lives of the Women's Commonwealth* (Columbus: Ohio State University Press), x.

51. Ibid., 131.

52. O'Brien, M., ed. (1993), *An Evening When Alone: Four Journals of Single Women in the South 1827–67* (Charlottesville: University Press of Virginia).

53. *The Art of the Brontës: Drawings and Manuscripts*, exhibit at the Pierpont Morgan Library, New York, January–April 1996.

54. Brontë, E. (1993), "The Night Is Darkening Around Me," *The Brontës' Selected Poems*, ed. J. R. V. Barker (London: Everyman), no. 30.

55. Brontë, C. (1993), "Evening Solace," ibid., no. 12.

56. Brontë, C. (1993), "On the Death of Anne Brontë," ibid., no. 15.

57. Letter M92696 to Ellen Nussey, in Henry Houston Bonnell Brontë Collection.

58. Dickinson, E. (1995), "Some Keep the Sabbath Going to Church," in *Skies in Blossom: The Nature Poetry of Emily Dickinson*, ed. J. Cott (New York: Doubleday), 1.

59. Ibid., 19.

60. Interview with William Irwin Thompson, in *Lightworks* (see n. 6), 53.

61. Maslow, A. (1970), *Motivation and Personality* (New York: Harper & Row).

62. Ibid., 46.

63. Some of the ideas here stem from a forthcoming paper: S. Hoff and E. S. Buchholz, "School Psychologist Know Thyself: Creativity and Aloneness for Adaptive Professional Coping," *Psychology in the Schools* (journal).

64. The *New York Times* carefully pointed this out in their 1996 series on downsizing in America.

65. Storr suggests that invaluable solitude, while hard to achieve in the fast-paced and high-pressured Western culture, can lead to profound moments of thought and inner peace that would not be harmful to a work environment. For example, he sees solitude as being closely linked to insight, change, and creativity.

The healing, growth-promoting aspects of aloneness, elaborated on by Moustakas, accept an existential position. He proposes that man is, in essence, a solitary being, who can achieve a fuller appreciation of life through embracing loneliness. He writes: "I have concluded that loneliness is within life itself, and that all creations in some way spring from solitude, meditation, and isolation"—C. E. Moustakas (1989), *Loneliness* (New York: Prentice Hall Press), xii. The experience of solitude, while sometimes alienating and terrifying, allows an individual to have access to otherwise untapped resources, which lead to unique realizations, increased awareness, improved human relations, and new experiences.

66. Pines, A. M., and E. Aronson (1988), *Career Burnout* (New York: The Free Press).

67. Ibid., 190.

68. Ibid., 189.

69. Storr (1988).

70. Suedfeld, P. (1982), "Aloneness As a Healing Experience," in *Loneliness: A Sourcebook of Current Theory, Research and Therapy*, ed. L. A. Peplau and D. Perlman (New York: John Wiley & Sons), 54–67.

71. Moustakas (1989).

72. Saltzman, A. (1991), *Downshifting: Reinventing Success on a Slower Track* (New York: Harper Perennial).

73. Rogers, C. R. (1983), *Freedom to Learn* (Ohio: Charles E. Merritt), 141.

74. Rogers, C. R. (1951), *Client-Centered Therapy* (Boston: Houghton Mifflin), and C. R. Rogers (1961), *On Becoming a Person* (Boston: Houghton Mifflin).

75. Rosten, L. (1956), *Captain Newman, M.D.* (New York: Harper Brothers).

76. Ibid., 89, 90.

77. Ibid., 106.

78. Coston, J. (1996), "Tracking a Serial Killer," New York University and Post Graduate Hospitals Alumni Association meeting, Apr. 25, New York City.

79. Oates, J. C. (1995), *Zombie* (New York: Putnam), 29.

80. Ibid., 6.

81. Solomon (1977).

82. Dreifus, C. (1996), "The Cyber-Maxims of Esther Dyson," *New York Times Magazine*, July 7, 16–19.

83. Gardner, H. (1993), *Creating Minds* (New York: Basic Books).

84. Ibid., 32.

85. Ueland, B. (1987), *If You Want to Write: A Book About Art, Independence, and Spirit*, 2nd ed. (St. Paul, Minn.: Graywolf Press), 111.

86. Giddens, A. (1991), *Modernity and Self-Identity* (Stanford: Stanford University Press).

87. Giddens, A., and J. Rainwater (1989), *Self-Therapy* (London: Crucible).

88. Giddens (1991), 77.

89. Ibid., 80.

90. Moustakas, C. E. (1967), *Creativity and Conformity* (Princeton, N.J.: D. Van Nostrand), 133.

91. Moustakas (1989), 48.

92. Ueland (1987), 89.

Chapter 11: Autism, Abuse, and Asylum

1. Quotation attributed to W. Somerset Maugham; source unknown.

2. Roth, G. (1992), *When Food Is Love* (New York: Plume).

3. Cicippio, J., and R. W. Hope (1993), *Chains to Roses: The Joseph Cicippio Story* (Waco, Tex.: WRS Group, Inc.).

4. As a teacher of psychological disturbances in childhood for over twenty years, I am well aware of the latest diagnostic criteria from DSM IV of the American Psychiatric Association, which places autistic disorder and other related syndromes under the category of pervasive developmental disorders. More important, I am familiar with some of the individuals who worked carefully and painstakingly on the research to achieve a consensus on current information in the field. But since my thesis is related mainly to the ability to form a self and develop regulatory skills and adaptive behaviors despite lack of social engagement, mutual regulation, language skills, and peer relationships, the degrees of difference between these syndromes are of lesser import than the functions related to the alone need that contribute to this highly skewed adaptation. For readers interested in these latest systems of classification, I refer them to the American Psychiatric Association, 1400 K Street N.W., Washington, D.C., 20005, and the *Diagnostic and Statistical Manual of Mental Disorders,* 4th ed. (1994).

5. There are those who would argue Jenny's behavior is self-controlled rather than self-regulated. Kopp, as a result of her thoughtful work showing the development of self-regulation, might be one such person. Kopp distinguishes developmentally between the two, signifying regulation as more flexibly adaptive than control. I prefer using the terms interchangeably as I see self-regulation even in the autistic person as adaptive and flexible as circumstances allow. See C. B. Kopp (1982), "Antecedents of Self Regulation: A Developmental Perspective," *Developmental Psychology* 18 (2): 199–214.

6. Jacobs, J. (1996), *A School Teacher in Old Alaska* (New York: Random House).

7. Esther Menaker, biographer and interpreter of Rank's theories, addressed this topic at an American Psychological Association meeting in New York City, on psychoanalysis and creativity, April 18, 1996.

8. Roser, K., and E. S. Buchholz (1996), "Autism from an Intersubjective Perspec-

tive," *Psychoanalytic Review* 83 (3): 15. Though many of my considerations on autism stem from the work reflected in this 1996 paper, the actual article was written in 1994 and my ideas have evolved since that time.

9. Sinclair, J. (1972), "Bridging the Gaps: An Inside-Out View of Autism (or, Do You Know What I Don't Know?)," in *High Functioning Individuals with Autism*, ed. E. Schopler and S. B. Mesibov (New York: Freeman), 294–301.

10. Lane, H. (1993), *The Mask of Benevolence: Disabling the Deaf Community* (New York: Random House). The deaf community itself distinguishes between those who later in life become deaf and those born without hearing.

11. Schaller, S. (1995), *A Man Without Words* (Berkeley: University of California Press), 44–45.

12. Williams, D. (1994), *Somebody Somewhere: Breaking Free from the World of Autism* (New York: Times Books), 96.

13. Ibid., 96.

14. Ibid., 97.

15. In 1809, the case of an autistic boy who had been admitted to an asylum in 1799 was described for the first time.

16. This continues to be apparent in the literature. In particular, biological and genetic approaches—C. Gillberg (1990), "Autism and Pervasive Developmental Disorders," *Journal of Child Psychology and Psychiatry* 31: 99–119; M. Prior (1987), "Psychological and Neuropsychological Approaches to Childhood Autism," *British Journal of Psychiatry* 150: 8–17—look for defects in the child's neurochemical or genetic makeup. Newer cognitive behaviorists —M. Rutter (1985), "Treatment of Autistic Children," *Journal of Child Psychology and Psychiatry* 26: 193–214; O. Lovaas (1987), "Behavioral Treatment and Normal Educational and Intellectual Functioning in Young Autistic Children," *Journal of Consulting Clinical Psychology* 55: 3–9—without entering the etiological debate full-swing, approach the autistic child from the vantage point of targeting behavioral and cognitive deficits. They emphasize in a "theory of the mind" the autistic child's lack of sensitivity to other people's minds or perhaps even to their own mind's development in contrast to young children's empathic recognition of others. This interesting theory is well summarized by L. C. Mayes and D. J. Cohen (1996), "Children's Developing Theory of Mind," *Journal of the American Psychoanalytic Association* 44 (1): 117–42. Most research points to children fully developing that perspective between ages four and six. Confounding the cognitive picture are a substantial minority of autistic people on the low end of general mental ability. Lorna Wing, a well-known British physician and expert on autism, delineates that the question is not "Is this child autistic or is he mentally retarded?" Rather, we should ask, "Is he autistic?" and, "What is his level of intellectual functioning?" See L. Wing (1985), *Autistic Children: A Guide for Parents and Professionals*, 2nd ed. (New York: Brunner/Mazel), 34–35. Removed from the cognitive debate, for a long while psychoanalysts—B. Bettelheim (1967), *The Empty Fortress* (New York: Macmillan); M. Mahler (1968), *On Human Symbiosis and the Vicissitudes of Individuation* (Madison, Conn.: International Universities

Press); and F. Tustin (1990), *The Protective Shell in Children and Adults* (London: Karnac Books)—focused on the child's internal conflicts around, respectively, parental rejection and loss of a sense of efficacy, inability to emerge from a "normal autistic" state, and loss of an illusion of oneness with the caregiver. Mahler's theory of development comes closest to, and in some sense ushers in, the recent move toward two-person psychology. Her stages of development—normal autistic, symbiotic, practicing, rapprochement, and libidinal object constancy—focus on the mother-child dyad. However, her theory of autism posits that the child has developed from within an objectless state, a one-person universe. See M. Mahler, F. Pine, and A. Bergman (1975), *The Psychological Birth of the Human Infant* (New York: Basic Books). The unfortunate term refrigerator mother was used by pioneer psychiatrist Leo Kanner in diagnosing the disorder of eleven children brought to his clinic at Johns Hopkins Hospital. See L. Kanner (1943), "Autistic Disturbances of Affective Contact," *Nervous Child* 2: 217–50. Although noted as happy in their alone self-sufficiency, these children were seen as suffering from disturbances in affective contact, in part, he thought, resulting from cold and distancing mothering. During the early 1940s, when Kanner, an emigré from Vienna, was writing his discoveries in Baltimore, Asperger was in Vienna contributing his now classic descriptions to the field. See H. Asperger (1944), "Die Autistischen Psychopathen im Kindesalter," *Archiv fur Psychiatrie and Neven Kankheiten* 117: 76–136 and H. Asperger (1991), "Autistic Psychopathy in Children," *Autism and Asperger Syndrome*, U. Furth, ed. (New York: Cambridge University Press). Other pioneering work was going on in this area. For example, Lauretta Bender in New York was composing studies on Childhood Schizophrenia and autism. See L. Bender (1942), "Childhood Schizophrenia," *Nervous Child* 1: 138–40 and L. Bender (1959), "Autism in Children with Mental Deficiency," *American Journal of Mental Deficiency* 4: 81–86. Unfortunately, the early link of autism with psychosis has continued to augment, in the eyes of practitioners, the level of disturbance seen in this disorder, making it nearly impossible to distinguish between which autistic characteristics interfere with development and which are actually extreme examples of, yet part of, a valuable developmental process.

17. See also G. Atwood and R. Stolorow (1984), *Structures of Subjectivity* (Hillsdale, N.J.: Analytic Press); R. Stolorow, B. Brandchaft, and G. Atwood (1987), *Psychoanalytic Treatment: An Intersubjective Approach* (Hillsdale, N.J.: Analytic Press).

18. Lorna Wing, an expert in the field of autism, originally coined the phrase "the autistic continuum" to account for differences in the population of people with diagnosable autistic features. See L. Wing (1988), "The Continuum of Autistic Characteristics," in *Diagnosis and Assessment in Autism*, ed. E. Schopler and G. G. Mesibov (New York: Plenum Press), 91–110.

19. A fine summary of the psychoanalytic search for understanding of autism is provided by R. P. Hobson (1990), "On Psychoanalytic Approaches to Autism," *American Journal of Orthopsychiatry* 60 (3): 324–36.

20. Mahler, M., A. Pine, and A. Bergman (1975).

21. Ogden, T. H. (1989), *The Primitive Edge of Experience* (Northvale, N.J.: Jason Aronson), 50.
22. Kanner (1943).
23. It is here where my ideas have evolved. While still supporting an intersubjective perspective, that is, that some of the autistic features formulate from a self in relationship, I now believe that the self can and does evolve removed from relationships with people.
24. For more information, also see T. Grandin (1995), *Thinking in Pictures and Other Reports from My Life in Autism* (New York: Doubleday).
25. Sachs, O. (1995), *An Anthropologist on Mars* (New York: Vintage).
26. Labbe, E., and D. Williamson (1980), "Behavioral Treatment of Elective Mutism: A Review of the Literature," *Clinical Psychology Review* 4: 273–93.
27. Kolvin, I., and T. Fundudis (1981), "Elective Mute Children: Psychological Development and Background Factors," *Journal of Child Psychology & Psychiatry* 22: 219–32.
28. Ibid.
29. Tylim, I. (1995), "*The Piano*: A Burial for the Undead," *Round Robin*, Apr., 17–19.
30. Elliot, J. M., ed. (1989), *Conversations with Maya Angelou* (Jackson, Miss.: University Press of Mississippi).
31. For a fuller account of this symptom see J. A. Yanof (1996), "Selective Mutism," *Journal of the American Psychoanalytic Association* 44 (1): 79–100.
32. Winnicott, D. W. (1951), "Transitional Objects and Transitional Phenomena," *Through Paediatrics to Psycho-analysis* (New York: Basic Books, 1975), 229–42.
33. Milne, A. A. (1926), *Winnie-the-Pooh* (London: Methuen).
34. Kanner (1943).
35. Tustin, F. (1980), "Autistic Objects," *International Review of Psychoanalysis* 7: 27–39, as interpreted by Roser and Buchholz (1996), 11.
36. Park, C. C. (1967), *The Siege* (New York: Harcourt, Brace and World).
37. Given that, in the description of behavioral treatment, virtually no mention is made of developing relationships as a part of the therapeutic process, it is interesting to note that the foundation that the tie provides is in one instance given weight in a passing observation: "Only a person who is familiar with a child (who knows how to play with him and otherwise care for him) will be able to elicit a full range of initial sounds"—O. Lovaas (1977), *The Autistic Child* (New York: Irvington Publishers), as reported in Roser and Buchholz (1996), 22.
38. Williams (1994), 25.
39. Probably among the most successful in helping autistic children, Tustin demonstrates her sensitivity to David's need to protect himself, via the making of a cardboard box, from the impending loss of an upcoming vacation. Tustin feels the role of the therapist is to disallow some of this to happen by not acceding to demands. Rather, verbal interpretation of the needs and wishes to merge will enable the child to move away from the need and to mourn the loss of the omnipotent illusion. Thus, for her the cardboard is a joining with both father and therapist and an enactment of a regressive theme. Alan Schore is a neuroscientist who has studied emotional regulation in depth, emphasiz-

ing the adaptive function of self-regulation in modulating reactive states. This alone skill intervenes positively to in part replace the comforts lost from failure to bond. See A. N. Schore (1994), *Affect Regulation and the Origin of the Self: The Neurobiology of Emotional Development* (Hillsdale, N.J.: L. Erlbaum Associates). Though the autistic child is aware of others in life, resistance to touch from the onset suggests a posture that self-soothing is far preferable to outward consolation. With the growing demands that face a two-year-old, the child whose sensitivity requires exquisite responses learns that the adult's actions are not isomorphic to needs and wishes, while all along the autistic child was not building the "neurophysical development" thought essential to supporting mutual regulatory functions.

40. Parker, B. (1962), *My Language Is Me* (New York: Basic Books), 1.

41. Ibid., 134. This is one of the few complete cases with all process notes published.

42. Bettelheim, B. (1974), *A Home for the Heart* (New York: Alfred A. Knopf).

43. Brooke, J., and D. Barboza (1996), "The Brothers Kaczynski: How Two Paths Diverged," *New York Times*, Apr. 12, A20. See also "The Mind of the Unabomber" *Newsweek*, April 15, 1996, 30–36.

44. Brooke and Barboza, ibid.

45. For a full understanding of this syndrome, see S. M. Johnson (1991), *The Symbiotic Character* (New York: W. W. Norton).

46. Bettelheim (1974).

47. Ibid.

48. See MacDonald, R. (1997), "A Mind of One's Own: The Pathology of Self-Sufficiency," Post-Graduate Psychoanalytic Society, New York City, March 14. See also E. Corrigan and P. E. Gordon, eds. (1995), *The Mind Object: Precocity and the Pathology of Self-Sufficiency* (Northvale, N.J.: Jason Aronson).

49. Wordsworth, W. (1939), "The World Is Too Much with Us," in *The Poet's Company*, ed. M. C. E. W. Parker (London: Longmans, Green).

50. *Othello, the Moor of Venice*, act 2, scene 3.

51. Bershman, B. J. (1993), "Human Aggression While Under the Influence of Alcohol and Other Drugs: An Integrative Research Review," *Current Directions in Psychological Science* 2, no. 5 (Oct.): 148–52.

52. A 1986 conference on helping the hidden victims of alcoholics describes the "I love you, go away" lessons. Children of alcoholic parents also learn loneliness as they learn to depend on themselves to make things happen too early on in their development.

53. Grotstein, J. (1991), "Nothingness, Meaninglessness, Chaos and the 'Black Hole III': Self and Interactional Regulation and the Background Presence of Primary Identification," *Contemporary Psychoanalysis* 27: 3–29, and J. Grotstein (1986), "The Psychology of Powerlessness: Disorders of Self-Regulation and Interactional Regulation As a Newer Paradigm for Psychopathology," *Psychoanalytic Inquiry* 6: 113–18. See also E. J. Khantzian (1990), *Addiction and the Vulnerable Self* (New York: Guilford Press).

54. Freud, S. (1888), "Hysteria," *The Standard Edition of the Complete Psychological*

Works of Sigmund Freud, vol. 1 (London: Hogarth Press), 41–57; S. Freud (1895), "Studies on Hysteria," *Standard Ed.,* vol. 2, 104.

55. Masson, J. (1984), *The Assault on Truth: Freud's Suppression of the Seduction Theory* (New York: Farrar, Straus and Giroux).

56. "Contemporary Approaches to Group Treatment with Children: Psychoanalytic Perspectives," 16th annual spring meeting of Division 39 APA, Ester Buchholz, discussant, April 20, 1996. Papers: S. A. Aronson, "Bereavement Group for Children of AIDS Families"; B. Cohler, "Group Work with the More Troubled Child"; C. J. Eagle, "A Developmental Perspective on the Use of Dissociation in Sexually Abused Girls."

57. Ellmann, M. (1993), *The Hunger Artists: Starving, Writing and Imprisonment* (Cambridge: Harvard University Press), 2.

58. Ibid., 93.

59. Roth, G. (1982), *Feeding the Hungry Heart: The Experience of Compulsive Overeating* (New York: Penguin Books), 100.

60. Quoted in *Women of the Asylum* (1994), by Jeffrey L. Geller and Maxine Harris (New York: Anchor Books), 322.

61. Storr, A. (1988), *Solitude* (New York: Ballantine).

62. As reported in R. Rymer (1994), *Genie: A Scientific Tragedy* (New York: Harper Perennial), 207.

63. Candland, D. K. (1993), *Feral Children and Clever Animals: Reflections on Human Nature* (New York: Penguin Books), 100.

64. The story of what went right and ultimately wrong in Genie's rehabilitation, the so-called scientific failure, is told poignantly by *New Yorker* journalist Russ Rymer. See Rymer (1994).

65. Quoted in Geller and Harris (1994), 324.

66. The American Psychological Association newsletter reported briefly on the importance of solitude. See H. McIntosh (1996), "Solitude Provides an Emotional Tune-up," *APA Monitor,* Apr. Psychologist Peter Suedfeld of the University of British Columbia, who has studied loneliness and solitude for many years, finds tendencies among people whose work demands social engagement to require longer periods of alone rest. One type of sensory-deprivation therapy, called restricted environmental stimulation technique (REST), is his antidote to combat social and sensory overload. See P. Suedfeld (1982), "Aloneness As a Healing Experience," in *Loneliness: A Sourcebook of Current Theory and Research and Therapy,* ed. L. A. Peplau and D. Perlman (New York: John Wiley).

67. Harrison, N. (1985), *Winnie Mandela: Mother of a Nation* (London: Victor Gollancz).

68. Quoted in Geller and Harris (1994), 314.

69. Ibid., 314.

70. Cicippio and Hope (1993), 23.

71. Keenan, B. (1992), *An Evil Cradling* (New York: Viking), 32.

72. Anderson, T. (1993), *Den of Lions* (New York: Crown Publishers), 75.

73. Morgenroth, L. (1996), "Silence Spoken Here," *New York Times,* March 17, Travel section, 37.

Chapter 12: Reclaiming Courage and Confidence

1. Poe, E. A. (1829), "Alone," in *Edgar Allan Poe*, ed. M. Alterton and H. Craig (New York: Hill and Wang), 28.
2. Milne, A. A. (1961), "Solitude," *Now We Are Six* (New York: E. P. Dutton).
3. Koch, P. (1994), *Solitude: A Philosophical Encounter* (Chicago, Ill.: Open Court).
4. Fromm, E. (1969), *Escape from Freedom* (New York: Holt, Rinehart and Winston).
5. Paz, O. (1961), *The Labyrinth of Solitude* (New York: Grove Press), 195.
6. Ibid., 205.
7. Coren, S. (1996), *Sleep Thieves* (New York: Free Press).
8. Ibid.
9. *New York Times*, Apr. 28, 1996, Week in Review.
10. Atlas, J. (1996), "Longing for a New Lone Genius," *New York Times*, Apr. 28, Week in Review, 1, 14.
11. Quoted ibid., 14.
12. Modell, A. H. (1993), *The Private Self* (Cambridge: Harvard University Press). Wouldn't you know? Just as I'm wrapping up my thoughts in this book, focusing on the overbearing pressures to connect at all levels of life and the increasingly difficult hunt for privacy, I receive mail about an important, May 1997 conference. A featured topic is "Relational Therapy in a *Non*-Relational World." Is this Rashomon? Then, of course, I, too, am talking about the difficulties in relating even in a world of attachment.
13. Larson, R. (1990), "The Solitary Side of Life: An Examination of the Time People Spend Alone from Childhood to Old Age," *Developmental Review* 10: 155–83.
14. Miller, J. (1996), *God Has Ninety-Nine Names: Reporting from a Militant Middle East* (New York: Simon & Schuster).
15. Campbell, J. (1949), *The Hero with a Thousand Faces* (New York: Pantheon Books), 11.
16. Fay, M. (1993), *Do Children Need Religion?: How Parents Today Are Thinking About the Big Questions* (New York: Pantheon), 49.
17. Coles, R. (1990), *The Spiritual Life of Children* (Boston: Houghton Mifflin), 104.
18. Van Manen, M., and B. Levering (1996), *Childhood's Secrets: Intimacy, Privacy and the Self Reconsidered* (New York: Teachers College Press).
19. Dowd, M. (1997), *New York Times*, March 15, op-ed page.
20. Henry Grunwald interviewed by David Gergen on *The Lehrer Report*, Feb. 11, 1997.
21. Karr, M. (1996), "Dysfunctional Nation," *New York Times Magazine*, May 12, 70.
22. Cheever, S. (1996), "Eating, Breathing, Drinking," *New York Times Magazine*, May 12, 48.
23. Quoted by Christopher Lehmann-Haupt (1996), "Thinking of Great Men Trying to Know God," *New York Times*, May 16, C19.
24. A theory that tries to expand an understanding of motivational systems while

incorporating the meaning within earlier psychoanalytic writings is to be found in J. D. Lichtenberg, F. M. Lachmann, and J. L. Foghage (1992), *Self and Motivational Systems* (Hillsdale, N.J.: Analytic Press). Psychoanalysis is being culturally and intellectually *revised*. This is as anticipated in any breathing psychological and social theory, but it does not need to be *revived*, as psychoanalysis is far from dead, as multiappearances in university discourse and treatment attest.

25. Freud, S. (1930), "Civilization and Its Discontents," *The Standard Edition of the Complete Psychological Works of Sigmund Freud*, vol. 21 (London: Hogarth Press), 57–146.

26. Chopin, K. (1972), *The Awakening* (New York: Avon).

27. Toth, J. (1993), *The Mole People: Life in the Tunnels Beneath New York City* (Chicago: Chicago Review Press), 109.

28. Ibid., 105.

29. Editorial, "Psychoanalysis, Society, and Politics," *International Forum of Psychoanalysis* 5, no. 4 (Dec. 1996): 251–52.

30. Gornick, V. (1987), *Fierce Attachments: A Memoir* (New York: Farrar Straus Giroux), 103–4.

31. Clara Hemphill, journalist, will have a guidebook to such schools in New York City published by SoHo Press.

32. Dertouzos, M. L. (1997), *What Will Be: How the World of Information Will Change Our Lives* (San Francisco: Harper San Francisco).

33. Fingarette, H. (1963), *The Self in Transformation: Psychoanalysis, Philosophy and the Life of the Spirit* (New York: Harper Torch Books), 226.

34. Zilboorg, G. (1938), "Loneliness," *Atlantic Monthly*, Jan. 16, 145.

35. Fraser, J. T. (1989), "The Many Dimensions of Time and Mind: An Epistemic Jigsaw Puzzle Game," in *Time and Mind: Interdisciplinary Issues: The Study of Time VI*, ed. J. T. Fraser (Madison, Conn.: International Universities Press), 11. Fraser is one of the leading authorities on time. My information on physical psychological time comes from one of his several edited volumes on the study of time.

36. *As You Like It*, act 3, scene 2.

37. Kakutani, M. (1996), "Tryst, Seduction, Pursuit and Life's Little Quirks," *New York Times*, May 14, C17.

38. Fraser (1989).

39. As referred to by Modell (1993).

40. If essayist and language maven William Safire reads this book, I shall eagerly await his reconstruction of alone terminology.

41. Lao Tsu (1988), *Tao Te Ching: A New English Version*, trans. Stephen Mitchell (New York: Harper Collins Publishers), 11.

42. Cicero, *Philippics* ii, 44, in *Familiar Quotations from Latin Authors*, ed. C. T. Ramage (London: Routledge), 44.

INDEX

Ester Schaler Buchholz, Ph.D., has been a licensed clinical psychologist for twenty-seven years. She is Associate Professor at New York University in the Department of Applied Psychology. She founded and directs the NYU Master's Program in the Psychology of Parenthood, and trains doctoral candidates in School Psychology. Educated early in her career as a psychoanalytic psychotherapist, she codirects psychoanalytic training at the Institute for Child, Adolescent, and Family Studies in New York City. She is former president of the Child section of the American Psychological Association's Division of Psychoanalysis, and a current member of the association's publication committee. Her book *Group Interventions with Children, Adolescents, and Parents* was recently reprinted. Author of numerous professional articles, she has also received several research and clinical grants. She is married and has three sons and two stepdaughters. She also has two grandchildren and is expecting a third. Oil painting is her favorite alonetime.

Dr. Buchholz can be contacted at eb5@is4.nyu.edu.

MH

THOMAS CRANE PUBLIC LIBRARY

3 1641 00370 7530

Public Library Core
Collection Non-Fiction
2013

OCT 14 1998